PHL

54060000202175

D1429582

A SURVEY OF MANUSCRIPTS
ILLUMINATED IN THE BRITISH ISLES
VOLUME THREE
ROMANESQUE MANUSCRIPTS 1066-1190

BY C · M · KAUFFMANN

THE
**PAUL HAMLYN
LIBRARY**

WITHDRAWN

TRANSFERRED FROM

THE
CENTRAL LIBRARY
OF THE
BRITISH MUSEUM

2009

Frontispiece: The Magi before Herod. Copenhagen, Royal Library, MS Thott 143 2°, f. 10 (Cat. 96)

British Museum
Education Office

A SURVEY OF MANUSCRIPTS ILLUMINATED IN THE
BRITISH ISLES ~ GENERAL EDITOR: J·J·G· ALEXANDER

ROMANESQUE MANUSCRIPTS 1066~1190

BY C·M·KAUFFMANN

WITH 350 ILLUSTRATIONS

 HARVEY MILLER ~ LONDON

A SURVEY OF MANUSCRIPTS
ILLUMINATED IN THE BRITISH ISLES

General Editor J. J. G. Alexander

Volume One: INSULAR MANUSCRIPTS FROM THE 6TH TO THE 9TH CENTURY

Volume Two: ANGLO-SAXON MANUSCRIPTS 900–1066

Volume Three: ROMANESQUE MANUSCRIPTS 1066–1190

Volume Four: EARLY GOTHIC MANUSCRIPTS 1190–1300

Volume Five: GOTHIC MANUSCRIPTS OF THE 14TH CENTURY

Volume Six: LATER GOTHIC MANUSCRIPTS—THE 15TH CENTURY

© 1975 Harvey Miller · 20 Marryat Road · London SW19 5BD · England

SBN 85602 017 6

745.670942 KAU

Designed by Elly Miller

Printed in Great Britain at the University Press, Oxford, by Vivian Ridler, Printer to the University

CONTENTS

9952

CENTRAL LIBRARY
WITHDRAWN
THE BRITISH MUSEUM

For T. C.
and in Memory of M. C.

Fig. 1. Canon Tables.
Paris, Bibl. Nat., lat. 14782, f. 9 (Cat. 2)

EDITOR'S PREFACE

CONCEIVED ORIGINALLY as a revision of Eric Millar's *English Illuminated Manuscripts* written nearly fifty years ago, the scope and plan of this series of volumes has altered somewhat. We have retained the idea of listing the most important illuminated manuscripts of each century but aimed at describing each in greater detail than Millar did.

It seemed desirable to enable the reader to get at three main sorts of information without having to consult a whole series of more or less inaccessible monographs, catalogues, or articles in learned journals. The first aim has been to list the type and content of the illumination and where it is to be found in the book. We are after all dealing not with independent panel paintings but with miniatures linked to a text, most of which have a specific illustrative purpose. Secondly it seemed desirable to set out briefly but clearly what evidence there might be of date or place of production. Too often conjectures are made on these matters which gradually come to pass as facts. The third object has been to provide an up-to-date list of secondary literature on each manuscript.

Since Millar wrote, the bibliography has grown considerably and this in turn reflects greater interest in this side of English medieval art. It has come to be realized that only in manuscript illumination can a continuous development of English medieval painting be traced. Very little monumental painting has survived in comparison and too much of this is either poorly preserved or of mediocre quality.

Manuscript illumination on the other hand often remains very much as the artist left it. The reason for this is, of course, that it has not been exposed to light and dirt. But unfortunately this very advantage brings with it a disadvantage. The manuscripts tend to be inaccessible to the public. They are too precious and too fragile to be frequently handled and cannot be often exhibited. Even when they are exhibited only one page can be shown at a time. Therefore our volumes aim as well by a generous selection of plates to put before the reader a sort of imaginary exhibition, an exhibition which could never be held. In this way we hope to make the great achievements of English medieval artists in this field, achievements which are not inferior to those of any western European country, more widely known and appreciated.

J. J. G. Alexander

FOREWORD

THIS BOOK contains a catalogue of just over a hundred illuminated manuscripts of the period 1066–1190. It should be stressed that this is not intended to be anything like a complete corpus, but rather a selection drawn from immensely rich material. Some fine manuscripts from particularly well-represented centres, such as Canterbury and St. Albans, have been omitted in favour of less well-known examples from, for instance, Worcester and Ely. It was felt that there should be a good selection of secular books to balance the inevitable predominance of Psalters and Bibles, but this does not imply the inclusion of every single illustrated astronomical text. Manuscripts not catalogued in detail will sometimes be found referred to briefly in the entries for related examples.

On the whole, only books with a secure English provenance have been included. Plausible attributions that remain controversial, such as the Pliny at Le Mans (MS 263) and the Bible at Coimbra (University Library MS 31432), have been omitted, as have those manuscripts—for example the Herbert of Bosham gift to Canterbury (see p. 27)—formerly thought to have been English but now placed in France. The introduction is intended to provide a historical framework for the catalogue entries and to highlight certain conclusions drawn from them. It is the wood to their trees.

An author working in this field is fortunate in the firmness of the anchor provided by previous literature. The last thirty years in particular have seen the pioneering articles of Francis Wormald, the specialist catalogues and studies of Fritz Saxl, Otto Pächt, C. R. Dodwell and Walter Oakeshott, and the admirable textbooks of Margaret Rickert and T. S. R. Boase. Without the fundamental support of Neil Ker's *Medieval Libraries of Great Britain*, the present work would hardly have been started. And, like a colossus astride the whole field, stands the figure of M. R. James. The debt to these and to other scholars will be apparent on every page of this book.

On a more personal note, the author would like to acknowledge help and stimulus gained in discussion with Mr. Malcolm Baker, Mr. John Beckwith, Professor Hugo Buchthal, Dr. Rosalie B. Green, Dr. Adelheid Heimann—who also read the introduction in typescript—Mr. R. W. Lightbown, Mr. Nigel Morgan and Mr. J. B. Trapp, as well as with the members of a graduate seminar on this subject held at Chicago University in 1969. Thanks are also due to the unfailingly helpful staff of the photographic libraries of the Courtauld and Warburg Institutes and of the Princeton Index of Christian Art at Utrecht University and, above all, to the librarians of the institutions housing the manuscripts described in this book. Both my wife and my father struggled manfully with what had become obsessively small handwriting in order to iron out endless irrelevancies and confusions, and for the same reason Mrs. Felicity Oldham must be congratulated on managing to type the text. Mrs. Isabel Hariades and Miss Dillian Gordon were most helpful in the preparation for publication. Lastly, more than formal thanks are due to the publisher and editor of this series, Mrs. Elly Miller and Dr. Jonathan Alexander, who, in their different spheres, provided help, encouragement and good humour well beyond the call of duty.

The Story of David. New York, Pierpont Morgan Library MS 619 verso (Cat. 84)

Fig, 2. Christ enthroned with Sword in mouth.
Cambridge, St. John's College, H.6. f. iii^v (Cat. 86)

Throughout this book Illustration Numbers refer to the main section of illustrations beginning on
page 129. Figure Numbers indicate the text illustrations accompanying the Introduction.
Numbers quoted in brackets refer to the Catalogue of Manuscripts beginning on page 53

INTRODUCTION

FOR WESTERN EUROPE, the century from 1050 was a period of startling change that divides it from the 'early' Middle Ages. For the first time since the Roman Empire, the West was free from invasions, for the late 10th and early 11th centuries had seen the defeat of the Hungarians in Germany, the gradual expulsion of the Moslems from Sicily and Northern Spain, and of the Vikings from northern Europe. Where the invaders remained they were converted to Christianity. In 1099 the first Crusade marked the first major expansionist movement of Western Europe since the Roman Empire.[1]

Largely as a result of this freedom from invasion, the period was one of an increasing prosperity that amounted to an economic revolution. Land reclamation, clearing of forests, and colonization, in sum a vast enlargement of cultivated land, which was itself linked with a rise in population, led to a rapidly increasing flow of trade and growth of capital.

Economic changes, resulting in more complex social relationships, led to attempts at more sophisticated administration by central governments. The Church, on the other hand, was able, to some extent, to assert its independence of lay control. The struggle over ecclesiastical investiture between Pope and Emperor that began with the pontificate of Gregory VII (1073–85) was mirrored at national and local level. Within the Church, this was the greatest age of monasticism, the period of monastic reform and the foundation of new orders, specifically the Cistercian monks and Augustinian canons. Many of the greatest churchmen including the majority of Popes, as well as archbishops of Canterbury, had been monks.[2]

It was a period, also, of intellectual revival, the age of Anselm, Abelard and John of Salisbury, long dubbed the '12th century Renaissance'. Not that it was a self-conscious renaissance based on classical civilization like the Italian Quattrocento, but there was definitely a quickening of intellectual life centred on the monasteries and cathedral schools.[3] Guibert, Abbot of Nogent, has been quoted in this context, for it was he who graphically described the increase in the teaching of grammar. Writing of his youth, c. 1060–70, he noted: 'One hardly finds teachers of grammar in any of the towns, indeed one hardly finds them in any of the large cities.' Later, in about 1100, the situation was so changed that he was able to say: 'grammar flourishes on all sides and many schools open their doors to the poor.'[4] Centred on France, but including the whole of Western Europe, the 12th-century Renaissance affected not only theological studies—though these were revolutionized at this period—but all other realms of intellectual activity from the study of classical literature and philosophy to civil and canon law, science and medicine. The effect on the production of books was incalculable. In quantity, the increase was tremendous and the number of manuscripts illuminated rose accordingly. For the first time since the introduction of the codex, illuminated manuscripts in the late 11th and 12th centuries can be counted by the hundred, whereas a reckoning by the dozen or the score would suffice for earlier periods.

All these changes—the growth of trade, the increasing centralization of the Church, and the quickening of intellectual life, led to a new degree of internationalism. The Archbishop of Canterbury had to go to Rome to receive his pallium, a nobleman would take a retinue on a pilgrimage to Compostela or a crusade to Jerusalem, and a scholar like John of Salisbury would be drawn to study in Paris. Quite apart from the influx of Norman clergy to England after the Conquest, the great churchmen of the 12th century were an international breed. Anselm, nephew of his great namesake the Archbishop of Canterbury, was born in Lombardy in *c.* 1080 and became in turn a monk at Chiusa, a monk at Canterbury, Abbot of San Saba in Rome (*c.* 1110–21), papal legate to England and Normandy and Abbot of Bury St. Edmunds (1121–48).[5]

This internationalism is reflected in all the arts. Without minimizing the importance of regional differences, one can say that Romanesque is the first international style in Western Europe since the fall of Rome.[6] The stylistic categories used to describe the arts of previous eras—Carolingian, Ottonian, Anglo-Saxon—are limited to clearly defined geographical areas. An illumination produced in Germany in about 1000 will be obviously and sharply distinguishable from its English counterpart of the same period. If the comparison is made again a century and a half later the distinctions have become blurred and the viewer's first reaction will be 'high Romanesque *c.* 1150' and only then will he turn to a more detailed examination to determine the country of origin.

THE PRODUCTION
OF MANUSCRIPTS IN ENGLAND

As far as the extant manuscripts can tell us, by far the greatest patrons of book illumination at this period were the monasteries. One of the undisputed changes wrought by the Norman Conquest was the reform of the English monasteries, of which there were thirty-five in 1066. Many of them were important and wealthy institutions and in the revised system of land tenure and service some of the great abbots were among the most important tenants-in-chief of the Crown. To ensure their loyalty, William the Conqueror appointed Normans to vacant abbacies, and through Lanfranc, himself a monk from Bec, who was Archbishop of Canterbury 1070–89, the English Church was reorganized on the model of Normandy. Between 1066 and 1135 there is evidence of over sixty overseas abbots being appointed to some twenty English houses, the majority from Bec, Caen, Jumièges, Mont-Saint-Michel, Fécamp and St. Evroul.[7] The Norman abbots, trained during the golden age of Norman monasticism, enforced reforms of discipline and liturgy embodied in Lanfranc's *Consuetudines*, organized major building programmes and introduced new ideas from overseas culture. At the same time many new abbeys were founded.

The monasteries with which we shall be most concerned as the main producers of illuminated manuscripts nearly all figure among the half dozen richest houses recorded in Domesday Book in 1086.[8] These include Christ Church, Canterbury (annual income £688), Bury St. Edmunds (£640), St. Augustine's, Canterbury (£635) and St. Swithun's (Old Minster), Winchester (£600) which between them provided almost forty of the manuscripts reproduced in this book. It is not surprising that the richest monasteries should have been the greatest patrons, but wealth had to be matched by the personalities of the abbots and priors. The wealthiest house at the time of Domesday was Glastonbury, which at this period has—as far as the surviving remains allow us to judge—a most undistinguished history; and the reason lies in the succession of abbots. After Thurstan, whose disastrous abbacy ended when a number of monks were killed and wounded by soldiers he had called in to restore discipline, there was a long vacancy, and then the Abbey was held in plurality by Henry of Blois, Bishop of Winchester, whose activities as a patron were focused on Winchester.[9] St. Albans, on the other hand, which in 1086 had the relatively modest, though still considerable, income of about £270 was fortunate in its abbots. Paul, a monk of Caen and nephew of Lanfranc, who became abbot in 1077 was one of the outstanding churchmen of the period who raised his house from a hitherto undistinguished position to intellectual and religious pre-eminence and we shall see that his successors were also men of rare ability as well as great patrons.

Before discussing the most relevant houses in more detail, a distinction must be drawn between the monasteries proper, ruled by an abbot, and the cathedral priories which came directly under the authority of the bishop—a peculiarly English institution. During the monastic revival of the 10th century, Benedictine monks had been introduced at certain cathedrals to carry out the liturgical functions in place of secular clerks. In this way monks were introduced at Winchester, Christ Church, Canterbury, Worcester and Sherborne. After the Conquest, Lanfranc increased the cathedral priories to nine, which was about half the cathedrals of medieval England. In the history of English Romanesque book illumination, the monasteries attached to the cathedrals of Canterbury and Winchester played a decisive role and those at Durham, Rochester and Worcester an honourable one.

From 1070 until about 1120 the field is dominated by the two houses at Canterbury. At Christ Church, the fire of 1067 followed by Lanfranc's accession as Archbishop three years later marked a break with the past. He brought with him monks from Bec and Caen, though Richard Southern estimates that there were probably not as many as a dozen foreigners among thirty to forty Englishmen.[10] Hostility between the two groups persisted into Anselm's time, yet this was a period of growing prosperity and increasing size for the community. The historian Eadmer, writing in c. 1110, estimated that there were about sixty monks in c. 1080; at Lanfranc's death in 1090 there were one hundred, and it has been estimated that there were about one hundred and forty in 1125.[11] Increases in land values raised the revenue from lands in Kent from £405 in 1066 to £678 in 1086 and Southern has reckoned the total annual revenue to have been as much as £1,000.[12] A considerable amount of money was clearly spent on the building programme, but equally a fair proportion must have been allocated to the library. In an illuminating comparison between the pre- and post-Conquest libraries, Southern characterized the former as 'redolent of the age of Bede rather than that of Lanfranc and Berengar',[13] whereas the new library embodied the intellectual revolution effected by the Conquest. Books in the earliest Norman hands at Christ Church included, apart from the works of the Church Fathers and other standard commentaries, Bede, Isidore of Seville, Hesychius on Leviticus, Angelomus on Kings, Haymo on Isaiah, Josephus, Aldhelm, Boethius and Solinus. A 12th-century library list contains an astonishing quantity of secular books including, among the Latin classics, five copies of Priscian's Grammar, nine copies of Cicero's *Rhetorica*, eleven copies of Macrobius, eight of Boethius, five of Terence, eight of Virgil and eight of Horace.[14]

The mixture of Norman and English traditions at Christ Church is, as we shall see, reflected in the style of its illuminations, but there was ultimately a reconciliation between the two groups, whereas at St. Augustine's, the Cathedral's near neighbour and an ancient abbey with a tradition of independence, the Normanization led to disaster. When in 1087 Lanfranc appointed a Norman monk of Christ Church, the community sought to assert its right of free election and there followed two years of turbulence which only ended when the community was dispersed and replaced by twenty-three monks from Christ Church after Lanfranc's death in 1089.[15]

The Abbey of St. Albans, which, with the work of the Master of the St. Albans Psalter, dominated English book illumination in the 1120s and influenced the other major centres in the following decades, owed its rise to Abbot Paul (1077–97), who introduced Lanfranc's Constitutions and began building a new abbey church immediately upon his arrival. He was succeeded by Abbot Richard (1097–1119), a Norman of noble birth, and then by Geoffrey (1119–46), another Norman and an outstanding churchman under whom the abbey attained an intellectual distinction which it did not lose even in the second half of the century, when the monasteries as a whole declined in importance as centres of learning in face of the Cathedral Schools.[16] Geoffrey was a great patron, not only of painters but also of goldsmiths and embroiderers as the chronicler's list of gifts to the abbey testifies. Not only the great Psalter but also the magnificent shrine of St. Alban, made by Anketil the goldsmith, to which the Saint's remains were translated in 1129, must have ranked among the major works of its kind. In the latter part of the century, under Abbot Simon (1167–83) and his successors, connections were maintained with St. Victoire and Paris which led to the introduction of the new scholastic learning and of a new, proto-Gothic style in the field of book illumination.

Bury St. Emunds offers something of a contrast, for its fame rests more on its wealth and power than on any claim to intellectual pre-eminence. Founded by Cnut in 1028 in honour of a royal saint and martyr, it was so richly endowed that it became at once one of the greatest monasteries in the country. From Edward the Confessor the Abbey received the privilege of governing the whole of West Suffolk, the 'liberty of St. Edmund'. The abbot had the right of minting coinage and received ancient royal revenues and profits of justice. Under Abbot Baldwin (1065–98), a monk of St. Denis famous for his medical skill who was physician to both Edward the Confessor and William the Conqueror, the Abbey was reformed and brought into the mainstream of European monasticism. Baldwin was sufficiently well connected to secure royal protection from rapacious nobles and to obtain papal privileges from Alexander II against interference from the Bishop of Thetford. He also carefully husbanded the Abbey's estates, drawing up an authoritative register of its lands. In his abbacy the eastern part of the Abbey church was built and into it the body of St. Edmund, encased in a great shrine, was translated in 1095. With the possible exception of a herbal (no. 11) there are no extant illustrated manuscripts of Baldwin's period, but it was at this time that the foundation of the library was laid.[17]

The next outstanding abbot was Anselm (1119–48), former Abbot of San Saba in Rome and papal legate in Normandy, who once more brought the Abbey into prominence. Yet, although the Abbey benefited from his connections with Henry I and the papal curia, his travels abroad were so frequent that on occasions the monks implored him to spend more time in Bury. Unlike Canterbury and St. Albans, Bury never developed a distinct school of book illumination, but in Anselm's abbacy two artists of major importance were employed by the Abbey. The first was the 'Alexis Master' from St. Albans who illustrated the Life and Miracles of St. Edmund (no. 34) in about 1130, the second, Master Hugo, the artist of the Bury Bible (no. 56, c. 1135) and both left their mark on the Bury scriptorium. Anselm himself has a niche in 12th-century theological and literary history for the part he played in the reintroduction of the feast of the Immaculate Conception of the Virgin and in the collection of a volume of miracles of the Virgin and it is likely that he was responsible for the splendidly illustrated edition of the Life of St. Edmund.[18] This has been attributed in part to Osbert of Clare, Anselm's friend who was at Bury in about 1130. Usually, however, patronage of the artists appears to have been the work of successive priors and sacrists rather than of the abbot himself. The sacrist was responsible for allocating a certain part of the revenue for the building programme and for the library, and in Anselm's abbacy Bury had two sacrists, Hervey (c. 1125–38) and Ralph (c. 1140–50), described in the *Gesta Sacristarum* as 'men of entire wisdom'. They were responsible for the building of the nave of the Abbey church—which was bigger than Durham Cathedral—and it was Hervey who, together with Prior Talbot, employed Magister Hugo to illuminate the great Bury Bible in c. 1135.

Winchester, the ancient capital of Wessex and for long after the Conquest the seat of the royal treasury, had, like Canterbury, two great monasteries: the Old Minster, or Cathedral Priory of St. Swithun, and the New Minster (Hyde Abbey). The New Minster was adjacent to the Cathedral but friction between the two houses led to its removal to Hyde in 1111. Even after that, it was less fortunate than St. Swithun's for it was burnt down during the civil war in 1141. From 1129 until 1171 the history of Winchester was dominated by its great bishop, Henry of Blois, nephew of Henry I and brother of King Stephen.[19] Formerly a monk at Cluny, he became Abbot of Glastonbury in 1126, an office he retained when he was made Bishop of Winchester three years later. Glastonbury was the wealthiest abbey in the land and St. Swithun's, Winchester, ranked sixth in wealth in Domesday book and the two together, ably figures, rhythmically parallel drapery folds, stylized curling beards and hair, symmetrical compositions, and heavy colouring—these are all features derived from the late Ottonian schools of Echternach or the Meuse and pointing towards the Romanesque style of the 12th century. However, as far as one can tell, this stylistic innovation did not bear fruit in the second half of the 11th century and it is possible that but for the Conquest the Romanesque style might have developed earlier in England than in fact it did.

For the Conquest, bringing Norman monasticism in its wake, ensured that the main artistic influence came from Normandy. At this period, Norman illumination is characterized by a dependence on Anglo-Saxon art and by a preoccupation with initials to the exclusion or relative absence of major illustrative picture cycles. The Normans were great conquerors, colonizers, builders and administrators, but as far as painting was concerned they lagged far behind their Anglo-Saxon contemporaries. Norman book illumination is permeated with Anglo-Saxon features; indeed to some extent it may be seen as a provincial version of an art at which pre-Conquest England excelled. Yet the Norman artist produced a harder, drier, more solid version of the Anglo-Saxon style and to this extent his art was more Romanesque in character. The Evangelists in a Norman book of the Gospels (B.L. Add. 11850; fig. 7), for example, show Anglo-Saxon influence, particularly in the fleshy acanthus leaves of the frame.[32] But the heavy colouring and solidly painted background which eliminates the last vestiges of classical illusionistic space, the weight of the figures, the hardening of outlines and the new dominance of pattern all bear witness to the emergence of a new style, despite the unsophisticated nature of the work. A comparable manuscript, in which the same mixture of Anglo-Saxon and Continental features can be detected is the Paris Gospels from Exeter (no. 2) which has also been placed in the last quarter of the 11th century.

The second important aspect of Norman illumination and its influence in England was the increasingly prominent place of the decorated initial. Here again the Norman illuminator owed much to Anglo-Saxon art. Splendid initials with fleshy 'Winchester' acanthus filling and interlace ribbonwork—derived from the Carolingian Franco-Saxon school—had appeared in English manuscripts from the 10th century (fig. 8). Fiercely biting animal heads, furthermore, formed part of the Insular tradition well before it was influenced by Carolingian art. Even the initials constructed entirely of winged dragons, which are such a feature of Norman and Anglo-Norman illumination, appeared in Anglo-Saxon books.[33]

In two respects, however, the Normans were ahead of their time. The first was in their greater use of decorated initials. These predominate in Norman manuscripts, while long illustrative cycles are scarce. As the elaborately decorated initial is an essential feature of Romanesque art, the Norman artist must be seen as innovating in this respect. The second was the introduction of the clambering human figure into initials. Plant scrolls inhabited by birds or beasts had originally been a classical motif which appeared in the margins and frames of manuscripts from Carolingian times on. Such inhabited scrolls were adapted to the decoration of initials occasionally in the 10th century (e.g. the English Psalter, Bodleian Library MS Junius 27)[34] and more commonly in northern French manuscripts of the early 11th century, such as the St. Vaast Bible at Arras (Bibl. Mun. MS 559).[35] What was new was the regular introduction of human figures into the foliage decoration of initials often in scenes of combat with dragons and beasts. An early example appears in a manuscript from Mont-Saint-Michel dating from the middle or third quarter of the 11th century (Avranches MS 72, f. 151; fig. 9) in which a man with an axe is attacking a lion enmeshed in foliage scrolls within the body of an initial P.[36] This kind of scene is not only the basis of the most typical and splendid of Romanesque decorative creations, but is also important for the development of the historiated initial, and its introduction must be considered the most important Norman contribution to English illumination.

The close link between the art of the two countries in the second half of the 11th century is amply illustrated by the fact that several manuscripts once thought to have been English are now considered Norman. Most famous are those written for William of St. Calais (Carilef), Bishop of Durham (Durham Cathedral Library MS A. II. 4, Bible; B. II. 13/14, St. Augustine on Psalms).[37] Illuminated with initials consisting of fleshy Anglo-Saxon acanthus decoration combined with clambering figures, these manuscripts were always seen as typifying the Anglo-Norman fusion of the late 11th century (fig. 10). This is a reasonable conclusion, but it now appears that they were produced in Normandy during the period 1088–91 when Bishop William was exiled for taking part in the rebellion of Odo of Bayeux against William II. The third volume of the St. Augustine on Psalms (MS B. II. 14, f. 200ᵛ) contains a verse suggesting that it was written during the exile, and Otto Pächt has shown that the illuminator Robert Benjamin, who drew his self-portrait in the second volume (MS B. II. 13, f. 102), was a Norman.[38] He compared the illuminations with those of a manuscript formerly believed to have been written at Exeter (MS Bodley 717), and with a Norman manuscript from La Croix St. Leufroi in Paris (Bibl. Nat., MS lat. 13765). These two were both illuminated by an artist who called himself Hugo Pictor, and Pächt concluded that Hugo, like Robert Benjamin, was a Norman. At the same time Hanns Swarzenski arrived at a similar conclusion for another manuscript of this group, the Carilef Bible, which he compared with manuscripts at Bayeux and Rouen.[39] We know from a contemporary source that Bishop William brought back many books from his exile in 1091, and it seems most likely that the school of illumination responsible for these late 11th-century Durham manuscripts is Norman rather than English.

If the Durham and Exeter books are taken from the English scene, only Canterbury remains as a centre producing a consistent series of illuminated manuscripts in the two generations after the Conquest and it is at Canterbury that the Anglo-Norman fusion can best be studied (see nos. 6–8). Equally, however, the manuscripts of Canterbury, and particularly of St. Augustine's, illustrate another major tendency in the period 1070–1120: the tenacious survival of the Anglo-Saxon figure style. This was first elucidated by Francis Wormald,[40] who traced the continuity of the nervous, expressive outlines and sketchy tinting of Anglo-Saxon art in the initials of St. Augustine's manuscripts, such as the Martyrology, Cotton, Vitellius C. XII (no. 18) and the Lives of Saints, Arundel 91 (no. 17) and, above all, in the full-page drawings of the *De Civitate Dei* of St. Augustine in Florence (no. 19). Elsewhere the Anglo-Saxon style survived into the second quarter of the 12th century, as can be seen, for example, in an Ely manuscript of *c.* 1130 (no. 40) and its influence may be detected later still in essentially Romanesque drawings such as the famous Virgin and Child in the Bodleian Library (no. 52).

It is possible, therefore, to summarize the developments between the Conquest and the St. Albans Psalter under the following headings: Continental influence in the mid 11th century, the fusion with Norman illumination, and the tenacious survival of the Anglo-Saxon style of drawing. And yet, in so far as the available evidence allows us to judge, the St. Albans Psalter itself marks a distinct break with the past, for it is the first manuscript with an extensive cycle of miniatures in a fully developed Romanesque style to be produced in England. Otto Pächt has clarified the contributory influences of Ottonian and Byzantine art. The overriding purple colour, the panelled backgrounds and the solid, hieratic figures are linked with Ottonian illumination, particularly of the 11th-century school of Echternach, while the architectural backgrounds and, above all, the draperies with their cobwebs of white highlights, betray the influence of Byzantine art. This stress on Ottonian and Byzantine sources must not be allowed to obscure the contributions of the Alexis Master himself—the creator of the St. Albans Psalter. In particular, the profile, with its straight line from brow to tip of nose and regular, curly black fringe, is idiosyncratic, though it became a hall-mark of St. Albans influence on later manuscripts.

The style of the St. Albans Psalter dominated English figure painting for one and a half decades from about 1120. Nearly all the major cycles of miniatures are attributable either to the Alexis Master himself (no. 34) or else to a follower (no. 35). An equally important land-

Fig. 4. St. Michael and the dragon.
London, B.L., Tiberius C.VI, f. 16

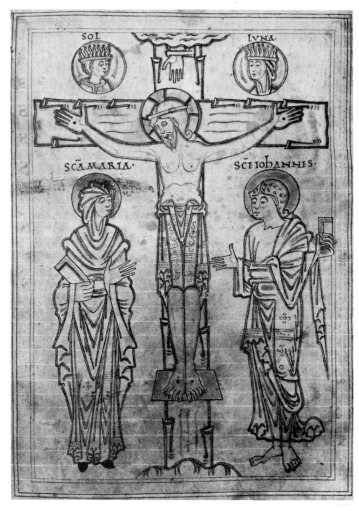

Fig. 5. Crucifixion.
London, B.L., Arundel 60, f. 12ᵛ (Cat. 1)

Fig. 6. The naming of John the Baptist.
London, B.L., Caligula A. XIV, f. 20ᵛ

Fig. 7. St. Mark.
London, B.L., Add. 11850, f. 61ᵛ

Fig. 8. Beatus Initial.
Cambridge, University Lib., ff. 1.23, f. 5

Fig. 9. Initial P.
Avranches 72, f. 151

Fig. 10. Beatus Initial.
Durham, Cath. Lib., A.II.4, f. 65

Fig. 11. Initial C.
Florence, Biblioteca Mediceo-Laurenziana,
Plut. XII. 17, f. 199ᵛ (Cat. 19)

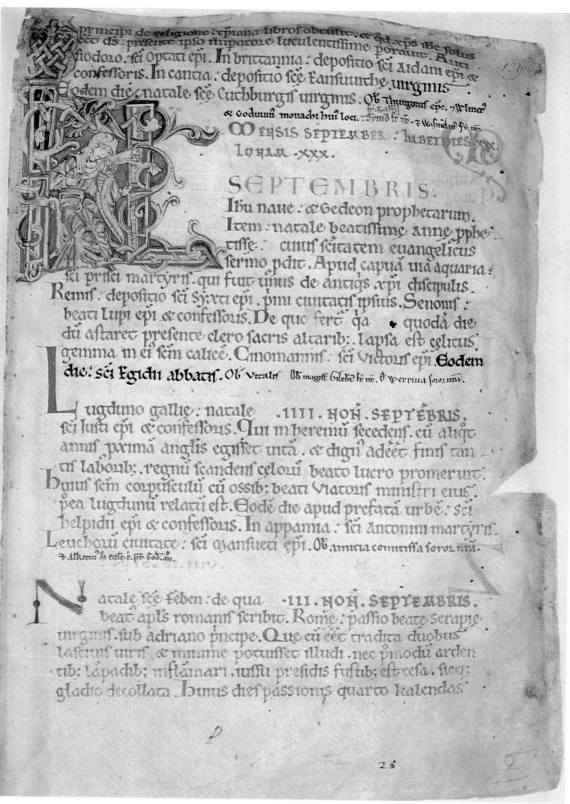

principi de religione xpiana libros obtulit. ce qd eps ille solus
sed ds presente ipso imperatore luculentissime poravit. Aue
siodoro. sci Optati epi. In brittannia: depositio sci Aidani epi &
confessoris. In cantia: depositio sce tansuurhe uirginis.
Eodem die: natale sce Cuthburgis uirginis. Ob Thingotus epe. Wlmer
& Goduini monachi huii loci. 25 mid fr m̄. & Wsnulai fr m̄.

MENSIS SEPTEMBER: HABET DIES XX.
LUNA .XXX.

SEPTEMBRIS:

Ihu naue: & Gedeon prophetarum.
Item: natale beatissime anne pphe
tisse: cuius scitatem euangelicus
sermo pdit. Apud capuam una aquaria:
sci prisci martyris. qui fuit unus de antiqs xpi discipulis.
Remis: depositio sci Syxti epi. pmi ciuitatis ipsius. Senonis:
beati Lupi epi & confessoris. De quo fert qa ⟨◆⟩ quodam die
du astaret presente clero sacris altarib;: lapsa est celitus
gemma in ei scm calice. Cinomannis: sci Victoris epi. Eodem
die: sci Egidii abbatis. Ob Vitalis. Ob magistr Giledd fr m̄. & Uerrina soror m̄.

Lugduno gallie: natale .IIII. NON. SEPTEBRIS.
sci Iusti epi. & confessoris. Qui in heremum secedens. cu aliqt
annis pximam anglis egisset uitam. & digm adeet finis tan
tis laborib;: regnu scandens celoru beato lucro promeruit.
huius scm corpusculu cu ossib; beati Viatoris ministri eius.
pea lugdunu relatu est. Eode die apud prefatam urbe: sci
helpidii epi & confessoris. In appamia: sci Antonini martyris.
Leuchoui ciuitate: sci Mansueti epi. Ob amicia commissa soror m̄.
& Alkerin ad cesse. r. pr. bod. m.

Natale sce feben: de qua .III. NON. SEPTEMBRIS.
beat apts romanis scribit. Rome: passio beate serapie
uirginis. sub adriano pncipe. Que cu eet tradita duobus
laseruis uiris. & minime potuisset illudi. nec pmodu arden
tib; lapadib; inflamari. iussu presidis fustib; est cesa. sicq;
gladio decollata. huius dies passionis quarto kalendas

p

25

September. London, B.L., Cotton Vitellius C. XII, f. 139 (Cat. 18)

Fig. 12. Moses. Detail of
Cambridge, Corpus Christi College 2,
f. 94 (Cat. 56)

Fig. 13. Evangelist. Detail of
Paris, Bibl. Nat., Gr.64, f. 10ᵛ

Fig. 14. Detail of Pentecost. Paris, Bibl. Nat.,
Nouv. acq. lat. 2246, f. 79ᵛ

Fig. 15. Initial D.
Oxford, Bodl. Lib., Auct.E.inf.6, f. 55ᵛ

Fig. 16. Initial D.
Cambridge, St. John's College C.18, f. 37ᵛ

Fig. 17. Initial Q. Cambridge, St. John's College C.18, f. 70ᵛ

mark is the great Bible illuminated by Magister Hugo for the Abbey of Bury St. Edmunds in about 1135 (no. 56). Here also the debt to St. Albans must be acknowledged, both for the use of full-page, framed miniatures—rare in Bible illustrations at this period—and for the style. Many of the principal features of the Bury Bible—the solidity of the figures, the strong contours, the elongated legs, the architectural features and the green and blue panelled backgrounds—would be unthinkable without the existence of the St. Albans Psalter, and even the typical St. Albans profiles reappear in one of the miniatures. Yet Master Hugo was also a great innovator. His faces are both more naturalistic and more sophisticated than those of the St. Albans manuscripts. This is due to their close adherence to Byzantine rules of facial contours and modelling. Dark facial shading in ochre and grey with greenish tints and white highlights, long flowing hair and the awe-inspiring features are Byzantinizing even down to the 'ᴗ' convention between the eyebrows.

However, it is the disposition of the draperies, with their rhythmical, sinuous double line folds dividing the body beneath into clearly defined areas, that has become the hall-mark of the Bury Bible figure style. Some years ago, Wilhelm Koehler characterized these clinging areas as damp folds, for they have the appearance of wet cloth stuck to the body, whose main features—stomach, thigh, knee, leg—thus become clearly delineated.[41] This is a western adaptation of the Byzantine method of articulating the human figure. The derivation from Byzantine forms can be seen by comparing the figure of Moses (fig. 12) with an Evangelist in the 11th-century Greek Gospels in Paris (Bibl. Nat. Gr. 64, f. 10ᵛ; fig. 13). Yet it is a highly stylized version of a Byzantine type and was probably adapted from an intermediate Continental source such as, for example, the Cluny lectionary of c. 1110–20 (Paris, Bibl. Nat., Nouv. acq. lat. 2246, f. 79ᵛ; fig. 14).

The damp fold is common throughout Western Europe from about 1100. It provides one of the international features of Romanesque art and this concern with the rendering of the structure of the human body has been interpreted as the visual counterpart of the 12th century's increasing stress on the importance of man in the universe. Yet, although the basic principle of the damp fold remains constant, its form in detail varies considerably. In an attempt to clarify the problem, Edward B. Garrison differentiated between three different kinds of drapery which have been grouped under the heading of damp fold.[42] He dubbed the Bury Bible style as 'clinging curvilinear' drapery and distinguished it from both the multilinear style of Burgundy—as it appears in the frescoes of Berzé-la-Ville—and the more widespread 'nested V' fold. This consists of oval- or pear-shaped areas terminating in a series of nested Vs to indicate hanging drapery. The earliest examples of damp fold drapery in England, such as the Anselm manuscript in Oxford (MS Bodley 271; no. 42) of c. 1120 belong to this type, of which perhaps the finest example is the St. Matthew in the Dover Bible (ill. 188). The clinging curvilinear style, on the other hand, with its flowing S-shaped lines, was more popular and ultimately became the hall-mark of English art from c. 1140–70. It characterizes the illumination of the finest English Romanesque manuscripts such as the Lambeth Bible, the Winchester Psalter and the Winchester Bible—and is also found on sculptures, wall-paintings and enamels. The Bury Bible is the earliest extant manuscript in which it appears fully developed and it is likely that it was an original English contribution to the repertoire of Romanesque abstractions of Byzantine forms.

This preoccupation with the minutiae of drapery folds may appear exaggerated and yet it should be recognized how very important they are in any discussion of Romanesque art. For their function was not limited to delineating the human figure and to giving it weight and solidity. In that they are highly stylized they also serve to cover the surface of the figures with a rhythmic pattern which enlivens the whole composition. The flowing lines of the clinging curvilinear folds, in particular, as we can see in the Bury Bible (ills. 149, 152), not only animate individual figures but also serve to reinforce postures and gestures in relating different figures and groups to each other.

There has been much emphasis on the solemn, hieratic figures and symmetrical compositions of Romanesque painting, but equal stress should be placed on the decoration so graphically described by St. Bernard in his attack on the carvings of Cluny:

> What signifies these ridiculous monsters, those amazing things horrible in their beauty and beautiful in their horror? To what purpose are these filthy monkeys? these savage lions? these monstrous centaurs? these half human creatures? These fighting soldiers? These huntsmen with horns? . . .[43]

St. Bernard, who spent his life criticizing the shortcomings of the Church, was the first in a long line of theologians to complain at the preoccupation of artists with such vanities, which in most cases are purely decorative and do not appear to 'signify' anything. Theophilus, the author of the early 12th-century treatise *De diversis artibus*, himself a priest and probably a monk, as well as an artist in various media, considered these features as 'enrichment'. He recommended 'branches, flowers and leaves' as well as 'little animals, birds, vermicular patterns and nude figures . . .' on, for example, stained glass as much as in illuminated initials.[44] Such enrichment of sacred texts existed for the greater glory of God even if it was devoid of deeper meaning. Certainly, the very levity of the decorative features acts as a perfect foil to the solemnity of the miniatures. Indeed, this contrast provides one of the most beguiling features of Romanesque illumination and of Romanesque art in all media, on capitals in churches, ivory carving and goldsmiths' work, as much as in manuscripts.

We have seen the emergence of the Romanesque initial, with its clambering figures and animals enmeshed in foliage scrolls, in the latter part of the 11th century. It reached its peak as a vehicle of artistic expression during the first half of the 12th century, and in England the most inventive period was *c.* 1120–50. Each school, and indeed each manuscript, differs one from the other, but three general tendencies can be discerned. To begin with, there is the increasing variety of animals, monsters and human figures—St. Bernard's 'monstrous centaurs' and 'half human creatures'—which people the initials, usually locked in combat or struggling with coils of the surrounding foliage. These creatures were derived from different sources, many of an ultimately classical origin, such as Near-eastern silks, astrological illustrations, calendar scenes and Bestiaries, but in the hands of the 12th-century artist they were highly stylized and bent and twisted into the framework of the initials.

The second discernible trend lies in the development of the foliage itself. In 11th-century initials the principal filling typically consisted of fleshy foliage derived from Anglo-Saxon decoration. Thick, striated stems were arranged in loose spirals with shoots growing in all directions terminating in a curled-over trefoil or quatrefoil (fig. 10). From about 1100 onwards increasing emphasis was placed on individualized flowers. Typically, the stem terminates in a small circle from which emerge a small central petal surrounded by two smaller ones. Other petals or leaves and blossoms were added until flowers of this kind usually placed in the centre of foliage spirals became the dominant motif in decorated initials. In the second quarter of the century they developed into large, luxuriant plant formations that extend in all directions like a fleshy octopus. This type of decoration reached its maturity in the Bury Bible, but the preliminary stages are clearly discernible in earlier English manuscripts from Canterbury and elsewhere.

Meanwhile the foliage spirals had become much more strictly controlled within the structure of the initial than they were in the 11th century, when the Winchester acanthus often grew beyond its framework. In spite of the luxuriant nature of the blossoms and the variety of creatures caught in the foliage, Romanesque decoration parallels the composition of miniatures in its symmetry, its strict control, and, above all, in the subjugation of the parts in the overriding interest of the whole. This, indeed, is perhaps the salient characteristic of Romanesque art. The peak of inventiveness achieved in English manuscripts of the 1120s–40s was never surpassed either in this country or on the Continent. In the mid-century the individual floral forms were sometimes exaggerated to an unprecedented extent (ills. 225–8) but there was no fundamental change until about 1170. When it came, this change was introduced from France.

Among the earliest datable manuscripts in the new style, are those given by Herbert of Bosham, Becket's faithful supporter, to Christ Church, Canterbury (fig. 15). These include a glossed Psalter (Trinity College, Cambridge, MS B. 5. 4 and Bodley MS Auct. E. inf. 6) and a glossed copy of the Epistles of St. Paul (Trinity College, Cambridge, MS B. 5. 6–7), both richly illuminated with decorated initials. They can be dated from internal textual evidence between 1170, the year of Becket's death, and 1177, when Archbishop William of Sens, to whom they are dedicated, was translated to Rheims.[45] If these dates are accepted, it follows that these books were produced in France, for Herbert of Bosham was in exile in France throughout this period. In script and decoration they are very similar to seven somewhat less lavish manuscripts given by Becket to Canterbury (especially glossed Pentateuch, Bodley MS Auct. E. inf. 7 and glossed Gospel Book, Trinity College MS B. 5. 5). The Becket books must date from before 1170 and, like the Bosham volumes, they were produced in Northern France, in the diocese of Sens, where both Becket and Herbert of Bosham spent their exile. It is reasonable, therefore, to place the origin and early development of the new style of decoration in France in about 1170, though whether Paris or Northern France was the original source remains to be clarified.

A glance at these initials (fig. 15) reveals the contrast with those of the mid-century (e.g. ill. 150). Foliage has become thinner, the spirals more regularly and tightly wound; the background is now usually of burnished gold. Many of the old floral forms have been retained, including the octopus flower, but they have become, on the whole, smaller and neater and usually circumscribed by rows of white dots. The principal animal decoration now consists of small white lions which inhabit the scrolls in great profusion. The initial itself is placed in a framing panel usually of blue, red, or gold, often itself decorated with small circles or dots. These initials are smaller and neater than their predecessors, but it may be felt that what has been gained in refinement has been lost in vigour and inventiveness.

If the Becket and Bosham books are French and may be compared with other Northern French manuscripts of the period, their style of decoration was soon as common in England as in France, and, as the representatives of the two countries are so often indistinguishable, the term Channel style has been coined to cover them all (see nos. 90 ff.). Yet these initials should not be seen in isolation, for they were invented to decorate a new type of book, smaller in size and written in a smaller hand. This is marked by the beginning of the substitution of angles for curves which ultimately led to the development of Gothic script.[46] Above all, the books of the later 12th century were adapted to contain the new biblical glosses of which the most popular was the expanded gloss of Peter Lombard on St. Paul and on the Psalter (c. 1136–43).[47] Their usage spread from Paris throughout Latin Christendom from the middle of the 12th century. These glosses were written in a small hand in columns surrounding the text, and they required a series of small initials running parallel to the larger ones of the main text. A page with the typically complex layout of the post-1170 book may be seen on ill. 287. It belongs to a different world from those of the earlier part of the century and marks the transition to the Gothic period.

The same time, c. 1170, saw an equally striking change in figure style. It is characterized by the renewed influence of Byzantine art, particularly in the careful modelling of the faces in heavy ochres and greys, producing a more naturalistic effect. An early group of manuscripts with illuminations in the new style is that associated with Abbot Simon of St. Albans (1167–83; nos. 90–1) and, as in the case of the initial-decoration, the Continental influence appears to have come from France. In particular, the illumination of these St. Albans books is related to that of the St. Bertin (or Troyes) Bible (Paris, Bibl. Nat., lat. 16743–6, Vols. II and IV) and to a St. Bertin Psalter which lacks Becket's festival and can therefore be reasonably dated before 1173 (figs. 16, 17, see no. 90). The greater realism of the faces is accompanied by a new naturalism in the fall of the drapery on which multiple folds gradually replace the abstract patterns formed by the damp fold. Smaller and neater figures accord with the reduced size of most books and the fine white outlines, usually considered a feature of Gothic illumination, make their first appearance at this date.

Variants of this style occur in the 1170s and 80s in manuscripts from Durham (nos. 98–100) and other centres (nos. 96, 101, 103), but a distinction should be made with the style embodied in the later initials of the Winchester Bible (no. 83). Here the Byzantine influence appears in a more direct form and it is likely that it reached England via the Sicilian mosaics, especially those of the Cappella Palatina, Palermo, if not from Byzantine manuscripts. Certainly, these Winchester hands are more strictly Byzantinizing than the St. Albans artists of the period, even reflecting the expressionistic phase of Byzantine painting of the second half of the 12th century; and yet it is they who appear more forceful and more highly individual and who represent the greatest achievement of late Romanesque art in England.

In this brief discussion of style it has often been necessary to speak of foreign influences in order to understand the developments in England. Northern France played a crucial part, especially from the time of the Conquest and again a century later with the beginning of the 'transitional' or Channel style. Equally the influence of Byzantine art was endemic throughout the 12th century and it was this Byzantine influence which gave Romanesque art its international aspect by the mid 12th century. The reader might well wonder at this stage what, if anything differentiates English illumination from that of the Continent? Briefly, the English idiosyncracies may be summarized under a few headings. To begin with, there was the survival well into the mid 12th century of Anglo-Saxon drawing technique, an emphasis on more or less sketchy outlines. Related to this tradition was the tendency to reduce forms to linear patterns, as exemplified in the transformation of the Byzantine damp fold into the all-pervasive rhythm of the clinging curvilinear fold. And thirdly, it was in the inventiveness of the decoration, particularly of the grotesques and monsters locked in interminable combat within exotic foliage scrolls, that the English artist surpassed his Continental colleagues.

Such a brief summary of stylistic development cannot aim to do justice to the outstanding quality of the illuminated manuscripts treated in this book. This period was the last in which English illumination was second to none in Europe. From the 13th century, Paris took a leading position in this field which it never relinquished. It was perhaps not until the period of Constable and Turner that English painting again achieved the kind of undisputed international stature that had been attained by the artists of the great 12th-century Psalters and Bibles.

ICONOGRAPHY OF THE RELIGIOUS MANUSCRIPTS

It is a truism concerning medieval art, and, indeed, religious art in general, that artists tended to work within an existing pictorial tradition rather than invent new scenes themselves. We know that they used pattern books, though the surviving evidence for these is fragmentary, and that they copied directly from manuscripts. Some copies are very literal, such as those made at Canterbury of the Utrecht Psalter (see nos. 67–8); more usually the artist adapted a composition to his own particular needs. This is not to suggest that medieval illuminators lacked inventive imagination. On the contrary, a glance at their work in the field of decoration shows us how extraordinarily inventive they were. But when it came to illustrating a text, older

traditions existed to be followed or to be adapted, so that family relationships of manuscripts can be reconstructed from their pictures as much as from a study of their textual variants.[48] Nor were these pictorial traditions limited to manuscripts; related scenes and picture cycles reappear in wall-paintings, monumental sculpture, ivory carvings, metalwork—particularly enamels—textiles and stained glass.

(a) *The New Testament*

In 12th-century England the series of New Testament illustrations form a reasonably coherent group. In particular there are three related picture cycles of the period 1120–40, all probably produced for Psalters, which influenced all subsequent New Testament illustrations in England. The first, and the artistic masterpiece among them, is the St. Albans Psalter which contains thirty-seven New Testament miniatures from the Annunciation to Pentecost. The second, probably also originally made for a Psalter but now bound with a book of the Gospels, the so-called Bury Gospels (Pembroke College, Cambridge, MS 120; no. 35) contains forty scenes mainly in three registers per page, from the Ministry of Christ to the Last Judgment. It was probably produced at Bury in about 1130. Lastly, there are the four separate leaves from a Psalter now conserved in London and New York (no. 66) with one hundred and fifty illustrations in small compartments, which originated at Canterbury in *c.* 1140. The iconography of the St. Albans Psalter has been examined in detail by Otto Pächt[49] and that of Pembroke College MS 120 by Elizabeth Parker;[50] our discussion here will be limited to the relationship between the three manuscripts.

A full comparison of the three cycles is impossible as the St. Albans Psalter does not include scenes from Christ's Ministry, while the Pembroke College manuscript no longer has any illustrations of the Infancy. By far the largest series of pictures is contained in the four separated leaves in which the Gospels are illustrated with some one hundred and fifty scenes. They have about thirty-three illustrations in common with the St. Albans Psalter (Infancy and Passion) and twenty-six with Pembroke 120 (Ministry and Passion) and in each manuscript about half the scenes shared are very similar in composition. If the comparison were limited to the very common scenes, these similarities might well be attributed to coincidence, but, on the contrary, it covers relatively rare ones, such as Zacchaeus in the fig tree, which are very similar in the four Canterbury leaves and the Pembroke College manuscript (figs. 18, 19). In particular, these two manuscripts are linked by their inclusion of several rare illustrations of the story of Christ appearing to the disciples on the shore of Lake Tiberias and that of the fish and the honeycomb (John 21; Luke 24: 42, figs. 20, 21). The relationship of Pembroke 120 and the St. Albans Psalter has long been accepted and it is unlikely that the four leaves belong to a completely independent tradition. Equally, however, as they contain a very much more extensive series of pictures than the other two, they can hardly be considered totally dependent upon them. It is therefore most likely that all three cycles were derived directly or indirectly from a common model, though clearly the outstandingly creative artist of the St. Albans Psalter set the stamp of his invention upon those scenes he painted.

The exact nature of the relationship between the three manuscripts is hard to trace, yet a comparison of all the miniatures leads to certain tentative conclusions. Pembroke 120 appears to be directly dependent, for its iconography as much as for its style, upon the St. Albans Psalter. For example, in the Entry into Jerusalem (figs. 22, 23), the Mocking, the Marys at the Sepulchre and the Emmaus scenes, Pembroke 120 is distinctly closer to the St. Albans Psalter than to the four leaves, and the Harrowing of Hell, which is omitted in the four leaves, is equally close in the other two manuscripts. On the other hand, Pembroke 120 shares a whole series of scenes with the four leaves which are not included in the Psalter and there is the evidence of certain compositions, such as the Last Supper, in which both manuscripts differ from the St. Albans Psalter, to indicate that the artist had access to the same cycle, or a very similar one, as the artist of the four leaves. Very tentatively, therefore, the relationship may be represented in the following way:

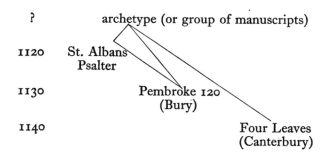

Clearly, in the present state of evidence this diagram is, at best, a considerable oversimplification. It omits the problems of ultimate parentage and of the extent of foreign influences upon each of the three cycles. The principal components are Anglo-Saxon, Byzantine and Ottonian.[51] Anglo-Saxon survivals may be seen, for example, in the long cycle dealing with the three Magi, the dragon mouth of hell in the Harrowing of Hell and in the disappearing Christ in the Ascension which are paralleled, respectively, in the Missal of Robert of Jumièges (Rouen MS Y6) and in the 11th-century Psalter in the British Library (Cotton, Tiberius C. VI). Byzantine influence is stronger on the St. Albans Psalter than on the other two manuscripts. For instance, in the Flight into Egypt, the Psalter follows the Byzantine pattern and has James leading the ass and Joseph bringing up the rear whereas the four leaves are in the Ottonian tradition of having Joseph leading the ass, and not including James. Indeed, for both Pembroke 120 and the four leaves by far the most important single source is that of Ottonian art. Extensive New Testament cycles were produced in the 10th–11th centuries at the major German centres, particularly Reichenau (or wherever the 'Reichenau' manuscripts were made) and Echternach. Elizabeth Parker has amply demonstrated the close link that exists between these and Pembroke 120 and the comparison can be extended to include the four leaves. Indeed, the rarity of the Parables and Miracles scenes they have in common underlines this connection, which is particularly strong with the manuscripts produced at Echternach in the 1040s.

Perhaps, therefore, the archetype in our diagram should be seen as one or more Echternach manuscripts, possibly circulating in England at the time of the marriage of Matilda, daughter of Henry I, with the German Emperor Henry V in 1114. However, the four leaves contain a much more extensive series of pictures than any of the extant Ottonian manuscripts and the possibility, often mooted, that even longer Early Christian cycles, of the type of the St. Augustine Gospels in Cambridge,[52] were known in 12th-century England, cannot be entirely excluded. But here, for lack of evidence, we enter the realm of pure speculation.

The fact remains that these three cycles dominate English New Testament illustration in the 12th century, and even, as Hanns Swarzenski has shown, in the 13th century.[53] The Winchester Psalter (no. 78), for example, also contains an extensive series of pictures, indebted in part to the earlier Winchester tradition but to a larger extent dependent on Pembroke 120. The compartments of the four leaves were copied into the last manuscript in the Utrecht Psalter tradition, now in Paris (Bibl. Nat., MS lat. 8846) and the St. Albans Psalter set the standard for the whole tradition of Psalters with preliminary cycles of full-page miniatures which characterizes English illumination in the 12th century.

(b) *Old Testament*

If the New Testament illustrations form a fairly coherent group dominated by three related cycles, those of the Old Testament appear to present an endless variety, not only of different scenes but of different systems of illustrations—picture cycles, frontispieces, historiated initials, often combined within the same book. The only extensive cycle which still exists is contained in the first of the four Psalter leaves (Morgan 521; no. 66) already discussed in connection with the New Testament illustrations. Its Genesis illustrations are no longer extant, but this single leaf does at least show that such cycles existed in 12th-century England. Psalters, on the whole, contain only a few early Genesis scenes as an introduction to the New Testament pictures, though on occasion, as in the Winchester Psalter (no. 78), the series was expanded to include illustrations of Jacob, Joseph, Moses and David. But for a wider selection of Old Testament scenes, it is to the great illuminated Bibles that we must turn rather than to the Psalters which provide the primary evidence for the Gospel illustrations. These Bibles usually had one historiated initial or frontispiece for each book, which contained a single scene or, more rarely, a sequence of scenes. This method of illustration may sound commonplace now, but it was relatively novel in the 11th and 12th centuries and to understand its origins we must look briefly at earlier systems of Old Testament illustration.[54]

In early Christian times the Old Testament was illustrated not as a complete book but in separate parts. Best known are the profusely illustrated Genesis manuscripts of the 5th–6th centuries such as the Cotton Genesis (B.L. Cotton, Otho B. VI) and the Vienna Genesis (Nationalbibl. cod. theol. gr. 31). In the Middle Byzantine period, there is an illustrated Joshua, the famous 10th-century Joshua Rotulus (MS Vat. Gr. 431), a book of Kings (MS Vat. Gr. 333), and several books of Job—all of which reflect pre-Iconoclastic models. Most popular, to judge from the number of surviving manuscripts, were the Octateuchs, illustrated manuscripts of the first eight books (five books of Moses, Joshua, Judges and Ruth), whose compositions were enormously influential in both Byzantine and Western art.[55] All these manuscripts contain extensive series of narrative illustrations interspersed with the text. There is only one example of a complete, illustrated Greek Bible—the 10th-century Reginensis Bible (Vat. Reg. Gr. 1) which contains frontispieces to individual books of the Old Testament. However, it remains an exception and its frontispieces were probably derived from the more extensive picture cycles in the separate books.

Meanwhile in the early medieval West there is a dearth of fully illustrated manuscripts of the Old Testament. Indeed, before the 11th century there is but one fully illustrated Bible— the Carolingian Bible at San Paolo fuori le Mura, Rome (fig. 27).[56] It has a full-page frontispiece, containing several scenes, to fourteen of the books in the Old Testament and some of them are, in general terms, similar to the frontispieces in the 12th-century Bibles. It is unfortunate that the San Paolo Bible has remained such an isolated monument. Ottonian art offers us hardly any Old Testament illustrations and it is not until the 11th century that we again have illustrated Bibles produced in the West. Frontispieces, and, from the late 11th century, historiated initials at the opening of each book, now become the usual method of Bible illustration. Bibles with extensive narrative cycles, such as the 11th-century Catalan Roda (Paris, Bibl. Nat., lat. 6) and Farfa (Vat. lat. 5729) Bibles[57] and the Anglo-Saxon Hexateuch (B.L. Cotton, Claudius B. IV)[58] remain extremely rare before the 13th century.

In discussing the origins of the illustrations of the English Romanesque Bibles it is essential to distinguish the immediate source from the ultimate parentage. For example, in the case of the single figures of Prophets illustrating their books, Dodwell was surely right in pointing to their ultimate origin in Byzantine art.[59] However, it is also true that this way of illustrating the books of Prophets had been taken over in the West during the 11th century. Standing or, less frequently, seated Prophets usually within an initial, appear not only in the Italian giant Bibles but also, nearer home, in those of Arras (MS 559), of the Meuse, such as the Lobbes (Tournai Seminary) and Stavelot Bibles (B.L. Add. 28106–7), and Normandy (Carilef Bible, Durham A. II. 4).[60] Clearly, by the time a composition or a system of illustration had become so widespread in Western Europe, there is no reason to believe that the English artist used Byzantine models, even if the ultimate source lay in Byzantine art.

Because of the wide diffusion of the Octateuchs and of their influence on compositions in other media, Byzantine influence was strongest on the illustrations of the earlier books of the Old Testament particularly Genesis to Joshua. The Bury Bible (no. 56) pictures for Numbers and Deuteronomy, for example, which include scenes of Moses and Aaron and of Moses expounding the law of the unclean beasts, are closer to the Octateuchs and other Byzantine manuscripts than to anything known from the West. In the Winchester Bible (no. 83) the initial to Leviticus contains the scene of the sons of Aaron offering unholy fire, a very rare illustration paralleled only in the Octateuchs. More usually, however, the scenes concerned had been adapted for use in Western Bibles in the later 11th century, so that their Byzantine origin is already at one remove. Moses slaying the Egyptian in the Winchester Bible occurs regularly in the Octateuchs but was early adapted for the Exodus initials in the Western Bibles, for instance in the French Bible of c. 1120 in the British Library (Harley 4772, f. 27ᵛ). An even clearer example of this process is provided by the initial to Joshua in the Winchester Bible (fig. 26). In two distinct compositions, it shows God's charge to Joshua and Joshua speaking to his officers. The same two scenes occur in a very similar form—clearly a forerunner of the Winchester composition—in the 11th-century Octateuch in the Vatican (Vat. Gr. 747, f. 215ᵛ, fig. 24). However, they had already been selected from the cycle and adapted for the two registers of the initial E in the Stavelot Bible, which dates from 1097 (fig. 25), and it was in this tradition that the Winchester artist followed.

For the illustrations to the other books of the Bible, notably Ruth, Kings (Samuel and Kings), Esther, Judith and Maccabees, the ultimate parentage was more often Western.[61] There is no evidence that Esther was ever illustrated in Byzantine manuscripts and for the other books comparison usually reveals a closer link with Western rather than with Byzantine cycles. This applies to the extended illustrations as much as to the historiated initials. The Kings cycle in the Morgan leaf of the Winchester Bible (no. 84) is related to the San Paolo Bible and the Bible of Stephen Harding (Dijon MS 14, f. 13) and not to the Greek Book of Kings in the Vatican (Vat. Gr. 333).

But where historiated initials are concerned, the process of detaching individual scenes from cycles and adapting them had, as we have seen, in most cases already taken place. For example, the illustration to 2 Samuel in the Dover, Winchester and Laud Misc. Bibles shows the Amalekite offering Saul's crown to David, who rends his clothes, while, below, the Amalekite is killed (fig. 27). These scenes form the full-page frontispiece to 2 Samuel in the San Paolo Bible; they were adapted for the opening initial in the later 11th century (for instance, again, in the Stavelot Bible and in the St. Bénigne Bible, Dijon MS 2; fig. 28) and reappear thereafter with minor variations in most illuminated Bibles (fig. 29). It can be shown that this process was typical whether the ultimate parentage was Western or Byzantine. When the new system of illustrating Bibles evolved in the late 11th century, key scenes, suitable for the role of frontispiece, were extracted from the extensive cycles and used for historiated initials just as they were adapted for the carved capitals in churches at the same period. Once the early Romanesque illustrated Bible had come into existence, a tradition was soon established, and, although the evidence is scant, there is every indication that on the whole artists were content to follow other such Bibles rather than having constant recourse to earlier cycles. In this way the English Bibles (see nos. 45, 56, 69, 70, 83, 98, 103) owe most to those of the Meuse and of Burgundy.

The same conclusion applies to the illustrations of the Sapiential books (Proverbs, Ecclesiastes, Song of Songs, Wisdom, Ecclesiasticus) though here there were no extensive cycles in the first place. One or more of these books usually show an author portrait of Solomon which, as Hugo Buchthal has shown, has a prototype in the frontispiece to Proverbs in a 10th-century Greek manuscript of Job and Proverbs (Copenhagen, Royal Library, Kongl. Saml. 6).[62] For the Song of Songs, on the other hand, the *Sponsus–Sponsa*, Bride and Bridegroom, illustration, showing Christ embracing the Church, was evolved in the West in the 11th century.

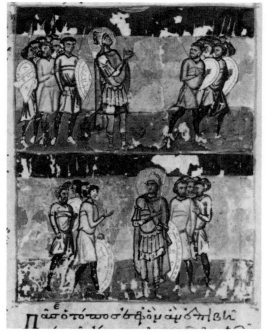

Figs. 24–6. Joshua commanded by God; Joshua and his officers.
Rome, Biblioteca Apostolica Vaticana, Vat.Gr.747, f. 215ᵛ;
London, B.L., Add. 28106, f. 78ᵛ; Winchester, Cath. Lib., f. 69 (Cat. 83)

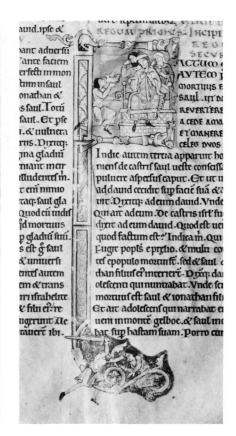

Figs. 27–9. The Amalekite before David; the Amalekite being killed. Rome, S. Paolo fuori le Mura, S. Paolo Bible, f. 91;
Dijon, Bibl. Mun. 2. f. 114; Cambridge, Corpus Christi College 3–4, f. 133 (Cat. 69)

Figs. 30–1. Ezekiel eating the scroll; Ezekiel shaving.
London, Lambeth Palace 3, f. 258ᵛ (Cat. 70);
Paris, Bibl. Nat., lat. 6³, f. 45

Fig. 32. Ezekiel.
London, Lambeth Palace 3, f. 258 (Cat. 70)

Fig. 33. Ezekiel.
Paris, Bibl. Nat., lat. 6³, f. 45ᵛ

Figs. 34–5. Obadiah feeding the Prophets.
Winchester, Cath. Lib., f. 203ᵛ (Cat. 83); Paris, Bibl. Nat., lat. 6³, f. 82

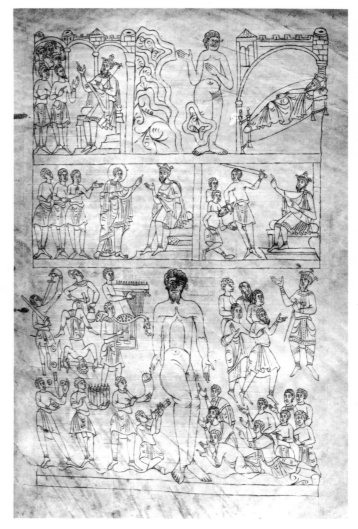

Figs. 36–7. The Story of Daniel.
London, Lambeth Palace 3, f. 285ᵛ (Cat. 70); Paris, Bibl. Nat., lat. 6³, f. 64ᵛ

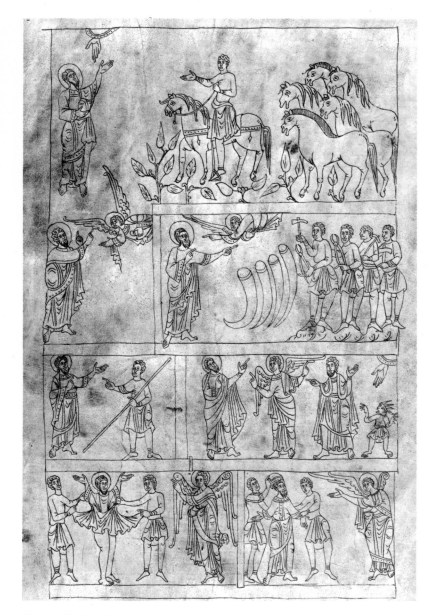

Fig. 38. Initial I (Zechariah).
Winchester, Cath. Lib., f. 210ᵛ (Cat. 83)

Fig. 39. Zechariah.
Paris, Bibl. Nat., lat. 6³, f. 91

Fig. 40. *Sponsus–Sponsa*.
Cambridge, King's College 19, f. 21ᵛ

It first appears in the Bible of St. Vaast, Arras (Arras MS 559) and soon became standard in Western Bibles (cf. fig. 40).[63]

Finally, in the books of Prophets, the English Bibles again followed the standard types having either single figures or common scenes, such as the Vision of Ezekiel and Daniel in the lions' den, which already occur in, for example, the initials of the Lobbes Bible of 1084. What has been insufficiently stressed, however, is that both the Lambeth and the Winchester Bibles contain extensive Prophet cycles which are not readily paralleled elsewhere. The Lambeth manuscript has full-page frontispieces of two or three registers to Ezekiel and Daniel, as well as several narrative scenes contained in the initials to Ezekiel and Zechariah (figs. 30, 32, 36). Many of these illustrations are remarkably similar to the Prophets scenes in the 11th-century Bible from Roda in Catalonia (Paris, Bibl. Nat., lat. 6; figs. 31, 33, 35, 37) but do not occur anywhere else (see no. 70).[64] The same conclusion applies to the Prophets initials with narrative scenes in the Winchester Bible. In particular, the Zechariah initial (fig. 38) contains four scenes in medallions: the calling of Zechariah; the vision of the man with the measuring line beside the city; the vision of the four horns; and the vision of Joshua reclothed. The last three of these are exceedingly rare but they are very close to the illustrations in the Roda Bible (fig. 39). Even more, the initial to Obadiah underlines this relationship (figs. 34, 35). It shows Obadiah bringing food to the Prophets hiding in the cave, a scene that illustrates not the book of Obadiah itself but a story in 1 Kings (18: 4) referring to Obadiah's actions at the time of Jezebel. This hardly seems a likely choice to illustrate the book of Obadiah, but the scene does occur in a similar composition in that context in the Roda Bible. This is not to claim that the artist of the Lambeth and Winchester Bibles had direct access to this particular Catalan manuscript, but to suggest that a similar cycle of Prophets illustrations was available in 12th-century England.

In outline, the origin of these Bible pictures is reasonably clear, but in points of detail the unanswered questions are legion, and the foregoing generalizations should not be taken as minimizing the richness and diversity of English Old Testament illustration in the 12th century. There are many examples of unusual iconography, sometimes dependent on particular Biblical commentaries, at others doubtless due to the inventiveness of the artist. Three of the Bibles have full-page frontispieces as well as initials, in some cases both were used to illustrate one book. Inexplicably, also, in the Winchester Bible there was a change of plan during which a full-page miniature appears to have been abandoned. One can show that very often the English illuminator followed the practice of an earlier English or Continental Bible, but any suggestion of rigid standardization is out of place. In book illumination, as in monumental sculpture and in the field of theological and other studies, the 12th century was an experimental age groping towards a uniformity which finally evolved in the 13th.

TABLE OF OLD TESTAMENT ICONOGRAPHY IN ROMANESQUE BIBLES

	BODLEY, LAUD MISC. 752 LAUD BIBLE c. 1180 (Cat. no. 103) Initials	DURHAM CATHEDRAL A. II. 1 PUISET BIBLE c. 1170–80 (Cat. no. 98) Initials	WINCHESTER CATHEDRAL WINCHESTER BIBLE c. 1150–80 (Cat. no. 83) Initials and 2 Miniatures	LAMBETH PALACE LAMBETH BIBLE c. 1140–50 (Cat. no. 70) Miniatures and Initials	CORPUS, CAMBRIDGE MS 3–4 DOVER BIBLE c. 1140–50 (Cat. no. 69) Initials	CHESTER BEATTY, MS 22 WALSINGHAM BIBLE c. 1140 (Cat. no. 59) Initials	CORPUS, CAMBRIDGE, MS 2 BURY BIBLE c. 1135 (Cat. no. 56) Miniatures	B.L., ROYAL I.C. VII ROCHESTER BIBLE c. 1130 (Cat. no. 45) Initials
GENESIS	Creation cycle in roundels	Lost	Genesis cycle (typological) in roundels	Creation cycle, roundels, Abraham and 3 Angels, Sacrifice of Isaac, Jacob's Ladder	Lost	Creation cycle in medallions	Lost	Volume not extant
EXODUS	Moses and the burning bush	Lost	Egyptian smiting the Hebrew; Moses slays the Egyptian	Lost	Busts of Jacob and 12 Patriarchs	Moses and the burning bush	Lost	,, ,,
LEVITICUS	Moses at Tabernacles before God	Lost	Two sons of Aaron offer unholy fire; devoured by fire from the Lord	Moses communicating with God. Aspersion of lamb's blood	Dec.	Dec.	Lost	,, ,,
NUMBERS	Destruction of Korah	Lost	Moses and brazen serpent	Moses and Israelites. Levites carrying ark. Offerings at Tabernacle	Angel and 5 busts in medallions	Moses	Moses and Aaron. Moses and Aaron addressing Israelites	,, ,,
DEUTERONOMY	Moses asleep. Moses blessing Israelites	Lost	Lost	Dec.	Moses teaching	Dec.	Moses and Aaron. Law of unclean beasts	,, ,,
JOSHUA	God's charge to Joshua. Joshua pierces Men of Ai	Lost	God's charge to Joshua; he speaks to his officers	Lost	Dec.	Moses and Joshua seated	Lost	God's charge to Joshua
JUDGES	Ehud kills Eglon	Lost	Lost	Lost	Joshua and Caleb armed	? Judah and Simeon (or Joshua and Caleb) armed	Lost	Dec.
RUTH	Dec.	Lost	Dec.	Ruth gleaning. Ruth and Naomi. Ruth and Boaz	Ruth	Dec.	Dec.	Dec.
I SAMUEL	Hannah's prayer	Lost	Elkanah, Hannah, Penninah under arcade	Lost	David and Goliath	Volume not extant	Elkanah, Hannah. Penninah. Hannah's prayer	Elkanah, Hannah, Penninah under arcade
II SAMUEL	Amalekite offers crown. Amalekite killed	David mourning; Saul and Jonathan dead	Amalekite takes Saul's crown; David rends clothes; Amalekite killed	Battle on Mt. Gilboa. Death of Saul	David rends clothes. Amalekite offers crown. Amalekite killed	,,	Dec.	David harpist
I KINGS	Anointing of Solomon. Burial of Dead	Lost	David gives charge to Solomon. David and Abishag	David enthroned	Dec.	,,	Dec.	Dec.
II KINGS	Ascension of Elijah. Elisha below	Lost	Elijah and messangers. Ascension of Elijah. Elisha below	Dec.	Ascension of Elijah. Elisha below	,,	Dec.	Ascension of Elijah
ISAIAH	Isaiah sawn in half	Lost	Calling of Isaiah	Tree of Jesse. Death of Isaiah	Isaiah portrait	,,	Lost	Volume not extant

JEREMIAH (and LAMENTATIONS)	,,	,,	Fall of Jerusalem	,,	Calling of Jeremiah	Lost	Calling of Jeremiah. Lamentations: God and Jeremiah	—	Jeremiah lowered into the well
EZEKIEL	,,	,,	Vision of Ezekiel	,,	Dec.	Ezekiel eating the roll; and shaving	Vision of Ezekiel	Lost	Calling of Ezekiel. Ezekiel beheaded
DANIEL	,,	,,	Dec.	,,	Daniel with scroll	Full-page Daniel cycle. Daniel in lions' den	(?) Belshazzar's feast	Lost	Daniel in the lions' den
MINOR PROPHETS	,,	,,	2 Prophet portraits	,,	11 Prophet portraits	8 Prophet portraits. Habbakuk: Crucifixion. Zechariah: cycle	Various scenes and cycles	3 Prophet portraits	3 Prophet portraits
JOB	,,	,,	Job, sons and daughters. Job and wife	,,	Lost	Lost	Blank	Lost	Job and friends
PSALMS	,,	,,	Volume not extant	,,	Beatus: David and choir	Historiated initials: Psalms 26, 38, 51, 52, 109	Historiated initials: Psalms 1, 51, 101	Lost	Beatus: David and choir
PROVERBS	,,	,,	,,	,,	Solomon teaching	Lost	Solomon with scribes	Solomon teaching	Solomon teaching
ECCLESIASTES	,,	,,	,,	,,	Dec.	Lost	Ecclesiastes the preacher	Shrouded corpse before king	Ecclesiastes the preacher
SONG OF SONGS	,,	,,	,,	,,	Solomon	Lost	Sponsus–Sponsa	Lost (Rex et regina)[1]	Sponsus–Sponsa
WISDOM OF SOLOMON	,,	,,	,,	,,	Judgment on a criminal	Lost	Solomon	Lost (Justitia et Sapientia)[1]	Solomon
ECCLESIASTICUS	,,	,,	,,	,,	Seated writer: Jesus ben Sirach	Lost	Wisdom enthroned	Lost (Sapientia)[1]	Jesus ben Sirach. Wisdom enthroned
CHRONICLES I/II	,,	,,	,,	,,	Descendants of Adam	Lost	Solomon at altar	Lost	I. David dancing before Ark. II. Solomon with God
EZRA	,,	,,	,,	,,	Dec.	Lost	King Cyrus, Zerubbabel and Jeshua. Ezra	Ezra seated	King Cyrus
ESTHER	,,	,,	,,	,,	Dec.	Lost	—	Esther and Ahasuerus. Haman hanging	Esther standing
TOBIT	,,	,,	,,	,,	Dec.	Lost	—	Lost	Tobit comforting fellow prisoners
JUDITH	,,	,,	,,	,,	Dec.	Lost	Full-page cycle	Lost	Judith killing Holofernes
MACCABEES I	,,	,,	,,	,,	Alexander divides kingdom	Lost	Full-page cycle	Execution of renegade Jew	Execution of renegade Jew. Battle scene
MACCABEES II	,,	,,	,,	,,	Dec.	Lost	Fire kindled at altar	Battle scene	Massacre scene

Dec.: Decorated only   [1] Inscription

SYMBOLISM, TYPOLOGY
AND THE PICTORIAL DIAGRAM

Typology, the interpretation of the Old in terms of the New Testament, has its basis in the Gospels themselves: '. . . all things must needs be fulfilled, which are written in the law of Moses, and the prophets and the psalms, concerning me' (Luke 24: 44). St. Paul saw the meaning of the Old Testament as covered by a veil until it could be understood through the New Testament (2 Corinthians 3) and upon this foundation the early Christian theologians, from Origen and Tertullian to St. Augustine and St. Gregory, built an elaborate theological system in which nearly every significant person and event in the Old Testament was interpreted as a prefiguration of a comparable scene in the Gospels. Their interpretations were so complete and so thorough that relatively little remained for subsequent authors—Isidore of Seville, Rabanus Maurus and their successors—except to elaborate on the work of the earlier commentators. In the 12th century, perhaps the best known typological system was that contained in the *Speculum Ecclesie* of Honorius Augustodunensis (died *c.* 1130).[65]

Illustrations of typological themes were common in the Early Christian period. The salvation of Daniel in the lions' den and of Jonah in the whale, for example, were used to explain the mystery of Christ's Passion, in catacomb paintings and on sarcophagi, and the late 4th-century ivory casket in Brescia provides the earliest example of an extensive typological cycle.[66] Yet typological illustrations appear only sporadically in the early Middle Ages and it was not until the 11th century, with, for example, the extensive picture cycle planned for Mainz Cathedral by Archbishop Aribo (d. 1031),[67] that the visual aspect of the early typological systems was fully exploited. In the 12th century there was an abundance of typological cycles in all the visual arts, some of the most famous being those produced in champlevé enamel by Mosan goldsmiths. English cycles were among the most important both for their extensive length and for their number, though little has survived. We have written evidence of 12th- and 13th-century typological cycles on paintings in Peterborough Cathedral and Worcester Cathedral Chapter House, in roundels on the high altar of Bury St. Edmunds Abbey Church, and on the stained glass in Canterbury Cathedral. Nothing remains of these except a record of the inscriptions that once served to explain the pictures, but we can obtain an impression of their appearance from the extant 12th-century enamel ciboria and from a mid 13th-century manuscript in Eton College Library, both of which are related to the lost picture cycle in Worcester Cathedral.[68] The earliest remaining example of a typological handbook, unfortunately not illustrated, is the *Pictor in Carmine* text, apparently compiled in England in the early years of the 13th century, which contains descriptions of anti-types, each with a large number of Old Testament types.[69]

With all this evidence to demonstrate the importance of English art in the development of extensive typological cycles, it is singularly unfortunate that so very few objects survive. No manuscript contains anything like the series of typological scenes that can still be seen on the 12th-century enamel ciboria, but one can reasonably assume that as such cycles were known in nearly all other media, they existed in manuscripts also. The most famous typological miniature of the period, the tree of Jesse in the Lambeth Bible (ill. 195) is discussed below, and the same manuscript contains a picture of the Crucifixion flanked by personifications of Church and Synagogue to illustrate the opening of Habakkuk (f. 307). The Prophet himself is shown below the Crucifixion, holding a scroll inscribed with a messianic prophecy which St. Isidore had interpreted as referring to the Crucifixion (Hab. 3: 3–4).[70] Church and Synagogue, which already appear on scenes of the Crucifixion in Carolingian times, are here used to underline the typological significance of the illustration. A rather different typological Crucifixion occurs in the Florence of Worcester Chronicle of about 1130–40 (no. 55, ill. 141) in which the two subsidiary characters prefigure the central theme. On the left, the widow of

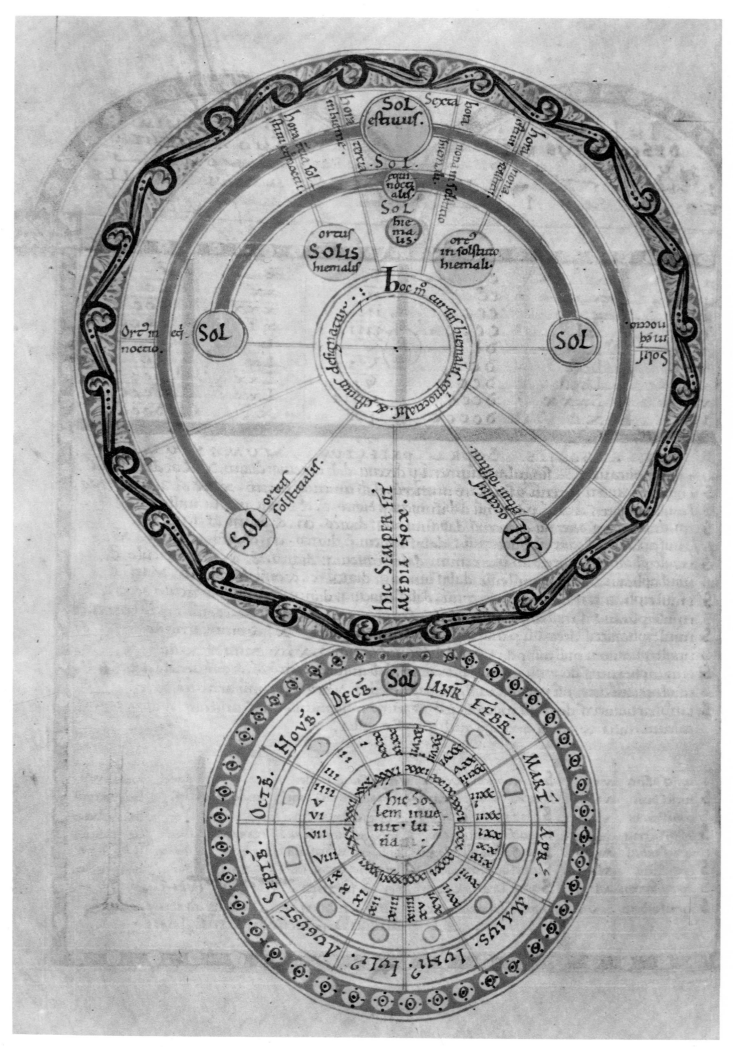

Fig. 41. Solar diagrams. Oxford, St. John's College 17, f. 35ᵛ (Cat. 9)

Fig. 42. Winged Cherub inscribed with virtues.
Cambridge, Corpus Christi College 66, p. 100 (Cat. 102)

Sarepta, encountered by Elijah (1 Kings 17: 8 ff.), holds the crossed sticks which were interpreted as a type of the cross. The man on the right is probably Tobias standing on the fish he caught, which cured his blind father and which was seen as a prefiguration of Christ.

Elsewhere many scenes serving purely as illustrations were selected for that purpose because they had been in the first place popular typological subjects.[71] The Ascension of Elijah, for example, which illustrates 2 Kings in nearly every illuminated Romanesque Bible, was the principal type of the Ascension of Christ since the Early Christian period. Under this heading, mention should also be made of the selection of Old and New Testament scenes to prefix the Psalter. Although these cycles are illustrative rather than typological, the juxtaposition of David and Christ and, indeed, the whole plan of prefixing pictures of the life of Christ to a book of the Old Testament, is due ultimately to typological ideas.

Figural and allegorical interpretations were not limited to the Scriptures. In the 12th century, particularly in the work of Hugh of St. Victor (d. 1142), they were used as the ultimate explanation of the whole visible universe. He argued that not only were the Scriptures allegorical from beginning to end but that, as the means of salvation are sacramental, they are essentially symbolical. 'For as there is body and soul in man, and in Scripture the letter and the sense, so in every sacrament there is the visible and external which may be handled and the invisible within which is believed and taught.'[72] In his works on Noah's Ark, every detail of the Ark, which is a symbol of the Church, is allegorically interpreted in terms of the Christian scheme of life and salvation.[73]

If symbolism was one of the cornerstones of 12th-century thought, the desire for classification was another. Classification and subclassification of all aspects of learning reached a climax in the revival of Aristotelianism in the late 12th and 13th centuries, but it already played a considerable part in the encyclopaedias of Isidore and Rabanus and in the classification of, for example, Boethius, Gerbert and Hugh of St. Victor. The method of listing concepts in groups of four (seasons, elements, temperaments, humours, ages of man, parts of the world) and seven (Liberal arts, planets, virtues, gifts of the Holy Spirit, sacraments) and of linking different members of each numerical group, attained ever increasing complexity.[74] These systems were embodied in diagrams which illustrated school books from the time of Isidore of Seville. The complexities of the universe were presented in diagrammatic form and there is an uninterrupted series of manuscripts containing such diagrams from the Carolingian period onwards (see especially nos. 9, 37, 74, 102, figs. 41, 42). However, it was in the 11th–12th century that pictures were first presented in this form. Indeed, the pictorial diagram, in which the picture plane is divided into a series of carefully organized circles, squares and other geometric shapes, became one of the typical features of Romanesque art.

One masterpiece illustrates perfectly this mixture of symbolism and classification in diagrammatic form: the tree of Jesse in the Lambeth Bible (no. 70, ill. 195). Isaiah's 'And there shall come forth a rod out of the stem of Jesse and a branch shall grow out of his roots' was one of the most famous prophecies of the coming of Christ. The Latin *Virga* (rod or stem) was identified with *Virgo* (Virgin) and the pictorial image of the tree of Jesse incorporating the ancestors of Christ, the Virgin and Christ himself originated in the 11th century and came to an elaborate fruition in the 12th.[75] In this miniature the rod leads straight from Jesse through the Virgin to Christ, who is surrounded by the seven gifts of the Holy Spirit (Isaiah 11: 2) in the form of seven doves. In the upper roundels, which are held up by the Virgin, the Church triumphant is flanked by two figures, probably apostles, while on the right the veil is torn from the face of Synagogue who is accompanied by Moses (horned) and another Old Testament elder. Synagogue's veil, a symbol of the blindness of the Jews, originated in the writings of early Christian authors from the time of Prudentius and St. Ambrose, and from the 11th century she is depicted not only veiled but blindfolded. However, towards the middle of the 12th century the stress on the antithesis of Church and Synagogue occasionally gave way to a conception of the ultimate concordance between them, particularly in the writings of St. Bernard of Clairvaux.[76] This new concept lies behind the famous window at St. Denis in which Christ crowns Ecclesia and lifts the veil from Synagogue, which provides a contemporary parallel to the scene in the Lambeth Bible.[77]

In the lower roundels, at the Virgin's feet, four prophets point upwards towards Christ. One is Isaiah who holds a scroll inscribed with his prophecy: 'Egredietur virga de radice Jesse, et flos de radice eius ascendet.' Four other prophets are shown in the roundels at the corners of the frame. Finally, in the middle roundels are personifications of the four virtues referred to in Psalm 84 (85): 'Mercy and Truth are met together; Righteousness and Peace have kissed each other.' Mercy holds a vase and Justice her scales. In this connection, Dodwell cites St. Jerome's commentary on Psalm 84 in which he says that Truth symbolizes the Jews, for their promise of a saviour was fulfilled in Christ, and Mercy represents the Gentiles.[78] Equally, Truth is similar to Righteousness and Mercy is equated with Peace, for in both pairs the second cannot exist without the first. Consequently, the verse refers to the union of Gentile and Jew under one shepherd, an interpretation which is relevant to the scenes in the upper medallions and to the concept of the tree of Jesse itself.

It would be difficult to imagine such a series of complex theological doctrines more simply and clearly expressed within the confines of a single picture. As Fritz Saxl put it: 'The 12th century did not invent the idea of representing a group of abstract notions in diagrammatic form, but it was not until then that this device played so considerable a part.'[79]

Finally, no discussion of Romanesque art can omit a brief reference to the new dignity accorded to man after centuries of self-abasement and the new recognition of his humanity. St. Bernard saw man as an elevated creature capable of reflecting the majesty of his creator and leading theologians like William of Saint-Thierry and Hugh of St. Victor wrote works on the harmony of body and soul.[80] Indeed, R. W. Southern has defined medieval humanism in terms of man's reawakened concept of his own dignity and of the importance of human friendship and of man's friendship with God.[81] The beginning of this change can be traced to the latter part of the 11th century.

These trends are reflected in the arts of the time. The damp fold itself, the expression of a desire to portray man's body in more naturalistic terms, was recognized by Wilhelm Koehler as the counterpart of 12th-century humanism.[82] A more human interpretation of the Crucifixion, with Christ shown dead on the cross, and a more personal, intimate concept of the relation of Virgin and Child have also been discussed in this context.[83] One of the most telling illustrations of this change in an English manuscript is the representation of *Sponsus-Sponsa*, the mystic Bride and Bridegroom (Christ and the Church), at the opening of the Song of Songs. Before the 12th century, Christ and Ecclesia had been depicted as solemnly enthroned figures in a strictly frontal position. By contrast, in an initial in a Song of Songs manuscript illuminated by the Master of the St. Albans Psalter (Kings College, Cambridge, MS 19; fig. 40), the hieratic solemnity has been abandoned and the couple are shown embracing.[84] The opening words of the Song of Songs 'Let him kiss me with the kisses of his mouth' have been portrayed in the human terms of conjugal love. Romanesque art is essentially solemn and hieratical, but it is also characterized by a new humanism which distinguishes it fundamentally from the more abstract tendencies endemic in earlier medieval art.

NOTES

1. The best historical introduction to this period is still Marc Bloch, *Feudal Society*.

2. For an illuminating summary see R. W. Southern, *Western Society and the Church in the Middle Ages*, Penguin, 1970.

3. The classic study in English is C. H. Haskins, *The Renaissance of the 12th Century*. Compare some of the essays in R. W. Southern, *Medieval Humanism and other studies*, 1970.

4. *The Autobiography of Guibert, Abbot of Nogent-sous-Coucy*, transl. C. C. S. Bland, 1925, 17; G. Paret, A. Brunet, P. Tremblay, *La Renaissance du 12ᵉ siècle*, 1933, 22.

5. See below, notes 17 and 18.

6. A. Grabar, C. Nordenfalk, *Romanesque Painting*, 1958, 135.

7. D. Knowles, *The Monastic Order in England*, 2 ed. 1963, 704.

8. *Ibid.*, 702 f.

9. D. Knowles, C. N. L. Brooke, V. C. M. London, *The Heads of Religious Houses in England and Wales 940–1216*, 1972, 3. For Henry of Blois see above, p. 14 and n. 19.

10. The history of the community at Canterbury at this period is given by R. W. Southern, *Saint Anselm and his Biographer*, 1963, chapt. VII.

11. Knowles, *Monastic Order*, 714.

12. Southern, *Anselm*, 256–9. As an example, he cites Orpington, which was bought for £53 in about 1032 and was worth £28 *a year* in 1086.

13. *Op. cit.*, 244.

14. M. R. James, *The Ancient Libraries of Canterbury and Dover*, 1903, xxxiii ff.; see also L. D. Reynolds, N. G. Wilson, *Scribes and Scholars, a guide to the transmission of Greek and Latin Literature*, 1968, 93 ff.

15. Knowles, *Monastic Order*, 115 f.

16. On St. Albans see, apart from Knowles, *op. cit.*: *Gesta Abbatum S. Albani*, ed. H. T. Riley, Rolls Series, 28, 1863–78, vol. IV; L. F. R. Williams, *History of the Abbey of St. Alban*, 1917; O. Pächt, C. R. Dodwell, F. Wormald, *The St. Albans Psalter*, 1960.

17. On Bury, see *Memorials of St. Edmund's Abbey*, ed. T. Arnold, Rolls Series, 96, 1890–6, in which the *Gesta Sacristarum* is Vol. II, 289; M. R. James, *On the Abbey of St. Edmund at Bury*, Cambridge Antiquarian Society, 1895; D. C. Douglas, ed. *Feudal Documents from the Abbey of Bury St. Edmunds*, British Academy, 1932; M. D. Lobel, *The Borough of Bury St. Edmunds*, 1935; R. H. C. Davis, 'The Monks of St. Edmund 1021–

48', *History*, 40, 1955, 227–39; Antonia Gransden ed., *Chronica Buriensis* (Nelson's Medieval Classics), 1964; R. M. Thomson, 'The Library of Bury St. Edmunds Abbey in the eleventh and twelfth centuries', *Speculum*, 47, 1972, 617–45.

18. R. W. Southern, 'The English Origins of the Miracles of the Virgin', *Medieval and Renaissance Studies*, 4, 1958, 183–200; E. W. Williamson, ed. *The Letters of Osbert of Clare*, 1929, 26 ff.

19. Knowles, *Monastic Order*, 286–93; *id., The Episcopal Colleagues of Thomas Becket*, 1951; L. Voss, *Heinrich von Blois*, 1932; Edmund Bishop, *Liturgica Historica*, 1918 (reprinted 1962), 392–401.

20. *Historia Pontificalis*, ed. R. L. Poole, 1927, 81 ff. On the icons see F. Wormald, *The Winchester Psalter*, 1973, 87 ff.

21. Kathleen Edwards, *The English Secular Cathedrals in the Middle Ages*, 1949, 187 ff.

22. See nos. 14, 33, 61, 62, 64. For example no. 14 from Lincoln is inscribed *pret(ium) XXs* (i.e. 20 shillings) and no. 62 from Hereford has two prices, *precii XXs* on f. 2ᵛ and *precii Vs* on the end leaf. The meaning of these inscriptions has never been fully clarified, but M. R. James's suggestion (in A. T. Bannister, *Descriptive Catalogue of MSS in Hereford Cathedral*, p. iii) that they are valuations 'taken . . . for a papal or other levy' does not seem convincing. The fact that these pricings occur in manuscripts from secular cathedrals and not from monastic foundations supports the supposition that they were in fact what they appear to be: the prices they cost. The second price, where it is given, could refer to the cost of the binding, or to a later valuation. See C. H. Talbot, 'The Universities and the Mediaeval Library', in *The English Library before 1700*, ed. F. Wormald and C. E. Wright, 1958, 72 f.

23. O. Pächt, 'Hugo Pictor', *Bodleian Library Record*, 3, 1950, 96–103.

24. Respectively Bremen MS b. 21 and Stockholm MS A. 144, see J. Prochno, *Das Schreiber-und Dedikationsbild in der deutschen Buchmalerei*, I, 1929, 49, and V. W. Egbert, *The Mediaeval Artist at Work*, 1967, 30, fig. 5.

25. O. Lehmann-Brockhaus, *Lateinische Schriftquellen zur Kunst in England, Wales und Schottland 901–1307*, Munich, 1955–60.

26. See lit. under no. 56.

27. Lehmann-Brockhaus, *op. cit.*, nos. 5265, 5294.

28. N. R. Ker, *English Manuscripts in the century after the Norman Conquest*, 1960, 1.

29. N. R. Ker, *Medieval Libraries of Great Britain*, 1964, 16–22.

30. V. Leroquais, *Les Psautiers: manuscrits latins des Bibliothèques Publiques de France*, 1940–1; G. Haseloff, *Die Psalterillustration im 13. Jahrhundert*, 1938. A useful summary in English of the illustrations of liturgical manuscripts is in J. A. Herbert, *Illuminated Manuscripts*, 1911 (1972, ed. J. I. Whalley), 324–9.

31. F. Wormald, 'Some illustrated manuscripts of the Lives of Saints', *Bulletin of the John Rylands Library*, 35, 1952–3, 248–66.

32. Dodwell, *Canterbury School*, 9, 11 ff.; *id.* in *Jumièges, Congrès Scientifique du XIIIᵉ Centenaire*, Rouen, 1955, 737–41.

33. F. Wormald, 'Decorated initials in English MSS from A.D. 900–1100', *Archaeologia*, 91, 1945, 107–35.

34. *Ibid.*, pl. IV*c*.

35. A. Boutemy, 'La Bible enluminée de Saint-Vaast à Arras', *Scriptorium*, 4, 1950, 67–81, pls. 1–8; S. Schulten, 'Die Buchmalerei des 11. Jahrhunderts im Kloster St. Vaast in Arras', *Münchner Jahrbuch der Bildenden Kunst*, 7, 1956, 49–90, figs. 1, 7.

36. J. J. G. Alexander, *Norman Illumination at Mont St. Michel 966–1100*, 1970, 71 f., pl. 12*a*.

37. Mynors, *Durham*, 32 ff.

38. O. Pächt, 'Hugo Pictor', *Bodleian Library Record*, 3, 1950, 96.

39. Swarzenski, 'Der Stil der Bibel Carilefs von Durham', *Form und Inhalt: Kunstgeschichtliche Studien für Otto Schmitt zum 60. Geburtstag*, 1950, 89–95. The same conclusions were reached by Dodwell, *Canterbury School*, 115–18.

40. Wormald, 'Survival'.

41. W. Koehler, 'Byzantine Art and the West', *Dumbarton Oaks Papers*, 1, 1940, 63–87. For a comparison of the Bury Bible with the frescoes in Asinou, Cyprus, see O. Demus, *Byzantine Art and the West*, 1970, 171, fig. 186.

42. E. B. Garrison, *Studies in the history of Mediaeval Italian painting*, 3, 1958, 200 ff.

43. *Apologia ad Guilelmum* (Migne, *P.L.*, 182, col. 916, quoted by Dodwell, *Canterbury School*, 60). Theologians continued to attack artists for painting such vanities throughout succeeding centuries: see M. Baxandall, *Painting and Experience in 15th century Italy*, 1972, 43.

44. Book II, chapt. 22. Recent translations are those of C. R. Dodwell (1961) and J. G. Hawthorne and C. S. Smith (Chicago, 1963).

45. Dodwell, *Canterbury School*, 104 ff.

46. Ker, *English MSS*, 2–3.

47. B. Smalley, *The Study of the Bible in the Middle Ages*, 1964, 64 f.

48. K. Weitzmann, *Illustrations in Roll and Codex*, Princeton, 2 ed. 1970, remains the standard introduction to this subject. For model books see R. W. Scheller, *A Survey of Medieval Model Books*, Haarlem, 1963.

49. *St. Albans Psalter*, chapt. 4.

50. E. Parker, 'A 12th century cycle of New Testament Drawings from Bury St. Edmunds Abbey', *Proceedings of the Suffolk Institute of Archaeology*, 31, 1969, 263–302, pls. 32–47.

51. *St. Albans Psalter*, chapt. 4.

52. F. Wormald, *The Miniatures in the Gospels of St. Augustine, Corpus Christi College MS 286*, 1954. Unfortunately only one of the full pages with narrative scenes survives.

53. H. Swarzenski, 'Unknown Bible pictures by W. de Brailes', *Journal of the Walters Art Gallery*, 1, 1938.

54. See especially K. Weitzmann, 'The Illustration of the Septuagint', in his *Studies in Classical and Byzantine manuscript illumination*, ed. H. L. Kessler, Chicago, 1971, 45–75, which contains bibliographical notes on the manuscripts cited here. See also M. R. James, 'Illustrations of the Old Testament', in S. C. Cockerell, *A Book of Old Testament Illustrations of the middle of the 13th century*, Roxburghe Club, 1927.

55. (*a*) Florence, Laurenziana, Plut. V. 38, 11th cent. (*b*) Vatican gr. 747, 11th cent. (*c*) Istanbul, Seraglio MS 8, 12th cent., see T. Ouspensky, *L'Octateuque de la Bibliothèque du Sérail à Constantinople*, Sofia, 1907. (*d*) Smyrna, Evangelical School, MS A. I, 12th century (destroyed in 1923), see D. C. Hesseling, *Miniatures de l'Octateuque grec de Smyrne*, Leiden, 1909. (*e*) Vatican gr. 746, 12th cent.

56. J. E. Gaehde, 'The Turonian Sources of the Bible of San Paolo fuori le Mura in Rome', *Frühmittelalterliche Studien*, 5, 1971, 359–400.

57. W. Neuss, *Die Katalanische Bibelillustration um die Wende des ersten Jahrtausends und die altspanische Buchmalerei*, 1922.

58. G. Henderson, 'Late antique influences in some English mediaeval illustrations of Genesis', *J.W.C.I.*, 25, 1962, 172 ff.

59. *Canterbury School*, 85 f.

60. For the Italian giant Bibles see E. B. Garrison, *Studies in the History of Mediaeval Italian Painting, passim*; one of the earliest is the Palatine Bible of *c.* 1080–90 (Vat. Pal. lat. 3–5), Garrison, I, 1953, 10 ff., II, 1956, 131 ff., figs. 145–8; for the Stavelot Bible see K. H. Usener, 'Das Breviar Clm. 23261 . . . und die Anfänge der romanischen Buchmalerei in Lüttich', *Münchner Jahrbuch der bildenden Kunst*, D. F. I, 1950, 78–92; for the Arras Bible, *c.* 1030, see above n. 35 (esp. Schulten, fig. 47); for the Carilef Bible see Mynors, *Durham*, p. 18.

61. Compare especially the iconographical analysis and conclusions in H. Buchthal, *Miniature Painting in the Latin Kingdom of Jerusalem*, 1957, 54 ff. For specific books see: H. Swarzenski, 'A Chalice and the Book of Kings', *De Artis Opuscula XL. Essays in honor of E. Panofsky*, ed. M. Meiss, 1961, 437–41; F. G. Godwin, 'The Judith illustration of the Hortus Deliciarum', *Gazette des Beaux-Arts*, 36, 1949, 25–46.

62. Buchthal, *op. cit.*, 64.

63. *Lexikon der Christlichen Ikonographie*, Herder, 1970, 2, 308 f.; see also below note 84.

64. Neuss, *op. cit.*, figs. 95, 96, 98; and for the Winchester Bible, figs. 91, 106, 117.

65. For the origins of typology see E. Auerbach, 'Figura', in *Scenes from the Drama of European Literature*, 1959. The best summary of typology illustration is in H. Cornell, *Biblia Pauperum*, Stockholm, 1925, 120–53, and a full list of types and anti-types in W.

Molsdorf, *Christliche Symbolik der Mittelalterlichen Kunst*, 1926. See also P. Bloch, 'Typologie', *Lexikon der Christlichen Ikonographie*, 4, 1972, 395; *id.*, 'Nachwirkung des Alten Bundes in der Christlichen Kunst', *Monumenta Judaica*, exh. Cologne 1963, Handbuch, 735.

66. J. Kollwitz, *Die Lipsanothek von Brescia*, 1933; R. Delbrueck, *Probleme der Lipsanothek in Brescia*, 1952.

67. U. Graepler-Diehl, in *Studien zur Buchmalerei und Goldschmiedekunst des Mittelalters. Festschrift für K. H. Usener*, Marburg, 1967, 167–80.

68. The Peterborough and Canterbury cycles have two Old Testament types to each anti-type; the Worcester-enamel Ciboria–Eton 177 cycles (of which the one at Bury is a shortened version) have three Old Testament types. See M. R. James, 'On the paintings formerly in the Choir at Peterborough', *Proceedings of the Cambridge Antiquarian Society*, 9, 1894–8 (1899), 178–94; *id.*, 'On the series of paintings formerly in Worcester Cathedral Priory', *ibid.*, 10, 1898–1903 (1904), 99–115; *id.*, *The verses formerly inscribed on twelve windows in the Choir of Canterbury Cathedral*, Cambridge, 1901; *id.*, *Catalogue of the manuscripts in the Library of Eton College*, 1895, 95 ff.; *id.*, *On the Abbey of St. Edmund at Bury*, Cambridge, 1895, 192–4; M. D. Cox, 'The 12th century design sources of the Worcester Cathedral misericords', *Archaeologia*, 97, 1959, 165–78; L. F. Sandler, 'Peterborough Abbey and the Peterborough Psalter in Brussels', *Journal of the British Archaeol. Asscn.* 33, 1970, 36–49.

69. M. R. James, 'Pictor in Carmine', *Archaeologia*, 94, 1951, 141–66. The Pictor in Carmine cycle is related to those at Peterborough and Canterbury and is similar also to that of the retable of Nicolas of Verdun at Klosterneuburg.

70. Dodwell, *Canterbury School*, 88.

71. P. Strohm, 'The Malmesbury medallions and 12th century typology', *Mediaeval Studies* (Toronto), 33, 1971, 180–2.

72. *De Sacramentis Christianae Fidei*, Migne, *P.L.*, 176, col. 317 (translation by R. J. Deferrari, Cambridge, Mass. 1951), quoted and discussed in H. O. Taylor, *The Mediaeval Mind*, 1911, II, 72. See also J. Chydenius, *The Theory of Medieval Symbolism*, Helsingfors, 1960.

73. Hugh of St. Victor, *Selected Spiritual Writings*, transl. by a Religious of the C.S.M.V., 1962, 45–153 (*De Arca Noe Morali*).

74. V. F. Hopper, *Medieval Number Symbolism*, Columbia U.P., 1938, chapt. VI.

75. A. Watson, *The Early Iconography of the Tree of Jesse*, 1934.

76. W. Seiferth, *Synagoge und Kirche im Mittelalter*, 1964, 149 f.

77. Seiferth, *op. cit.*, fig. 31; also reproduced in E. Mâle, *L'Art réligieux du 12ᵉ siècle en France*, 1953, fig. 130, and discussed at length in L. Grodecki, 'Les Vitraux allégoriques de Saint-Denis', *Art de France*, I, 1961, 32 f.

78. Dodwell, *Canterbury School*, 89, where St. Bernard's interpretation of these Virtues is also discussed. For a full discussion of this subject, see H. von Einem, *Das Stützengeschoss der Pisaner Domkanzel*, 1962, 12 ff.

79. F. Saxl, 'A Spiritual Encyclopaedia of the later Middle Ages', *J.W.C.I.*, 5, 1942, 107. On 12th-century pictorial diagrams see also A. Katzenellenbogen, *Allegories of the Virtues and Vices in Mediaeval Art*, 1964, part II, chapt. 2; A. Watson, 'The Speculum Virginum . . .', *Speculum*, 3, 1928, 445 ff. See also below, nos. 9, 37, 102.

80. These are discussed by M.-M. Davy, *Initiation à la Symbolique Romane*, 1964, 45 f. See also note 82 below.

81. R. W. Southern, *Medieval Humanism and other Studies*, 1970, 29 ff.

82. Koehler, *op. cit.* (note 41). For a fuller discussion of this subject see G. B. Ladner, *Ad Imaginem Dei. The Image of Man in Mediaeval Art*, Wimmer Lecture, 1962, esp. 42–65, with further lit.

83. R. W. Southern, *The Making of the Middle Ages*, 1953, chapt. 5, esp. 237 ff. For a more detailed study, see R. Haussherr, *Der tote Christus am Kreuz: zur Ikonographie des Gerokreuzes*, Diss. Bonn, 1963.

84. *St. Albans Psalter*, 160 f. (with further lit.).

Fig. 43. Lions. Oxford, Laud. Misc. 247, f. 139ᵛ (Cat. 36)

GLOSSARY

Calendar
Placed at the beginning of liturgical manuscripts to record, month by month, the feasts and saints' days celebrated locally.

Canon Tables
A concordance table, usually arranged in columns under arches, showing parallel passages occurring in two or more of the four Gospels.

Colophon
Passage appearing at the end of a manuscript recording information comparable to that contained on the title-page of a book.

Evangelist Symbols
The four Evangelists were frequently represented symbolically by four winged creatures derived from Ezekiel's vision (Ezek. 1: 5–14; Rev. 4: 6–8): the Lion (St. Mark), the Angel (St. Matthew), the Eagle (St. John) and the Calf (St. Luke).

Gospel Lectionary
A selection of passages from the Gospels, arranged in order of the liturgical year, to be sung at Mass.

Historiated Initial
Initial letter enclosing a picture which illustrates or refers to the text it introduces.

Hours, Book of
A Prayer Book used by laymen for private devotion. It included the Office of the Virgin, Psalms, Litanies and Offices of the Dead. From the fifteenth century Books of Hours became very common and the Hours of the Office of the Virgin were illustrated by eight miniatures, each connected with a particular hour.

Mandorla
An almond shaped line or series of lines surrounding the body of a person endowed with divine light, usually reserved for Christ or the Virgin.

Psalter
A service book containing the Psalms and a selection of prayers. Common in the Middle Ages both because Benedictine monks had to sing all the Psalms each week and because it was used for private devotion. The present catalogue uses the Vulgate numeration of the Psalms.

Techniques
Medieval manuscripts were, on the whole, written on vellum until the fifteenth century. The script usually came first and then the unbound leaves were handed to the illuminator. Three main techniques were in use:

1. Outline drawings in ink;

2. Drawings tinted with water-colour;

3. Miniatures painted in gouache and sometimes gold or silver.

For the miniatures it was customary first to draw the composition in pencil, then to ink it in. Then the gold, if any, and next the colours were applied. The final stage was the application of shadows and highlights and any necessary redrawing. Finally the folios in their quires were handed to the binder.

Typology
The interpretation of the Old in terms of the New Testament (see p. 42).

ABBREVIATIONS

Bannister, *Catalogue*	A. T. Bannister, *A descriptive catalogue of the manuscripts in the Hereford Cathedral Library*, Hereford, 1927.
Barcelona, 1961	Barcelona, *L'Art Roman, exposition*, 1961.
B.F.A.C.	Burlington Fine Arts Club.
Boase, *English Art*	T. S. R. Boase, *English Art 1100–1216* (Oxford History of English Art, III), 2nd edn., Oxford, 1971.
Brussels, 1973	Bibliotheque royale, Brussels, *English illumination 700–1500*, 1973.
Coxe, *Catalogue*	H. O. Coxe, *Catalogus Codicum MSS qui in Collegiis Aulisque Oxoniensibus hodie Adservantur*, Oxford, 1852.
Dodwell, *Canterbury School*	C. R. Dodwell, *The Canterbury School of Illumination 1066–1200*, Cambridge, 1954.
H.B.S.	*Henry Bradshaw Society.*
James, *Bestiary*	M. R. James, *The Bestiary, being a reproduction in full of the manuscript Ii.4.26 in the University Library, Cambridge* (Roxburghe Club), 1928.
James, *Catalogue*	M. R. James, *Descriptive catalogue of the manuscripts in the library of:* *Corpus Christi College, Cambridge, 1912.* *Pembroke College, Cambridge, 1905.* *St. John's College, Cambridge, 1913.* *Western manuscripts in the library of Trinity College, Cambridge, 1900–4.*
J.W.C.I.	*Journal of the Warburg and Courtauld Institutes.*
Kendrick, *Late Saxon*	T. D. Kendrick, *Late Saxon and Viking Art*, London, 1949.
Ker, *Catalogue*	N. R. Ker, *Catalogue of manuscripts containing Anglo-Saxon*, Oxford, 1957.
Ker, *English MSS.*	N. R. Ker, *English Manuscripts in the century after the Norman Conquest*, Oxford, 1960.
Ker, *Medieval Libraries*	N. R. Ker, *Medieval libraries of Great Britain*, London, 1964.
Manchester, 1959	City of Manchester Art Gallery, *Romanesque Art c. 1050–1200 from collections in Great Britain and Eire*, 1959.
Millar, I	E. G. Millar, *English illuminated manuscripts from the xth to the xiiith century*, Paris and Brussels, 1926.
Mynors, *Durham*	R. A. B. Mynors, *Durham Cathedral Manuscripts to the end of the twelfth century*, Durham, 1939.

New Pal Soc., I and II	*New Palaeographical Society, Facsimiles of Ancient Manuscripts, etc.*, 1st and 2nd series, London, 1903–30.
Pächt and Alexander, III	O. Pächt, J. J. G. Alexander, *Illuminated manuscripts in the Bodleian Library, Oxford, III, British school*, Oxford, 1972.
Pal. Soc., I and II	*Palaeographical Society, Facsimiles of Manuscripts and Inscriptions*, 1st and 2nd series, London, 1874–94.
Rickert, *Miniatura*, I	M. Rickert, *La Miniatura Inglese, 1, Dalle origine alla fine del secolo xii*, Milan, 1959.
Rickert, *Painting in Britain*	M. Rickert, *Painting in Britain. The Middle Ages* (Pelican History of Art), 2nd edn., 1965.
R. A.	Royal Academy.
St. Albans Psalter	*The St. Albans Psalter (Albani Psalter), 1. The full-page miniatures*, by O. Pächt. *2. The initials*, by C. R. Dodwell. *3. Preface and description of the manuscript*, by F. Wormald, London, 1960.
Saunders, *English illumination*, I and II	O. E. Saunders, *English illumination*, 2 vols., Florence and Paris, 1928.
Saxl and Meier, III	F. Saxl, H. Meier, *Verzeichnis astrologischer und mythologischer illustrierter Handschriften des lateinischen Mittelalters, III. Handschriften in Englischen Bibliotheken* (Herausgegeben von H. Bober), 2 vols., London, 1953.
Schiller, *Iconography*	G. Schiller, *Iconography of Christian Art*, 3 vols., London, 1971 ff.
S.C.	*Summary catalogue of Western Manuscripts in the Bodleian Library*, Oxford, 7 vols., 1895–1953.
Swarzenski, *Monuments*	H. Swarzenski, *Monuments of Romanesque Art. The art of Church Treasures in north-western Europe*, 2nd edn., London, 1967.
Talbot Rice, *English Art*	D. Talbot Rice, *English Art 871–1100* (Oxford History of English Art, II), Oxford, 1952.
Warner and Gilson	G. F. Warner, J. P. Gilson, *Catalogue of Western Manuscripts in the Old Royal and King's Collections*, 4 vols., London, British Museum, 1921.
Woolley, *Catalogue*	R. M. Woolley, *Catalogue of manuscripts of Lincoln Chapter Library*, Oxford, 1927.
Wormald, 'Development'	F. Wormald, 'The development of English illumination in the 12th century', *Journal of the British Archaeol. Asscn.*, 3rd series VIII, 1943, 31–49.
Wormald, *English Drawings*	F. Wormald, *English Drawings of the tenth and eleventh centuries*, London, 1952.
Wormald, 'Survival'	F. Wormald, 'The survival of Anglo-Saxon illumination after the Norman Conquest', *Proceedings of the British Academy*, 30, 1944, 127 ff.

CATALOGUE

1. London, British Library MS Arundel 60

Psalter, with Anglo-Saxon gloss
306 × 192 mm.
c. 1060 and *c.* 1080. Winchester (?New Minster)
Ills. 1, 2; Fig. 5

Outline drawings: signs of the Zodiac for each month in the Calendar (ff. 2–2ᵛ) in red ink; Crucifixion with Mary and St. John before the Psalter text (f. 12ᵛ) tinted drawing.

Framed, painted pages: Beatus page with David and another figure in scrolls in the initial (f. 13); the Crucifixion with the Evangelist symbols in medallions at the corners of the frame (f. 52ᵛ); decorated page for Psalm 51 with dragons in the Q (f. 53); decorated page for Psalm 101, D (f. 85).

The Calendar and Litany indicate an origin in Winchester (SS. Judoc, Eadburg, Leothfred, Swithun, Haedde, Grimbald, Aethelwold, Birinus and Byrnstan are included in the Calendar), but it is difficult to decide between St. Swithun's and the New Minster. Warner pointed out that the main New Minster saints—Judoc, Eadburg and Grimbald—are marked with a red cross in the Calendar, but Wormald found that in the Litany a number of bishops buried at St. Swithun's are placed before Grimbald and Judoc.

A pre-Conquest date is suggested by the fact that the gloss is Anglo-Saxon. The illustrations are in two sharply contrasting styles: the outline drawings present a hardened version of the Anglo-Saxon tradition, whereas the painted pages are in a later style. These painted pages all have an elaborate frame with stylized acanthus decoration of the Anglo-Saxon type, except that it is drier and more strictly controlled, rather like that in the Gospels in Paris (Bibl. Nat., lat. 14782; no. 2). On the other hand, the initial with a clambering figure on f. 13 is derived from Norman illumination of the second half of the 11th century. The Crucifixion itself is fully Romanesque in character. The nervous calligraphy of Anglo-Saxon art has given way to thick, firm outlines and contours which stress the anatomy of Christ and delineate the abstract patterns on the loin-cloth. The heavy colours dominated by deep blue and green, are also unlike Anglo-Saxon illumination; only the unpainted backgrounds provide a link with Anglo-Saxon drawings.

Dodwell has argued convincingly that these miniatures were not part of the original manuscript but were added later. The text may be dated *c.* 1060, but part of it (ff. 47–52, 133–42ᵛ) is in an Anglo-Norman hand of the last quarter of the century. Two of the later illuminations immediately follow these folios (ff. 52ᵛ, 53) and two are on pages where the interlinear Anglo-Saxon gloss is in a different hand from that of the main part of the manuscript (ff. 13 and 53). Dodwell's arguments are supported by the fact that the later miniatures either start a quire (ff. 13, 53) or end one (f. 52ᵛ). Stylistically, the miniature on f. 52ᵛ shows the influence of Continental painting. The original source is probably Ottonian, but Dodwell has made a telling comparison with Norman and Northern French manuscripts, in particular with a Crucifixion in a manuscript from Angers (Amiens, MS fonds Lescalopier 2; Dodwell, pl. 72e). This is similar in style and has the same S-shaped body of Christ, unusual at this early date.

The trees on either side of the cross represent the two trees of Paradise described in Genesis 2: 9: the tree of life and the tree of the knowledge of good and evil. The symbolism of the two trees in this context was not fully exploited until the later Middle Ages, but they occasionally appear on Crucifixions in Ottonian art. They are found, for example, in the Gospels of Bernward of Hildesheim, *c.* 1000 (Thoby, *Crucifix*, fig. 38), where they resemble the trees of Arundel 60 in form, and in an early 11th-century relief from a doorway now in the museum at Strasbourg (R. L. Füglister, *Das lebende Kreuz*, 1964, 150, fig. 10).

PROVENANCE: Thomas Howard, Earl of Arundel (1585–1646); 1681 presented by Henry Howard to the Royal Society; bought by the British Museum in 1831.

LITERATURE: J. O. Westwood, *Miniatures and Ornaments of Anglo-Saxon and Irish MSS*, 1868, 121, pl. 49; Guido Oess, *Untersuchungen zum altenglischen Arundel Psalter* (Anglistische Forschungen, Heft 30, 1910), with whole text and glosses; Warner, *Illuminated MSS in the British Museum*, 1903, pl. 11; O. Homburger, *Die Anfänge der Malschule zu Winchester im X. Jahrh.*, 1912, 24, 64, 68 f.; Millar, I, 81, pl. 31; F. Wormald, *English Kalendars before 1100*, 1934, no. 11; *id.*, 'English Saints in the Litany of Arundel 60', *Analecta Bollandiana*, 64, 1946, 73; *id.*, 'Survival', 5 f., pl. 3; *id.*, *English Drawings*, no. 25, pp. 47, 50, 52, 66, 78, pl. 33; *id.*, in *Archaeologia*, 91, 1945, 126, 129, pl. 1c; T. D. Kendrick, *Late Saxon and Viking Art*, 1949, 19 f., pls. 21, 89; Talbot Rice, *English Art*, 216 f., pl. 79; Rickert, *Painting in*

Britain, 55, pls. 52–3; Dodwell, *Canterbury School*, 118, pl. 72; J. E. Hunt, *English and Welsh Crucifixes*, 1956, 28 ff. rep.; P. Thoby, *Le Crucifix des Origines au Concile de Trente*, 1959, 41, pl. 14, no. 31; G. Zarnecki, *Romanesque Art*, 1972, 174, fig. 189; D. Pearsall, E. Salter, *Landscapes and Seasons of the Medieval World*, 1973, 40.

2. Paris, Bibliothèque Nationale MS lat. 14782
Gospels
245 × 170 mm., ff. 132
c. 1080. Exeter Cathedral   *Ills. 3–6; Fig. 1*

Decorated Canon tables (ff. 9–16); four full-page, framed Evangelist portraits: St. Matthew (f. 16ᵛ); St. Mark (f. 52ᵛ); St. Luke (f. 74ᵛ); St. John (f. 108ᵛ). Small decorated initial N to preface (f. 1); four large, framed decorated initials to the Gospels: Matthew (f. 17); Mark (f. 53); Luke (f. 75); John (f. 109).

Jonathan Alexander has placed this manuscript in Exeter primarily because the miniatures of Mark and John were copied from the Leofric Gospels (Bodl. Lib. MS Auct. D. 2. 16), given by Bishop Leofric (1050–72) to Exeter Cathedral. The two Evangelist portraits of this manuscript are Flemish work of about 1040 and it is these that were copied in the Paris manuscript. The other two are no longer extant, but it is likely that the artist of the Paris Gospel Book derived all four Evangelist portraits from the same source. The Exeter provenance is supported by the fact that the text of the Canon tables is also copied from the Leofric Gospels and the script is close to other Exeter books. Jonathan Alexander argues that the manuscript was produced not long after Leofric's death in 1072.
The style of the Evangelists of the Leofric Gospels, characterized by a two-dimensional monumentality and a stylized treatment of pleated drapery, marks a stage in the development from Ottonian to Romanesque art and the Paris Gospels demonstrate the influence of these Continental developments in England. The figures are solid, with strong, firm outlines, without any sign of the agitated lines and zigzag hems of Anglo-Saxon drawings. The frames on the other hand, are clearly derived from Anglo-Saxon acanthus decoration, though the leaves themselves are thinner and drier and the decorative structure more tightly controlled (cf. B.L. Arundel 60; no. 1). There are in fact only four different designs for the eight framed pages (1. ff. 16ᵛ and 109; 2. ff. 17 and 74ᵛ; 3. ff. 53ᵛ and 75; 4. ff. 53 and 108ᵛ), though the colours vary. Type 1, in particular, contains a variety of individualized flowers emerging from the mass of acanthus foliage. These do not occur in Anglo-Saxon manuscripts but are derived from Norman decorations and their appearance marks another stage in the development from Anglo-Saxon to Romanesque decorative forms.

PROVENANCE: Exeter Cathedral (see above); Abbey of St. Victor, Paris, since 16th century (shelf-mark and arms f. 1).

LITERATURE: A. Boeckler, *Abendländische Miniaturen*, 1930, 56; J. J. G. Alexander, 'A little known Gospel Book of the later 11th century from Exeter', *Burlington Magazine*, 108, 1966, 6–16.

3. Cambridge, Corpus Christi College MS 391
Calendar, Psalter, Hymns, Collects, private prayers, etc.
223 × 134 mm., 724 pages
c. 1080. Worcester Cathedral Priory   *Ill. 8*

Full-page, framed, tinted drawing of David playing the harp (p. 24); decorated Beatus initial (p. 25).

This manuscript bears the title *Portiforium Oswaldi*, but the connection with St. Oswald (Bishop of Worcester, Archbishop of York, died 992) is difficult to substantiate for an 11th-century manuscript. The limits of the Easter table on p. 22 indicate that it was written between 1064 and 1093, and it has been argued that it was probably made for St. Wulfstan, Bishop of Worcester, 1062–95.
The figure of David represents a hardened and solidified version of the Anglo-Saxon tradition of outline drawing. Wormald compared the red, green, and yellow stripes on the drapery to the colouring of the William of St. Carilef manuscripts at Durham (Mynors, *Durham*, pls. 16–18) which are now generally held to be Norman work of *c.* 1088–91. The Beatus initial has a multi-coloured background of blue, red, green, purple, and yellow patches which indicates a degree of Norman influence, but is otherwise firmly in the Anglo-Saxon tradition.

PROVENANCE: Worcester Cathedral Priory (inscription f. 1 *Liber sce. Marie Wygorniens(is) . . .*).

LITERATURE: James, *Catalogue*, II, no. 391; C. H. Turner, *Early Worcester MSS*, 1916, lviii; Laurentia McLachlan, 'St. Wulfstan's Prayer Book', *Journal of Theological Studies*, 50, 1928–9, 174–7; F. Wormald, *English Kalendars before A.D. 1100*, 1934, No. 17, pp. 212 ff.; id., *English Drawings*, 56 f., 61, no. 11, pl. 39; F. P. Pickering, *Literature and art in the Middle Ages*, 1970, pl. 10a.

4. Cambridge, Clare College MS 30
Gregory the Great, Dialogues, etc.
322 × 205 mm., ff. 207 (not foliated)
Late 11th century. Worcester Cathedral Priory
Ills. 7, 9, 10

Five decorated initials: Preface, Q (f. 2), Bk. I, V (f. 5); Bk. II, F, Bk. III, D, Bk. IV, P.

The Worcester provenance is confirmed by the presence of 13th-century copies of four letters relating to the Priory on f. 1ᵛ. On the fly-leaf, in a late 12th-century hand, there is a set of fifty-eight verses which appear to have been written to accompany a set of illustrative pictures of Maccabees. Whether these pictures ever existed at Worcester, or elsewhere, we do not know. The only series of pictures of Maccabees recorded are those of the 13th century, formerly in the Painted Chamber at Westminster (see Stothard's drawings in *Vetusta Monumenta*, VI, 1897, 32 f., pls. xxxv–vi).

The lively decorated initials are typical of Anglo-Norman ornamentation, containing foliage spirals with palmettes and curling trumpet leaves, animal masks, human and animal profile terminals, and large, winged dragons, all on a multi-coloured ground of red, green and pale purple. Only the purple buds sprouting from the stems (f. 5) are idiosyncratic. Similar initials appear in other Worcester manuscripts of this period, such as Bodleian Library, MSS Hatton 23 and Lat. th. d. 33 (Pächt and Alexander, III, nos. 55–6, pls. 5–6) and there are points of contact also with those of Corpus Christi College, Cambridge, MS 391 (no. 3).

PROVENANCE: Worcester Cathedral Priory; subsequent history not recorded.

LITERATURE: James, *Catalogue*, no. 30; *id.*, 'On two series of paintings formerly at Worcester Priory', *Proceedings of the Cambridge Antiquarian Society*, x, 1898–1903, 110–15.

5. Oxford, Wadham College MS A. 10. 22
Gospels
206 × 136 mm., ff. 130
Late 11th century   *Ills. 17, 18*

Two red ink outline drawings, framed: St. Matthew seated, holding scroll and pen (f. 12ᵛ); St. John's Gospel: the Three Marys at the Sepulchre (f. 104ᵛ). Facing St. Matthew: a painted decorative frame containing the opening words of the Gospel and a faint pencil drawing of St. Matthew, barely visible to the naked eye, but in an ultra-violet photograph appearing very similar to the drawing opposite (f. 10); for St. Mark's Gospel there is only a decorative frame, the drawing was never carried out (f. 44ᵛ).
One historiated initial in outline: St. Luke's Gospel, Q with an angel standing on a dragon (fig. 67).
One decorated initial, painted: large opening B, St. John's preface to Pope Damasus (f. 3). Three decorated initials in red outlines: P, opening to St. Mark (f. 45), H, St. John's prologue, I, St. John's Gospel (f. 105ᵛ).

The two drawings of St. Matthew, the empty frame for St. Mark, and the curious substitution of the Marys at the Sepulchre for St. John's portrait at the opening to St. John's Gospel, all indicate that there was a change of plan in the illustration of this book, which was never completed. Alexander has pointed

out that the St. Matthew portrait is similar to that in the Winchester 'Grimbald' Gospels (B.L. Add. 34890) and the Marys at the Sepulchre to the same scene in the Benedictional of St. Ethelwold (B.L. Add. 49598, f. 51ᵛ), another Winchester manuscript of the late 10th century. However, the composition of the Marys at the Sepulchre differs too considerably from the Benedictional to warrant an attribution of the Wadham manuscript to Winchester on grounds of iconographical similarity. The crossed legs, which are found neither in the Grimbald Gospels nor in the faint drawing on f. 13 of this manuscript may be compared with a mid 11th-century Canterbury drawing (Durham Cathedral MS B. III. 32; Wormald, *Drawings*, pl. 29).

The style of both the figures and the acanthus decoration represents a hardened, solidified version of Anglo-Saxon drawings and is comparable to that in the Exeter Gospels in Paris (Bibl. Nat., lat. 14782; no. 2). The post-Conquest date is confirmed by the script which is Norman rather than English in form (Alexander, 13). The initial H on f. 105 differs from the rest of the decoration in containing large, individualized flowers within circular foliage stems. This is a clearly developed Romanesque form and indicates either that it is a precocious example at this early date or that the initial was added to the manuscript in the first half of the 12th century.

PROVENANCE: Given to Wadham by William Boswell, Scholar (1613) and Fellow (1622) of the College in 1625 (inscription f. 2).

LITERATURE: Coxe, *Catalogus*, II, 1; Waagen, *Treasures of Art in Great Britain*, III, 1854, 111; Talbot Rice, *English Art*, 200, 209, pls. 64a, 73b; J. J. G. Alexander, *Anglo-Saxon illumination in Oxford Libraries*, Bodleian Picture Book, 1970, 12 f., pls. 31–4.

6. Cambridge, Trinity College MS B. 5. 26
St. Augustine, Commentary on the Psalms, Part I
240 × 333 mm., ff. 179
c. 1070–1100. Canterbury, Christ Church
Ill. 11

Beatus initial f. 1, David enthroned playing harp, below musician playing rebec and juggler with knives.

This is one of the eight manuscripts in the script of the earliest monks brought over to Christ Church, Canterbury from the Norman abbey of Bec after the Conquest. Another is Trinity MS B. 5. 28 which formed the third volume of this commentary (the second volume is lost) and which contains four decorated initials (ff. 45, 60, 60ᵛ, 87ᵛ; Dodwell, pl. 10d). The form of the B is basically Anglo-Saxon (cf. Winchester Psalter, Cambridge University Library, MS Ff. 1, 23, f. 5; Dodwell, pl. 8a) but the style of the figures and the brightly coloured yellow background is Norman rather than English. The iconography is Anglo-Saxon—David is enthroned with a musician and a juggler in the Psalter B.L. Cotton, Tiberius C. VI (Dodwell, pl. 10a)—but the practice of placing the figures within the initial developed in Normandy. For French and Spanish versions of the theme of the juggler among David's choir see H. Steger, *David Rex et Propheta*, Nürnberg, 1961, pp. 85–94, pls. 15, 18, 19, 34.

PROVENANCE: Christ Church, Canterbury (f. 171ᵛ, 15th cent. inscription *de claustro ecclesie Christi Cant*); given to the college by John Whitgift, Master of Trinity, 1567–77, Archbishop of Canterbury, 1583–1603/4.

LITERATURE: James, *Catalogue*, I, no. 172; Dodwell, *Canterbury School*, 17 f., 76, 120, pl. 10b.

7. London, British Library MS Arundel 16
Osbern, Life of St. Dunstan
248×155 mm., ff. 45
c. 1090. Canterbury, Christ Church   *Ill. 12*

Decorated initial U, with angel (f. 1, damaged); historiated initial R with St. Dunstan (not Osbern as the inscription might suggest) and a censing monk (f. 2).

Osbern was Precentor at Christ Church and internal evidence suggests that his Life of St. Dunstan was written at the very end of Lanfranc's archiepiscopate or during the interval between his death and the appointment of Anselm (1089–93). Boase compared the initial to that in a Canterbury manuscript belonging to William of St. Carilef, Bishop of Durham, who died in 1096 (Durham B. II. 10; Mynors, *Durham*, pl. 26), and argued that Arundel 16 was also produced in about 1090. Some twenty manuscripts of the text survive, but this appears to be the earliest and it may have been the original Christ Church copy. The figure-style and the colouring, in particular the bright yellow and orange of the background, are Norman in origin.

PROVENANCE: Christ Church, Canterbury; Dover Priory (press mark). Thomas Howard, Earl of Arundel (1585–1646); 1681 presented by Henry Howard to the Royal Society; bought by the British Museum in 1831.

LITERATURE: W. Stubbs, *Memorials of St. Dunstan*, Rolls Series, 1874, xxxi, xliii; Boase, *English Art*, 42, pl. 10a; Dodwell, *Canterbury School*, 48 n. 1, 120.

8. Cambridge, Trinity College MS O. 2. 51
Priscian, Grammar
150×217 mm., ff. 160; bound with
a 10th-century Prudentius manuscript
c. 1070–1100. Canterbury, St. Augustine's Abbey
Ills. 13–16

Decorated initial for each of the eighteen Books (that on f. 121, Bk. 17, is a late 12th-century addition; initial to the Prologue, f. 1, cut out): Bk. 1, P (f. 2); Bk. 2, S (f. 9); Bk. 3, C (f. 16); Bk. 4, D (f. 21); Bk. 5, Q (f. 26); Bk. 6, Q (f. 34); Bk. 7, T (f. 46); Bk. 8, V (f. 58); Bk. 9, D (f. 74); Bk. 10, I (f. 81ᵛ); Bk. 11, Q (f. 91); Bk. 12, P (f. 96); Bk. 13, C (f. 100); Bk. 14, Q (f. 105); Bk. 15, A (f. 111ᵛ); Bk. 16, C (f. 116ᵛ); Bk. 18, I (f. 139).

This manuscript is a storehouse of early Romanesque initials, characterized by figures clambering in shafts or entwined in foliage scrolls, and by human heads in medallions. Such figured initials were developed in Normandy in the middle of the 11th century and were perfected in England in the period *c.* 1100. Dodwell (p. 26, pl. 15d) has described the figures clambering up the shafts of the initials on ff. 46, 81ᵛ as the earliest developed English examples of this popular type. The style of the figures, however, characterized by a calligraphic technique of nervous, almost zig-zag outlines only lightly tinted, is very much in the Anglo-Saxon (rather than the Norman) tradition.

PROVENANCE: Probably St. Augustine's Canterbury; the hand is the same as a St. Augustine's book in the Bodleian Library, Ashmole 1431, and the style of initials is close to B.L. Arundel 91 (no. 17); subsequently (?)Christ Church, Canterbury—end fly-leaves taken from Christ Church manuscript, B.L. Cotton, Otho D. VIII. Dr. Thomas Gale (1635/6–1702) Regius Professor of Greek, High Master of St. Paul's School; given to his college by his son, Roger Gale, in 1738.

LITERATURE: James, *Catalogue*, III, no. 1155; Dodwell, *Canterbury School*, 17, 19, pls. 11c, 15b, d; Ker, *Medieval Libraries*, 1964, 33, 41.

9. Oxford, St. John's College MS 17
Natural Science text-book
342×242 mm., ff. 177
5 leaves now in British Library,
MS Cotton, Nero C. VII, ff. 80–4
c. 1090. Ramsey or Thorney Abbey
Ill. 21, p. 127; Fig. 41

Large coloured diagrams throughout, especially: world map (f. 6), tree of consanguinity (f. 6ᵛ), divisions of philosophy (f. 7), Byrhtferth's diagram, harmony of the 'physical and physiological fours': elements, seasons, humours, etc. (f. 7ᵛ), lunar tables (ff. 22–8), the sun and signs of the Zodiac (f. 35ᵛ), measurement of time (f. 37), graph of planetary course in Zodiac (f. 38), microcosmic–macrocosmic harmony: elements, seasons, humours (f. 39ᵛ), celestial and terrestrial climate zones (f. 40ᵛ).
Calendar ff. 16–21ᵛ with outline drawings of signs of the Zodiac: January, Aquarius (f. 16); February, Pisces (f. 16ᵛ); May, Gemini (f. 18); July, Leo (f. 19).

Folios 139–55 of St. John's 17 and the five leaves of Cotton, Nero C. VII contain the annals of Thorney Abbey, near Peterborough, written in the margin of tables of years. Ker argued that the annals up to 1111 were mainly in one hand, which occurs also in the corrections and notes throughout St. John's 17 and is nearly contemporary with the text hand. There is a reference to the 'present time 1110' on f. 3ᵛ, which accounts for the date traditionally given to this manuscript (Coxe, Singer, Ker). However, this date was queried by C. W. Jones (manuscript note at St. John's) on the grounds that f. 3 could be a later addition to the manuscript, and, more recently, Cyril Hart has put forward arguments for placing the origin of the manuscript in nearby Ramsey rather than Thorney, and in c. 1080–90 rather than 1100. Ramsey Abbey had been the home in England of Abbo of Fleury (c. 945–1004), the author of certain sections of this manuscript, and it remained an important centre in the field of scientific study in the 11th century, when Byhrtferth, Abbo's pupil, produced his manual. Hart suggested that the manuscript was written at Ramsey and then obtained for Thorney by the Norman Abbot, Gunter, 1083–92 (whose name appears in capitals in the annals) for his newly rebuilt monastery. From an examination of the script, he concluded that the annals up to 1081 were contemporary with the main hand and were written by Ramsey monks, but that the entries from 1092 were added at Thorney. The link with the scientific tradition at Ramsey is very convincing, but whether the manuscript was actually written there or at Thorney remains in doubt. The text book character of the manuscript has been analysed by Harry Bober. It is a compilation of excerpts principally from Isidore of Seville, Bede and Abbo of Fleury for use in monastic teaching. Other English 12th-century manuscripts with similar contents are B.L. Royal 13. A. XI (early 12th cent.), Cotton, Tiberius E. IV (Winchcombe, early 12th cent.), Cotton, Tiberius C. I (see no. 37), and Walters Art Gallery, Baltimore, 73 (c. 1190–1200). The tradition of Isidore (*De Natura Rerum*) and Bede (*De Natura Rerum*; *De Temporum Ratione*) was expanded at the Abbey of Fleury in the 10th century, and, in particular, under the aegis of Abbo, who was a monk there and who became Abbot after his return from Ramsey in 998.

R. W. Southern has characterized the diagrams as a 'marriage of science and art'. Some of them originated in Isidore manuscripts, others were added to the tradition by later compilers (Bober, 185). Their function was to illustrate the text, but often they go beyond this to convey fundamental themes of Christian cosmological doctrine. Thus, the three circular diagrams of the harmony of the four elements, seasons and humours (f. 39ᵛ) convey, in a perfectly ordered manner, the microcosmic–macrocosmic harmony in the constitution of the universe. These schemata are of particular interest for their relationship with the didactic, diagrammatic layout of so much of Romanesque art in which the picture plane is divided into compartments. The connection

with the cosmological diagrams is underlined by the inscriptions, which are often included to clarify the typological or cosmological meaning of the figures and scenes depicted. Mosan enamels, such as the Stavelot portable altar in Brussels, form perhaps the most diagrammatic group of works, but the Tree of Jesse picture in the Lambeth Bible (no. 70, ill. 195) provides an almost equally good comparison. The diagrams in St. John's 17 may be described as works of art in their own right, and it was during this period, also, that a work of art often took on the character of a diagram.

PROVENANCE: Thorney Abbey, c. 1100; 16th century, Robert Talbot who lent it to Leland; Hugh Wickstead, early 17th century, who gave it to St. John's College. Borrowed by Sir John Cotton who, presumably, tore out five leaves between ff. 143 and 144 which now form part of B.L. Cotton, Nero C. VII.

LITERATURE: Coxe, *Catalogus*, II, 5; John Leland, *De Rebus Britannicis Collectanea*, 2 ed. 1770, IV, 97; Charles and Dorothea Singer, 'Byrhtferd's Diagram', *Bodleian Quarterly Record*, II, 1917, 47–51, fig. 3; C. Singer, 'A review of medical literature in the Dark Ages', *Proc. Royal Soc. of Medicine*, 10, 1917, 107; C. H. Haskins, *Studies in the History of Mediaeval Science*, 1924, 83 f.; A. van de Vyver, 'Les Œuvres inédites d'Abbon de Fleury', *Revue Bénédictine*, 1935, esp. 144 ff.; N. R. Ker, 'Membra disiecta', *British Museum Quarterly*, 1938, 131; C. W. Jones, *Bedae Pseudepigrapha*, 1938, 60–3, 127 f.; id., *Bedae, Opera de Temporibus*, 1943, *passim*; H. Bober, 'An illustrated Mediaeval School-Book of Bede's De Natura Rerum', *Journal of the Walters Art Gallery*, 19–20, 1956–7, esp. 77 f., figs. 9, 11, 12, 18; M. Destombes, *Mappemondes*, Amsterdam 1964, no. 25, 8; *Byrhtferth's Manual*, ed. S. J. Crawford, 1966 ed., frontispiece; R. W. Southern, 'The Place of England in the 12th century Renaissance', *Medieval Humanism and Other Studies*, 1970, 164 ff., pls. 3, 5, 6; Cyril Hart, 'The Ramsay Computus', *English Historical Review*, 85, 1970, 29–44.

10. Oxford, Bodleian Library MS Ashmole 1431

Herbal, 237×150 mm., ff. 43
Last quarter 11th century. Canterbury,
St. Augustine's Abbey   *Ills. 22–5*

About one hundred and fifty coloured drawings of plants.

The herbal, a collection of descriptions of plants listing their medicinal qualities, can be traced back to the 4th century B.C. It was, and remained, essentially a medical manual and not a book of natural history. The most popular herbal in the Middle Ages was traditionally linked with the name of Dioscorides, a physician of the first century A.D., whose *De Materia Medica*, written in Greek, was translated into Latin in the 6th century. The popularity of this work is attested by the existence of many manuscripts in Greek and Latin. From the 7th century onwards (see Leyden, MS Voss Q. 9) the Dioscorides Herbal was often combined with another selection of plants attributed, for no known reason, to 'Apuleius Barbarus'. From the 9th century, there is a proliferation of illustrated herbals of which the main recensions are listed by Charles Singer, 'The Herbal in Antiquity', *Journal of Hellenic Studies*, 47, 1927, 1–52. The plant drawings were copied from one manuscript into another and remained essentially schematic rather than naturalistic.

Ashmole 1431 contains only the pseudo-Apuleius text. It is related to Bodley 130 (no. 11) but contains a fuller selection of plants, including the famous Mandrake, which is missing in Bodley 130. However, its drawings are considerably cruder in execution than those of Bodley 130.

PROVENANCE: St. Augustine's, Canterbury (ex libris and press mark, 15th century f. iv; no. 1264 in 15th-century catalogue, see M. R. James, *The Ancient Libraries of Canterbury and Dover*, 346, no. 1264, 520).

LITERATURE: R. T. Gunther, *The Herbal of Apuleius Barbarus*, Roxburghe Club, 1925, xvii, xxvi, pl. 2; Ker, *Catalogue*, 350, no. 289; Ker, *English MSS*, 30; Dodwell, *Canterbury School*, 26, 122; Bodleian Picture Book, *English Rural Life*, 1965, pl. 15*b*; L. MacKinney, *Medical illustrations in medieval MSS*, 1965, 160; Pächt and Alexander, III, no. 50, pl. 6.

11. Oxford, Bodleian Library MS Bodley 130 (S.C. 27609)
Herbal and 'Sextus Placitus', de virtutibus bestiarum in arte medicinae
244 × 180 mm., ff. 95
c. 1100. Bury St. Edmunds Abbey

Ills. 26–9

One hundred and forty-two paintings of plants (ff. 1–67); drawing of a man and woman embracing (f. 68); twenty-six tinted outline drawings of animals (ff. 76–95ᵛ).

The contents include the herbals of pseudo-Apuleius (ff. 1–56) and pseudo-Dioscorides (ff. 57–67), both in an incomplete form. For a note on the tradition of medieval herbals see MS Ashmole 1431 (no. 10). Bodley 130 belongs to the tradition of the 9th-century manuscript at Schloss Herten, but it is unique in this period in that several of its illustrations are convincing naturalistic studies, apparently painted with reference to actual plants rather than copied from earlier texts. Singer suggested, for example, that for the plant *viperina* (f. 37ᵛ) the artist adopted a milk thistle *cardurus marianus*

which would have been known to him. With the exception of this single 12th-century manuscript, this process of correcting the transmitted tradition by consulting nature was not renewed until the late 14th century in Italy.

The last part of this manuscript contains the treatise on the 'medicinal qualities of animals' attributed to Sextus Placitus, of whom nothing is known. Much of the treatment prescribed, for example 'drink the saliva of a horse', was unpleasant, and this text never approached the popularity of the herbal. Nevertheless, there are several illustrated manuscripts of the early Middle Ages, usually combined with herbals (9th century: Florence, Laurenziana, Plut. 73. 41; Schloss Herten; Lucca, Bibl. Gov., MS 269; 10th century: Monte Cassino MS 97; 11th century, English: B.L. Cotton, Vitellius C. III). The birds and animals in Bodley 130 are reminiscent of Anglo-Saxon drawings; J. J. G. Alexander (*Anglo-Saxon Illumination*, 1970, 14) compares the style with the late 10th-century astronomical manuscript, B.L. Harley 2506, and suggests a prototype of this period. Indeed, Pächt has taken the Anglo-Saxon derivation of the animals to indicate that the plants in the herbal owe their naturalism to an Anglo-Saxon prototype rather than to direct reference to nature, but this remains an open question.

PROVENANCE: Bury St. Edmunds Abbey (press mark M. 44, inscription, 14th century, *Herbarium Dioscorid de armario monachorum Sancti Edmundi*, f. 1); given by Sir Thomas Knyvett (d. 1594) to Augustine Styward (inscription f. 1); given to the Bodleian Library by Dr. Edward Tyson in 1706.

LITERATURE: R. T. Gunther, *The Herbal of Apuleius Barbarus*, Roxburghe Club, 1925 (facsimile ed.); C. Singer, 'The Herbal in Antiquity', *Journal of Hellenic Studies*, 47, 1927, 1–52, esp. 39 ff.; *Corpus medicorum latinorum*, IV, ed. H. Howald, H. E. Sigerist, 1927, xi; O. Pächt, 'Early Italian nature studies and the early Calendar landscape', *J.W.C.I.*, 13, 1950, 29 n. 2; Ker, *Catalogue*, 357, no. 302; Bodleian Picture Book, *English Rural Life*, 1965, pl. 14; L. MacKinney, *Medical illustrations in medieval MSS*, 1965, 160; R. H. Rouse, 'Bostonus Buriensis', *Speculum*, 41, 1966, 489 n. 52; J. J. G. Alexander, *Anglo-Saxon illuminations in Oxford Libraries*, 1970, pls. 35–6; A. Gransden, 'Realistic Observation in 12th century England', *Speculum*, 47, 1972, 51, figs. 9–10; Pächt and Alexander, III, no. 53, pl. 6.

EXHIBITED: Brussels, 1973, no. 19, pl. 8.

12. London, British Library MS Sloane 2839
Medical tracts
184 × 127 mm., ff. 112
Early 12th century

Ills. 19, 20

Four pages of pen outline drawings of cautery figures: surgeon heating cautery irons; naked male patient with cautery points marked (f. 1ᵛ); two naked male cautery figures (f. 2); surgeon with cautery iron and bowl, male patient on right with relevant sickness inscribed (f. 2ᵛ); two cautery figures with inscriptions *ad elefantiacos incenditur sic* and *Ad renum et coxarum dolores incenditur sic* (f. 3).

Traditionally described as 11th-century, both the drawings and the script suggest a date *c.* 1100. These cautery illustrations are among the earliest surviving examples of their kind. Indeed, apart from one 9th-century manuscript from Southern Italy, which attests to the ancient nature of the tradition, this is the earliest of medieval cautery manuscripts of which over twenty have survived (see Sudhoff, *loc. cit.*). A fairly close comparison can be made with MS Hunter 100 from Durham (see no. 27). In particular the two figures on f. 2 are in similar postures as those on f. 119 of the Hunter manuscript, though in the latter they are partially clothed.
Cautery was, together with blood-letting, one of the principal forms of medical treatment in the Middle Ages. Its use spread far beyond the cauterization of wounds, as the inscriptions here show. Cautery illustrations differ in detail, but they all show figures on which the points where the iron is to be applied have been clearly marked.

PROVENANCE: Sir Hans Sloane Bt., M.D. (1660–1753); his manuscripts bought for the British Museum in 1753.

LITERATURE: K. Sudhoff, *Beiträge zur Geschichte der Chirurgie im Mittelalter*, I, Leipzig, 1914, 81 ff., pl. xvii; W. Bonser, *The Medical Background of Anglo-Saxon England*, 1963, 303; L. MacKinney, *Medical illustrations in Medieval MSS*, 1965, 52 f., fig. 49.

13. Lincoln, Cathedral Library MS A. 1. 2 & Cambridge, Trinity College MS B. 5. 2

Bible, Vol. I, Cathedral Library, Lincoln,
Genesis–Job, 492×322 mm., ff. 235
Vol. II, Trinity College, Cambridge,
480×318 mm., ff. 180
c. 1100. Lincoln   *Ills. 30–3*

Vol. I:
Six historiated initials: Joshua, large T, God and Joshua in shaft (f. 70ᵛ), I, Ruth standing (f. 85ᵛ), I, Joel standing (f. 184), I, Jonah standing (f. 187), I, Haggai seated (f. 191), I, Zechariah (f. 191ᵛ).
Forty-two decorated initials: F, Jerome prologue, uncoloured (f. 2), D (f. 5), I, Genesis (f. 6), H, Exodus (f. 22ᵛ), V, Leviticus (f. 35ᵛ), L, Numbers (f. 45), H, Deuteronomy (f. 58ᵛ), P, Judges, (f. 78ᵛ), V, preface to 1 Samuel (f. 86ᵛ), F, 1 Samuel (f. 87), F, 2 Samuel (f. 97), E, 1 Kings (f. 105ᵛ), C, 2 Kings (f. 115ᵛ), N, V, Isaiah prologue (f. 125), V, Jeremiah (f. 140), E, E, Ezekiel and prologue (ff. 158ᵛ, 159), D, A, Daniel and prologue (ff. 174ᵛ, 175), N, V, Hosea and prologue (f. 182), V, Joel (f. 184),

A, V, Amos and prologue (f. 185), A, V, Obadiah and prologue (f. 186ᵛ), E, Jonah (f. 187), M, V, Micah and prologue (f. 187ᵛ), N, O, Nahum and prologue (f. 189), A, O, Habakkuk and prologue (f. 189ᵛ), S, V, Zephaniah and prologue (f. 190), A, Haggai prologue (f. 191), Z, Zechariah prologue (f. 191ᵛ), D (f. 193ᵛ), M, O, Malachi and prologue (f. 194), V, Job and prologue (f. 195, 195ᵛ).

Vol. II:
Seven historiated initials: I, Ezra standing (f. 55), I, Esther standing (f. 62ᵛ), A, Judith holding the head of Holofernes (f. 70), L, Matthew's Gospel, angel with book (f. 98ᵛ), I, Mark seated, and lion (f. 110), I, Christ, John, eagle in medallions (f. 129ᵛ), P, Acts, Luke in mandorla (f. 139ᵛ).
Forty-four decorated initials: P, Proverbs (f. 1ᵛ), V, Ecclesiastes (f. 8ᵛ), O, Song of Songs (ff. 10ᵛ), D, Wisdom of Solomon (f. 12ᵛ), M, O, Ecclesiasticus and prologue (ff. 17, 18), S, A, Chronicles and prologue (ff. 31, 32ᵛ), C, 2 Chronicles (f. 43), V, Ezra prologue (f. 54), L, Esther prologue (f. 62ᵛ), C, T, Tobit and prologue (f. 66ᵛ), A, Judith prologue (f. 69ᵛ), E, 1 Maccabees (f. 75), F, 2 Maccabees (f. 85ᵛ), B, S, P, E, prefaces etc. to New Testament (ff. 93, 93ᵛ, 97, 97ᵛ), M, Matthew prologue (f. 98), M, Mark prologue (f. 109ᵛ), L, Q, Luke and prologue (ff. 116ᵛ, 117ᵛ), H, John prologue (f. 129), L, Jerome's preface to Acts (f. 139), N, Epistles prologue (f. 150), I, James (f. 150ᵛ), P, Peter (f. 151ᵛ) S, Simon (f. 153), Q, John (f. 154), S, S, 2, 3 John (f. 155), A, Apocalypse (f. 156), 11 initials to Paul Epistles, mainly P's (ff. 162–176ᵛ).

The second volume, which had long been considered lost, was first published by Ker in 1964. The Lincoln Bible is the earliest illustrated English Romanesque Bible, though most of the twelve historiated initials are limited to single figures and there are no narrative scenes.
The uncoloured foliage scrolls of the initials are shown against a background of small areas brightly coloured in green, blue, red and yellow. Apart from the thick foliage stems with curling leaf endings, there are small trefoil plants in the spirals—a combination that occurs in late 11th-century Norman manuscripts (e.g. Paris, Bibl. Nat., lat. 11636 from Préaux, see F. Avril, 'Manuscrits Bénédictins Normands . . .', *Mélanges d'Archéologie et d'Histoire*, 77, 1965, repr. p. 235). The figures, usually shown in mandorlas applied to the shafts, are also predominantly Norman in style though the spread-out, fluttering hems are reminiscent of Anglo-Saxon drawings. They are characterized by thin bodies, and very long hands and fingers, which occur in all the Lincoln manuscripts of this period: A. 3. 17 (see no. 14), B. 3. 5, and B. 2. 3 (one initial only).

PROVENANCE: given to Lincoln Cathedral library by *Nicholaus Canonicus et archidiaconus*, probably to be identified with Nicholas, Archdeacon of Huntingdon, who was appointed by Bishop Remigius (1073–94) and died about 1109. No. 1 in the catalogue of Hamo, Chancellor of the Cathedral from *c.* 1150 (which gives the above provenance and which appears on f. 1 of this manuscript) and in the 15th-century catalogue. It is not known when Vol. II was acquired by Trinity College.

LITERATURE: Woolley, *Catalogue*, no. 1; Giraldus Cambrensis, *Opera*, VII, ed. J. F. Dimock, Rolls Series, 1877, 153 ff., 165 (reprints the obituary, ff. 203ᵛ–206 and Hamo's catalogue, which is also given in Woolley, *op. cit.*, v–ix); Boase, *English Art*, 41, 160; Ker, *Medieval Libraries*, 116.

14. Lincoln, Cathedral Library MS A. 3. 17
St. Augustine, Sermons
334×213 mm., ff. 242
Early 12th century. Lincoln   *Ills. 34–6*

Initials to most of the eighty-eight sermons (eight have been cut out). Nine historiated initials: opening initial E, Christ preaching repentance (f. 8ᵛ), D, (?) St. Matthew standing (23ᵛ), T, St. Luke (f. 85ᵛ), I, St. John (f. 96), D, Trinity (f. 142), Q, St. Augustine (f. 188ᵛ), O, St. Paul (f. 235), Q, (?) David (f. 231), Q, Synagogue holding a broken flag (f. 233).
Seventy-one decorated initials, mainly small, a few with figures: ff. 7, 10, 11ᵛ, 12ᵛ, 14, 17ᵛ, 25, 27ᵛ, 30, 48ᵛ, 51, 55ᵛ, 56, 64ᵛ, 65ᵛ, 67, 70, 73ᵛ, 74ᵛ, 76ᵛ, 78, 79ᵛ, 82ᵛ, 86ᵛ, 88ᵛ, 90, 93ᵛ, 95, 101ᵛ, 103, 105, 106ᵛ, 110ᵛ, 115, 116ᵛ, 119, 121, 126, 130, 131ᵛ, 133, 136, 137ᵛ, 138ᵛ, 139, 139ᵛ, 146, 147ᵛ, 149ᵛ, 150, 156, 161, 162ᵛ, 165ᵛ, 169, 173ᵛ, 178, 182ᵛ, 185ᵛ, 191, 192ᵛ, 196ᵛ, 200ᵛ, 204ᵛ, 211ᵛ, 217ᵛ, 220ᵛ, 223ᵛ, 227ᵛ, 239, 241.

The style of both the decoration and the figures is very close to that of the Lincoln Bible (no. 13). Yet the initial on f. 8ᵛ is more sophisticated than any in the Bible and this may indicate a slightly later date for this manuscript. The fact that there is a group of related illuminated manuscripts in the Cathedral library suggests that there was a local scriptorium at Lincoln. However, as there was no priory attached to the cathedral one cannot be sure whether there was a cathedral scriptorium or whether its manuscripts were produced elsewhere. Many of the Lincoln manuscripts, like those of other non-monastic cathedral libraries such as Hereford, are marked with a price (in this case 20 shillings), but this in itself does not answer the question of where they were actually produced.

PROVENANCE: Lincoln Cathedral Library (inscribed f. 2ᵛ *liber sancte Marie Linc*; and ...*pret(ium) XXs*) no. 4 in the Catalogue of Hamo, Chancellor of the Cathedral from *c.* 1150, and no. 73 in the 15th-century catalogue.

LITERATURE: Woolley, *Catalogue*, no. 90; Boase, *English Art*, 40 f., pl. 10*b*.

EXHIBITED: Manchester 1959, no. 3.

15. London, British Library MS Royal 6. C. VI
Gregory the Great, Moralia in Job (Parts 4–6)
332×238 mm., ff. 260
1108–14. Rochester Cathedral Priory
                                              Ill. 37

Large initials to each Part (ff. 6, 79ᵛ, 142ᵛ), smaller decorated initials to most Books. Bk. 17, Job on the dunghill, his wife brings him bread on a stick (f. 6), Bk. 18, P with lamb of God (f. 15), Bk. 19, Q with Michael and the dragon (f. 33ᵛ), Bk. 20, Q (f. 45ᵛ), Bk. 22, Q (f. 68ᵛ), Bk. 23, P, a knight pierces a dragon (f. 79ᵛ), Bk. 24, H (f. 91), Bk. 25, I (f. 101ᵛ), Bk. 27, Q with a bust of Christ (f. 128), Bk. 28, P with a nimbed eagle (f. 142ᵛ), Bk. 29, D with Samson and the lion (f. 152ᵛ), Bk. 30, B (f. 167ᵛ), Bk. 32, S (f. 206), Bk. 33, A (f. 218ᵛ), Bk. 34, Q (f. 236), Bk. 35, Q (f. 247).

The Radulphus mentioned on f. 1, Ralph d'Escures, was Bishop of Rochester from 1108 to 1114 and Archbishop of Canterbury from 1114 to 1122. As the manuscript may be firmly placed in Rochester on stylistic and palaeographical grounds, it is likely that it was commissioned by Ralph while he was bishop there, even though he is given the title of archbishop in the 14th-century inscription.
The initials, particularly on ff. 79ᵛ, 91, 206, 218ᵛ, and 236, are very similar to those in Royal 5. D. I (see no. 16). The somewhat crude but solidly constructed figures are in the Norman rather than Anglo-Saxon tradition. The scene of Job receiving bread on a stick from his wife appears in Early Christian and Byzantine illustrations of Job's patience. A comparable scene occurs in a 9th-century Greek manuscript in Venice (Marciana Gr. 538, see K. Meyer, 'St. Job as a Patron of Music', *Art Bulletin*, 36, 1954, 26, fig. 13).

PROVENANCE: Rochester Cathedral Priory (inscribed f. 6: *Liber de Claustro Roffensi per Radulfum Archiepiscopum*). Entered Royal Library at time of the Dissolution, *c.* 1540 (no. 548 in Catalogue of 1542), given to the British Museum by George II in 1757.

LITERATURE: Warner and Gilson, I, 110; Boase, *English Art*, 62, pl. 18*b*; D. Tselos, 'Unique Portraits of the Evangelists in an English Gospel Book', *Art Bulletin*, 34, 1952, 263, fig. 9.

16. London, British Library MS Royal 5. D. I–II
St. Augustine, Commentary on Psalms, Vols. II and III
5. D. I: 362×220 mm. ff. 249
5. D. II: 372×240 mm. ff. 237
(?) 1107–13 and 1115–24. Rochester, Cathedral Priory   *Ills. 38, 39*

5. D. I:
Eleven decorated initials: large opening initial P

(f. 1), T (f. 45), E (f. 101), P (f. 129ᵛ), P (f. 167), N (f. 175ᵛ), O (f. 196ᵛ), S (f. 203), P (f. 210ᵛ), D (f. 226ᵛ), C (f. 235ᵛ).

5. D. II:

Historiated initial M, Psalm 118, angels clambering up shaft, one is held by a haloed youth (f. 70ᵛ); seven decorated initials: P (f. 43), Q, man as tail (f. 52), A (f. 90), P, rider with sword (f. 197ᵛ), D (f.208), I (f. 213), M, two men attacking a third (f. 227ᵛ).

Prior Arnulph (see below) probably held office from c. 1107 to 1113 (D. Knowles, C. N. L. Brooke, V. London, *Heads of Religious Houses in England and Wales 940–1216*, 1972, 63), Bishop Ernulph from 1115 to 1124. The similarity of these names could have led to confusion, but if the 14th-century inscription is regarded as authoritative, Royal 5. D. I should be dated c. 1107–13 and Royal 5. D. II 1115–24. The precise length of the interval is unknown, but there can be no doubt, to judge from the initials that the two volumes were produced at different times. The initials of 5. D. I, characterized by thick, fleshy, striated foliage, large winged dragons and lions' masks are in the late 11th-century Anglo-Norman style, not unlike the Carilef manuscripts of c. 1090 at Durham or some of the manuscripts from St. Ouen (e.g. Rouen MS 467, Dodwell, pl. 9).

The initials of Vol. II vary in style, but they are quite different from those in Vol. I. The thick Anglo-Norman foliage has been replaced by smaller, neater initials with rows of flattened palmettes in the shafts and more human figures. It clearly represents a later stylistic phase than Vol. I and also than Royal 6. C. VI (see no. 15).

Boase has raised the question of the meaning of the (?)illustrative initials to Psalms 118 (119) and 148 (149), but it is hard to discover any relevance to the texts of these Psalms.

PROVENANCE: Rochester Cathedral Priory (5. D. I inscribed 14th century f. 1 *liber de claustro Roffensi prima pars psalterii S. Augusti Arnulphi prioris*; 5. D. II inscribed f. 1 *secunda pars psalterii Ernulphi episcopi liber de claustro Roffensi*). Entered Royal Library at time of Dissolution, c. 1540 (No. 81 in Cat. of 1542), given to the British Museum by George II in 1757.

LITERATURE: Warner and Gilson, I, 110; Boase, *English Art*, 62, 106.

17. London, British Library MS Arundel 91

Passionale (Lives of Saints)
333 × 222 mm., ff. 229
1100–20. Canterbury, St. Augustine's Abbey
Ills. 40, 41, 43, 44

Twelve of the Saints' lives have historiated initials: E, beheading of St. Matthew (f. 2), M, St. Michael spearing the Dragon (f. 26ᵛ), Q, Jerome and the lion (f. 32ᵛ), I, St. Picaton (f. 33), B, St. Bavo (f.

36), P, St. Denis (f. 86), C, martyrdom of St. Demetrius (f. 107), C, SS. Tharacus, Probus and Andronicus (f. 119ᵛ), C, martyrdom of SS. Crispin and Crispianus (f. 161ᵛ), B, martyrdom of St. Foillan (f. 179), I, St. Benigne (f. 186ᵛ), T, St. Cesarius: above, the Saint watches a pagan sacrifice—Lucian, the victim, first sacrifices in the temple (left medallion) and then hurls himself from the mountain as a sacrifice in honour of Apollo, on the right spectators watch his suicide; below, St. Cesarius is judged for sorcery; in the last medallion he is sewn into a sack and thrown into the sea (f. 188).

Sixteen decorated initials: I (f. 6), T (f. 9ᵛ), I (f. 20ᵛ), D (f. 23), I (f. 28ᵛ), L (f. 40ᵛ), B (f. 47ᵛ), S (f. 55), V (f. 81ᵛ), C (f. 116ᵛ), T (f. 156ᵛ), B (f. 158ᵛ), I, the Devil urging a monk to gluttony (f. 190, cf. Royal 1. B. XI, no. 65), B (f. 206ᵛ), T (f. 218ᵛ), T (f. 222ᵛ).

The figure style is still very much in the Anglo-Saxon tradition of flimsy, agitated pen outlines which survived at St. Augustine's well into the 12th century (see also Trinity College MS O. 2. 51, and B.L. Cotton, Vitellius C. XII; nos. 8 and 18). This is one of the few early Canterbury manuscripts with historiated initials, and it is the only one in the first quarter of the century to contain narrative scenes. The initial to St. Cesarius, in particular, contains a complex narrative cycle which has been compressed with considerable ingenuity to fit within the confines of a small initial.

PROVENANCE: Thomas Howard, Earl of Arundel (1585–1646); 1681, presented by Henry Howard to the Royal Society; bought by the British Museum in 1831.

LITERATURE: J. Raine (ed.) *The Historians of the Church of York*, Rolls Series, 1, 1879, xlix, 161 ff. (Eadmer's *Life of Wilfrid*, ff. 125ᵛ–144 of this MS); Wormald, 'Survival', 10, pl. 5b; Kendrik, *Late Saxon*, 135; Wormald, *English Drawings*, 55, 61; id., *Archaeologia*, 91, 1945, 110, 128, pl. 8c; Talbot Rice, *English Art*, 198, 221; Boase, *English Art*, 40, 53, 73, 157, pl. 6b; Dodwell, *Canterbury School*, 26 ff., 31, 34, 62, 74, 79, pls. 15, 16, 19b, 21a, 35c; Rickert, *Painting in Britain*, 50 f., pl. 46B; Swarzenski, *Monuments*, fig. 199; *St. Albans Psalter*, 170 n 7.

18. London, British Library MS Cotton, Vitellius C. XII

Martyrology of St. Augustine's Abbey, Canterbury
290 × 203 mm. (size of original leaf), leaves damaged through fire in 1731 and remounted.
ff. 156, 12th-century text ff. 114–56
1100–20. Canterbury, St. Augustine's Abbey
Ill. 42; Colour Plate p. 23

Historiated initials KL (Kalendae) originally for each month, of which only seven remain:
January, Capricorn (f. 114); February, Aquarius,

warming, (f. 117ᵛ); March, Pisces, pruning trees (f. 121); May, Taurus (f. 127); August, Leo (?)harvesting grapes (f. 134); September, Virgo (f. 139); October, Libra (f. 143ᵛ).

These initials present an unusual mixture of the signs of the Zodiac, the occupations of the months, and purely decorative motifs. Aquarius appears to be warming himself by the fire as the occupation for February and Pisces could almost be mistaken for a decorative motif beside the occupation of pruning. Other months have the signs of the Zodiac only; some entwined in the foliage scrolls (Capricorn), others perched on top of the shafts (Taurus, Leo). Only Virgo fills the body of the initial. The style of the figures is still firmly rooted in the Anglo-Saxon tradition.

PROVENANCE: Sir Robert Cotton, Bt. (1571–1631); his library presented to the nation by his grandson, Sir John Cotton, Bt. in 1700, incorporated in the British Museum in 1753.

LITERATURE: M. R. James, *The Ancient Libraries of Canterbury and Dover*, 1903, 502, 531; British Museum, *Schools of Illumination*, II, 1915, 7, pl. 5e; F. Wormald, 'Survival', 10; id., *English Drawings*, 55, 61, pl. 37; Boase, *English Art*, 39 f., 87, pl. 30b; Rickert, *Painting in Britain*, 49 f., pl. 46c; Dodwell, *Canterbury School*, 27, 62, 123, pls. 16b, 35 a–b; Ker, *English MSS*, 30, pl. 10a.

19. Florence, Biblioteca Mediceo-Laurenziana MS Plut. XII. 17

St. Augustine, De Civitate Dei
350 × 250 mm., ff. 226
c. 1120. Canterbury, (?)St. Augustine's Abbey
Ills. 49, 50, 56; Fig. 11

Four full-page miniatures prefixed to the text:
f. 1ᵛ: top, weighing of souls; centre, sudden death—the bad regiment; bottom, peaceful agriculture—the good regiment.
f. 2ᵛ: the City of God: top, Christ in mandorla surrounded by musician-angels; 2nd register, apostles holding palms; 3rd register, Ecclesia enthroned surrounded by saints; bottom register, angel with fiery sword guarding the gates of paradise, surrounded by saints and kings.
f. 3ᵛ: author portrait: St. Augustine surrounded by scholars.
f. 4: scholars in discussion, the left-hand figure in each register points to St. Augustine on the opposite page.
Nine illuminated initials:
Bk. 1, C with figures in scrolls (f. 5), Bk. 4, D with man expounding (f. 107), Bk. 15, D, Christ in Majesty (f. 118), Bk. 16, P decorated (f. 130ᵛ), Bk. 17, P decorated (f. 145), Bk. 18, D, man preaching (f. 157), Bk. 19, Q decorated (f. 174ᵛ), Bk. 20, D, man with flask and lily (f. 185ᵛ), Bk. 21, C, enthroned man with book (f. 199ᵛ), Bk. 22, decorated (f. 211).

There is no mark of provenance, but the style of the illuminations leaves little doubt that this is a Canterbury manuscript. The treatment of the figures is very much in the sketchy, calligraphic Anglo-Saxon tradition and this is paralleled in St. Augustine's Abbey manuscripts of the early 12th century, such as B.L. Arundel 91 and Cotton, Vitellius C. XII (nos. 17 and 18). The initials, on the other hand, are closer to Christ Church manuscripts of c. 1130, in particular Cambridge University Library Dd. i. 4 (no. 43) and Trinity College R. 15. 22 (Dodwell, pls. 13 and 18). Nevertheless, the Anglo-Saxon appearance of the illustrations suggests an origin in St. Augustine's Abbey, for it was there that this tradition persisted most tenaciously. For either of the Canterbury houses, the manuscript is exceptional in having full-page illustrations.

Dodwell has drawn attention to the harder outlines and greater monumentality of the author portrait (f. 3ᵛ) when compared to the other figures and he described this figure as one of the links between Anglo-Saxon impressionism and the fully developed Romanesque style of, for example, the Eadwine portrait (no. 68). The same observation may be made of the figure of Christ on f. 2ᵛ, which is similar to the Byzantinizing Christ in the Anselm manuscript, Bodley 271 (no. 42).

This is one of the earliest extant illustrated manuscripts of St. Augustine's City of God (see also no. 54). Indeed, the text remained rarely illustrated until the time of the 14th-century translation of Raoul de Praelles. Of the sixty-one illuminated manuscripts examined by De Laborde, four can be dated c. 1120–c. 1310; the remaining fifty-seven are all after 1376. There is, therefore, very little comparative material for these early manuscripts, and it is hard to say whether the artist of the Laurenziana manuscript could draw on earlier *De Civitate Dei* manuscripts or whether he assembled his illustrations from other sources. The drawing of the City of God (f. 2ᵛ) is paralleled in MS Prague, Chapter Library A. 7., a German book of c. 1250 (De Laborde, pl. IV) which suggests that this frontispiece may go back to an earlier tradition. The illustration of the good and bad regiment (f. 1ᵛ), on the other hand, is not paralleled in any of the other early manuscripts and may have been assembled from a variety of sources: the top is a Last Judgment, the centre is reminiscent of a battle of Virtues and Vices with Superbia falling off her horse in Prudentius' *Psychomachia* manuscripts (see no. 30), while the bottom register may be compared with Anglo-Saxon calendar illustrations (e.g. Cotton, Julius A. VI). Dodwell has compared the author-portrait with an 11th-century illustration of St. Benedict with his monks (B.L. Arundel 155).

PROVENANCE: Piero di Cosimo dei Medici (1554–1604) (inscribed f. 226, *Liber Petri de Medicis Cos. fil.*).

LITERATURE: A. M. Bandini, *Catalogus Codicum*

Latinorum, I, 1774, 24; A. de Laborde, *Les Manuscrits à peintures de la Cité de Dieu de Saint Augustine*, 1909, I, 216 f., no. 1, III, pl. I; *New Pal. Soc.* I, ii, pl. 138 f.; G. Biagi, *Reproductions from Illuminated MSS in the Mediciean Laurentian Library*, 1914, 9, pls. 10–12; M. Schapiro, 'From Mozarabic to Romanesque in Silos', *Art Bulletin*, 21, 1939, 314 n. 4; Wormald, 'Survival', 11; D. Tselos, 'Unique Portraits of the Evangelists . . .', *Art Bulletin*, 34, 1952, 260 267, fig. 21; Dodwell, *Canterbury School*, 28 ff., 35 ff., 64 f., 122, pls. 13*b*, 17*a*, 17*d*, 18*c*, 22; Boase, *English Art*, 46, pls. 11*c*, 52*b*; Rickert, *Painting in Britain*, 51, pls. 54–5; O. Pächt, 'The illustrations of St. Anselm's prayers and meditations', *J.W.C.I.*, 19, 1956, 80 f.; Swarzenski, *Monuments*, figs. 201, 203; M. W. Evans, *Medieval Drawings*, 1969, pl. 47.

EXHIBITED: *Mostra della Biblioteca di Lorenzo*, Florence, Biblioteca Mediceo-Laurenziana, 1949, no. 74; *Mostra Storica Nazionale della Miniatura*, Rome, Palazzo Venezia, 1953, no. 146.

20. London, British Library MS Cotton, Cleopatra E. I

Register of Privileges of the See of Canterbury (forming part of a collection of documents compiled by Sir Robert Cotton in *c.* 1604)
400×210 mm., ff. 17–57
1120–1. Canterbury, Christ Church

Ill. 55

Decorated initial R (f. 40) originally at the beginning of the manuscript.

This is the only illuminated Canterbury manuscript which can be securely dated from internal evidence. It concerns the rights and privileges of the see of Canterbury and it contains—apart from the forged evidence proving the primacy of Canterbury over York—bishops' professions of obedience to the Archbishop of Canterbury beginning in 814 and continuing to 1163. The whole text appears to be in the same hand up to and including the profession of David, Bishop of Bangor, on 4 April 1120 (f. 32). After that, beginning with the profession of Everard, Bishop of Norwich, who was consecrated on 12 June 1121, the hands vary. From this point the professions were inserted from time to time as they were made. The original manuscript, therefore, including the initial, may be placed in the period April 1120–June 1121. The initial, fully painted in red, blue and green body-colour, with only a few areas on the drapery left uncoloured, has spiral foliage stems curling round the shaft. The leaves show a variety of developed Romanesque palmettes, as yet rather small when compared to their successors in the following decades, but already with tendrils large enough to curl round the shaft. The same features occur in the following two manuscripts.

PROVENANCE: Sir Robert Cotton, Bt. (1571–1631); his library presented to the nation by his grandson Sir John Cotton, Bt., in 1700, incorporated in the British Museum in 1753.

LITERATURE: *New Pal. Soc.* I, i, pls. 60–2; D. Tselos, 'Unique Portraits of the Evangelists in an English Gospel Book', *Art Bulletin*, 34, 1952, 265 ff., fig. 19; Boase, *English Art*, 43, pl. 12*a*; Dodwell, *Canterbury School*, 7, 120; R. W. Southern, 'The Canterbury Forgeries', *English Historical Review*, 73, 1958, 219.

21. London, British Library MS Cotton, Claudius E. V

Corpus of Canon Law
430×330 mm., ff. 256
c. 1120–30. Canterbury, Christ Church

Ills. 51, 52

Four historiated initials: St. Jerome's letter to Pope Damasus, B, two men with animal offerings (f. 7); Letters of St. Clement of Rome, D, St. Clement enthroned (f. 21ᵛ); Pope Alexander, D, saying Mass, angel brings scroll (f. 35ᵛ); Pope Fabrianus, F, two men in a boat (transporting the relics of Pope Pontianus to Rome) (f. 55ᵛ).
Thirty-eight decorated initials: I (f. 2ᵛ), B, R (f. 4); H (f. 4ᵛ), C (f. 7ᵛ), C (f. 14), C (f. 16ᵛ), C (f. 20), A (f. 22ᵛ), A (f. 25ᵛ), A (f. 28), D (f. 30), C (f. 31), A (f. 32ᵛ), A (f. 36), O (f. 36ᵛ), S (f. 37ᵛ), I (f. 38), C (f. 39), C (f. 39ᵛ), O (f. 40), P (f. 40ᵛ), A (f. 41ᵛ), S (f. 42), D (f. 42ᵛ), C (f. 43), V (f. 44), V (f. 44ᵛ), Z (f. 45), I (f. 45ᵛ), C (f. 46ᵛ), D (f. 47), U (f. 49), P (f. 50ᵛ), P (f. 51), I (f. 52), D (f. 54), T (f. 93).

At the end of the manuscript (ff. 249ᵛ–255) there is a copy of the correspondence begun in 1119 between Ralph d'Escures, Archbishop of Canterbury 1114–22, and Pope Calixtus II (1119–24) concerning the Canterbury–York controversy. This has given rise to various conjectures as to the date of the manuscript (Boase; Tselos) and it could be argued that it should be placed in the period 1119–22 when the original letters must have been written. However, these are only copies of those letters and they are not in the same hand as the bulk of the manuscript. They can, therefore, be taken as no more than an approximate indication of the date of the manuscript, which at any rate is unlikely to be much earlier than 1119.
The initials contain a good repertory of fish, birds, beasts and humans, including a cynocephalus (f. 4ᵛ), a horned man eating grapes (f. 28), and a man gathering fruit while an animal plays the lute (f. 49). Frequently, the outline of the initial itself is constructed of these creatures (ff. 22ᵛ, 25ᵛ, 41ᵛ, 45, 46ᵛ). Zarnecki has compared the initial on f. 49 with carved capitals at Castor, Northamptonshire, and at Canterbury itself as an example of the influence of the Canterbury scriptorium on contemporary decorative sculpture. For further comparisons of

Canterbury manuscripts and carved capitals see Dodwell, pl. 42.

PROVENANCE: Sir Robert Cotton, Bt. (1571–1631); his library presented to the nation by his grandson, Sir John Cotton, Bt., in 1700, incorporated in the British Museum in 1753.

LITERATURE: J. Raine, *Historians of the Church of York*, II, Rolls Series, 1886, xvi, 238 ff.; British Museum, *Schools of Illumination*, II, 1915, 7, pls. 5 *a–d*; G. Zarnecki, *English Romanesque Sculpture 1066–1140*, 1951, 32, pl. 40; D. Tselos, 'Unique Portraits of the Evangelists in an English Gospel Book', *Art Bulletin*, 34, 1952, 262, 266 f., figs. 11, 14, 22; Boase, *English Art*, 42 f.; Dodwell, *Canterbury School*, 38, 41, 65 f., 71–4, 121, pls. 26*b*, 38*d*, 39 *d, e*, 43 *e, f*, 44 *b, f*.

22. London, British Library MS Harley 624
Lives of Saints (Passionale)
372×228 mm., ff. 84–143
c. 1120–30. Canterbury, Christ Church

Ills. 53, 54

The text is divided between this manuscript, Cotton, Nero C. VII (ff. 29ᵛ–78), and Harley 315 (ff. 1–39ᵛ).

Twenty-four decorated initials at opening of Saints' lives (one cut out, f. 99): D (f. 84ᵛ), V (f. 89ᵛ), O (f. 93ᵛ), headpiece with six heads in medallions (f. 94), A (f. 100), Q (f. 101ᵛ), R (f. 104ᵛ), T (f. 106ᵛ), T (f. 107ᵛ), N (f. 108ᵛ), P (f. 112), E (f. 112ᵛ), E (f. 113ᵛ), D (f. 114ᵛ), B (f. 115), R (f. 120), V (f. 121), O (f. 126), F (f. 128ᵛ), T (f. 132), T, St. Michael and the dragon (f. 134), Q (f. 137), I (f. 140), T (f. 141ᵛ).

The order of the original manuscript is reconstructed by Ker: Cotton, Nero C. VII now has six decorated and two historiated initials, Harley 315 has two decorated initials including a fine one of a monk pulling the devil's nose with a pair of pincers (f. 15ᵛ).
Apparently the work of several hands, the initials of this manuscript contain, in embryo, two features that were to become the hall-mark of mature Romanesque painting. The first is the circular or pear-shaped damp fold indicating the human body beneath the drapery (f. 137; Boase, pl. 11*b*); the second, the very large leaf or flower with blossoms in the centre of the foliage spirals (f. 120). This is more fully developed than those in Cotton, Cleopatra E. 1 and foreshadows the enormous floral creations of the mid-century.

PROVENANCE: Sir Simonds D'Ewes (1602–50), antiquary; Harleian manuscripts collected by Robert (1661–1724) and Edward Harley (1689–1741), 1st and 2nd Earls of Oxford. Bought by the British Museum in 1753.

LITERATURE: N. R. Ker, 'Membra disiecta, 2nd series', *British Museum Quarterly*, 14, 1939–40, 83–5; Boase, *English Art*, 43 ff., pl. 11*b*; Dodwell, *Canterbury School*, 28, 41, 51, 65, 67, 72, 74 f., 79, 121, pls. 17 *b, c*, 29*a*, 37*h*, 40 *d, f*, 45 *a*.

23. Cambridge, Trinity College MS O. 4. 7
St. Jerome, Various Commentaries on Books of the Old Testament
335×235 mm., ff. 170
c. 1120. Rochester Cathedral Priory

Ills. 47, 48

Historiated pen outline initial F, Commentary on Kings, with David playing a viol (f. 112); seven decorated pen outline initials: Q, rider fighting bear (f. 1), I (f. 2), S (f. 32ᵛ), A (f. 48ᵛ), P (f. 74), A, man teaching bear the ABC (f. 75), I, dragons seen from above (f. 132).

The text is identical with a Christ Church manuscript of the same work (Trinity College B. 2. 34) and M. R. James believed that it was written at Canterbury and then acquired by Rochester. The style of the initials—in which human figures play a greater part than they do in Trinity R. 3. 30—is closely comparable to Royal 12. E. XX, formerly thought to be from Canterbury (Boase, 44, 63, pl. 7*b*) but given by Dodwell to Rochester (p. 24). Pächt (*St. Albans Psalter*) has drawn attention to the fact that David (f. 112) is playing a rebec or viol instead of the more usual harp. The viol occurs in Byzantine art in the 11th century (Psalter of 1066, B.L. Add. 19352) and from the early 12th century in the West, where it appears at Canterbury (Laurenziana, MS Plut. 12. 17) and St. Albans (Psalter) as well as in this Rochester manuscript.

PROVENANCE: Rochester Cathedral Priory (f. 1 inscribed *liber de claustro Roffensi per G. Camerarium*). Dr. Thomas Gale (1635/6–1702), Regius Professor of Greek, High Master of St. Paul's School; given to his college by his son Roger Gale in 1738.

LITERATURE: James, *Catalogue*, III, no. 1238; *id., The Ancient Libraries of Canterbury and Dover*, lxxxviii; Dodwell, *Canterbury School*, 74, 119; Boase, *English Art*, 45, pl. 7*c*; *St. Albans Psalter*, 51 n. 3, 154 n. 2.

24. Cambridge, Trinity College MS R. 3. 30
Lucan, Pharsalia
214×133 mm., ff. 109
c. 1120. Rochester Cathedral Priory

Ills. 45, 46

Decorated initial to each of the ten Books: B with three armed knights peering round shaft (f. 1); I (f. 17ᵛ), P (f. 26ᵛ), I (f. 35), S (f. 44), P (f. 54), S (f. 64), I (f. 75), A (f. 84ᵛ), V (f. 98).

The initials are very similar to those of Canterbury and M. R. James took this to be a Christ Church manuscript. However, the quires are numbered by letters (a–n), a practice common in Rochester but unknown in Canterbury manuscripts (see Dodwell, p. 119). The relationship between the two houses had been close ever since Benedictine monks were established at Rochester in about 1080. Their privileges were consciously modelled on those of the priory of Christ Church, Canterbury, and under a special agreement the Archbishop of Canterbury looked after the see of Rochester when there was no bishop, while the Bishop of Rochester had a similar responsibility for Canterbury. It is, therefore, not surprising that the decoration of Rochester manuscripts is dependent on that of Canterbury.

Nevertheless, Rochester books are different in script and construction, and in their decoration certain distinctive features can be isolated. The rows of flattened palmettes in the curved outlines of the initials and the predilection for horses and riders are comparable with Royal 5. D. II. At the same time, the initials on ff. 26ᵛ and 54 are characterized by the elongated animals twisting in and out of the hollow shafts which were to become the hall-mark of Rochester manuscripts of the 1130s (see no. 45).

PROVENANCE: Given to Trinity College by William Greaves, D.D., in 1705.

LITERATURE: James, *Catalogue*, II, no. 610; Dodwell, *Canterbury School*, 24, 67, 68, pl. 8e; Boase, *English Art*, 63, pl. 11a; *St. Albans Psalter*, 148 n. 1, pl. 146c.

25. New York, Pierpont Morgan Library, M 777
Gospels (The Mostyn Gospels)
263 × 168 mm., ff. 76
c. 1120   *Ills. 57, 58*

Four portraits of Evangelists seated on their symbols: Matthew (f. 3ᵛ), Mark (f. 24ᵛ), Luke (f. 37ᵛ), John (f. 58ᵛ).
Four decorative initials at the beginning of the Gospels: Matthew, M (f. 4), Mark, I (f. 25), Luke, Q (f. 38), John, I (f. 59).

A tentative attribution to Canterbury appears in the catalogue of the 1933 New York exhibition, but Tselos was the first to compare the initials in detail with those of Canterbury and Rochester manuscripts of c. 1110–20 (B.L. Royal 6. C. VI, Cotton, Nero C. VII, and Claudius E. V), and to decide firmly in favour of a Canterbury origin. It is true that there are similarities in the structure of these initials (esp. Tselos, figs. 8, 9), yet the winged dragons upon which Tselos based much of his argument are ubiquitous in Anglo-Norman illumination of the period. On the other hand, the fine cross-hatching on the floral decoration, which is so pronounced a feature of the initials in the Gospels (esp. f. 38), is not paralleled in the Canterbury manuscripts.

The Evangelist portraits are highly unusual, both for their close stylistic dependence on Carolingian models and because of their being seated on their symbols. Stylistically, a close comparison can be made with the 9th-century Ebbo Gospels from Rheims (Épernay, Bibl. Mun., MS 1). The outlines have become harder, but the heads, facial types, and postures are closely similar (Tselos, figs. 39–40). The frontal posture of St. John has been compared with another Rheims manuscript, the Vienna Schatzkammer Gospels.

The large Evangelist symbols on the other hand, are not found in these Carolingian manuscripts. Panofsky (quoted in the 1933 New York exhibition catalogue) suggested that there might be a connection with an oriental type of planet illustration showing the planet divinities riding upon their zodiacal signs (e.g. Bodl. Lib., MS Or. 133, see F. Saxl in *Der Islam*, III, 1912, 171, cf. figs. 26, 35). In both the Gospels and the astronomical manuscript, human figures, invested with divine powers, are shown seated on symbols of animal forms and a transference from the one to the other would not be unlikely. Tselos, however, did not accept their oriental source, but compared the Evangelist symbols, for scale and general appearance, with those in certain insular manuscripts, such as the Canterbury Gospels (Royal I. E. VI) and the Book of Cerne (Cambridge University Library MS Ll. 1. 10). For the Evangelist seated upon his symbol, he drew a parallel with illustrations of the four elements in a 12th-century German astronomical manuscript (Vienna, National-bibliothek, MS 12600, f. 30), in which the human personifications of air, fire, earth and water are seated, respectively, on an eagle, a lion, a centaur and a griffin. The correlation between the four Evangelists and the four elements—the four spiritual and the four physical constituents of the universe—was discussed in medieval texts from the 9th century and it may well be that the artist of the Morgan Gospels adapted his 'riding Evangelists' from comparable illustrations of the four elements.

PROVENANCE: Stephen Batman (d. 1584), chaplain to Archbishop Matthew Parker (name on St. Mark's scroll, St. John's book and note f. 2ᵛ); Sir Thomas Mostyn, Bt. (armorial bookplate and signature, dated 1744, on f. 2); Mostyn sale, Sotheby's, 13 July 1920, lot 40; A. Chester Beatty, sold Sotheby's, 7 June 1932, lot 4; Pierpont Morgan Library.

LITERATURE: E. G. Millar, *The Library of A. Chester Beatty*, 1927, I, 72, no. 19, pls. 57–9, frontispiece; D. Tselos, 'Unique Portraits of the Evangelists in an English Gospel-Book of the 12th Century', *Art Bulletin*, 34, 1952, 257–77; Boase, *English Art*, 157; Swarzenski, *Monuments*, fig. 283; Rickert, *Painting in Britain*, 62, pl. 63b; W. M. Hinkle, 'A mounted Evangelist in a 12th century Gospel Book at Sées', *Aachener Kunstblätter*, 44, 1973, 193.

EXHIBITED: New York Public Library, *The Pierpont Morgan Library*, 1933–4, no. 29, pl. 28; Pierpont Morgan Library, *Fiftieth Anniversary Exhibition*, 1957, no. 14, pl. 9.

26. Oxford, University College MS 165

Bede, Life of St. Cuthbert

197 × 122 mm., ii + 203 pages

c. 1100–20. Durham Cathedral Priory

Ills. 59–63

One historiated initial D with Bede writing (p. 1) and two decorated initials (pp. 9, 170). One painted and framed miniature, Bede writing and presenting his book to the Bishop of Lindisfarne (damaged, p. 1), fifty-five multi-coloured outline drawings illustrating the text, one per chapter:

Chapt. 1, Cuthbert as a boy playing games (p. 8).

Chapt. 2, the angel cures his knee (p. 12).

Chapt. 3, he changes the wind by prayer and saves the monks on their raft (p. 14).

Chapt. 4, he sees the soul of Bishop Aidan carried to heaven (p. 18).

Chapt. 5, his horse miraculously discovers a loaf and some meat in a barn (p. 20).

Chapt. 6, on arriving at Melrose, where he becomes a monk, he is greeted by Boisel (p. 23).

Chapt. 7, at Ripon he entertains an angel and is rewarded with heavenly bread (p. 26).

Chapt. 8, he reads to Boisel before his death (p. 29).

Chapt. 9, now Prior of Melrose, he preaches (p. 33).

Chapt. 10, he bathes in the sea at Coldingham; two others dry his feet (p. 35).

Chapt. 11, cut off by a storm with two companions, he finds three pieces of dolphin's flesh (p. 38).

Chapt. 12, he tells his companions that an eagle will bring them food; the eagle brings a fish (p. 41).

Chapt. 13, he foretells a fire; the people are unable to extinguish it (p. 43).

Chapt. 14, he speaks to a woman, and extinguishes a fire through prayer (p. 45).

Chapt. 15, the reeve asks him to drive out his wife's demon; when they arrive she is cured (p. 47).

Chapt. 16, he teaches the monks at Lindisfarne (p. 50).

Chapt. 17, on the isle of Farne he receives angelic help (p. 55).

Chapt. 18, he digs for water in the rock, and then washes his brethren's feet (p. 58).

Chapt. 19, with a word he drives away the birds eating his crops (p. 61).

Chapt. 20, he appeals to the ravens to leave the straw on his roof; the ravens return with a gift (p. 63).

Chapt. 21, monks forget to bring him some timber; it is brought by the tide (p. 65).

Chapt. 22, he instructs visitors (p. 67).

Chapt. 23, Abbess Aelfflaed and a nun cured by Cuthbert's girdle (p. 69).

Chapt. 24, on the island of Coquet, Aelfflaed tells him he is to become a bishop (p. 72).

Chapt. 25, he cures a nobleman's servant (p. 76).

Chapt. 26, as a bishop, he prays and teaches (p. 78).

Chapt. 27, at a fountain in Carlisle, he feels that King Ecgfrith has died in battle (p. 79).

Chapt. 28, at Carlisle, with the hermit Herebert (p. 84).

Chapt. 29, his host's wife is cured with holy water (p. 86).

Chapt. 30, hearing of a nun's illness, he cures her with holy oil (p. 88).

Chapt. 31, the reeve is cured by eating bread blessed by Cuthbert (p. 89).

Chapt. 32, he cures a dying youth by his prayers (p. 91).

Chapt. 33, he restores a dying boy to his mother (p. 92).

Chapt. 34, at a meal he sees the soul of a man, who was killed by falling off a tree, carried to heaven (p. 94).

Chapt. 35, he tastes water and gives it the flavour of wine (p. 97).

Chapt. 36, two monks fail to take a goose and are imprisoned by a storm (p. 98).

Chapt. 37, taken ill, he tells the monks of his forthcoming death (p. 102).

Chapt. 38, he is carried to his oratory on Farne by his monks (p. 108).

Chapt. 39, Cuthbert's death (p. 110).

Chapt. 40, his body is taken by boat to Lindisfarne (p. 113).

Chapt. 41, a demoniac boy is healed by the water in which Cuthbert's body was bathed (p. 115).

Chapt. 42, after eleven years the monks find his body still incorrupt (p. 118).

Chapt. 43, Bishop Eadbert is buried in Cuthbert's tomb (p. 121).

Chapt. 44, a sick man is cured by praying at the tomb (p. 122).

Chapt. 45, a paralytic is cured by putting on Cuthbert's shoes (p. 124).

Chapt. 46, the hermit Felfild is cured of a swelling on his face by a calf skin on the oratory wall (p. 126).

Chapt. 47, a monk is cured of paralysis by praying at the tomb (p. 130).

Chapt. 48, the relics of the saint heal a monk's diseased eye (p. 132).

Chapt. 49, King Alfred gives food to a pilgrim and is afterwards rewarded by Cuthbert (p. 135).

Chapt. 50, threatened by Danes, Eardulf, Bishop of Lindisfarne, tries to take Cuthbert's body to Ireland, but is forced by a storm to land it near Crayke (p. 143).

Chapt. 51, King Raegnald is struck motionless and killed for dividing Cuthbert's land among his followers (p. 149).

Chapt. 52, the Scottish army attacking Lindisfarne is swallowed up in the ground (p. 153).

Chapt. 53, Barcwith is struck down when he attempts to break into the church to capture an escaped prisoner (p. 157).

Chapt. 54, fleeing from William the Conqueror in 1069, the monks take the Saint's body to Lindisfarne and arrive with dry feet in spite of the high tide (p. 159).

Chapt. 55, a Norman soldier dies of torment after stealing treasures from Durham Cathedral in 1080 (p. 163).

Bede, who was two generations younger than St. Cuthbert (d. 687) wrote this work in about 721, basing it on an anonymous Life of *c.* 699–705. Bede's actual text ends at chapter 44; the following two chapters are taken from his Ecclesiastical History (IV, 31–2) from where they became attached to the Life of St. Cuthbert as early as the 10th century. The last seven chapters (47–55) contain a group of miracles dating from the time of Alfred to 1080 which were added to manuscripts of Bede's Life by the early 12th century. It may be assumed that these miracles were collected soon after 1083, when the community of Benedictine monks was installed at Durham by Bishop William of St. Calais, and certainly before 1104, the date of the translation of the relics, a key event which is not included in this text. Univ. 165 has no secure date or provenance, but the subject, style, and palaeography all point to an origin in Durham and a date c. 1120. Durham was the home of St. Cuthbert's relics, and it was at Durham that the additional chapters were composed. The style of the drawings is related to that of MS Hunter 100 (no. 27) and other Durham manuscripts of c. 1120, characterized by a similar mixture of the nervous, zigzag lines of Anglo-Saxon art and the new solidity of the Romanesque period. Finally, Neil Ker has shown that the handwriting is similar to that of Simeon of Durham's Chronicle (Durham University, MS Cosin V. II. 6), a Durham manuscript dated before 1128.

Univ. 165 is not only the earliest extant illustrated Life of St. Cuthbert but also the earliest post-Conquest manuscript with a cycle of religious narrative illustrations (cf. no. 34). There is a group of later Cuthbert cycles which are clearly related: 1. Trinity College, Cambridge, MS O. 1. 64, second half of the 12th century (only two drawings completed); 2. B.L. Add. 39943, c. 1190–1200 (forty-five out of the original fifty-five illustrations remain; the last seven miracles not illustrated); 3. York Cathedral windows, early 15th century (fifty-five panels); 4. Carlisle Cathedral choir stalls, late 15th century (seventeen panels). The relationship of these cycles to each other and to Univ. 165 has been clarified by Malcolm Baker. Although it is the earliest extant, Univ. 165 is not the archetype of these cycles as it differs in too many particulars from the others. If, therefore, the later cycles were not derived from Univ. 165, one must assume that they had a common origin in a lost archetype. Whether this dated from the Anglo-Saxon or post-Conquest period it is no longer possible to say, though there is little evidence of artistic activity at Durham before the introduction of regular monastic life in 1083. The fact that the last seven chapters were composed after 1083 also supports the view that Univ. 165 was copied from a manuscript of about that date.

Otto Pächt has drawn attention to the fact that the illustrations frequently consist of two episodes and he compared this with the pictures in an 11th-century Life of St. Benedict and St. Maur from Monte Cassino (MS Vat. lat. 1202) in which two neighbouring scenes make up one incident. Bede himself draws attention to parallels with St. Benedict's life (chapters 13 and 18) and it is possible that the original illustrated Life of St. Cuthbert was influenced by the pictures in a Life of St. Benedict. However, this hypothesis does not alter the likelihood that Univ. 165 was copied from an illustrated Cuthbert manuscript of the 11th century.

PROVENANCE: Southwick Priory, near Southampton (erased ex libris ff. 1–2). Other inscriptions on fly-leaves list several names: Joh. Theyer of Cowpers Hill near Gloucester; Fulke Wallwyn (gift of John Daniell); William and Thomas Leigh. In 1666 it belonged to William Rogers of Painswick, Gloucestershire, who gave it to his college.

LITERATURE: Coxe, *Catalogus*, I, 1852, 45; *New Pal. Soc.* II, pl. 67; B. Colgrave, 'The St. Cuthbert Paintings on the Carlisle Cathedral Stalls', *Burlington Magazine*, 73, 1938, 21; id., *Two Lives of St. Cuthbert*, 1940, 26 f., no. 12 (with text and translation in full); id., 'The Post-Bedan miracles and translations of St. Cuthbert', *The Early Cultures of N.W. Europe* (*H. M. Chadwick Memorial Studies*), ed. Sir Cyril Fox and B. Dickens, 1950, 307–32; F. Wormald, 'Some illustrated MSS of the Lives of Saints', *Bulletin of the John Rylands Library*, 35, 1952–3, 259 f.; Boase, *English Art*, 28, pl. 6c; Rickert, *Painting in Britain*, 63, pl. 59b; Bodleian Library Picture Book, *English Romanesque Illumination*, 1951, pl. 6; 'The medieval home of the illustrated life of St. Cuthbert', *Bodleian Library Record*, 5, 1954, 6; Ker, *English MSS*, 24; O. Pächt, *The Rise of Pictorial Narrative in 12th century England*, 1961, 14–18, 20 f., figs. 2–3; J. J. G. Alexander, *Norman illumination at Mont St. Michel 966–1100*, 1970, 141, pl. 34D; Malcolm Baker, forthcoming study.

EXHIBITED: B.F.A.C. *Illuminated MSS*, 1908, no. 16; Manchester, 1959, no. 5; Brussels, 1973, no. 20.

27. Durham, Cathedral Library MS Hunter 100

Medical and astrological treatises
170 × 122 mm., ff. 124
c. 1100–20. Durham Cathedral Priory

Ills. 64, 66–8

ff. 1–42: Calendar with texts and tables in connection with it; the Calendar itself illustrated with outline drawings of the signs of the Zodiac (ff. 2–7).
ff. 43–84ᵛ: treatise on the Calendar of Helperic of Grandval and selections from astronomical writings of Bede, Abbo of Fleury and Isidore; historiated initials: C, author portrait of Helperic (f. 43); A, consisting of a master beating a pupil's naked behind *Afficitur plagis qui non vult discere gratis* (f. 44). Small outline drawings of the constellations (ff. 61ᵛ–64ᵛ), a fragment of a larger cycle.
ff. 85–101ᵛ (formerly at the beginning of the volume, inscribed *Liber ecclesie Cathedr. Dunelm.*): medical texts, principally from Isidore's Etymologies (not illustrated).

ff. 102–18: lists of remedies, notes on the four humours and their effects (not illustrated).
ff. 119–20: cautery illustrations; f. 119 top, under arcades a surgeon cauterising the temples of a recumbent patient; below, heating the cautery irons. The drawings are framed, but only those in the upper register are tinted. f. 119ᵛ, two registers of standing, partially dressed cautery figures with physicians, unframed outline drawings; f. 120, cautery figure and physician.

The Durham provenance is supported by the saints in the Calendar and there is internal evidence to indicate a date in the first quarter of the century. The marginal annotation to the chronological tables (ff. 27ᵛ–42) include references to the deaths of Bishop Carilef (1096) and William II (1100) and it is, therefore, possible to conclude that the manuscript was written after 1100 and before 1128, the year of the death of Bishop Ranulph Flambard which is not recorded. An early 12th-century date accords well with the style of the drawings which is characterized by the nervous outlines of Anglo-Saxon art. The calendar illustrations, in particular, are very close to the Anglo-Saxon tradition; the cautery drawings are less delicate in execution. Drawings in this style appear in other Durham manuscripts of this period: in initials in the Life of St. Cuthbert, Bodl. Lib. MS Digby 20, f. 194 (Bodleian Picture Books, *English Romanesque Illumination*, 1951, fig. 1), and the Durham Cathedral MSS B. IV. 14 (Mynors, no. 55, pl. 35) and B. II. 26, f. 90 (see no. 28), and in the extensive series of drawings in the Life of St. Cuthbert at Oxford (University College MS 165, see no. 26).
The illustrations of the constellations are related to those of B.L. Royal 13. A. XI. They are derivatives of the original Aratus illustrations rather than of the Cicero recension to which most of the English medieval astronomical cycles belong (see nos. 37, 38, 74).
The cautery figures on ff. 119–20 are similar to those of Sloane 2839 (see no. 12), while the treatment of a recumbent patient is found in an earlier cautery manuscript (Florence, Laurenziana, MS Plut. 73. 41, South Italy, 9th century). The practice of placing such medical illustrations under elaborate arcades is also traditional at this date (for an early example see the 10th-century Byzantine medical manuscript, Florence, Laurenziana, Plut. 74. 7; MacKinney, *op. cit.*, fig. 91A).

PROVENANCE: Dr. Christopher Hunter (1675–1757); bought by the Dean and Chapter of Durham in 1757.

LITERATURE: A description of the manuscript by J. P. Gilson is MS Hunter 100A. Mynors, *Durham*, no. 57, pls. 36 f.; Charles Singer, 'Early English Magic and Medicine', *Proceedings of the British Academy*, 9, 1920, 4, fig. 1; H. D. Hughes, *A History of Durham Cathedral Library*, 1925, 32 (repr.); *New Pal. Soc.*, II, pl. 125; Millar, I, 125; Wormald, *English Drawings*, 57; Saxl and Meier,

III, pp. xxv, 441 ff., pl. LXX; N. R. Ker, *English MSS*, 24; Rickert, *Painting in Britain*, 63; Boase, *English Art*, 27 f., pl. 6a; W. Bonser, *The Medical Background of Anglo-Saxon England*, 1963, 303; Loren MacKinney, *Medical Illustrations in Medieval MSS*, 1965, 120; M. W. Evans, *Medieval Drawings*, 1969, pl. 62.

28. Durham, Cathedral Library MS B. II. 26
St. Augustine, On the Trinity
347×217 mm., ff. 143 (58 used twice)
c. 1120–30. Durham Cathedral Priory

Ill. 65

Fifteen decorated initials (one at the opening and one for each of the 15 books, except Book VII): L (f. 5ᵛ), I (f. 6), C (f. 17), C (f. 28), S (f. 37), H (f. 48), C (f. 53ᵛ), D (f. 64), T (f. 71ᵛ), H (f. 77), N (f. 83), A (f. 90), I (f. 97), N (f. 108ᵛ), V (f. 119).

The initials are decorated with a wide variety of men and beasts in foliage scrolls. These are outline drawings on a background of small coloured fields of blue, red, green and yellow, a technique reminiscent of late 11th-century Anglo-Norman manuscripts, to be found, for example, in Durham Cathedral MS B. III. 10 (Mynors, pl. 28). The figure in the initial on f. 90 is similar to, though somewhat more solid than, those in MS Hunter 100 (see no. 27).

PROVENANCE: Durham Cathedral Priory (inscription f. 5).

LITERATURE: Mynors, *Durham*, no. 62, pl. 39.

29. Hildesheim, St. Godehard
Psalter (St. Albans Psalter)
276×184 mm., 418 pages (separated leaf in the Schnütgen Museum, Cologne)
c. 1119–23. St. Albans Abbey

Ills. 72–4, 76, 78; Fig. 22

Calendar illustrations, signs of the Zodiac; and occupations of the months represented by single seated figures (pp. 3–14):
January, Janus, combined with feasting (p. 3); February, warming (p. 4); March, man holding up flowering branch on which a bird is perched (p. 5); April, man holding flowering plants (p. 6); May, man holding falcon (p. 7); June, man holding scythe (mowing) (p. 8); July, man holding sickle and plant (reaping) (p. 9); August, man holding sheaf of corn (reaping) (p. 10); September, man holding grapes (vintage) (p. 11); October, wine-tasting (p. 12); November, man holding axe (? ox-killing) (p. 13); December, pig-killing (p. 14).
Forty full-page miniatures at the beginning of the book: The Fall (p. 17), The Expulsion (p. 18), The Annunciation (p. 19), The Visitation (p. 20),

The Nativity (p. 21), The Annunciation to the Shepherds (p. 22), The Magi before Herod (p. 23), The Magi guided by the star (p. 24), Adoration of the Magi (p. 25), Dream of the Magi (p. 26), Return of the Magi (p. 27), Presentation in the Temple (p. 28), Flight into Egypt (p. 29), Massacre of the Innocents (p. 30), Return from Egypt (p. 31), The Baptism (p. 32), First Temptation (p. 33), Second Temptation (p. 34), Third Temptation (p. 35), Christ in the house of Simon the Pharisee (p. 36), Entry into Jerusalem (p. 37), The Washing of the Feet (p. 38), The Agony in the Garden (p. 39), Christ and the Sleeping Apostles (p. 40), The Last Supper (p. 41), The Betrayal (p. 42), The Mocking (p. 43), The Flagellation (p. 44), Pilate washes his hands (p. 45), The Carrying of the Cross (p. 46), The Descent from the Cross (p. 47), The Entombment (p. 48), The Harrowing of Hell (p. 49), The Three Marys at the Sepulchre (p. 50), Mary Magdalene announces the Resurrection to the Apostles (p. 51), The Incredulity of St. Thomas (p. 52), The legend of St. Martin: St. Martin's vision and the division of the cloak (p. 53), The Ascension (p. 54), Pentecost (p. 55), David as a musician (p. 56). There are two further full-page miniatures at the end of the manuscript: Martyrdom of St. Alban (p. 416), David and his Musicians (p. 417).

Five tinted drawings:
Scenes from the life of St. Alexis illustrating the *Chançon* of St. Alexis (p. 57), Christ on the road to Emmaus (p. 70), Christ breaking bread at Emmaus (p. 71), Christ disappears from the table at Emmaus (p. 72), Two armed warriors on horseback in combat illustrating the dissertation relating to the spiritual battle, written in the margins on pp. 71–2.

Two hundred and eleven historiated initials, of which one hundred and eighty-five are to Psalms and twenty-six to Canticles, and Prayers and Collects at the end (initial cut out p. 386).

This is one of the key manuscripts of the English 12th century, and it is treated in a magisterial volume by Pächt, Dodwell, and Wormald (*St. Albans Psalter*, 1960). The date is now placed before 1123 as the obit of Roger the Hermit, Christina of Markyate's patron, who died in *c.* 1121–3, is a later addition. The manuscript is also linked with Abbot Geoffrey (*c.* 1119–47) who was a friend and patron of Christina, so that the date may be tentatively given as *c.* 1119–23.

The St. Albans Psalter is, therefore, the first extant English manuscript with a cycle of full-page miniatures (as opposed to tinted drawings) since the early Winchester school in the 10th century. All the full-page miniatures, except the two at the end, the tinted drawings, and the Beatus initial, are by the same hand, dubbed by Pächt the Alexis Master, from the drawings of the Life of St. Alexis. The style of the miniatures, characterized by hieratic, symmetrical compositions, background panels providing compartments for different figures, and an extensive use of purple, betrays a considerable debt to Ottonian art and particularly to the 11th-century school of Echternach. The figures have heavy

contours and most of them are shown in profile, which is marked by an almost straight line from the brow to the tip of the nose. An early stage of the damp fold convention is visible on the draperies, which are modelled by a series of fine, comb-like, white highlights. This practice of picking out the drapery surface is Byzantine in origin, though Pächt has argued that it reached England via Italian models. The hand of the Alexis Master has been recognized in several other manuscripts (see nos. 31, 33–4) and his influence on English illumination in the next two decades was considerable.

In his detailed analysis of the iconography of the New Testament cycle, Pächt provides examples of Anglo-Saxon, Ottonian and, in particular, Byzantine influence, but he concludes that the Alexis Master invented the cycle, making use of a variety of sources in the process. Pächt's iconographical parallels are always illuminating, but in stressing the inventiveness of the Alexis Master he does not deal convincingly with the salient factor of the relationship with two longer New Testament cycles: the four Psalter leaves in London and New York (no. 66) and the Bury Gospels, Pembroke College MS 120 (no. 35), with which the St. Albans Psalter shares thirty-three and sixteen scenes respectively. The possibility that the three cycles had a common English model should also be considered (see above, Introduction, p. 31 f.).

The initials are not by the Alexis Master, though he appears to have been responsible for their design. The figures in the initials—and also in the Calendar medallions and the two miniatures at the end—are in a coarser, flatter style characterized by the heavily striped effect of broad parallel lines on the drapery, which Dodwell attributes to Norman or Flemish influence. Nevertheless, in spite of these differences, the initials are clearly dependent on the Alexis Master's style.

In each Psalm, one line is singled out for illustration in the initial, as in the 10th-century Corbie Psalter (Amiens MS 18), and the 11th-century St. Augustine Commentary on the Psalms from St. Amand (Paris, Bibl. Nat., lat. 1991 and Valenciennes MS 39). However, the St. Albans Psalter initials are not similar to these, and Dodwell argues that they are to a large extent original creations formed to illustrate an often specifically monastic interpretation of the Psalms. Yet there are links with the Utrecht Psalter tradition (Schiller, III, 70) and the possibility that the artist knew the Utrecht Psalter or one of its English derivatives cannot be excluded.

PROVENANCE: St. Albans, brought together for Christina, anchoress of Markyate (evidence of calendar and litany); manuscript still in England in 16th century (under Henry VIII the word *pape* erased from the calendar); by 1657, Benedictine Abbey of Lampspringe, near Hildesheim (inscription, p. 1); probably came to St. Godehard's, Hildesheim, when Lampspringe was suppressed in 1803.

SELECT LITERATURE: Adolph Goldschmidt, *Der*

Albanipsalter in Hildesheim, 1895; Millar, I, 82, pl. 34; Wormald, 'Development'; Rickert, *Painting in Britain*, 64-6, pls. 61-2; Boase, *English Art*, 101-13, pls. 31, 34-8; C. H. Talbot, *The Life of Christina of Markyate*, 1959; O. Pächt, C. R. Dodwell, F. Wormald, *The St. Albans Psalter*, 1960; H. Swarzenski, review of the latter, *Kunstchronik*, 16, 1963, 77-85; H. Roosen-Runge, *Farbgebung und Technik Frühmittelalterlicher Buchmalerei*, 1967, I, 81-94; Schiller, *Iconography*, I, 1971, 144, figs. 394-6; III (German ed.), 37 f., 61, 70, 101, 111, 129, figs. 79, 81, 152, 186, 300, 312-14, 355, 413. For the Schnütgen Museum leaf see also Brussels, 1973, no. 22.

30. London, British Library MS Cotton, Titus D. XVI

Prudentius, Psychomachia (ff. 1ᵛ–35)
and other tracts
152 × 105 mm., ff. 128
c. 1120. St. Albans Abbey   *Ills. 69–71*

Forty-six tinted pen drawings, mainly one third or one quarter page size, distributed among the text: verse 1 of the Preface, Sacrifice of Isaac (f. 1); v. 15, Lot's capture, v. 19, Abraham's pursuit (f. 2ᵛ); v. 34, Abraham and Lot (f. 3); v. 38, Abraham and Melchisedek (f. 3ᵛ); v. 45, Abraham and the angels (f. 4); v. 1 of Psychomachia, Prudentius kneeling before Christ (f. 4ᵛ); vv. 21, 28, Fides attacked by Cultura Deorum, two drawings (f. 5ᵛ); v. 30, Fides conquers Cultura Deorum; v. 36, Fides crowns the Martyr (f. 6); v. 40, Pudicitia attacked by Libido (f. 6ᵛ); v. 46, Pudicitia disarms Libido, v. 49, Pudicitia slays Libido (f. 7); v. 53, Pudicitia inveighs against Libido (f. 7ᵛ); v. 98, Pudicitia washes her sword in the Jordan (f. 8ᵛ); v. 109, Patientia (f. 9); v. 113, Patientia accosted by Ira (f. 9ᵛ); v. 121, Ira throws lance at Patientia (f. 10); v. 137, Ira attacks Patientia with a sword (f. 10ᵛ); v. 151, Ira falls on her sword (f. 11); v. 178, Superbia on horseback (f. 12); v. 194, Superbia threatens Humilitas and Spes (f. 12ᵛ); v. 253, Superbia attacks Humilitas (f. 14); v. 257, Superbia falls into pit (f. 14ᵛ); v. 280, Humilitas beheads Superbia (f. 15); v. 305, Spes goes to heaven, v. 310, Luxuria feasting (f. 16); v. 332, Luxuria persuades men to throw down arms (f. 17); v. 344, Sobrietas reproaches renegades (f. 17ᵛ); v. 407, Sobrietas halts Luxuria (f. 19); v. 417, Sobrietas stones Luxuria (f. 197ᵛ); v. 454, Avaritia gathers spoils (f. 20ᵛ); v. 551, Avaritia disguised as Thrift (f. 23); v. 596, Largitas defeats Avaritia (f. 24ᵛ); v. 604, Largitas rejoices (f. 25); v. 667, Discordia stabs Concordia (f. 26ᵛ); v. 705, Discordia seized by Virtues (f. 28); v. 715 Fides strikes Discordia; v. 719, Discordia dismembered (f. 28ᵛ); v. 726, Virtues build a tribunal (f. 29); v. 734, Concordia (Caritas) and Fides mount the tribunal (f. 29ᵛ); v. 746, Concordia addresses the Virtues (f. 30); v. 868, the temple (f. 33); v. 875, Sapientia seated on the temple (f. 33ᵛ); v. 888, Prudentius offers prayers (f. 34).

Dating from the first decade of the 5th century, Prudentius' *Psychomachia* is a Christian poem written in the manner of a classical epic. It relates how virtues and vices, personified as female figures, battle for possession of the human soul. It was an immensely popular work in the early Middle Ages and some twenty illustrated manuscripts survive, most of them dating from the 9th to 11th centuries. It is clear from their close relationship that all these manuscripts go back to a common archetype. The archetype no longer exists, but, as several of the extant manuscripts (e.g. Paris, Bibl. Nat., lat. 8318; Leyden, University Library, MS Voss. Lat. Oct. 15), are very classical in appearance, it is generally accepted that it was produced as early as the 5th century. The virtues and vices are depicted in classical female dress and the style of these 9th- and 10th-century manuscripts clearly reflects the impressionism of Roman painting. Three of the extant manuscripts were written in England (Cambridge, Corpus Christi, MS 23; B.L. Add. 24199 and Cotton, Cleopatra C. VIII); others originated in France and Germany.

Of these twenty manuscripts, Cotton, Titus D. XVI is, with one exception, the last. It is partly based on its Anglo-Saxon forerunners (Group I), but Stettiner also detected the influence of manuscripts of a different recension which he characterized as 'Group II'. For example, while Group I represents most of the virtues in long garments and Group II shows them wearing chain-mail and helmets, this manuscript alternates between these two types. The complete manuscripts all contain ninety illustrations, whereas this one, also textually complete, has only forty-six. The first quire (ff. 1–8) is fully illustrated and only after that do the drawings become much sparser than in the other manuscripts. This led Stettiner to conclude that the artist copied a complete model but decided after the first quire to reduce the number of illustrations. In some cases the omitted pictures have left a trace on the following illustrations (e.g. ff. 11ᵛ, 20, 21).

The impressionist outlines have hardened and both the actions and the figures are more realistically portrayed than in the pre-Conquest manuscripts.

The date has traditionally been rendered *c.* 1100 (e.g. Rickert), but Pächt (*St. Albans Psalter*) has argued that this manuscript was produced in the atelier of the 'Alexis Master', the great artist of the St. Albans Psalter, not long after 1120. Certainly the figures—elongated and usually shown in profile—are similar to those in the St. Albans Psalter in spite of their calligraphic technique. Pächt has pointed out that the prominent beak-shaped noses, in particular, are close to those in the Josephus manuscript (no. 32) which was illuminated by an assistant of the Alexis Master in *c.* 1120–30. It may be, on the other hand, though it is less likely, that this Prudentius manuscript represents the St. Albans style of the first decades of the century which influenced the formation of the Alexis Master's style. It is unfortunate that no illustrated St. Albans manuscripts of this period survive. The relationship of the Psalter to earlier St. Albans illumination would have been more readily defined had earlier manuscripts such as the Missal of Abbot Richard (d. 1119), described in the *Gesta Abbatum*, survived.

PROVENANCE: St. Albans Abbey (inscriptions ff. 36ᵛ, 37); Egidius Watson, 16th cent. (inscription f. 1ᵛ); Sir Robert Cotton, Bt. (1571–1631); his library presented to the nation by his grandson Sir John Cotton, Bt. in 1700; incorporated in the British Museum in 1753.

LITERATURE: Westwood, *Anglo-Saxon and Irish MSS*, 1868, 108; A. Goldschmidt, *Der Albanipsalter in Hildesheim*, 1895, 41; R. Stettiner, *Die illustrierten Prudentius Handschriften*, 1895, 138–43, 193–6, *Plates*, 1905, 193–6; British Museum, *Schools of Illumination*, II, 1915, 6, pl. 1; Helen Woodruff, 'The illustrated manuscripts of Prudentius, *Art Studies*, 7, 1929, 47, 66; A. Katzenellenbogen, *Allegories of the Virtues and Vices in Mediaeval Art*, 1964 ed., 4, 7; Boase, *English Art*, 101, 112, pl. 34a; *St. Albans Psalter*, 166, 168, pl. 151; Rickert, *Painting in Britain*, 63 f., pl. 59a.

EXHIBITED: British Museum, *The Art of Drawing*, 1972, no. 61.

31. Verdun, Bibliothèque Municipale MS 70

St. Anselm, Prayers and Meditations
265 × 180 mm., ff. 106
c. 1120–30. St. Albans Abbey   *Ills. 77, 84–7*

Originally contained fourteen full-page miniatures facing the text to which they belonged; their offsets are still visible on the opposite pages, but only one survives: Christ handing the keys to St. Peter, for the prayer to St. Peter (f. 68ᵛ).
One historiated initial: D with a priest holding the Eucharist (f. 45ᵛ).
Twenty-four decorated initials, many with human figures and animals: D (f. 1), O (f. 8), A (f. 12), A (f. 15ᵛ), C (f. 21ᵛ), D (f. 24ᵛ), A (f. 26ᵛ), A (f. 29ᵛ), M (f. 33), C (f. 35ᵛ), D (f. 39ᵛ), S (f. 42ᵛ), A (f. 49), D (f. 52), V (f. 54), M (f. 56), S (f. 61ᵛ), S (f. 62ᵛ), S (f. 69), S (f. 81), S (f. 87), S (f. 89), P (f. 96), S (f. 101).

Anselm wrote his Prayers and Meditations in his early years; at any rate most of them were written before he became Abbot of Bec in 1078. They are the first examples of what was to become a vogue for fervid and personal devotion, especially to the Virgin. As he wrote them, he sent copies to monastic friends or ladies of noble birth, from Adelaide, a daughter of William the Conqueror, the first recipient in 1071, to Mathilda, Duchess of Tuscany, the last in 1104 (see R. W. Southern, *St. Anselm and his biographer*, 1963, 34–47).
This manuscript is the earliest extant illustrated text of the Prayers and Meditations but it is likely, from the evidence of other extant manuscripts, that earlier illustrated texts existed. The miniature of

Christ handing the keys to St. Peter, combined with the injunction 'feed my sheep', is very similar to the small illumination of the same scene in Bodleian MS Auct. D. 2. 6. of about 1150 (no. 73). This also belongs to the Bec–Canterbury recension, as opposed to the manuscript in Admont (Stiftsbibliothek, MS 289) which is derived from Mathilda of Tuscany's copy.

The style of the miniature and of the initials is clearly that of the St. Albans Psalter (no. 29). Pächt (*St. Albans Psalter*) has attributed the full-page miniature to the Master of the St. Albans Psalter himself and the initials to an assistant. The scenes of combat in the initials are as lively and inventive as those of contemporary Canterbury manuscripts, though they are somewhat stiffer in treatment. There are close similarities with those of other St. Albans manuscripts, notably the Josephus in the British Library (no. 32, ill. 88; *St. Albans Psalter*, pl. 151), but for figured initials the present manuscript is the most important of the group. The mask-like face on f. 39ᵛ (ill. 84) is similar to the lion's head of St. Mark in the Gospels at Hereford (no. 33, ill. 75) and looks forward to the mid-century Bodleian Terence (no. 73, ills. 198–202).

PROVENANCE: uncertain, possibly brought from England by Henry, Archdeacon of Winchester, Bishop of Verdun, 1117–29.

LITERATURE: H. Swarzenski, *The Berthold Missal*, 1943, 45, fig. 63; Boase, *English Art*, 107; O. Pächt, 'The Illustrations of St. Anselm's Prayers and Meditations', *J.W.C.I.*, 19, 1956, 74 f., pl. 18b; *St. Albans Psalter*, 156, 165, pls. 151–3; Schiller, *Iconography*, III (German ed.), 118, fig. 387.

EXHIBITED: *Manuscrits à Peintures du 7ᵉ au 12ᵉ siècle*, Paris, Bibliothèque Nationale, 1954, no. 277; Barcelona, 1961, no. 178; Brussels, 1973, no. 21.

32. London, British Library MS Royal 13. D. VI–VII

Flavius Josephus, Antiquities, and Jewish Wars
Vol. I, 385 × 273 mm., ff. 218;
Vol. II, 405 × 273 mm., ff. 211
c. 1120–30. St. Albans Abbey   *Ills. 88, 89*

Vol. I:
One historiated initial to Bk. I of the Jewish Antiquities, I with eight medallions of the Creation (f. 3); twenty-eight decorated tinted outline initials, in the two volumes one to each book: H, Prologue (f. 1), P, Bk. 2 (f. 17ᵛ), I, Bk. 3 (f. 33), H, Bk. 4 (f. 47), M, Bk. 5 (f. 61ᵛ), T, Bk. 6 (f. 77ᵛ), P, Bk. 7 (f. 96ᵛ), D, Bk. 8 (f. 115ᵛ), I, Bk. 9 (f. 134ᵛ), C, Bk. 10 (f. 147), P, Bk. 11 (f. 158ᵛ), A, Bk. 12 (f. 171), Q, Bk. 13 (f. 186), A, Bk. 14 (f. 201ᵛ).
Vol. II:
S, painted with gold outlines, Bk. 15 (f. 1), I, Bk. 16 (f. 16), A, Bk. 17 (f. 28), C, Bk. 18 (f. 45), C, Bk. 19

(f. 62), M, Bk. 20 (f. 74ᵛ), Q, opening of the Jewish Wars (f. 83ᵛ), C, Bk. 1 (f. 85), T, Bk. 2 (f. 114), N, Bk. 3 (f. 138ᵛ), Q, Bk. 4 (f. 153), A, Bk. 5 (f. 161ᵛ), T, Bk. 6 (f. 170ᵛ), C, Bk. 7 (f. 187).

The style of the decoration is derived from the St. Albans Psalter and may be compared with the spandrels of the David miniature in the Psalter (*St. Albans Psalter*, pl. 34). Pächt (*St. Albans Psalter*) has attributed the initials to the same hand as the Anselm manuscript at Verdun (see no. 31).

The initial I containing eight roundels of the Creation is ultimately derived from Genesis initials in Bibles, but there are early 12th-century Josephus manuscripts in which this transposition has already taken place (Florence, Biblioteca Laurenziana, MS Plut. 66. 5, see *Mostra della Biblioteca di Lorenzo*, Florence, 1949, no. 84, pl. VI). These medallions show the Creation scenes reduced to a bare minimum; in most of them the Creator himself does not appear. This particular cycle is distinguished by its Creation of Adam scene in which God is seen moulding the human figure as a potter with clay. This type belongs to the tradition of the 5th-century Cotton Genesis of which the best-known extant example is the mosaic in the atrium of San Marco, Venice, but which was known in England in the 11th and 12th centuries when it appears in Aelfric's Heptateuch (B.L. Cotton, Claudius B. IV. f. 4), the St. Albans Psalter (no. 29), and the Lambeth Bible (no. 70) (see O. Pächt, *The Rise of Pictorial Narrative in 12th century England*, 1962, 24 f., pl. IV).

The Genesis initial in this manuscript was apparently copied by the artist of the Lambeth Bible (Dodwell, *Canterbury School*, frontispiece). This raises the problem of the artistic connection between St. Albans and Canterbury in the first half of the 12th century (see nos. 71–2).

PROVENANCE: St. Albans Abbey (inscriptions f. 1 of each vol.); acquired by Leland for the Royal Library at the dissolution in 1540 (inventory of 1542), given to the British Museum by George II in 1757.

LITERATURE: Warner and Gilson, II, 110; Boase, *English Art*, 98 f., 157, 167; Dodwell, *Canterbury School*, 50, 82; *St. Albans Psalter*, 156 f., 166, 168, pls. 148*b*, 151*h*, 152 *a*, *d*, 153*b*.

33. Hereford, Cathedral Library MS O. 1. VIII
Gospels
237 × 153 mm., ff. 141
c. 1120–30. St. Albans Abbey   *Ill. 75*

Framed miniature, three quarters' page, to Mark: lion-headed Evangelist writing (f. 45ᵛ).
Historiated initial I to John with Evangelist seated in shaft (f. 113ᵛ); three decorated initials: L, Matthew (f. 6), I, Mark (f. 46), F, Luke (f. 72ᵛ). Small drawing of a bearded head above the initial on f. 72ᵛ.

Pächt firmly placed this manuscript in the immediate circle of the St. Albans Psalter. The decoration, characterized by small flowers like spinning tops, is very close to that in the spandrels of the David picture in the Psalter (*St. Albans Psalter*, pls. 56, 155*e*). The profile figure of St. John is in a pure St. Albans style, as is the drapery, with its toothcomb white highlights, of St. Mark. Of the script, only the text of St. John appears to be in a characteristic St. Albans hand, but the manuscript was certainly illuminated by a St. Albans artist, perhaps by the Alexis Master himself working with an assistant.

The type of the St. Mark portrait, consisting of a mixture of the Evangelist and his symbol, occurs as early as the 8th century in the Gellone Sacramentary (Paris, Bibl. Nat., lat. 12048) and in the Book of Kells. These early examples, however, show the Evangelist standing, and Garrison has distinguished between this group and the rarer cases of animal-headed Evangelists seated, in the manner of ordinary Evangelist portraits. This is the earliest English example of this type—others occur in the Bury Gospels (Cambridge, Pembroke College, MS 120; no. 35) and in a later 12th-century Durham manuscript (A. IV. 10, Mynors, pl. 56)—and it is likely that the St. Albans artist derived his model from abroad. The closest comparison occurs in a 12th-century Italian Bible (Rome, Casanatense, MS 723; Garrison, figs. 127–8) but as this dates from the third quarter of the century, and as French examples are also known (Carolingian ivory book-cover, Metz Museum, A. Goldschmidt, *Elfenbeinskulpturen*, I, no. 78, pl. XXXII; St. Bénigne Bible, Dijon MS 2, repr. W. W. S. Cook, *Art Bulletin*, 8, 1925–6, fig. 19) the nationality of the model remains in doubt. For a wider view of animal-headed figures in art see Z. Ameisenowa, *J.W.C.I.*, 12, 1949, 21 ff.

PROVENANCE: Hereford Cathedral Library (typical inscription f. 2: *De concordia evangeliorum prec. XIIIs IIId*).

LITERATURE: Bannister, *Catalogue*, 11; H. H. Glunz, *History of the Vulgate in England*, 1933, 188 f.; Boase, *English Art*, 165; E. B. Garrison, *Studies in Mediaeval Italian Painting*, II, 1955–56, 115 n.; *St. Albans Psalter*, 157 n. 1, 165, pl. 155.

EXHIBITED: B.F.A.C., *Illuminated MSS*, 1908, no. 9, pl. 24; Manchester, 1959, no. 30; Brussels, 1973, no. 23, pl. 9.

34. New York, Pierpont Morgan Library M 736
Life and Miracles of St. Edmund, King and Martyr (d. 869)
273 × 184 mm., ff. 100
c. 1130. Bury St. Edmunds Abbey
Ills. 79–83, 90

Thirty-two full-page miniatures preceding the text:

Saxons, Jutes, and Angles cross the sea to Britain (p. 11), they fight the Britons and dispossess them (p. 12), the three tribes divide the island (p. 13), St. Edmund crowned King of East Anglia (p. 14), he bestows alms on the poor (p. 15), Danes under Ingvar and Ubba land in England (p. 16), Ingvar attacks East Anglia (p. 17), Ingvar sends an envoy to Edmund to demand submission (p. 18), Edmund consults a bishop who advises him to yield (p. 19), the envoy reports to Ingvar that Edmund refuses to yield unless Ingvar becomes a Christian (p. 20), Edmund is dragged from his throne (p. 21), he is bound and mocked (p. 22), he is maltreated and beaten (p. 23), he is tied to a tree and scourged (p. 24), his body is riddled with arrows (p. 25), his head is struck off and hidden in a thicket (p. 26), the Danes leave the country (p. 27), Edmund's friends discover his headless body (p. 28), they search for the head and find it guarded by a wolf (p. 29), they carry it to where the body lies and the wolf follows (p. 30), they fit it on to the shoulders and prepare the body for burial (p. 31), they bear the body in procession, the wolf still follows (p. 32), they lay the body in a wrought tomb (p. 33), eight thieves try and break into the church but are miraculously fixed motionless until morning (p. 34), they are brought before Bishop Theodred for judgement (p. 35), they are hanged (p. 36), the monk Egelwin, guardian of the shrine, for fear of the Danes, brings the relics to London; the house of a priest who refused hospitality burns (p. 37), the cart with the relics miraculously crosses a narrow and broken bridge at Stratford (p. 38), Egelwin, at the command of St. Edmund, prays to King Sweyn to exempt his church from tribute but is rudely repulsed (p. 39), St. Edmund appears to Sweyn at night, hands him the money and kills him (p. 40), the death of Sweyn is miraculously announced by a dying man in Essex (p. 41), St. Edmund King and Martyr crowned by angels, two others making him a sceptre and palm branch (p. 42).

Thirteen historiated initials:
Lesson for the vigil of St. Edmund, I with St. Edmund (p. 7), Preface to the Miracles, C with Edmund killed with a spear (p. 43), Miracles chapt. 2, C, a light shines on the shrine (p. 50), chapt. 3, I, King Sweyn standing (p. 53), chapt. 7, C, Canute enthroned (p. 80), chapt. 8, O, St. Edmund standing (p. 84), chapt. 11, Q, William the Conquerer enthroned (p. 95), chapt. 12, Q, St. Edmund cures a sick soldier (p. 97), Bk. 2, chapt. 2, C, Cnut (p. 113), Q, (?)St. Edmund (p. 145), Opening of the *Passio*, D with Abbo of Fleury presenting his book to Dunstan (p. 151), Lessons for the office of St. Edmund, C, martyrdom (p. 186), C, wolf guarding head (p. 191).

Twenty-five decorated initials to chapters and lessons:
E (p. 51), P (p. 60), I (p. 77), N (p. 89), D (p. 92), A (p. 99), T (p. 101), E (p. 103), N (p. 104), I (p. 108), N (p. 109), L (p. 125), N (p. 129), M (p. 131), A (p. 153), S (p. 178), B (p. 179), P (p. 181), D (p. 182), S (p. 185), S (p. 187), Q (p. 189), S (p. 193), S (p. 194), I (p. 195).
One initial has been cut out (p. 45).

Edmund was an obscure East Anglian king killed by the Danish invaders in 869. Within forty years he had come to be honoured as a saint in East Anglia and the community that guarded his relics at Bury was to become one of the most important monasteries in the country. There are many manuscripts of his life and miracles, but this is the only one, before the 15th century, which is illustrated. The text consists of:
1. *Miracula Sancti Edmundi regis et martyris* (pp. 43–149) attributed to Osbert of Clare (*c.* 1130) but based on an earlier compilation by Herman the Archdeacon (*c.* 1100).
2. *Passio Sancti Edmundi* by Abbo of Fleury (pp. 151–70) dedicated to St. Dunstan and therefore datable before 998 the year of Dunstan's death.
These texts are published in Arnold, *Memorials*, I, 3–25, 26–92, 107–208.)
3. Lessons for the office of St. Edmund and hymns (pp. 170–98).
Out of the thirty-two miniatures in the manuscript, the first twenty-six illustrate Abbo of Fleury's *Passio*, though the text comes towards the end of the manuscript. Only five illustrations, dealing with the miracles during the second wave of Danish raids (*c.* 1009–14) refer to the *Miracula*, the greater part of which is not illustrated at all. In one instance, the illustrator, or whoever devised the illustrations, appears to have corrected the order of events in the Miracles text. The transportation of the relics to London, which may be dated 1010, the year of the worst plundering of East Anglia, is correctly placed before the illustration of Sweyn's death (1014), whereas the text has these events the other way round.
The style of the miniatures is very like that of the St. Albans Psalter pictures, though the colours are brighter—royal blue and bright green predominate—and the scenes more violently expressionistic. Rickert ascribed the miniatures to an assistant of the Alexis Master, but Pächt (*St. Albans Psalter*) convincingly argued that they are by the same hand. The initials, however, are in a different style and do not belong to the St. Albans tradition. The historiated initials are simple and usually contain only a single figure, but some of the decoration is elaborate, with large dragons forming the sides of initials that contain foliage spirals inhabited by beasts and humans. These initials are similar to those in the Bury Gospels, Pembroke College MS 120 (no. 35). However, some of the initials towards the end of the book are characterized by very large, luxuriant blossoms (pp. 178, 179) of a kind that foreshadows the decoration of the Bury Bible.
The close stylistic link with the St. Albans Psalter, datable just before 1123, suggests a date around 1130, or slightly earlier, for this manuscript. The letters from Henry I and Prior Talbot at the beginning of the book were written to Anselm

abroad to ask him to return to Bury. R. M. Thomson has connected them with events of 1125–6, when Anselm was in Normandy, and suggests that the whole manuscript was written at this time. However, these letters are copies in book hand which could have been made at a later date. Even so, it is more likely that they were added to the manuscript because they were topical, and, although they cannot be accepted as firm evidence, they do serve to confirm an approximate date *c.* 1130 for the manuscript. Iconographically, as well as stylistically, the Life of St. Edmund is dependent upon the St. Albans Psalter. In general terms, the persecution and martyrdom of St. Edmund (pp. 22–32) is paralleled in the Passion cycle of the Psalter. Two of these scenes, St. Edmund scourged and his burial, are very similar to the Flagellation and the Entombment in the Psalter. Pächt (*St. Albans Psalter*, 118, pl. 138*a*) has pointed out the coronation picture on p. 14 is based on an Ottonian model, such as the Sacramentary of Henry II (Munich Clm. 4456, f. 11). Unlike the contemporary Life of St. Cuthbert (no. 26) which may well be based on an earlier cycle, the St. Edmund miniatures must have been created for this particular manuscript. Again unlike St. Cuthbert there are no extant later cycles of these pictures, though several of the scenes reappeared in a hanging in the Abbey church at Bury described in MS Arundel XXX at the Royal College of Arms (reprinted in M. R. James, *On the Abbey of St. Edmund at Bury*, 1895, 187). The 15th-century illustrations of Lydgate's *Life of St. Edmund* (B.L. Harley 2278) are not very similar.

PROVENANCE: Bury St. Edmunds Abbey (copies of letters from Henry I to Abbot Anselm and from Prior Talbot to Anselm and a memorandum concerning Anselm's care of his monks, pp. 1–3). George Roche, 16th cent. (p. 1); W. Stonehouse, 17th cent. (p. 1); Robert Parker, 17th cent. (p. 7); John Towneley, sale 8 July 1814 lot 904, bt. Booth for £168; sold by Payne & Foss to R. S. Holford, (sale catalogue 1841 no. 1) for £300; Sir George Holford; 1927, Pierpont Morgan Library.

LITERATURE: G. F. Waagen, *Treasures of Art in Great Britain*, II, 1854, 215; T. W. Arnold, *Memorials of St. Edmunds Abbey*, Rolls Series, 96, 1890–6, iii, xxxvi; *New Pal. Soc.* I, vol. 2, 51–8, pls. 113–15; *The Holford Collection, Westonbirt*, Oxford, privately printed 1924, no. 2, 35 f., pls. 3–5; Millar, I, 29 f., 82, pl. 36; E. W. Williamson, ed., *The Letters of Osbert of Clare*, 1929, 28–32, 195; *The Pierpont Morgan Library 1924–29*, 1930, 19, pls. 5–6; O. E. Saunders, *History of English Art in the Middle Ages*, 1932, 67; W. A. Bloar, 'The proper of the Mass for the Feast of St. Edmund', *Douai Magazine*, 7, no. 4, 1933; Boase, *English Art*, 112 f., pl. 38*a*; G. Zarnecki, 'A Romanesque bronze candlestick in Oslo and the problem of Belts of Strength', *Oslo Kunstindustrimuseet, Årbok*, 1963–4, 54 f.; Rickert, *Painting in Britain*, 66, 89, pls. 64–5; Swarzenski, *Monuments*, figs. 275–6; *St. Albans Psalter*, 118, 141 f., 167, pl. 139; C. M. Kauffmann, 'The Bury

Bible', *J.W.C.I.*, 29, 1966, 80, pl. 30*c*; A. N. L. Munby, *Connoisseurs and Medieval Miniatures*, 1972, 149; R. M. Thomson, 'The dates of the Pierpont Morgan Vita S. Edmundi and the Bury Bible', *Viator*, II, 1971, 211–25.

EXHIBITED: B.F.A.C., *Illuminated MSS*, 1908, no. 18, pl. 23; Morgan Library, *Exhibition of Illuminated MSS held at the New York Public Library*, 1933–4, no. 30, pl. 29.

35. Cambridge, Pembroke College MS 120
Gospels
416×270 mm., ff. 182
c. 1130 and *c.* 1140. (?)Bury St. Edmunds Abbey
Ills. 91–102; Figs. 18, 20, 23

Twelve pages of drawings containing forty subjects from the Gospels (ff. 1–6) tinted ff. 1–3, outlines only, ff. 3ᵛ–6ᵛ:
1. The Wicked Husbandman, 2. Cleansing of the Temple, 3. Miracle of the Loaves and Fishes (f. 1), 4. Healing of the man born blind, 5. The Woman taken in adultery, 6. Raising of Lazarus (f. 1ᵛ), 7. The Good Samaritan, 8. The Good Samaritan tends the traveller's wounds, 9. Zacchaeus in the tree (f. 2), 10. Christ disputing with the Jews; they stone him, 11. Parable of the guest without the wedding garment, 12. Entry into Jerusalem (f. 2ᵛ), 13. The Last Supper, 14. Christ washes the disciples' feet, 15. The Betrayal (f. 3), 16. The Flagellation, 17. Christ crowned with thorns, 18. Simon bearing the Cross, 19. The Crucifixion (f. 3ᵛ), 20. The Deposition, 21. The Entombment, 22. The Jews ask Pilate for a guard, 23. The Holy Women at the Sepulchre (f. 4), 24. The Harrowing of Hell, 25. Noli me tangere, 26. The Journey to Emmaus, 27. Supper at Emmaus, 28. Return from Emmaus, 29. Incredulity of St. Thomas (f. 4ᵛ), 30. The fish and honeycomb (Christ and four disciples; Luke 24: 42), 31. Christ and St. Peter on Lake Tiberias, 32. Miraculous draught of fishes, 33. Fish and bread laid on the fire, 34. Christ on the mountain (Matthew 28: 16–19), 35. Christ appears to the Eleven at table (Mark 16: 14) (f. 5), 36. The Ascension, 37. The dance of Salome and the beheading of the Baptist, 38. God and Christ between cherubim, 39. Pentecost (f. 6), 40. The Last Judgement (f. 6ᵛ). Five historiated initials: Matthew, L with the Saint enthroned (f. 11), Prologue to Mark, M, St. Mark with tetramorph heads cutting off his thumb (cf. *Legenda Aurea*) (f. 31ᵛ), L, Luke, with bull (f. 45ᵛ), I, John, with eagle-headed Evangelist in medallion, Christ in mandorla (f. 70), P, Peter Epistles, St. Peter enthroned (f. 113).
About forty decorated initials: ff. 7, 7ᵛ, 8ᵛ, 32ᵛ, 45ᵛ, 69, 86ᵛ, 88, 110, 110ᵛ, 112ᵛ, 115ᵛ, 117, 117ᵛ, 119ᵛ, 120, 121, 121ᵛ, 122, 123, 124ᵛ, 132, 133ᵛ, 141, 141ᵛ, 146ᵛ, 147, 150, 153, 155ᵛ, 157ᵛ, 158ᵛ, 161, 163ᵛ, 165, 166, 167, 174.

The illustrations are on six leaves tipped in at the beginning of the manuscript. The size of the pages is fairly consistent throughout, but whereas the text is contained in an area of 305×190 mm. the pictures cover 320×213 mm. which leaves them with an inadequate margin at the sides. This supports the view, widely expressed, that the illustrations were not part of the original manuscript but were later bound with the text, at which time the pages were trimmed to fit those of the text. This leaves two questions unanswered: what kind of manuscript did these drawings originally illustrate? And secondly, were either the pictures, or the text, or both produced at Bury? James and Swarzenski argued that, as there was no parallel in the 12th century for a manuscript of the Gospels containing a picture cycle of the Life of Christ, the drawings were probably produced for a Psalter. Elizabeth Parker, on the other hand, pointed out that Pembroke 120 has no Old Testament scenes—which occur in all Psalter cycles—and suggested that the illustrations may, after all, have been made for a New Testament manuscript comparable to the 6th-century 'Gospels of St. Augustine' (Corpus Christi College, Cambridge, MS 286).

The question of the Bury provenance is equally imponderable. The inscription on the first page of the text (f. 7) tells us that the text volume was given to Bury by Reginald of Denham who was Sacrist in the early 14th century. Elizabeth Parker has concluded that, as both the handwriting and the decoration are quite unlike Bury manuscripts, Pembroke 120 was produced elsewhere and did not reach Bury until Sacrist Reginald's time. Certainly many of the initials with gold backgrounds and tight, somewhat dry foliage spirals, are different to those in Bury manuscripts and suggest a date in the 1140s. A few of them, however, are similar to those of the Morgan Library Life of St. Edmund, produced at Bury c. 1130 (cf. Pembroke 120 ff. 155ᵛ, 174 with Morgan 736 ff. 60, 153) and it must be admitted that the evidence is inconclusive on this point. The pictures, on the other hand, probably were produced at Bury. The design of the frames, which appear to be, like the colouring, slightly later additions look as though they are inferior copies of the Bury Bible's frames (ff. 2, 3, cf. Bury Bible, ff. 147ᵛ, 344ᵛ). The style of the drawings fits with a Bury provenance, for it is closely related to that of the St. Albans Psalter and the St. Albans Psalter style was known at Bury ever since the Life of St. Edmund was produced there in c. 1130 (no. 34). Pembroke 120 has the same elongated figures and the same characteristic and predominant use of profile. If the Life of St. Edmund is by the St. Albans Psalter Master himself, the drawings of Pembroke 120, characterized by a greater stylization, are by a close follower. Elizabeth Parker (1969, p. 265) has isolated several compositional motifs which are found in the St. Edmund manuscript, but not in the Psalter, thereby strengthening the argument of a Bury provenance.

The picture cycle opens with the Ministry of Christ and it used to be thought that extensive illustrations to the Nativity and Infancy had been lost. Elizabeth Parker, however, has recently argued from an examination of the gatherings that only one leaf could have been lost at the beginning of the series. Clearly, therefore, the Infancy was not as fully illustrated as the Ministry and Passion. The iconography shows some links with Anglo-Saxon tradition (for example the 'disappearing Christ' in the Ascension) and, equally, some influence from Byzantine art (e.g. the Raising of Lazarus from a rock-cut tomb). But by far the most important source was provided by the Ottonian cycles and in particular those produced at Echternach in the 1040s (*Codex Aureus Epternacensis*, Germanisches Museum, Nürnberg; Golden Gospels of Henry III, Escorial) in which some of the rarest scenes from the Parables and Miracles are paralleled. However, the iconography of Pembroke 120 cannot be considered in isolation, for the cycle is closely related to two others produced in England in the period c. 1120–40: the St. Albans Psalter (no. 29) with which it has sixteen scenes in common, and the four Psalter leaves in London and New York (no. 66) with which it shares twenty-six scenes. The relationship between these cycles is discussed in the Introduction (see above, p. 31 f.).

PROVENANCE: Given to the Abbey of Bury St. Edmunds by the Sacrist Reginald of Denham who held office in the early 14th century (inscription f. 7). Probably presented to Pembroke College by Edmund Boldero, D.D., Master of Jesus College, 1663–79.

LITERATURE: James, *Catalogue*, no. 120; Millar, I, 29, 82, pl. 35; H. H. Glunz, *History of the Vulgate in England*, 1933, 187 f.; A. Boeckler, *Abendländische Miniaturen*, 1930, 90 f., pl. 87; M. R. James, 'Four Leaves of an English Psalter', *Walpole Society*, 25, 1937, 1 ff.; H. Swarzenski, 'Unknown Bible Pictures of W. de Brailes', *Journal of the Walters Art Gallery*, 1, 1938, 65 n. 20; Wormald, 'Development', 37; Boase, *English Art*, 111, pl. 39a; Swarzenski, *Monuments*, fig. 282; Rickert, *Painting in Britain*, 67, 82, pl. 66; Dodwell, *Canterbury School*, 46; *St. Albans Psalter*, 75 f., 142 n., 169, pls. 122 f., 157a; C. M. Kauffmann, 'Bury Bible', *J.W.C.I.*, 29, 1966, 61, 65; Elizabeth Parker, 'A 12th century cycle of New Testament Drawings from Bury St. Edmunds Abbey', *Proceedings of the Suffolk Institute of Archaeology*, 31, 1969, 263–302, pls. 32–47; Schiller, *Iconography*, III (German ed.), 101, 107, figs. 291, 332.

EXHIBITED: B.F.A.C., *Illuminated MSS*, 1908, no. 23, pl. 28; R. A., *British Primitive Paintings*, 1923, no. 97; Victoria and Albert Museum, *English Medieval Art*, 1930, no. 62; Manchester, 1959, no. 13; Barcelona, 1961, no. 177, pl. 12; Brussels, 1973, no. 24, pl. 10.

36. Oxford, Bodleian Library MS Laud. Misc. 247 (S.C. 1302)
Bestiary
272×168 mm., ff. 139ᵛ–168ᵛ
c. 1120   *Ills. 103, 104; Fig. 43*

Thirty-six pen outline drawings: lions reviving whelps (f. 139ᵛ), antelope (f. 141), male and female stones, shown as men and women, causing a fire; serra, a winged fish (f. 141ᵛ), Caladrius bird looks at sick man (f. 142), pelican biting herself to feed her young (f. 143), night crow, eagles (f. 143ᵛ), phoenix (f. 144), hoopoe (f. 145), siren, calling centaur (f. 147), hedgehog (f. 147ᵛ), ibex (f. 148), fox (f. 149), capture of the unicorn (f. 149ᵛ), beaver hunt (f. 150ᵛ), hyena (f. 151ᵛ), hydrus (dragon) and crocodile (f. 152ᵛ), goats, onager, a donkey (f. 153), monkeys tormenting a man (f. 153ᵛ), fulica, a coot (f. 154), panther (f. 154ᵛ), whale with ship on its back (f. 157), partridge (f. 157ᵛ), weasel (f. 158), viper (158ᵛ), ostrich (f. 159), stag (f. 160), salamander (f. 161), doves (f. 161ᵛ), serpent eating doves (f. 161ᵛ), elephants (f. 163ᵛ), Amos and his goats (f. 165), diamonds (f. 165ᵛ), pearl oyster (f. 166ᵛ).

The medieval Bestiary was directly descended from the Greek *Physiologus*, a compilation in which fantastic descriptions of real and fabulous animals and birds were used to illustrate Christian allegories and moral lessons. The *Physiologus* was translated into Latin perhaps as early as the 5th century, though there are no surviving manuscripts until the 8th century. There is no extant intermediary between the 8th–10th-century Latin *Physiologus* and the 12th-century Bestiaries whose descendants they were. Laud Misc. 247 is the earliest extant Bestiary. Its illustrations are similar to those of a *Physiologus* manuscript at Brussels (Bibliothèque Royale, MS 10074, 10th century) but its text is closest to that of a manuscript at Berne (MS 233, 8th–9th century). This is not illustrated and Laud Misc. 247 is presumably descended from a manuscript of this textual recension containing illustrations similar to those in the Brussels manuscript. However, it also contains additional material taken from Isidore of Seville's *Etymologiae* (Bk. 12, *De Animalibus*) in the form of fantastic etymologies. This marked the beginning of a process which culminated in the expanded medieval Bestiary in the later 12th century. M. R. James categorized the earlier manuscripts, containing thirty-five to forty chapters, including Laud Misc. 247, as the first family and the later ones, containing over one hundred chapters and further additional texts as the second family (see nos. 105–6). This broad distinction has been upheld by Florence McCulloch. Other 12th-century Bestiaries belonging to the first family are B. L. Stowe 1067, with twenty-eight somewhat crude drawings, and Corpus Christi College MS 22 (no. 104).
The tradition of the *Physiologus* and Bestiary was one of the main channels through which classical representations of animals and fabulous beasts remained known throughout the Middle Ages. The appearance of the animals has become thoroughly Romanesque. They are, indeed, indistinguishable from the decorative beasts inhabiting the scrolls of initials, but the fact that they occur in this book confirms their classical origins. The Bestiary remained a fruitful source of decorative motifs

throughout the Middle Ages (see lit. below and also to nos. 104–6).
This manuscript may be dated *c.* 1120–30 on stylistic grounds, but there is no evidence as to its provenance. Rickert drew attention to the links with Anglo-Saxon drawings, such as the Cædmon and Ælfric manuscripts, particularly in the treatment of the trees and landscape.

PROVENANCE: William Laud, Archbishop of Canterbury, 1633 (inscription f. 2).

LITERATURE: James, *Bestiary*, 7 ff., pls. 2, 10; G. Zarnecki, 'The Coronation of the Virgin on a Capital from Reading Abbey', *J.W.C.I.*, 13, 1950, 5, pl. 2; Saxl, Meier, III, 384; Boase, *English Art*, 88, 244, pl. 51A; Rickert, *Painting in Britain*, 62, 87; Bodleian Picture Book, *English Romanesque Illumination*, 1951, pl. 7; Florence McCulloch, *Mediaeval Latin and French Bestiaries*, N. Carolina, 1960, 29; Swarzenski, *Monuments*, fig. 287; F. Klingender, *Animals in art and thought*, 1971, 387, fig. 219a; Pächt and Alexander, III, no. 111, pl. 11.

EXHIBITED: *The Bodleian Library in the 17th Century*, 1951, no. 72.

37. London, British Library MS Cotton, Tiberius C. I.

Computistic and astrological treatises
292 × 197 mm., ff. 41;
MS Harley 3667 is a fragment from the same MS
310 × 210 mm., ff. 10
c. 1122. Peterborough Abbey

Ills. 105, 106

Tiberius C. I:
Computistic and cosmological diagrams (ff. 1–17); pen drawings of the signs of the Zodiac, constellations, and planets (ff. 20–33ᵛ) (detailed description in Saxl and Meier, III).

Harley 3667:
Diagrams, including life and death (f. 4ᵛ), winds (f. 5ᵛ), divisions of knowledge (f. 6ᵛ); typological diagrams: Christ and Apostles with O.T. Kings and Prophets (f. 7ᵛ), Byrhtferth's diagram (f. 8), world map (f. 8ᵛ).

These are two fragments of a comprehensive scientific manuscript. Neil Ker has established that the script is the same almost throughout. Harley 3667 (ff. 1–2) contains the Annals of Peterborough Abbey, and these are written by the main hand up to 1122. The manuscript, therefore, probably originated at Peterborough in about 1122.
The text and diagrams—excluding the astrological material—belong to the tradition of St. John's College MS 17 (no. 9). The astrological drawings, on the other hand, are an exact copy of a 9th-century manuscript, probably written at Fleury, of a Cicero text describing the constellations (Harley 647). Cicero had written a Latin verse version of a Greek

poem on the constellations by Aratus. Subsequently, in the late classical period, further explanatory material was added to the text and this was written within the figures which were left without outlines. Harley 647 is clearly an accurate copy of a classical model, down to its use of rustic capitals (see Saxl and Meier). In Tiberius C. I. the textual filling is in lower case letters rather than rustic capitals and the figures have firm outlines, but otherwise it follows Harley 647 very closely. It is the only 12th-century representative of this type.

It should be stressed that it was through the survival of the classical tradition of illustrated astrological manuscripts (see also nos. 27, 38, 74) that the pictorial images of classical gods and mythical creatures remained known throughout the Middle Ages.

PROVENANCE: Peterborough Abbey (14th-century catalogue, see M. R. James, *List of MSS formerly in Peterborough Abbey Library*, Supplement to the Transactions of the Bibliographical Society, 5, 1926, 16, 34).

LITERATURE: A. van de Vyver, 'Les Œuvres inédits d'Abbon de Fleury', *Revue Bénédictine*, 2, 1935, 142 *passim*; Neil Ker, 'Membra Disiecta', *British Museum Quarterly*, 12, 1937–8, 132; Saxl and Meier, III, xvii, 128–134; F. Saxl, 'Illuminated Science MSS in England', *Lectures*, 1957, 102, 108, pl. 55A.

38. Oxford, Bodleian Library MS Bodley 614 (S.C. 2144)

Astrological manuscript and Marvels of the East
143 × 100 mm., ff. 51
c. 1120–40.   *Ills. 107–11*

Drawings of four seated learned men, framed, two with coloured backgrounds (ff. 1ᵛ–2).
Calendar, ff. 2ᵛ–14, with three full-page drawings: January, Janus, feasting (f. 3); February, warming (f. 4); March, pruning (f. 5), ff. 6ᵛ–13ᵛ framed panels left empty for pictures. Framed, full-page outline drawing on red and blue ground, sun and moon in chariots (f. 17ᵛ).
Framed drawings on coloured ground of the signs of the Zodiac, planets, and constellations (ff. 18–34; detailed description in Saxl and Meier, III).
Table of winds (f. 34ᵛ); drawing of an astronomer with an astrolabe (f. 35ᵛ), De Rebus in Oriente mirabilibus, ff. 36–51, with forty-eight framed pen drawings on coloured ground, including: Caenocephalus, man with dog's head (f. 38ᵛ), man with two heads (f. 40), headless man (f. 41), Sciapod, using his enormous foot to shield himself from the sun; Antipod, with feet turning backwards; Hippopod, with horse's hoofs (f. 50), Hermaphrodite (f. 50ᵛ).

In combining astrological texts and Marvels of the East, this manuscript is in the tradition of B.L.

Cotton, Tiberius B. V, an Anglo-Saxon manuscript of *c.* 1000, though it is not a direct copy. The astrological illustrations of both Bodley 614 and Digby 83 (no. 74) go back to a model related to Tiberius B. V. This may be characterized as a derivative of the Carolingian manuscript Harley 647 but one in which the text had already been omitted from the bodies of the figures (cf. no. 37). The drawings of the constellations are of classical descent, but drawn in a solid Romanesque style, no different in appearance from the decorative creatures in Romanesque manuscripts and sculpture. Bodley 614 and Digby 83 also differ from the Harley 647–Tiberius B. V. tradition in that the Cicero text and illustrations have been supplemented by material taken from a manuscript of Hyginus' *Astronomica*.

The Marvels of the East had their origin in ancient Greek descriptions of the fabulous peoples of India. The earliest text of the actual Marvels of the East treatise, which probably originated in the 4th century A.D., is written in the form of a letter from a certain Fermes to the Emperor Hadrian purporting to comment on a journey to the East. The earliest complete illustrated Marvels of the East manuscripts are Anglo-Saxon and date from about 1000: B.L. Cotton, Vitellius A. XV (Anglo-Saxon text) and Tiberius B. V (Anglo-Saxon and Latin texts). Bodley 614 is closely similar in its text and illustrations to Tiberius B. V; if it was not a direct copy, it must, as James believed, descend from the same archetype. On stylistic grounds this manuscript, with its simple treatment of the drapery, not yet developed into fully formed damp folds, may be dated *c.* 1120–40.

The illustrations of Marvels of the East provided a useful fount for the Romanesque painter and sculptor. These fabulous creatures could be used for purely decorative motifs, as in the architrave at Aulnay, or, in the case of the Vézelay tympanum, to portray the pagan peoples from the borders of the world. Wittkower (see below) traced the continuation of the tradition throughout the Middle Ages and into the 17th century.

PROVENANCE: Ralph Hopwood, 16th century (inscription f. 1ᵛ); acquired by the Bodleian Library in 1605–11.

LITERATURE: Waagen, *Treasures of Art in Great Britain*, III, 1854, 68 f.; R. T. Gunther, *Early Science in Oxford*, II, 1923, 4, 28, 221; M. R. James, *Marvels of the East*, Roxburghe Club, 1929; E. Panofsky, F. Saxl, 'Classical Mythology in Mediaeval Art', *Metropolitan Museum Studies*, 4, 1932–3, 238, fig. 15; J. C. Webster, *The Labors of the Months*, 1938, 173, no. 97, pl. 63; R. Wittkower, 'Marvels of the East', *J.W.C.I.*, 5, 1942, 172 n., pl. 47a; Saxl and Meier, III, 313–16; Bodleian Picture Book, *English Romanesque Illumination*, 1951, figs. 8, 10; Boase, *English Art*, 86 f., 240, pl. 28b; F. Saxl, 'Illuminated Science MSS in England', *Lectures*, 1957, 108 ff., pl. 60; K. Malone, *The Nowell Codex* (Early English MSS in Facsimile,

XII), 1963, 115; Pächt and Alexander, III, no. 156, pl. 16.

39. Cambridge, St. John's College MS B. 20
Calendar, St. Isidore, Homilies, etc.
330×202 mm., ff. 136
c. 1120–40. (?)Worcester Cathedral Priory

Ill. 112

Occupations of the months and signs of the Zodiac in roundels linked in pairs (f. 2ᵛ):
January, feasting, Janus seated holding loaf and horn; February, warming, man wrapped in hairy cloak; March, digging; April, pruning; May, falconry; June, weeding; July, mowing; August, reaping; September, vintage; October, sowing; November, killing hogs; December, gathering wood.
Tinted pen drawing of the Nativity (f. 4).
Illuminated initial N, made up of two dragons, to Isidore (f. 6).

M. R. James suggested that the Calendar, which contains the feasts of Archbishop Oswald and St. Egwin, indicated a Worcester origin, though the name of Wulfstan (Bishop of Worcester, 1062–96) is apparently a later addition. A date c. 1120 proposed by Zarnecki is reasonable, to judge from the style of the figures, though the gold background and large flowers of the initial on f. 6 may indicate a slightly later period, in the second quarter of the century.
The occupations of the months follow a well-established pattern which is ultimately derived from classical models. The English cycles are similar to the French but adapted for the climate: the pruning of vines is replaced by digging in March and appears in April instead; mowing, reaping, and threshing occur a month later; the gap in June is filled by weeding, which does not appear in other countries. As opposed to the Anglo-Saxon Calendars (e.g. B.L. Cotton, Julius A. VI) which showed complex scenes with several figures, most Romanesque manuscripts have simplified illustrations with single figures or small groups, usually in roundels. The St. Albans Psalter (c. 1120, no. 29) has the occupations in roundels, but they are simplified to the point of obscurity. St. John's B. 20 and the Shaftesbury Psalter (B.L. Lansdowne 383, c. 1130–40, no. 48) are early examples of the developed form of Romanesque calendar illustration; later examples include Bodl. Lib. MS Auct. D. 2. 6 (no. 71), the Winchester Psalter (no. 78) and the 'York' Psalter (no. 95). St. John's B. 20 is unusual in showing the roundels grouped together on one page, instead of distributed in their appropriate months in the calendar, but otherwise it is a representative example of this tradition.

PROVENANCE: William Crashaw, Puritan divine; bought by Henry Wriothesley, Earl of Southampton, c. 1615; Thomas Wriothesley, Earl of South-ampton, who gave his library to St. John's College in 1635.

LITERATURE: James, *Catalogue*, no. 42; J. C. Webster, *The Labors of the Months*, 1938, 93, 171, no. 92, pl. 58; Boase, *English Art*, 109 n.; Dodwell, *Canterbury School*, pls. 38e, 39b; G. Zarnecki, *Early Sculpture of Ely Cathedral*, 1958, 34, 50, pl. 82.

40. Cambridge, Corpus Christi College MS 393
Historia Eliensis
224×148 mm., ff. 82
c. 1130. Ely Cathedral Priory

Ill. 114

Historiated initial O with St. Withburga (sister of St. Ethelreda) holding palm and crown (f. 59).
Two decorated initials: A (f. 1), B (f. 3).

The contents include a description of Ely and the Lives of various Saints venerated there, principally SS. Ethelreda, Withburga and Werburg. Among the miracles in the Life of St. Ethelreda (ff. 1–33), Ernest Blake found that there were three that occurred in the time of Bishop Hervey (1108–31) of which one is dated 1116 (Zarnecki, 43 n. 20). The fact that the miracles of the period of Bishop Nigel (1133–63)—one of which dates from 1141—are not included in this text, further helps to fix the date of the manuscript at c. 1130.
The drawing of St. Withburga is in a somewhat hardened Anglo-Saxon calligraphic style, with contours strengthened by greenish tinting. It is a late survival of the Anglo-Saxon technique, later even than the Canterbury Passionale with which it is closely comparable (B.L. Arundel 91, f. 31ᵛ; no. 17). This survival of an earlier style at Ely may also be seen in the carved relief on the tympanum of the Prior's door (Zarnecki, pls. 40, 43–5). The decorated initials contain fleshy, striated stems and an animal mask reminiscent of late 11th-century Anglo-Norman work but the blossoms, formed of three petals growing out of a small circular centre, are large and individualized and are clearly typical of the second quarter of the 12th century. George Zarnecki has shown how very similar they are to the flowers decorating the jambs of the Monks' and Prior's doorways and suggested that the design for the decoration of these doorways originated in the Ely scriptorium (e.g. Zarnecki, pls. 52–3, 72–4).

PROVENANCE: Ely Priory (press mark f. 1; erased inscription f. 82ᵛ). Bequeathed to his college by Matthew Parker, Archbishop of Canterbury (d. 1575).

LITERATURE: James, *Catalogue*, II, no. 393; Boase, *English Art*, 40, pl. 10a; Dodwell, *Canterbury School*, 27 n. 2; G. Zarnecki, *The Early Sculpture of Ely Cathedral*, 1958, 31 f., 43 n. 20.

41. Cambridge, University Library MS Ii. 3. 12

Boethius, De Musica, De Arithmetica

291×203 mm., ff. 137 (A list of books belonging to Christ Church Cloister is appended on ff. 135–7)

c. 1130. Canterbury, Christ Church

Ills. 113, 115

Half-page outline drawing, frontispiece to *De Arithmetica*: Boethius presenting his book to Symmachus (f. 1), full-page tinted drawing; frontispiece to *De Musica*: Boethius and Pythagoras above, Plato and the neo-Platonist Nichomacus below (f. 61ᵛ). Historiated initial O at the beginning of *De Musica* with the Virgin and Christ standing on the devil (f. 62ᵛ); six decorated initials: I (f. 1ᵛ), O (f. 4ᵛ), S (f. 25ᵛ), P (f. 65ᵛ), S (f. 93ᵛ), C (f. 106ᵛ), the last two uncoloured.

The frontispiece to *De Arithmetica*, which is cruder in execution than that to *De Musica* (the facial outlines may have been redrawn), shows Boethius handing his book to his father-in-law Symmachus for whom it was written. Like the other Boethius illustrations (see also nos. 49, 50) this drawing is derived from earlier Boethius manuscripts, ultimately, perhaps, from a late classical model. A similar dedication scene appears, for example, in a 9th-century manuscript from Tours now in Bamberg (Staatsbibliothek, class 5, f. 2ᵛ; Courcelle, 1967, pl. 1). The more elaborate scene on f. 61ᵛ, which shows Boethius as a patron of music together with three philosophers who had influenced *De Musica*, has a parallel in a 10th-century Boethius manuscript in Vienna (Nationalbibliothek, MS 51, f. 3ᵛ; Courcelle, 1967, pl. 5).

The historiated initial with the Virgin holding the lamb, and Christ (f. 62ᵛ) is characterized by the nervous lines of the Anglo-Saxon tradition—a persistent survival at this late date. It appears to have been adapted from an Anglo-Saxon model, for the iconography is derived from illustrations of the *Gloria in Excelsis* in the 9th-century Utrecht Psalter (which was copied at Canterbury in the 11th century) showing the Virgin and Child, and God and the lamb, and of Psalm 109—God and Christ treading a devil underfoot—in the same manuscript. The illustration to Psalm 109 was enlarged by an Anglo-Saxon artist to include the Virgin and Child as well as the Trinity (B.L. Cotton, Tiberius D. XXVII, see E. H. Kantorowicz, 'The Quinity of Winchester', *Art Bulletin*, 29, 1947, 73 ff., esp. figs. 1–2, 13, 15).

The Anglo-Saxon appearance of the initial on f. 62ᵛ contrasts sharply with the solid, almost massive weight of the figures in the full-page drawing (f. 61ᵛ). This may be described as the first fully Romanesque whole-page illustration produced at Canterbury. Dodwell (p. 35) compared the style with that of the frescoes in the St. Gabriel Chapel in Canterbury Cathedral (c. 1130), yet these frescoes are much more strongly under Byzantine influence, as may be seen in the dark, heavily painted facial

shading, particularly around the eyes, which is entirely absent in the Boethius drawing (for the frescoes see O. Demus, *Romanesque Mural Painting*, 1970, pl. 235 f.).

PROVENANCE: Christ Church, Canterbury (*De Claustro* inscription ff. 2, 62); bequeathed to Cambridge University Library by Richard Holdsworth, Master of Emmanuel College, 1664.

LITERATURE: *Catalogue of Manuscripts preserved in the Library of the University of Cambridge*, III, 1858, 418; M. R. James, *The Ancient Libraries of Canterbury and Dover*, 1903, xxxi ff., 3–12 (reproduces the catalogue of books); Boase, *English Art*, 40; Dodwell, *Canterbury School*, 23, 35 f., 37, 39, 64, 66, 74, 121; Swarzenski, *Monuments*, fig. 296; *St. Albans Psalter*, 123; P. Courcelle, *La Consolation de Philosophie dans la tradition littéraire*, 1967, 67 f., 70 f., pl. 2.

EXHIBITED: Manchester, 1959, no. 16; Barcelona, 1961, no. 181.

42. Oxford, Bodleian Library MS Bodley 271 (S.C. 1938)

St. Anselm, Works

403×280 mm., ff. ii+239 (ff. 1–166)

c. 1130. Canterbury, Christ Church

Ills. 119, 120

Illuminated initial at the beginning of each work, one historiated: Q (*De Libertate arbitrii*), Christ enthroned (f. 43ᵛ); twelve decorated: C (*Proslogion*, f. 24ᵛ), T. (*De Veritate*, prologue, f. 36), Q (*De Veritate*, f. 36ᵛ), I (*De Casu diaboli*, f. 50), D (*De Incarnatione Verbi*, f. 62ᵛ), S (*Cur Deus homo*, f. 72), C (*De conceptu virginali*, f. 98), N (*De Processione Spiritus Sancti*, f. 109), A (*Meditatio Redemptionis*, f. 125ᵛ), D (*De Concordia Praescientia*, f. 127ᵛ), D (*Orationes sive Meditationes*, f. 139), D (*Tractatus de grammatico*, f. 160).

Of all the Canterbury manuscripts of the period, this is perhaps the one most closely related in style to the wall-paintings in St. Gabriel's Chapel, Canterbury Cathedral. Both the heavy facial shading and the drapery, with its panels made up of nested V folds, are closely paralleled in the wall-paintings (Demus, *Romanesque Mural Painting*, 1970, pl. 235 f.). Behind these new forms, and the greater naturalism they imply, lies Byzantine influence, but whether this reached England from Italy, as Dodwell suggests, or through the intermediary of manuscripts from another source, perhaps the Crusading Kingdom, remains an open question. Some of the initials are similar to those in the Josephus manuscript in Cambridge University Library and St. John's College (nos. 43, 44). The main hand can be compared, for example with St. John's MS 8, f. 102 or University Library Dd. 1. 4, f. 220 (ill. 122). The historiated initial on f. 43ᵛ (ill. 120), which is by a different hand, is paralleled in St. John's MS 8, f. 219 (Dodwell, pl. 37*d*).

PROVENANCE: Christ Church, Canterbury (Prior Eastry's catalogue, 14th cent., see M. R. James, *Ancient Libraries*, 23, no. 62, 357, no. 144); given to the Bodleian Library by Abraham, Isaac and Jacob Colfe in 1616.

LITERATURE: Dodwell, *Canterbury School*, 22, 39, 41, 73, 121, pls. 26*c*, 31*b*; Boase, *English Art*, 47 n. 2; F. S. Schmitt, 'Die unter Anselm veranstaltete Ausgabe seiner Werke und Briefe', *Scriptorium*, 9, 1955, 64–70, pl. 15*e*; Ker, *English MSS*, 41; *St. Albans Psalter*, 123, 158 n. 3, pl. 142*e*; Pächt and Alexander, III, no. 86, pl. 8.

EXHIBITED: *The Bodleian Library in the 17th Century*, Oxford, 1951, no. 58

43. Cambridge, University Library MS Dd. 1. 4.

Flavius Josephus, Jewish Antiquities I–XIV
404×280 mm., ff. 239. For the second volume (St. John's College MS A. 8.) see next number
c. 1130. Canterbury, Christ Church

Ills. 116, 122

Thirteen initials, one for each Book (that for Bk. I missing):
Bk. II, P, Christ with the cross, angels in medallions (f. 18ᵛ),
Bk. III, I, decorated, man with dragon (f. 34ᵛ),
Bk. IV, H, Prophet with Scroll, two censing monks (f. 50),
Bk. V, M, decorated, man with two dragons (f. 64ᵛ),
Bk. VI, T, decorated, two figures in scrolls (f. 81),
Bk. VII, P, decorated, man in scroll (f. 100ᵛ),
Bk. VIII, D, decorated, lion and birds (f. 121),
Bk. IX, I, heads of King Jehosophat and two angels in medallions (f. 142ᵛ),
Bk. X, C, bust of Christ in medallion carried by two angels (f. 157),
Bk. XI, P, decorated, man wielding axe (f. 170),
Bk. XII, A, decorated, man wielding axe, acrobat above (184ᵛ),
Bk. XIII, Q, two monks holding chalices (f. 202ᵛ),
Bk. XIV, A, decorated, man piercing beast which is swallowing a woman (f. 220).

Several artists collaborated on these splendid initials and there are three distinct styles:
(1) ff. 64ᵛ, 100ᵛ, 121, 170, 184ᵛ: initials with figures in the Anglo-Saxon calligraphic tradition clambering in foliage coils similar to those in manuscripts of about 1100 such as Trinity College O. 2. 51 and Laurenziana, Plut. 12. 17 (see nos. 8, 19).
(2) ff. 18ᵛ, 50, 142ᵛ: more solid figures, initials characterized by human heads in medallions.
(3) f. 220: a more fully developed Romanesque initial with solid figures modelled by nested V folds.

The foliage is more firmly controlled and no longer flows freely over the initial and beyond its confines. Large, luxuriant flowers appear in the centre of the foliage spirals.

PROVENANCE: not recorded.

LITERATURE: *Catalogue of Manuscripts preserved in the Library of the University of Cambridge*, I, 1856, 6; Boase, *English Art*, 45; Dodwell, *Canterbury School*, 22, 29, 33, 39, 68, 73, 78 f., 120, pls. 13*a*, 20*a*, 30*a*, 36*a*, 41*c*, 46*b*; J. Beckwith, *Ivory Carvings in Medieval England*, 1972, fig. 112.

EXHIBITED: Barcelona, 1961, no. 180; Brussels, 1973, no. 25.

44. Cambridge, St. John's College MS. A. 8

Flavius Josephus, Jewish Antiquities XV–XX; Jewish Wars
382×270 mm., ff. 249. For the first volume (Cambridge University Library MS Dd. 1. 4) see previous number.
c. 1130. Canterbury, Christ Church

Ills. 117, 118, 121

Fourteen initials, one for each Book:
Bk. XV, S, Cain's sacrifice, Cain slaying Abel (f. 1ᵛ),
Bk. XVI, I, decorated (f. 16ᵛ),
Bk. XVII, A, Moses, the golden calf, massacre of the Levi (f. 39ᵛ),
Bk. XVIII, F, decorated (f. 61),
Bk. XIX, C, decorated, (f. 76ᵛ),
Bk. XX, M, two naked men bitten by serpents (f. 91),
Opening to the *Jewish Wars*, Q, decorated (f. 102),
Bk. I, C, scribe Samuel before Josephus (f. 103ᵛ),
Bk. II, T, decorated (f. 136ᵛ),
Bk. III, N, decorated (f. 164),
Bk. IV, Q, decorated (f. 180ᵛ),
Bk. V, A, decorated (f. 191),
Bk. VI, T, decorated, with peacock (f. 200ᵛ),
Bk. VII, C, decorated (f. 219).

The hands are not the same as in Vol. I, though a similar technique of lightly tinted outline drawing on blue ground occurs on f. 91 and the medallion heads are paralleled in the initial on f. 219. The latter is very close to an Anselm manuscript in the Bodleian Library, MS Bodley 271 (no. 42, Dodwell, pl. 26*c*).
Dodwell argued that the two historiated initials are only intelligible when transferred to different Books—both in Vol. I. The initial on f. 1ᵛ (Bk. XV) shows Cain offering to God the fruits of the earth and Cain slaying Abel. This is of no relevance to Book XV, which deals with Herod, but it does illustrate Book I, chapter 2. Equally, the Moses initial (Bk. XVII, f. 39ᵛ) only becomes relevant as an illustration to Book III. Canterbury artists were not used to historiated initials; this is one of the few manuscripts in which they occur, which may account

for the apparent mistake in their order. However, King Jehosophat appears correctly in the initial to Book IX (C.U.L. Dd. 1. 4, f. 142ᵛ).

PROVENANCE: Christ Church, Canterbury (inscription f. 2); William Crashaw (1572–1626); *c.* 1615 Henry Wriothesley, Earl of Southampton; presented by his son Thomas in 1635.

LITERATURE: James, *Catalogue*, no. 8; Boase, *English Art*, 45, pl. 12; Dodwell, *Canterbury School*, 22 f., 32, 36 ff., 63, 70, 77, 121, pls. 14*c*, 25 *a*, *b*, 37 *a*, *d*, 47*b*; Swarzenski, *Monuments*, fig. 278; F. Saxl, *English Sculptures of the 12th century*, 1954, 17 n., 21, fig. 16.

EXHIBITED: Manchester, 1959, no. 15.

45. London, British Library MS Royal 1. C. VII
Bible (Joshua–Kings)
395 × 265 mm., ff. vi + 189
The associated New Testament volume is
Baltimore, Walters Art Gallery MS 18
368 × 273 mm., ff. 247
c. 1130. Rochester Cathedral Priory

Ills. 123–6

Four historiated initials: E, Joshua receiving the book of the law from Moses (f. 2), F, 1 Samuel, Elkanah, Hannah and Penninah seated under arcades (f. 58), F, 2 Samuel, David playing the harp, with a fiddler and trumpeter seated under arcades (f. 92), P, 2 Kings, Ascension of Elijah (f. 154ᵛ).
Six decorated initials: T, preface to Joshua (f. 1), P, index to Joshua (f. 2), P, Judges (f. 27ᵛ), I, Ruth (f. 52ᵛ), V, preface to 1 Samuel (f. 55ᵛ), E, 1 Kings (f. 120ᵛ).
Walters Art Gallery, MS 18 has twenty-six decorated initials: ff. 1, 29, 81, 107ᵛ, 142, 146, 149, 152, 155ᵛ, 156ᵛ, 157, 161ᵛ, 175, 195, 199, 203, 206ᵛ, 209, 212, 213ᵛ, 216ᵛ, 219, 220ᵛ, 221ᵛ, 231, 232ᵛ.

The initials are characterized by thin, attenuated animals entwined in the shafts and by rows of palmettes in the curved outlines. The beasts in the foliage are frequently in facing or addorsed pairs. The Bible itself bears no Rochester inscription, but very similar initials occur in two manuscripts with a certain Rochester provenance: Royal 5. D. III and Royal 6. B. VI. The latter contains the addorsed griffins reproduced by Dodwell (pl. 46*e*) as an example of the influence of Byzantine silks. The same griffins occur on f. 120ᵛ of the Bible.
This manuscript has the distinction of being the earliest of the series of English Romanesque Bibles illustrated with narrative scenes. Its illustrations are sparse compared to the later examples and the tentative nature of the illustrative scheme is indicated by the Joshua initial in which the figures are shown horizontally to fill the two halves of the letter E.

The initial to 1 Samuel, showing Elkanah with his two wives seated under arcades belongs to a tradition exemplified by the Anglo-Saxon Heptateuch B.L. Cotton, Claudius B. IV in the 11th century and, in the 12th century, by the St. Omer Bible (Bibl. Mun., MS 1). The Ascension of Elijah—a scene that was popular already in Early Christian art because of its typological significance as a forerunner of the Ascension of Christ—occurs in almost every Western illustrated Bible from the 11th century as an illustration to 2 Kings. Comparable earlier examples include the Lobbes Bible of 1084 (Tournai, Seminary, MS 1, f. 159). This initial is unusual in not including the figure of Elisha receiving the mantle. The River Jordan, on the other hand, is depicted with great clarity.

PROVENANCE: entered Royal Library at time of the Dissolution, *c.* 1540 (no. 507 in the Catalogue of 1542), given to the British Museum by George II in 1757.

LITERATURE: Warner and Gilson, I, 14; Walters Art Gallery, *Illuminated Books of the Middle Ages and Renaissance*, exhibition catalogue, 1949, no. 19, pl. xiii; Dodwell, *Canterbury School*, 77, pls. 18*a*, 19*a*; Boase, *English Art*, 63 f., pls. 18*a*, 19; *St. Albans Psalter*, 170 n. 7; C. M. Kauffmann, 'The Bury Bible', *J.W.C.I.*, 29, 1966, 69, pl. 29*c*.

EXHIBITED: Brussels, 1973, no. 26, pl. 11.

46. Durham, Cathedral Library MS B. II. 8
St. Jerome, Commentary on Isaiah
403 × 290 mm., ff. 213
c. 1130. Durham Cathedral Priory

Ills. 127, 128

Eight historiated initials: V, Isaiah (f. 1ᵛ), F, Isaiah (f. 10ᵛ), V, (?)God seated (f. 22), I, (?)God seated, two men with scrolls below (f. 34ᵛ), F, Isaiah seated cross-legged (f. 43ᵛ), S, Isaiah (f. 87), V, Isaiah (f. 97), D, Isaiah (f. 118).
Eight decorated initials: C (f. 1), D (f. 109), N (f. 128), M (f. 138ᵛ), D (f. 149ᵛ), C (f. 162), Q (f. 185), D (f. 198).

The lightly tinted figures and the multicoloured backgrounds are similar to those of MS B. II. 26 (see no. 28).
The scrollwork initials (not listed above) include examples of what Mynors has called the 'clove curl' type (ff. 73ᵛ, 106, 172ᵛ; cf. Mynors, p. 7, pl. 38*b*) common in Durham manuscripts in the first half and, particularly, the second quarter of the century.

PROVENANCE: Durham Cathedral Priory (inscription f. 1).

LITERATURE: Mynors, Durham, no. 68, pl. 42; Boase, *English Art*, 229, pl. 33*b*.

47. Durham, Cathedral Library MS A. I. 10

1. Commentary on St. Matthew's Gospel (ff. 1–168)
2. Berengaudus, Commentary on the Apocalypse (ff. 170–234^v)
3. Cassiodorus, De Anima (ff. 235–242^v)

403 × 288 mm., ff. 242
c. 1130–40. Durham Cathedral Priory

Ills. 129, 130

Three historiated initials in the Apocalypse Commentary: opening initial A, Christ seated wearing a white robe (f. 170), D with bust of Christ (f. 197), D with St. John (f. 223).

Ten decorated initials: five in the St. Matthew manuscript, four in the Apocalypse manuscript, and one to Cassiodorus: C (f. 1^v), L (f. 4), I (f. 99^v), S (f. 146), V (f. 164^v), P (f. 179), C (f. 183), V (f. 212^v), S (f. 227), C (f. 235).

The initials in these three manuscripts, characterized by foliage scrolls with cinqfoil palmettes in green and purple on bare ground, are in the same style. The regularity of the foliage spirals and the emergence of the very large flowers with blossoms suggest a date c. 1130–40. Similar initials in a somewhat later version appear in MS A. III. 10 (Mynors, no. 124, pl. 45).

The scrollwork initials (not listed above) include an example of what Mynors has called the 'clove curl' type (f. 52^v; cf. Mynors, p. 7, pl. 38b) common in Durham manuscripts in the first half and, particularly, the second quarter of the century.

PROVENANCE: Durham Cathedral Priory (inscription f. 1) read in the Refectory (15th-cent. note on f. 104).

LITERATURE: Mynors, *Durham*, no. 66, pls. 40 f.

48. London, British Library MS Lansdowne 383

Psalter with Prayers etc. (Shaftesbury Psalter)
220 × 130 mm., ff. 179
c. 1130–40. West Country

Ills. 131–4; Colour Plate, p. 29

Calendar illustrated with signs of the Zodiac in medallions and occupations of the months:
January, Janus, standing (f. 3); February, warming (f. 3^v); March, horn blower (f. 4); April, flower bearer (f. 4^v); May, falconry (f. 5); June, mowing (f. 5^v); July, mowing, raking into piles (f. 6); August, reaping (f. 6^v); September, threshing (f. 7); October, vintage (f. 7^v); November, killing hogs (f. 8); December, gathering wood (f. 8^v).

Eight full-page miniatures, of which six precede the Psalter text:
God sending forth the angel Gabriel (f. 12^v), the three Marys at the sepulchre (f. 13), the Ascension (f. 13^v), Pentecost (f. 14), Christ in Majesty, an abbess in supplication at His feet (f. 14^v), Tree of Jesse with Abraham and Moses (f. 15).

The other two miniatures illustrate prayers to the Virgin and to St. Michael respectively: Virgin and Child enthroned within an architectural framework, an abbess kneels at her feet (f. 165^v), St. Michael holds souls in a napkin for the Last Judgment (f. 168^v), (the page containing the opening of the prayer to St. Lambert is missing, see f. 172).

Four historiated initials, three illustrating the Psalter: Psalm 1, Beatus initial, whole page, Christ and Evangelist symbols above David and his musicians, one of whom is dressed in an animal's skin (f. 15^v); Psalm 51, Q, David kills Goliath and afterwards carries his head (f. 57); Psalm 109, D, God and Christ seated, their feet resting on their enemies (f. 108), (the page containing the opening of Psalm 101 has been cut out). The other initial illustrates a prayer to the Holy Ghost, O, with the Virgin and the dove on her head (f. 159^v).

Lansdowne 383 was attributed to the nunnery at Shaftesbury by G. F. Warner (1903). The recurring figure of a nun in the miniatures (ff. 14^v, 165^v) indicates that the manuscript was produced for a nunnery and the prominence of St. Edward in the Calendar (red capitals) and Litany (invoked among the martyrs immediately behind St. Stephen) suggests a house dedicated to this royal saint. Warner concluded that Shaftesbury, where St. Edward was buried in 979 was effectively the only choice. B. Garfield (unpublished study) points out that St. Edith of Wilton appears twice in red capitals in the Calendar (16 September and 3 November), which might be taken as evidence in favour of an origin in Wilton. But the Shaftesbury provenance is further supported by the fact that St. Aelgifu (Elgiva), wife of King Edmund and a nun at Shaftesbury, where she was buried, is invoked in the Litany immediately after St. Edith.

Farley and Wormald assumed that the Shaftesbury Calendar implied a Shaftesbury origin, but Swarzenski discounted, perhaps rashly, the possibility that the manuscript was written and illuminated by nuns. Women are recorded as illuminating manuscripts in the earlier Middle Ages (some references in V. W. Egbert, *The Medieval Artist at Work*, 1967, 82) and at least one, a nun called Guda, has left us her self-portrait in a 12th-century manuscript in Frankfurt (MS. Batt. 42).

The problem of the origin of the Shaftesbury Psalter is complicated by the fact that there are two other manuscripts illuminated in the same style, perhaps even by the same hand: a Boethius in the Bodleian Library (MS Auct. F. 6. 5; no. 49), and a John Chrysostom in Hereford Cathedral Library (no. 51). The fact that the latter may have been at Hereford in the Middle Ages has led to the suggestion that the whole group was produced there. Furthermore, Swarzenski and Rickert draw attention to stylistic similarities with two mid 11th-century manuscripts presumed to have come from Hereford (B.L. Cotton, Caligula A. XIV; Pembroke College, Cambridge, MS 302, with a map of the diocese of Hereford), to support the theory of a Hereford origin of the Shaftesbury

Psalter. However, there is no evidence that the Chrysostom manuscript was produced at Hereford and although there are stylistic affinities with the two 11th-century manuscripts, particularly in the faces and beards of the apostles in the Pentecost miniature, these are certainly not sufficient to allow for any firm attribution. Perhaps the closest stylistic comparison is provided by an ivory figure of a King from an Adoration of the Magi relief excavated at Milborne St. Andrew, Dorset and likened to the picture of God in the Shaftesbury Psalter (f. 12ᵛ) by Eric Maclagen in 1924 (Beckwith, 1972, 75, fig. 146). It is worth noting, as Maclagen pointed out, that Milborne St. Andrew is scarcely twenty miles from Shaftesbury. The likelihood is that the Psalter and the two related manuscripts were produced at a centre in the South West of England rather than at Hereford, but there is no firm evidence.

Apart from this ivory, the style of the Psalter and of the two related manuscripts is difficult to parallel elsewhere. The profiles are clearly based on those of the St. Albans Psalter, but the frontal faces, characterized by their oblong shape, curling hair and beard, long mandarin moustaches, and large, protruding eyes are not of the St. Albans type. The draperies on f. 12ᵛ have the St. Albans white-cobweb highlights, but elsewhere they are strongly modelled by regular, curving, parallel bandage folds with prominent white highlights applied round each curve. There is little sign here of the damp fold which became ubiquitous in English painting from the 1140s. B. Garfield has convincingly compared the figure style with that of the Stephen Harding Bible (Dijon MS 14, see C. Oursel, *Miniatures Cisterciennes*, 1960, esp. pl. 2), produced at Cîteaux in *c.* 1109. This may indicate French influence, but it should be remembered that Abbot Harding was an Englishman and the illumination of his Bible has many features usually considered as English. A somewhat archaic feature of the Shaftesbury Psalter is the use of vertically and horizontally banded backgrounds (ff. 13, 13ᵛ, 168ᵛ) which are common in the 11th century rather than the 12th. The decoration (esp. f. 15) has some large, elaborate flowers but they are not as yet vast and luxuriating as those of the Bury Bible and the Winchester Psalter, which again supports a date *c.* 1130–40. In the other manuscripts of the group (though not in the Shaftesbury Psalter itself) there is a characteristic decorative form consisting of a head emerging from a curled-over acanthus leaf terminating in a series of long curling spurs. This is a feature of the Bodleian Winchester Bible (MS Auct E. inf. 1–2; no. 82) but as Pächt has pointed out (*St. Albans Psalter*, 168, pl. 156c) it already appears in a St. Albans manuscript of *c.* 1130.

Lansdowne 383 follows in the tradition of the St. Albans Psalter in having a cycle of full-page miniatures prefixed to the Psalter text. Indeed, the relationship is very close, for three of the miniatures—the Marys at the tomb, the Ascension and Pentecost—appear to be direct copies from the St. Albans Psalter (*St. Albans Psalter*, pls. 31, 33 see pp. 67 ff., 93 ff. for a discussion of the iconography of these scenes). The first miniature, on the other hand, is of a very rare subject: God sending out Gabriel for the Annunciation to the Virgin. The origin of this scene is Byzantine (Homilies of the monk Jacobus Kokkinobaphos, early 12th-century MSS Vat. Gr. 1162; Paris, Bibl. Nat. gr. 1208, see, e.g., C. Stornajolo, *Miniature delle Omelie di Giacomo Monaco*, 1910, pl. 48). The only Western 12th-century example is in the Winchester Psalter (B.L. Cotton, Nero C. IV; no. 78) and the two pictures are, indeed, so similar as to suggest a common model. As the Tree of Jesse is also closely paralleled in the Winchester Psalter, a link between the two must be presumed. The comparison remains tantalizing but impossible to pursue, because the Shaftesbury cycle, consisting of only six miniatures, is so very much shorter than the St. Albans and Winchester cycles with both of which it is clearly related. Farley and Wormald, followed by Boase, argued that the short length of the cycle was due to a careful selection made to illustrate basic Christian beliefs. However, as it stands, the cycle appears to have an inordinately long gap between the first (pre-Annunciation) scene and the following four (post-Crucifixion) pictures, and it is at least possible that the intervening illustrations have been lost. This theory is not contradicted by the make-up of the manuscript, for the first miniature is on a separate leaf, tipped in, while the post-Crucifixion group is together on two double leaves.

Of the two miniatures illustrating the prayers at the end of the book, the Virgin and Child may be considered an obvious choice (for a comparable composition see MS Bodley 269; no. 52), but the picture of St. Michael holding up souls is, again, most unusual at this date. The image is derived from that of the angel weighing souls in Byzantine compositions of the Last Judgment, but this angel was not at first identified as St. Michael. Michael had long been recognized as the guardian of souls and came gradually to be identified with the angel weighing souls at the Last Judgment (see L. Kretzenbacher, *Die Seelenwage*, 1958, 82 ff., and Wiegand, *op. cit.*) but this is the first time that he is shown on his own in this context. The choice of St. Michael as a theme for illustration may be connected with the prominence given to Gabriel in the first miniature, for the two archangels were represented together from the earliest times (e.g. mosaic in San Apollinare in Classe, Ravenna).

The nun shown as a kneeling suppliant in two of the miniatures (ff. 14ᵛ, 165ᵛ) was presumably the Abbess of Shaftesbury who commissioned the manuscript. There is, unfortunately, singularly little evidence concerning abbesses of Shaftesbury in the first half of the 12th century.

The likeliest candidate is Emma, who was abbess in the latter half of Henry I's reign. However, references to her in documents of 1135 and 1136 do not show whether she was still in office at that date (Shaftesbury register, B.L. Harley 61, ff. 23–4; see also D. Knowles, C. N. L. Brooke and V. C. M. London, *The Heads of Religious Houses in England and Wales 940–1216*, 1972, 219).

Quite apart from the interest of its miniatures, the Shaftesbury Psalter has the distinction of being the earliest Western Psalter with historiated initials at the liturgical divisions of the Psalms. The system, which later became standardized, of having historiated initials at the eight liturgical divisions as well as for Psalms 1, 51, and 101 is here in its infancy, for only Psalms 1, 51, 101 (lost) and 109 are illuminated. The Beatus initial, showing David and his choir of musicians, belongs to a conventional type, but the figure dressed in an animal skin and presumably representing the devil is an unusual feature (cf. the Rheims Psalter, St. Johns College, Cambridge B. 18; the subject is described at length by Steger, 1961, 138–46). David slaying Goliath reappears as an illustration to Psalm 51 in some later 12th- and 13th-century Psalters such as Paris, Bibl. Nat., lat. 1315 and Harley 5102 (Haseloff, 1938, 10, 100).

Finally, the initial to Psalm 109 showing God and Christ with their feet resting on their enemies is a literal illustration of the opening lines: 'Dixit dominus domino meo sede a dextris meis donec ponam inimicos tuos scabellum pedum tuorum'. The only eccentric feature is that Christ is seated on God's left, whereas the text clearly states 'sit thou at my right hand'. This composition was adapted in England from the Utrecht Psalter and became the usual illustration for Psalm 109 (see E. H. Kantorowicz, 'The Quinity of Winchester', *Art Bulletin*, 29, 1947, 73–85, and also above no. 41).

PROVENANCE: Shaftesbury Abbey, Dorset (see above), 1612, William Adlard of (?) Skendleby, Lincs (f. 2); 1627, Dorothy Berington (f. 2); William Petty, first Marquess of Lansdowne (1737–1805), library bought by Parliament from his executors in 1807.

LITERATURE: C. Rohault de Fleury, *La Sainte Vièrge*, 1878, I, 18, 239; II, 428; Friedrich Wiegand, *Der Erzengel Michael*, 1886, 37; A. Goldschmidt, *Der Albani-Psalter in Hildesheim*, 1895, 8; G. F. Warner, *Illuminated MSS in the British Museum*, ser. I–IV, 1903, no. 13; *Reproductions from Illuminated MSS in the British Museum*, II, 1907, pl. 9; id., *Schools of Illumination*, II, 1915, pl. 1; N. Kondakov, *Iconography of the Mother of God* (in Russian), 1914, II, 349, fig. 196; C. Sachs, *Handbuch der Musikinstrumentenkunde*, 1920, 96; E. Maclagen, 'A 12th century ivory . . .', *Antiquaries Journal*, 4, 1924, 214, fig. 2; A. Watson, *The Early Iconography of the Tree of Jesse*, 1934, 22 ff., pl. 18; Millar, I, 81, pls. 32–3; Günther Haseloff, *Die Psaltertillustration im 13. Jahrhundert*, 1938, 8 f.; J. C. Webster, *The Labors of the Months*, 1938, 92, 172 no. 96, pl. 62; M. A. Farley and F. Wormald, 'Three Related English Romanesque MSS', *Art Bulletin*, 22, 1940, 157–60; H. Swarzenski, (review of Farley–Wormald), *Art Bulletin*, 24, 1942, 295; Boase, *English Art*, 108 f., 174, pls. 31, 37b; T. D. Kendrick, *Late Saxon and Viking Art*, 1949, 135, 147, pl. 95; Rickert, *Painting in Britain*, 69 f., pl. 68b; Laura Sydenham, *Shaftesbury and its Abbey*, 1959, 16;

St. Albans Psalter, 52, n. 1, 163, 170, 200; H. Steger, *David, Rex et Propheta*, 1961, 138, 223 f.; G. Zarnecki, *The early sculpture of Ely Cathedral*, 1958, 51, fig. 101; R. Mellinkoff, *The horned Moses in medieval art and thought*, 1970, 62, fig. 48; Schiller, *Iconography*, I, 1971, 10, 15, 19, figs. 13, 28, 32, III (German ed.), 28, fig. 31; J. Beckwith, *Ivory Carvings in Early Medieval England*, 1972, 76.

49. Oxford, Bodleian Library MS Auct. F. 6. 5 (S.C. 1856)
Boethius, The Consolation of Philosophy
192 × 117 mm., ff. vii + 75
c. 1130–40. West Country   Ills. *137, 138*

Full-page opening miniature, Boethius in prison, comforted by Philosophy who stands before him holding a palm sceptre with two muses blowing trumpets on the right (f. 1ᵛ).
Small opening initial C with Boethius, seated, writing (f. viiᵛ).

Closely related to and perhaps by the same hand as the Shaftesbury Psalter (see no. 48 for a discussion of the style). The composition of the miniature of Boethius in prison is very similar to that in the Cambridge University Library Boethius (see no. 50). It belongs to the same tradition, differing only in showing Boethius more clearly in a walled prison and with a chain round his neck.

PROVENANCE: Given to the Bodleian Library by William Harwood, Prebendary of Winchester in 1611.

LITERATURE: M. A. Farley and F. Wormald, 'Three related English Romanesque MSS', *Art Bulletin*, 22, 1940, 157–61; F. Saxl and R. Wittkower, *British Art and the Mediterranean*, 1948, pl. 29. 6; Boase, *English Art*, 109; Bodleian Picture Book: *English Romanesque illumination*, 1951, fig. 2; Rickert, *Painting in Britain*, 70, pl. 68a; Swarzenski, *Monuments*, fig. 274; P. Courcelle, *Histoire littéraire des grandes invasions germaniques*, 3 ed. 1964, 371, pl. 41b; id., *La Consolation de Philosophie dans la tradition littéraire*, 1967, 72, pl. 8; Pächt and Alexander, III, no. 103, pl. 10.

EXHIBITED: Manchester, 1959, no. 28; Brussels, 1973, no. 29, pl. 14.

50. Cambridge, University Library MS Dd. 6. 6
Boethius, The Consolation of Philosophy
207 × 138 mm., ff. 89
c. 1140   Ill. *136*

Tinted drawing with blue background, Boethius in prison, comforted by Philosophy who stands before

him holding a palm sceptre, with three Muses blowing trumpets in the right tower (f. 2ᵛ).
Opening initial decorated with foliage scrolls (f. 2).

Boethius (c. 480–524/5) was one of the formative influences on medieval philosophy and many manuscripts of his work survive. Although the majority of these are not illustrated, there is a tradition of including either a dedication miniature (e.g. no. 41 *De Musica, De Arithmetica*) or, for the Consolation of Philosophy, a picture of Philosophy visiting Boethius in prison (see Bodley, Auct. F. 6. 5; no. 49). Although Boethius was Theodoric's minister, he had sided with the Eastern Emperor in the controversy with the Gothic rulers of Italy and these circumstances led to his downfall. Between his condemnation and his execution in 524/5 he was imprisoned at Pavia where he had sufficient freedom to write the Consolation. The book begins with a poem setting forth his change of fortune and explaining that he is still accompanied by the Muses of Poetry:

> 'While I was quietly thinking these thoughts over to myself and giving vent to my sorrow with the help of my pen, I became aware of a woman standing over me. She was of awe-inspiring appearance, her eyes burning and keen beyond the usual power of men. . . . It was difficult to be sure of her height, for sometimes she was of average human size, while at other times she seemed to touch the sky with the top of her head. . . .'

The earliest extant illustrations of this scene are German, 10th century. Boethius is shown either lying on a couch (Vienna, Nationalbibliothek, MS 271; Courcelle, pl. 37b) or seated, in the posture of an Evangelist writing (Maihingen, Oettingen Wallerstein collection, MS I 2. 40. 3; Courcelle, pl. 38). Philosophy is always standing, usually holding a book and sceptre, and the form of the prison is also standard, consisting of a crenellated arcade with towers. The three Muses first appear in an 11th-century northern French manuscript (Paris, Bibl. Nat., lat. 6401; Courcelle, pl. 40a, Swarzenski, *Monuments*, fig. 164). The composition was, therefore, fully formed and widely disseminated by the time the two 12th-century English manuscripts— Auct. F. 6. 5 and C.U.L. Dd. 6. 6—were illustrated. C.U.L. Dd. 6. 6. has a more fully developed prison building, with a baldachin rather than a simple arcade, but is otherwise essentially similar to Auct. F. 6. 5. Indeed, these two manuscripts are more closely related to each other than to any of the other versions of the scene—in particular, the Muses do not appear blowing trumpets in the earlier manuscripts—and it is likely that they are derived from the same model.
The style of both the figures, with predominant nested V folds rather than fully formed damp folds, and of the decorated initial suggest a date c. 1140.

PROVENANCE: Sam Hoadly (inscription, 17th–18th cent., f. 1).

LITERATURE: *Catalogue of Manuscripts preserved in the Library of the University of Cambridge*, I, 1856, 291; H. R. Patch, *The tradition of Boethius*, 1935, pl. 1; M. Farley and F. Wormald, 'Three related English Romanesque MSS', *Art Bulletin*, 22, 1940, 160; Boase, *English Art*, 109 n. 3; P. Courcelle, *Histoire littéraire des grandes invasions germaniques*, 3 ed. 1964, 371, pl. 40a.

51. Hereford, Cathedral Library MS O. 5. XI
St. John Chrysostom, Commentaries and Homilies
272 × 170 mm., ff. 148
c. 1140. West Country   *Ill. 140*

Framed outline drawing at end of book illustrating the Life of John Chrysostom on f. 147: the vision of a holy man, Marcus, who saw St. John Chrysostom in heaven surrounded by cherubim; below, two monks, probably Marcus and Macharias who told the story (f. 148).
Opening decorated initial M (f. 1).

Closely related to and perhaps by the same hand as the Shaftesbury Psalter and the Bodleian Boethius manuscript (see no. 48 for a discussion of the style). The figure of Christ may be closely compared with that in the Shaftesbury Psalter (f. 14ᵛ); even the orb with the cross reappears. However, the draperies are more naturalistically articulated in this drawing; those of the monks at the bottom have damp folds of the clinging curvilinear variety, which indicate a date in the 1140s, slightly later than the Shaftesbury Psalter and the Boethius manuscript.
George Zarnecki (1958) has drawn attention to the peculiar posture of the angels who walk away from the mandorla they are holding but turn their heads towards it. Of all the varieties of angels carrying Christ, this particular one appears to be an English peculiarity, paralleled, for example, on the tympanum of the Prior's doorway at Ely (Zarnecki, fig. 40). The general compositional scheme, showing the monks with their books squeezed into a narrow compartment below the more important figures, is reminiscent of Anglo-Saxon dedication drawings, such as the one in the Regularis Concordia (B.L. Cotton, Tiberius A. III; Wormald, *Drawings*, pl. 23).

PROVENANCE: Hereford Cathedral Library, no record of other provenance.

LITERATURE: Bannister, *Catalogue*, 56 f.; M. A. Farley and F. Wormald, 'Three related English Romanesque MSS', *Art Bulletin*, 22, 1940, 157–61; Boase, *English Art*, 109; Rickert, *Painting in Britain*, 69 f.; G. Zarnecki, *The early sculpture of Ely Cathedral*, 1958, 47, fig. 42.

EXHIBITED: B. F. A. C., *Illuminated MSS*, 1908, no. 21, pl. 26; Victoria and Albert Museum, *English Medieval Art*, 1930, no. 63; Manchester, 1959, no. 29.

52. Oxford, Bodleian Library MS Bodley 269 (S.C. 1935)

St. Augustine, Commentary on Psalms
(Ps. 101–50)
420 × 275 mm, ff. iii+233
c. 1130–40. (?)Eynsham Abbey

Ills. 135, 143

Large frontispiece with Virgin and Child, lightly tinted drawing on a painted background (f. iii). Decorated opening initial E (f. iii^v)

Wormald characterized this drawing as 'one of the most imposing examples of English Romanesque art'. He analysed the style as containing Anglo-Saxon components—the head of the Child, for example, is remarkably similar to that of St. Dunstan in the 11th-century Regularis Concordia manuscript (B.L. Cotton, Tiberius A. III)—but being essentially Romanesque in its solid structure and its frontal, geometric composition. Fritz Saxl, who compared the style with that of the stone relief of the Madonna in York Minster, suggested an Eastern Mediterranean origin of the frontal Mother and Child formula in which the Virgin holds the Child on her left arm. This type was known in England as early as the 10th century (Benedictional of St. Ethelwold), but the 12th-century examples are more closely related to Eastern models and are clearly the result of renewed Byzantine influence. The double mandorla, on the other hand, the animal head throne and the meander frame are derived from Carolingian and Ottonian art (for the frame see *St. Albans Psalter*, 99, pl. 132; for the throne, P. E. Schramm, *Herrschaftszeichen und Staatssymbolik*, I, 1954, figs. 35–7, 41).

The sceptre has a knob at the bottom, irregular in shape and different in appearance from the knobs which sometimes appear on medieval sceptres (e.g. P. E. Schramm, *Sphaira, Globus, Reichsapfel*, 1954, figs. 15, 80). This may, as Wormald suggested, be an allusion to the 'stem of Jesse', as it somewhat resembles a root. The association of *virga* (a rod or stem), as defined in the Messianic prophecy in Isaiah 11: 1–3, with the Virgin (*virgo*), originated in the time of Tertullian at the beginning of the 3rd century and was a commonplace by the 12th century. There are representations of the Virgin holding a stem sceptre in the 12th century in which the link with the tree of Jesse is not in doubt (A. Watson, *The Early Iconography of the Tree of Jesse*, 1934, pl. 8, cf. pl. 5; cf. also the Shaftesbury Psalter, no. 48). The root sceptre would have the double significance of a royal sceptre and a symbol of the Virgin.

The splendid initial on f. iii is similar to those in the Winchcombe Psalter of c. 1130–40 (no. 53). The structure of the initial, the beaded clasps on the stems, and the speckled tops of the flowers are closely paralleled on f. 36 of the Winchcombe Psalter. Eynsham is quite near Winchcombe and although there is no proof that this manuscript was written at Eynsham, it was there in the 13th–14th centuries and Neil Ker (quoted by Wormald) suggested that the script indicates a West Country origin.

PROVENANCE: Eynsham Abbey, Oxfordshire (press-mark B. III, 13th–14th cent., f. 1). Given to the Bodleian Library by the Dean and Canons of Windsor, 1612.

LITERATURE: F. Wormald, 'A Romanesque drawing at Oxford', *Antiquaries Journal*, 22, 1942, 17 ff., pl. 1 f.; F. Saxl, R. Wittkower, *British Art and the Mediterranean*, 1948, pl. 27 f.; Bodleian Picture Book, *English Romanesque Illumination*, 1951, pl. 5; 'The provenance of Bodley 269', *Bodleian Library Quarterly*, 5, 1954–6, 173; Boase, *English Art*, 110; Rickert, *Painting in Britain*, 79, pl. 79; Ker, *English MSS*, 41.

EXHIBITED: *The Bodleian Library in the 17th Century*, 1951, no. 61; Manchester, 1959, no. 22, repr. cover; Barcelona, 1961, no. 185; Brussels, 1973, no. 27.

53. Dublin, Trinity College MS 53

New Testament and Psalter
432 × 292 mm., 192 ff.
c. 1130–40. Winchcombe Abbey, Gloucestershire

Ills. 144–6

Miniature of St. Matthew writing, with initial L containing twenty-eight of Christ's ancestors (f. 7^v); outline drawings of St. Mark (f. 24^v), St. Luke (f. 36^v), and St. John (f. 54^v).
Two historiated Beatus initials (for the Vulgate and Hebrew translations of the Psalms) with David the Psalmist, with his choir, and David dancing (f. 151).
Nine decorated initials: B (f. 1), Mark, I with winged lion (f. 24^v), Luke, Q (f. 36), John, I with eagle (f. 55), Acts, P with man threatening peacock with an axe, Peter, P (f. 88), Psalm 51, two Qs (f. 164), Psalm 101, two Ds (f. 178^v).
Decorated canon tables (f. 2–4^v).

The Winchcombe provenance, suggested by Abbot Richard's ownership of the manuscript is confirmed by the existence of several contemporary manuscripts from Winchcombe with similar initials. These include Hereford Cathedral Library, MS P. VIII. 4, B.L. Cotton, Tiberius E. IV, and Bodl. Lib. MS Douce 368 (see Heimann, p. 107 f., pl. 18). Dr. Heimann compared the facial style of the figures and their parallel drapery folds to the historiated initials of the Pierpont Morgan Life of St. Edmund c. 1130 (no. 34). A comparison, both of the figures and of the large, luxuriant blossoms, may also be made with the Shaftesbury Psalter (no. 48) which confirms the date of c. 1130–40.
Dr. Heimann has discussed the iconography of the Matthew initial, showing the ancestors of Christ from Abraham to Jechonias (Matthew 1: 17) and of the Beatus initials with David as Psalmist and David

dancing. The Matthew initial is in the tradition of an Anglo-Saxon Gospel Book from St. Bertin (Boulogne MS 11) which shows Matthew seated, with busts of the ancestors under arcades (Heimann, pl. 14c–d). However, this series is unusual in that each of the twenty-eight ancestors is endowed with an attribute. The Beatus initial with David and his choir follows a well-known tradition (see H. Steger, *David Rex et Propheta*, 1961). The second initial, to the Hebrew version of the Psalms, has a figure of an acrobat which Dr. Heimann identified as David dancing before the Ark of the Covenant (2 Samuel 6 and 1 Chronicles 15). The Ark, looking very much like a reliquary, appears at the top of the initial, and Michal, David's wife who watched from a window, is shown in a medallion below. This scene is usually illustrated in terms of a religious procession (cf. the English Bible, Bodl. Lib. Laud. Misc 752, f. 279ᵛ, see no. 103) and the ingenious treatment here appears to be unique.

PROVENANCE: Richard of Kidderminster, Abbot of Winchcombe 1488–1525, gave the manuscript to his monastery. James Usher, Archbishop of Armagh (1580–1656) whose books were acquired at the Restoration by Trinity College, Dublin.

LITERATURE: Boase, *English Art*, 157, 213, pl. 49b; A. Heimann, 'A Twelfth Century MS from Winchcombe . . .', *J.W.C.I.*, 28, 1965, 86–109, pls. 13–18.

54. Oxford, Bodleian Library MS Laud Misc. 469
St. Augustine, City of God
404×256 mm., ff. 225
c. 1130–40   *Ill. 147*

Full-page unframed frontispiece, tinted drawing; upper register: Christ and the Apostles seated under arcade with towers—the City of God; lower register: on the left, Christ defending the City of God against the devil; on the right, a dead man lies on a bed, the Virgin holds out a naked infant, representing his soul, to an angel, while a devil attempts to gain possession, of the soul from below (f. 7ᵛ).
Twelve decorated initials: Bk. 1, G (f. 8), Bk. 2, S (f. 16), Bk. 4, D (f. 31ᵛ), Bk. 5, Q (f. 40), Bk. 6, Q (f. 50), Bk. 7, D (f. 55ᵛ), Bk. 10, D (f. 79), Bk. 11, C (f. 91), Bk. 18, D (f. 157), Bk. 19, Q (f. 173), Bk. 21, C (f. 198ᵛ), Bk. 22, S (f. 209ᵛ).

The upper half of the composition is similar to the Canterbury City of God manuscript in Florence (no. 19). The lower part is not paralleled in the City of God manuscripts but appears to be adapted from Revelation 12 (Michael fighting the dragon and the dragon presenting the woman with the child; cf., e.g., MS Bodley 352, ff. 8ᵛ–9, 12th century). Both the faces in the upper register and the patterns of the drapery are similar to those of the St. Albans Terence manuscript (no. 73).

The initials, decorated with dragons and foliage scrolls, may be compared with those in Canterbury manuscripts of c. 1130.

PROVENANCE: given to the Bodleian Library by William Laud, Archbishop of Canterbury (ex-libris, 1633, f. 1).

LITERATURE: A. De Laborde, *Les MSS à Peintures de la Cité de Dieu*, I, 1909, 103; Boase, *English Art*, 46; Ker, *English MSS*, 41; Swarzenski, *Monuments*, fig. 291; Pächt and Alexander, III, no. 112, pl. 12.

EXHIBITED: *Bodleian Library in the 17th Century*, 1951, no. 73.

55. Oxford, Corpus Christi College MS 157
Florence and John of Worcester, Chronicle
325×237 mm., 398 pages (p. 77 is triple)
(Companion volume in Bodleian Library, MS Auct. F. 1. 9)
c. 1130–40. Worcester Cathedral Priory
Ills. 139, 141, 142

Five tinted drawings: Crucifixion (p. 77b); Visions of Henry I in Normandy, 1130, when the king saw himself visited by infuriated peasants, armed and threatening knights (p. 382), and aggrieved prelates (p. 383), all complaining of high taxation. The king's physician, Grimbald, is seated on the left of each illustration, explaining the visions. In the last scene Henry is overwhelmed by a storm at sea which is only abated by his promise to withhold the Danegeld for seven years and go on a pilgrimage to Bury St. Edmunds.

The Worcester Chronicle, attributed to two monks, Florence and John, is one of the major works of historical writing in 12th-century England. Down to 1095 it consists mainly of a translation into Latin of the Anglo-Saxon chronicle grafted on to a world history compiled by Marianus Scotus in the 11th century. The attribution to Florence is based on an entry in the annal for 1118 recording his death and praising his great contribution to the chronicle without actually stating that he was the author. For the period 1118 until the chronicle ends in 1140, the author was another Worcester monk, John, and, indeed, it has been argued that it was he who wrote the whole book (summary by R. R. Darlington, 1947). Corpus 157 is the earliest and most accurate manuscript of the chronicle (cf. Bodley 297, from Bury St. Edmunds, also with a drawing of the Crucifixion, Pächt and Alexander, III, no. 167, pl. 17) and it is generally accepted that it was written for, or perhaps even by, John of Worcester himself. John tells us that he was away at Winchcombe c. 1134–9 and it was there that he learnt from the royal physician Grimbald of Henry I's dreams which he subsequently inserted under the year 1130. It appears that the bulk of the manuscript was written before c. 1130 and the last entries, including those describing the visions, added in *c.* 1140.

The pictures are in two different styles. The Crucifixion, which illustrates a short text on the dimensions of the cross, is an outline drawing lightly tinted in red and green. The style of the drawing is reminiscent of Anglo-Saxon art, so much so that Wormald characterized it as a copy of the Crucifixion in a 10th-century Psalter (Harley 2904). However, Rosalie Green has shown that the subject is not, like Harley 2904, a straightforward Crucifixion with Mary and John, but a typological composition in which the two subsidiary characters prefigure the Crucifixion. She identified them as the Widow of Sarepta encountered by Elijah (1 Kings 17: 8 ff.) and Job standing on the sea monster (Job 40: 20). The Widow of Sarepta holds the crossed sticks, which were interpreted as a type of the cross, while Job stands on Leviathan, prefiguring the victory of Christ over Satan. On the other hand, L. Wehrhahn-Stauch has argued that the man represents Tobias standing on his fish, which drove out the devil and which was interpreted as a symbol of the Crucifixion.

The four illustrations of Henry I's reign are also lightly tinted drawings, but the figures are more solidly drawn, without reminiscence of Anglo-Saxon sketchiness, and the backgrounds are painted in ochre or red. The facial types bear some resemblance to those of the St. Albans Terence manuscript (no. 73).

These are among the earliest extant chronicle illustrations. The Chronicle of S. Martin des Champs, Paris (*c.* 1070; B.L. Add. 11662) provides some earlier examples, but—the Bayeux tapestry notwithstanding—narrative illustrations in chronicles are rare before the Matthew Paris manuscripts in the 13th century and do not become common until the 14th century. Here, the recumbent figure of the king dreaming recalls illustrations of the dreams of Pharaoh in Genesis 41, but in detail these compositions must have been invented for this manuscript. John of Worcester refers to the illustrations in his text as 'sicut compositum est' which may be taken to indicate that they were made before the text which surrounds them.

PROVENANCE: Worcester Cathedral Priory. In 1480 Frater Thomas Straynsham exchanged it with Thomas Powycke for a copy of Guido's *De Bello Trojano* (inscription f. i); given to the college by Henry Parry, a fellow, in 1618.

LITERATURE: Coxe, *Catalogus*, I, 1852, 1; J. R. H. Weaver, *The Chronicle of John of Worcester* (Anecdota Oxoniensia, ser. IV, no. 13) 1908, 7 ff. (for the text concerning the miracles, see 32–4); Sir Henry Howarth, 'The Chronicle of John of Worcester previously assigned to Florence of Worcester', *Archaeological Journal*, 73, 1916, 2 ff., 166; *New Pal. Soc.* II, pl. 86 f.; Millar, I, 9, 159, 163, 166; N. R. Ker, 'William of Malmesbury's handwriting', *English Historical Review*, 59, 1944, 375; Wormald,

'Survival', 141 f., pl. 7; *id.*, *English Drawings*, 58; R. R. Darlington, *Anglo-Norman Histories*, 1947, 13 ff.; Boase, *English Art*, 157, 165; Rickert, *Painting in Britain*, 64, pl. 60; Swarzenski, *Monuments*, fig. 279; J. E. Hunt, *English and Welsh Crucifixes*, 1956, 38, 40, fig. 16; Rosalie B. Green, 'A Typological Crucifixion', in *Festschrift Ulrich Middeldorf*, 1968, 20–3, pl. xii; Schiller, *Iconography* II, 1972, 126, fig. 434; Bodleian Picture Book, *English Rural Life*, 1965, pl. 17*a*; L. Wehrhahn-Stauch, 'Christliche Fischsymbolik', *Zeitschrift für Kunstgeschichte*, 35, 1972, 39, fig. 45; D. J. A. Matthew, *The Norman Conquest*, 1966, 301, pl. 7.

EXHIBITED: Manchester, 1959, no. 21; Brussels, 1973, no. 28, pl. 13.

56. Cambridge, Corpus Christi College MS 2

Bible, Part I, Genesis–Job (Bury Bible)
514×355 mm., ff. 357, rebound in 3 vols:
I, ff. 1–121; II, ff. 122–241; III, ff. 242–357
c. 1135. Bury St. Edmunds Abbey

Ills. 148–53; Fig. 12

Six miniatures: Numbers, full-page, Moses and Aaron enthroned; Aaron and Moses numbering the people of Israel (f. 70); Deuteronomy, full-page, Moses and Aaron expounding the Law to the People of Israel; Moses expounding the Law of the Unclean Beasts (f. 94); 1 Samuel, full-page, Elkanah, Hannah and Penninah; Hanna's prayer before Eli and the birth of Samuel (f. 147ᵛ); Jeremiah, two-thirds page, Jeremiah pointing to the attack on Jerusalem (f. 245ᵛ); Ezekiel, one-third page, Ezekiel's vision of God (f. 281ᵛ); Job, two-thirds page, the children of Job; Job seated on ashes asked by his wife to renounce God (f. 344ᵛ).

Miniatures stripped off or cut out: between ff. 6 and 7 (Genesis), ff. 32ᵛ (Exodus), 54 (Leviticus), 115 (Joshua), 129 (Judges), 219ᵛ (Isaiah).

Three historiated initials: V, Isaiah, seated (f. 220ᵛ),[1] V, Amos seated (f. 324), Micah standing (f. 328ᵛ).

Thirty-nine decorated initials: Jerome's letter to Paulinus, F, whole-page, with medallions containing a centaur, a mermaid, and a one-legged man shearing a rabbit (f. 1ᵛ),[1] Jerome's Prologue, D (f. 5ᵛ),[1] Exodus, H (f. 33),[1] Leviticus, V (f. 54ᵛ), Numbers, L (f. 70ᵛ), Deuteronomy, H (f. 94ᵛ), Preface to Joshua, T (f. 113ᵛ), Joshua, E (f. 115ᵛ), Judges, P (f. 129ᵛ), Ruth, I (f. 143ᵛ), Preface to Kings, E (f. 145ᵛ), 1 Samuel, F (f. 148),[1] 2 Samuel, F (f. 167ᵛ),[1] 1 Kings, E (f. 183),[1] 2 Kings, C (f. 201ᵛ), N, a man with a bear (f. 220), Jeremiah, V (f. 246),[1] Baruch, H, with a monkey (f. 275),[1] Jeremiah epistle, P (f. 277), Lamentations, E (f. 278ᵛ),[1] Preface to Ezekiel, E (f. 281), Ezekiel, E (f. 281ᵛ),[1] Preface to Daniel, D (f. 307), Daniel, A (f. 307ᵛ),[1] Hosea, V (f. 318),[1] Preface to Amos, A (f. 323), Jonah, E (f. 327ᵛ), Nahum, O (f. 331), Preface to Habakkuk, Q (f. 332), Habakkuk, O (f. 333),[1] Preface to

[1] Initials painted on a separate sheet of vellum and stuck on.

Zephaniah, T (f. 334), Zephaniah, V (f. 334ᵛ),[1] Haggai, M, I (f. 335ᵛ), Preface to Zechariah, S (f. 336ᵛ), Zechariah, I (f. 337ᵛ), Malachi, O (f. 342), Preface to Job, C (f. 343), Job, V (f. 344ᵛ).[1]

The Bury Bible is the only one among the major English Romanesque manuscripts to be individually described, in more than a passing reference, in a contemporary document. The *Gesta Sacristarum Monasterii S. Edmundi* contains the following passage:

> 'This Hervey, the sacrist, brother of Prior Talbot, commissioned a large Bible for his brother the Prior and had it beautifully illuminated by Master Hugo. As Hugo was unable to find any suitable calf hide in these parts, he bought some parchment in Ireland.'[2]

By 1912 M. R. James had identified Master Hugo's Bible with a two-volume Bible, the only extant volume of which was in Corpus Christi College, Cambridge. He adduced the evidence of the Bury press-mark, of a small drawing of St. Edmund on a 15th-century repair to one of the leaves (f. 322), and of the fact that the miniatures and some of the initials in this Bible are painted on separate sheets of parchment pasted to the leaves of the book, which could well have relevance to Hugo obtaining special parchment from Ireland. There is, furthermore, evidence that Hugo's Bible was definitely a two-volume work, and, as there is only one such Bible listed in the 12th–13th-century catalogue of Bury books, the identification of it with the Corpus Christi Bible may be considered as certain (Kauffmann, 62 f.). Master Hugo was not only a renowned painter but also a sculptor and worker in metal, for he is recorded in the Bury *Gesta Sacristarum* as casting the bronze doors for the west front of the abbey church, casting a great bell, and carving a cross in the choir and statues of the Virgin and St. John.

As well as identifying the artist, the *Gesta Sacristarum* gives us the names of the patrons of the Bible and hence also the approximate date. Sacrist Hervey and his brother Prior Talbot held office under Abbot Anselm (1121–48) but there is evidence to show that they had been replaced by their successors before 1138/41 (Kauffmann, 64 f.; Thomson, 218). This means that the Bible must have been begun before c. 1138. A much earlier date is ruled out because of the advanced style of the illumination, and it would seem reasonable to date it c. 1135. R. M. Thomson has argued from the wording of the reference in the *Gesta Sacristarum* that the Bible was commissioned during Anselm's absence in 1137, but this evidence is inconclusive. The style of the miniatures—the solid, monumental figures and more especially the characteristic profiles—and the very fact that they are full-page and framed, betrays Master Hugo's debt to the Master

of the St. Albans Psalter, probably through the intermediary of the manuscript of the Life of St. Edmund (no. 34). Yet Hugo was also a great innovator. The very strong, rich colours—the prevalence of royal blue, magenta, bright red, purple and green—are unparalleled in earlier English illumination. The faces are both more naturalistic and more sophisticated than those of the St. Albans manuscripts. This is due to their close adherence to Byzantine rules of facial contours and modelling, characterized by dark shading in ochre and grey with greenish tints and white highlights. However, it is the disposition of the draperies, with their sinuous double-line folds dividing the body beneath into clearly defined areas, that has become the hallmark of the Bury Bible figure style. This is the clinging curvilinear variety of the damp fold, a highly stylized version of the Byzantine method of articulating the human figure. The Bury Bible is the earliest known representative of this style which probably developed from a north European stylized damp fold of the early 12th century, of the kind seen in the Pentecost miniatures of the Cluny Lectionary (Paris, Bibl. Nat., Nouv. Acq. lat. 2246, c. 1110–20, f. 79ᵛ; fig. 14). The probability that Master Hugo himself was the originator of this particular drapery convention is supported by the fact that it does not appear equally clearly in all the miniatures of the Bury Bible. It may be seen in its fully developed form in the Numbers, Deuteronomy and Ezekiel miniatures, but is less developed in the other scenes and hardly apparent at all in the portrait of Isaiah. It seems likely that Master Hugo was experimenting with different methods of treating drapery, but once the clinging curvilinear style had been perfected, it can be found in nearly all the major English paintings between about 1140 and 1170.

The illuminated initials contain foliage stem spirals terminating in large luxuriant plant formations that extend in all directions like the tentacles of a fleshy octopus. This is perhaps the earliest fully developed example of a decorative form that was to become the hall-mark of English illumination in the middle and third quarter of the century.

The iconography of the miniatures has been examined in detail (Kauffmann, 66–74) though for several scenes close parallels have yet to be found. The strongest influence was derived from Byzantine models. Of the eleven scenes contained in the six remaining miniatures one, that is the Vision of Ezekiel, is of obviously Western origin. Four, on the other hand, were probably derived from Byzantine sources (Moses and Aaron enthroned, Moses teaching and expounding the Law of Unclean Beasts; and Job's prayer). Since these conclusions were published, Beryl Smalley identified the source of an unusual feature in the illustration to 1 Samuel. Elkanah is handing robes to his two wives where the Bible simply refers to 'portions'. The identification of these portions with clothes was made by

---

[1] Initials painted on a separate sheet of vellum and stuck on.

[2] 'Iste Herveus, frater Taleboti prioris, omnes expensas invenit fratri suo priori in scribenda magna bibliotheca, et

manu magistri Hugonis incomparabiliter fecit depingi. Qui cum non inveniret in partibus nostris pelles vitulinas in Scotiae partibus parchamena comparavit.' (T. Arnold ed., *Memorials of St. Edmunds Abbey*, Rolls Series 1890–6, II, 290.)

pseudo-Jerome, an unknown author of *c.* 800 (*Quaestiones in libros Regum*, P.L. 23, col. 1331) and taken up by Andrew of St. Victor, and it therefore emerges that Master Hugo, or the monk who instructed him, derived this feature from a Western and not a Byzantine source.

PROVENANCE: Abbey of Bury St. Edmunds (press-mark B. 1, f. 2). Bequeathed to his college by Matthew Parker, Archbishop of Canterbury (d. 1575).

LITERATURE: James, *Catalogue*, no 2; *id.*, *Proceedings of the Cambridge Antiquarian Society*, 7, 1888–91 (1893), 32 ff., pl. 8; *New Pal. Soc.* II, ii, pls. 172–4; Millar, I, 30 ff., pls. 37–40; A. Boeckler, *Abendländische Miniaturen bis zur Ausgang der Romanischen Zeit*, 1930, 90 f.; G. Swarzenski, in *Städel-Jahrbuch*, 7–8, 1932, 355 f., fig. 283; Wormald, 'Development', 39 f., pl. 16; Millar, I, 83, pl. 37 f.; W. Weisbach, *Ausdrucksgestaltung in mittelalterlicher Kunst*, 1948, 67 f.; Boase, *English Art*, 161 ff., pls. 54, 55*a*, 59; Rickert, *Painting in Britain*, 70 f., pl. 69*a*; Swarzenski, *Monuments*, fig. 302; G. Zarnecki, *Later English Romanesque Sculpture 1140–1210*, 1953, pl. 68, *id.*, *English Romanesque Lead Sculpture*, 1957, 5 ff.; E. B. Garrison, *Studies in the History of Mediaeval Italian Painting*, 3, 1958, 200 ff.; C. R. Dodwell, *The Great Lambeth Bible*, 1959, 8 ff.; J. Beckwith, *Early Medieval Art*, 1964, 194 f., fig. 186; C. M. Kauffmann, 'The Bury Bible', *J.W.C.I.*, 29, 1966, 60–81, pls. 14–30; Beryl Smalley, 'L'Exégèse Biblique du 12e siècle', in *Entretiens sur la Renaissance du 12e siècle*, ed. M. de Gandillac and E. Jeauneau, 1965, 278 f.; H. Roosen-Runge, *Farbgebung und Technik frühmittelalterlicher Buchmalerei*, I, 1967, 94–104, repr.; R. Mellinkoff, *The horned Moses in medieval art and thought*, 1970, 61, fig. 47; R. M. Thomson, 'The dates of the Pierpont Morgan Vita S. Edmundi and the Bury Bible', *Viator*, II, 1971, 218 ff.; O. Demus, *Byzantine Art and the West*, 1970, 171, fig. 186.

EXHIBITED: Manchester, 1959, no. 14 (Vol. I only).

57. Cambridge, Pembroke College MS 16
St. Gregory the Great, Homilies
304 × 230 mm., ff. ii+124
c. 1140. Bury St. Edmunds Abbey
The gloss occupies more than half the page on the outer side.
Initial to each Homily (initials ff. i, 29, 32ᵛ, 85 etc. cut out)

Ills. 154, 156, 157

Four historiated initials: Hom. 10, S with the Adoration of the Magi (f. 19ᵛ), Hom. 14, A with David or Samson and the lion (f. 30), Hom. 28, L with Christ seated and the crowned nobleman (John 4) kneels before him (f. 70), Hom. 29, Q

with Christ surrounded by apostles standing on a dragon (f. 71ᵛ).
Twenty-four decorated initials: I (f. 1), I (f. 3ᵛ), S (f. 6), I (f. 7ᵛ), I (f. 9ᵛ), I (f. 13), I (f. 15ᵛ), I (f. 17), S (f. 27ᵛ), I (f. 32), I (35ᵛ), P (f. 39), R (f. 41ᵛ), M, two men with shields (f. 47), P (f. 50), L (f. 56), P, man playing fiddle (f. 63), L (f. 75), Q (f. 82ᵛ), E, seated figure (f. 90ᵛ), Q (f. 98ᵛ), H (f. 102ᵛ), S (f. 108ᵛ), L (112ᵛ).

The style of both the figures and the decoration is dependent on the Bury Bible. The clinging drapery and the profiles may be compared to the Micah initial of the Bible (f. 328ᵛ). The large, luxuriant flowers are closely related to those of the Bible and the floral and geometrical decoration of the shafts of the initials are derived from the frames of the Bible's miniatures. This is the most richly illuminated of the manuscripts produced at Bury under the influence of Master Hugo; others include Pembroke College MSS 64, 72, and 78 (see no. 58).

PROVENANCE: Abbey of Bury St. Edmunds (f. 1 inscription . . . *de armario claustri monachorum S. Edmundi* and press-mark G. 8) given to the college by William Smart, Portreeve of Ipswich, in 1599.

LITERATURE: James, *Catalogue*, no. 16; Boase, *English Art*, 161, pl. 49*a*.

58. Cambridge, Pembroke College MS 78
St. Paul's Epistles, glossed
330 × 242 mm., ff. 132
c. 1140. Bury St. Edmunds Abbey

Ill. 158

Large decorated outline initial P to Romans (f. 1).

See note to no. 57.

PROVENANCE: Abbey of Bury St. Edmunds (f. 1 inscription and press-mark B. 205); given to the college by William Smart, Portreeve of Ipswich, in 1599.

LITERATURE: James, *Catalogue*, no. 78; Boase, *English Art*, 161.

59. Dublin, Chester Beatty Library MS 22
Bible (Genesis–Ruth)
473 × 317 mm., ff. 137
c. 1140. Walsingham Priory   *Ills. 159–62*

Six historiated initials: Jerome's epistle to Paulinus, F with Jerome writing (f. 3ᵛ), Genesis, I, with Christ in mandorla and seven Genesis roundels, six of the Creation plus one of the Temptation (f. 8ᵛ), Exodus, H, Moses holding the serpent and removing his shoes before the burning bush which contains the head of God (f. 32ᵛ), Numbers, H, same composi-

tion as Exodus, except that an animal (? a donkey) playing a harp has replaced the burning bush at the top of the shaft (f. 67ᵛ), Joshua, E, at right angles to the text, with Moses and Joshua seated under arcades (f. 108), Judges, P, with (?) Judah and Simeon, armed (f. 120ᵛ).
Four decorated initials: D (f. 6ᵛ), Leviticus, V (f. 53), Deuteronomy, H, with a pig with human head cutting out a dragon's tongue (f. 89ᵛ), Ruth, I (f. 133).

On account of its celebrated image of the Virgin, the Augustinian Priory of Walsingham in Norfolk was an important place of pilgrimage in the Middle Ages. Nothing is known of its library, but the provenance of this manuscript seems assured from the contemporary rental of the Priory used as a fly-leaf, even though there is no other mark of ownership. Sir Henry Spelman, the first recorded owner of the manuscript after the Dissolution, lived at Congham in Norfolk and was educated at Walsingham Grammar School.
Stylistically, some of the figures, in particular the profiles, are reminiscent of one of the hands of the Dover Bible (e.g. Vol. II, ff. 58, 84ᵛ). However, the distinctive striped and dotted drapery is not readily paralleled elsewhere. The decoration of the initials also suggests a date c. 1140. On f. 3 there is a list of books of the whole Bible which confirms that this was the first volume of a three- or four-volume Bible of which the others have been lost. A detailed comparison with other Bibles is therefore impossible, but, as far as can be judged from the single surviving volume, the Walsingham Bible was neither as fully illustrated nor as sumptuously produced as the more famous English 12th-century giant Bibles. It should be grouped, rather, with the slightly earlier, sparsely illustrated but richly decorated Bible from Rochester (no. 45) which contains an almost identical initial to Joshua, also placed at right angles to the text. The other illustrations are paralleled elsewhere: the Creation roundels in the Lambeth Bible (no. 70) though they differ in detail, Moses and the burning bush in the somewhat later Bible at Oxford (Laud Misc. 752; no. 103), while the two knights in the initial to Judges are similar to the pair inscribed as Joshua and Caleb in the Dover Bible (no. 69), though from the Biblical text they could more fittingly represent Joshua's successor, Judah and his brother Simeon (Judges 1:3). The calling of Judah illustrates the opening of Judges in, for example, the Bible of St. Martial Limoges of c. 1100 (Paris, Bible. Nat., MS lat 8; J. Porcher, *French Miniatures*, 1960, pl. 26).

PROVENANCE: Walsingham Priory (fly-leaf, now f. 2, contains part of a contemporary rental of Walsingham Priory); Sir Henry Spelman (1564?–1641) antiquary (f. 3: *Henrici Spilmani Liber*); sold in Spelman sale, J. Harding, Temple Change, London 28 Nov. 1709, no. 1, p. 55; Hon. Richard Bateman, sale Christie's, 7, 9 May 1774, lot 118; John Jackson, F.S.A., sale, 28 April 1794, lot 372, bought Thane; Sir Thomas Phillipps, Cheltenham

(1792–1872) MS 4769; bought by Sir A. Chester Beatty from the Phillipps Collection in 1921.

LITERATURE: E. G. Millar, *The Library of A. Chester Beatty: A Descriptive Catalogue of the Western MSS*, I, 1927, 84–90, pls. 64–7; Boase, *English Art*, 169.

60. London, British Library MS Add. 46487
The Sherborne Chartulary
275×183 mm., ff. 88 (recently rebound in the correct order in its original oak covers)
c. 1146. Sherborne Abbey   *Ill. 155*

Two miniatures of Evangelists, St. Mark, half-page (f. 43ᵛ), St. John, full-page (f. 52ᵛ).
Several decorated initials, ff. 39, 56, 57ᵛ (with the eagle of St. John), 61ᵛ.

The contents of this manuscript fall into two distinct parts:
(1) Documents relating to Sherborne Abbey including royal and papal charters, the latter in particular relating to a quarrel between the monks of Sherborne and Jocelin, Bishop of Salisbury, over the election of an abbot. This quarrel was won by the Abbey in February 1146, when Pope Eugenius III wrote to Bishop Jocelin ordering him not to impede the election.
(2) Liturgical texts including narratives of the Passion from the four Gospels; Gospels preceded by Collects for feasts throughout the year, and a selection of prayers for liturgical ceremonies.
The documents were copied into a liturgical manuscript used by the abbot in order that they would be protected within the covers of a holy book and provide a weapon for any future attempts at interference by a Bishop of Salisbury. Wormald surmised that the manuscript was written not long after February 1146, the date of Pope Eugenius' final letter and this conclusion has been generally accepted.
Wormald has pointed out that both the snake-like scroll held by St. Mark and the standing posture of St. John are unusual in Evangelist portraits. Indeed, the standing St. John looks more like a Prophet (prophets usually appear standing) than like the usual western representation of an Evangelist. The treatment of the drapery, with its damp folds of an almost clinging curvilinear type, is probably derived from the Bury Bible (see no. 56). Swarzenski provides a close comparison between the Sherborne St. John and the Bury Bible Moses which underlines similarities not only in the draperies but also in the dark, Byzantinizing facial modelling. However, the white cross-hatching, forming arrowhead patterns is most closely paralleled in the Shaftesbury Psalter (see no. 48, f. 12ᵛ).

PROVENANCE: Sherborne Abbey, Dorset; c. 1712 Lord Digby, when it was seen by the antiquary Thomas Hearne; early 19th century, Thomas

Lloyd, sold Sotheby's 10 May 1828, lot 202, bought by Thorpe for Sir Thomas Phillipps of Cheltenham; bought by the British Museum in 1947.

LITERATURE: ed. Thomas Hearne, *The Itinerary of John Leland the Antiquary*, II, 1744, 57–9 with a drawing of the cover; F. Wormald in *Annual Report of the Pilgrim Trust*, 18, 1948, 7, frontispiece; *id.*, 'The Sherborne "Chartulary"', *Fritz Saxl Memorial Essays*, ed. D. J. Gordon, 1957, 101–19; Boase, *English Art*, 164 f., pl. 56a; Swarzenski, *Monuments*, fig. 303; M. A. F. Borrie, 'The binding of the Sherborne Chartulary', *British Museum Quarterly*, 32, 1968, 96–8, pls. 31–3.

61. Lincoln, Cathedral Library MS A. 1. 18
St. Augustine Commentary on the Psalms, Part I
363 × 245 mm., ff. 182
c. 1140. Lincoln   *Ills. 163–5*

More than thirty-six decorated initials: U (f. 2ᵛ), P (f. 7), I (f. 9ᵛ), P (f. 12), P (f. 18ᵛ), I (f. 26), T, P with (?)David (f. 28), I (f. 31ᵛ), D (f. 32ᵛ), Q (f. 37), P (f. 41), S (f. 43), I (f. 45ᵛ), D (f. 46ᵛ), P (f. 50ᵛ), I (f. 55), Q (f. 62ᵛ), E (f. 71ᵛ), P (f. 72), P (f. 80), Q (f. 82ᵛ), P (f. 88), N (f. 99), P (f. 109), P (f. 118ᵛ), O (f. 125), O (f. 135ᵛ), P (f. 140), P (f. 142), H (f. 145ᵛ), I (f. 152), D (f. 156), T (f. 159), M (f. 177).

Many of the initials contain a single bird, animal or naked figure. The foliage decoration includes the very large luxuriant blossoms of the period *c.* 1140 (ff. 12, 18ᵛ, 50ᵛ, 71ᵛ), but the figures have retained the peculiarly large hands and long fingers that characterized the earlier Lincoln manuscripts (see nos. 13, 14).

PROVENANCE: Lincoln Cathedral Library (inscribed f. 1ᵛ *Liber Sancte Marie linc.* and f. 1 *pr. XL.s*) no. 25 in the catalogue of Hamo, Chancellor of the Cathedral from *c.* 1150 and no. 56 in the 15th-century catalogue.

LITERATURE: Woolley, *Catalogue*, no. 155.

62. Hereford, Cathedral Library MS O. 6. XII
Glossed Psalter
265 × 173 mm., ff. 193
c. 1140. (?) Hereford   *Ill. 169*

Four decorated initials: Psalm 1, B (f. 2ᵛ), Psalm 51, Q (f. 63ᵛ), Psalm 101, D (f. 121ᵛ), Psalm 109, D (f. 139).

The Beatus initial (f. 2ᵛ) is unusual and has gold fillings with geometrical patterns in blue; the others consist of birds and monsters entwined with foliage decoration on blue ground. At the end of the book (f. 193ᵛ) there is a document recording a compact between Robert Foliot, Bishop of Hereford, and

Hugh de Laci dated 1177 which Bannister described as being apparently by the same hand as the text. Yet the style of the initials suggests a rather earlier date, probably *c.* 1140. Similar initials occur in other Herefordshire manuscripts, for example the Josephus from Monkland Priory (Trinity Hall, Cambridge, MS 4, see no. 63).

PROVENANCE: Hereford Cathedral Library (f. 2ᵛ: *precii XXs*, end fly-leaf: *precii Vs*).

LITERATURE: Bannister, *Catalogue*, 70–2.

EXHIBITED: Manchester, 1959, no. 27.

63. Cambridge, Trinity Hall MS 4
Flavius Josephus, Jewish Antiquities
368 × 263 mm., ff. 213
c. 1140. ? Hereford   *Ill. 166*

Sixteen decorated initials to Books (MS not foliated); Preface I with fiddler, harpist, and horn blower (f. 1), small Q containing a face (f. 2); Bk. 1, I with profile head terminals (f. 2ᵛ); Bk. 3, I; Bk. 4, H with a tall, nimbed figure standing on a man; Bk. 5, M made up of dragons; Bk. 6, T; Bk. 7, P; Bk. 8, D; Bk. 9, I; Bk. 13, Q; Bk. 14, A with dragons; Bk. 15, S; Bk. 16, I with dragons; Bk. 18, C; Bk. 20, M. (Other Books have simple scroll-work initials).

Monkland Priory near Leominster, some fifteen miles from Hereford, was a cell of the Norman abbey of Conches.
The initials of this manuscript are characterized by uncoloured foliage scrolls decorated with rows of small red circles exactly as in the Hereford Psalter (Hereford Cathedral, O. 6. XII; no. 62). The appearance of very large hairy blossoms (e.g. Bks. 15, 16) suggests a date in the 1140s.

PROVENANCE: Monkland Priory, Herefordshire (inscribed f. 1 *Lib. fratris Willelmi de Monkeland*).

LITERATURE: James, *Catalogue*, no. 4; Boase, *English Art*, 99, pl. 28a.

64. Hereford, Cathedral Library MS P. 4. III
Minor Prophets glossed; Jeremiah Lamentations glossed
287 × 186 mm., ff. 189;
medieval binding with chain
Mid 12th century. (?) Hereford
Ills. 167, 168

Two historiated initials: Hosea, V, with the prophet and God (f. 3); Habbakkuk, O, with the prophet, half-length, standing (f. 93).
Five decorated initials: Joel, V (f. 29ᵛ), Amos, V (f. 39ᵛ), Jonah, E (f. 63ᵛ), Micah, V (f. 70ᵛ), Nahum, O (f. 86).

A note dated 1876 now attached to the manuscript contains the comment: '. . . as far as the evidence before me goes it points to Kilpec(k)'. What this evidence consisted of we are not told, but the striking stylistic links with the Kilpeck sculptures were summed up by Boase. He compared the figures with their drooping moustaches, heavy cheekbones, large eyes, and their thin bodies with clinging draperies spread out in a fan at the feet, with those carved on the chancel arch at Kilpeck church and on the Castle Frome font (G. Zarnecki, *Later English Romanesque Sculpture*, 1953, figs. 21, 30).

This link with the Kilpeck sculpture (which probably had its source in Hereford) supports the Herefordshire provenance of the manuscript, but does not provide evidence to identify the actual scriptorium. Most of the initials have gold shafts and blue ground but the fact that three of them are on gold ground (ff. 29ᵛ, 63ᵛ, 70ᵛ) indicates a mid century date, slightly later than MS O. 6. XII (no. 62). This is confirmed by the connection with the carvings at Kilpeck which are usually dated *c.* 1150.

PROVENANCE: Hereford Cathedral Library (14th-century inscription f. 1 *Liber Herefordensis ecclesie precii dimid. marc.* and f. 2 *precii XXs*).

LITERATURE: Bannister, *Catalogue*, 140; Boase, *English Art*, 82, pl. 22b.

65. London, British Library MS Royal I. B. XI
Gospels
310×178 mm., ff. 147
ff. 145ᵛ–147ᵛ contain records relating to
St. Augustine's
c. 1140–50. Canterbury, St. Augustine's
Ills. 171, 172

Eleven outline initials (ten decorated, one historiated) to the prologues and Gospels: P (f. 2ᵛ), A (f. 5), M, St. Michael and the dragon (f. 6), S and side piece, devil urging monk to gluttony (f. 6ᵛ), L, initial to Matthew, partially coloured (f. 9), M, prologue to Mark (f. 44), I (f. 46), L, prologue to Luke, partially coloured (f. 70), Q (f. 72), H, prologue to John (f. 112), I, lamb with cross in medallion (f. 114).

This is one of the last decorated manuscripts of the period of Canterbury's greatness. Two of the initials (ff. 6, 6ᵛ) are copied from Arundel 91, (no. 17) a St. Augustine's manuscript of the early 12th century, but the impressionistic technique has been replaced by more solid, stiffer outlines. The large, octopus-like leaves with fine, hairy veins, unusual in Canterbury, are typical of Bury and Winchester in the 1140s.

PROVENANCE: St. Augustine's, Canterbury (documents ff. 145ᵛ–147ᵛ). John Theyer (1597–1673), whose library was acquired by the Royal Library in about 1678, given to the British Museum in 1743.

LITERATURE: Warner and Gilson, I, 12; British Museum, *Schools of Illumination*, II, 1915, 7, pl. 5g; Boase, *English Art*, 157; Dodwell, *Canterbury School*, 28 n. 1, 34, 79, 123, pl. 21b.

66. I. New York, Pierpont Morgan Library M 724 (400×292 mm.)
II. British Library MS Add. 37472 (1)
(405×300 mm.)
III. New York, Pierpont Morgan Library M 521 (400×292 mm.)
IV. Victoria and Albert Museum MS 661
(400×300 mm.)
c. 1140. Canterbury, (?)Christ Church
Ills. 173–80; Figs. 19, 21

Four leaves of a Psalter painted with biblical scenes in twelve or more compartments per page.

I. Morgan 724
1. Pharaoh enthroned, two Israelite midwives, Shiphrah and Puah before him; Jochebed holding Moses; Moses floating in the Nile
2. Moses taken out of the Nile and given to Pharaoh's daughter; Pharaoh crowns the boy Moses; the boy steps on the crown
3. Moses and the burning bush; his rod turned into a serpent; Moses and Aaron, with the serpents, before Pharaoh
4. Moses parts the Red Sea
5. The Jews pass over the Red Sea
6. The camp of Israel (?)
7. Moses on Mount Sinai; Moses and the brazen serpent
8. Joshua conquers a city (? Jericho)
9. Saul crowned
10. David before Saul
11. David fighting Goliath
12. David beheads the fallen Goliath

Verso:
13. David offered the crown of Judah
14. David entering Jerusalem (?)
15. (larger compartment) Tree of Jesse with the Annunciation; the wedding of Mary and Joseph, and Zacharias swinging the censer
16. Visitation
17. Birth of John
18. Naming of John
19. Nativity

II. B.L. Add. 37472 (1)
1. Annunciation to the Shepherds
2. The Magi follow the star
3. The Magi before Herod
4. The Jews before Herod
5. The Magi ride to Bethlehem
6. Adoration of the Magi
7. The Magi are warned

8. Presentation in the Temple
9. Joseph is warned
10. Flight into Egypt
11. Massacre of the Innocents
12. Herod's suicide

Verso:

13. Baptism of Christ
14. The Wedding at Cana: Christ orders the wine
15. Wine is brought
16. First Temptation
17. Second Temptation
18. Third Temptation
19. Healing the Leper
20. Peter's mother-in-law healed (mistakenly depicted as a man)
21. Foxes have holes; Christ with apostles
22. The Storm stilled; Christ cures the demoniac
23. Curing the Paralytic
24. Jairus before Christ; Jairus' daughter healed

III. Morgan 521

1. The two blind men healed
2. Apostles plucking corn; Christ disputing with Pharisees
3. The withered hand; the dumb man healed
4. Feeding of the five thousand
5. Christ prostrate; He walks on the water
6. Christ and the Woman of Canaan; the dogs eat crumbs that fall from the table
7. Peter receives keys from Christ; the Transfiguration
8. The unmerciful servant; the debtor led to prison
9. Parable of the Vineyard
10. The Woman taken in Adultery
11. Dives and Lazarus (four scenes)
12. The Prodigal Son

Verso:

13. The Wise and Foolish Virgins
14. Parable of the Talents
15. Zacchaeus in the tree; he offers Christ a dish
16. Simon the leper; at the feast Mary wipes Christ's feet with her hair
17. Christ and the Samaritan Woman at the well
18. Christ in the house of Mary and Martha; a woman pours ointment on His head
19. Mary and Martha greet Christ; the raising of Lazarus
20. The apostles obtain the ass; the entry into Jerusalem
21. Judas receives his money
22. Christ with two apostles; the Last Supper
23. The Washing of Feet; the Agony in the Garden
24. The Betrayal (two scenes)

IV. Victoria and Albert Museum MS 661

1. Christ before Annas and Caiaphas; Peter's first denial
2. A man hits Christ; Peter's second denial
3. Christ led before Pilate; Peter's third denial
4. Christ in the Hall of Judgment
5. The Mocking; the Scourging

6. The Crown of Thorns
7. Christ carrying the cross; Simon of Cyrene takes the cross from Him
8. The crosses erected; Christ and the thieves on the crosses
9. Longinus pierces Christ's side while two men break the thieves' legs; the Earthquake
10. Crucifixion with Mary and John
11. Joseph begs Pilate for the Body
12. The Deposition

Verso:

13. Three Jews ask Pilate for a guard; soldiers cast dice for the tunic
14. The swathing of the Body; the Entombment
15. Three Marys at the tomb; Peter and John at the tomb
16. Mary Magdalen at the tomb; Noli me tangere
17. Journey to Emmaus (two scenes)
18. Supper at Emmaus; Christ rises to leave
19. Christ appears to the disciples
20. Incredulity of Thomas; Thomas prostrate
21. Christ appearing to the disciples on the shore of Tiberias; Christ eats bread and fish with the disciples (John 21: 1–14)
22. The disciples touch Christ's arm; they give Him the fish and the honeycomb (Luke 24: 36–44)
23. The Ascension
24. Pentecost.

These four leaves, painted on both sides, contain by far the largest New Testament cycle produced in England in the 12th century. The Old Testament cycle is fragmentary and probably incomplete, but the Gospels are illustrated with some one hundred and fifty scenes covering twelve compartments per page, many of them subdivided. In format, choice of subject, and composition of individual scenes, these leaves are closely similar to the prefatory cycle contained in Paris, Bibl. Nat., lat. 8846, the latest Psalter in the Utrecht Psalter tradition written at Canterbury not long before 1200 (see James, and Dodwell, *op. cit.*, for a comparison between lat. 8846 and these four leaves). It has in the past been accepted that Paris lat. 8846 was copied from the Eadwine Psalter (Trinity College MS R. 17. 1), and hence it was argued by both Swarzenski and Dodwell that these four leaves were originally part of the Eadwine Psalter, from which they too were copied by the artist of the Paris Psalter. Certainly, the style of these leaves is similar to that of the Eadwine Psalter, though they were fully painted, whereas the Eadwine illustrations are, like the Utrecht and Harley Psalters, in tinted outline. As opposed to the Swarzenski–Dodwell thesis, however, A. Heimann has recently argued, in an unpublished lecture, that Paris lat. 8846 is a copy, not of the Eadwine Psalter, but of a lost manuscript in the Utrecht Psalter tradition (see no. 68 for a summary of her conclusions). If this is the case, these four leaves could well have belonged to this lost manuscript rather than to the Eadwine Psalter. A Canterbury origin remains likely, as all the English manuscripts in the Utrecht Psalter tradition were produced at Canterbury, though we know nothing of their provenance before their appearance in the collection of William Young Ottley, the well-known collector of medieval miniatures and early Italian paintings, in the opening years of the 19th century (on Ottley's collection see Munby, 1972, 62–8).

The New Testament picture cycle of the four leaves clearly belongs to the same family as the St. Albans Psalter and Cambridge, Pembroke College, MS 120 (see nos. 29 and 35 and introduction). They have thirty-three scenes in common with the St. Albans Psalter (Infancy and Passion) and twenty-six with Pembroke 120 (Ministry and Passion; the Infancy scenes are missing in this manuscript) and in each manuscript about half the scenes shared are very similar in composition. Such a close relationship suggests that these three cycles were derived from a common model. This must have been similar to the 11th-century Echternach manuscripts, which are the most closely related of extant New Testament illustrations, as has been shown in the discussion on the iconography of Pembroke 120 (no. 35).

Yet the fact remains that the four leaves have a much more extensive cycle and contain some forty illustrations not found in either the St. Albans Psalter or in Pembroke 120. Of these, ten occur in the mid 11th-century Golden Gospels of Echternach (Nürnberg, Germanisches Museum; facsimile ed. P. Metz, 1957) and three in particular—Christ healing the leper, the storm stilled, and the parable of Dives and Lazarus—are very similar. A further three scenes (the withered hand, Christ walking on the water, and the breaking of the thieves' legs on the cross) are paralleled in the Codex Egberti (Trier MS 24, ff. 23ᵛ, 27ᵛ, 84ᵛ; facsimile ed. H. Schiel, 1960). Clearly, this enables one to extend the link with these Ottonian cycles which has already been established for Pembroke 120. Nevertheless, there are still about twenty-five illustrations which do not occur in extant Ottonian manuscripts. The Byzantine Gospel cycles (e.g. Paris, Bibl. Nat., gr. 74, see H. Omont, *Evangiles avec Peintures Byzantines*, 1908) are equally extensive but, with the exception of the scenes of the Prodigal Son, they are not very similar in detail. One very rare scene, the 'foxes have holes' (Add. 37472) is paralleled in the 6th–7th-century Gospels in Corpus Christi College, Cambridge, in which the illustrations are also arranged in small compartments, and this has led to the suggestion that our cycle echoes an early Christian one.

The same has been said of the Old Testament scenes, which are not paralleled in the St. Albans Psalter or in Pembroke 120. Indeed, there is nothing comparable in England until the time of Paris lat. 8846, c. 1200. The Paris Psalter has one folio containing twenty-four scenes from Genesis, in addition to the Exodus scenes that appear here in Morgan 724, which would suggest that a Genesis leaf is missing from the present series. H. Swarzenski (1938) used the scene of the two midwives, Shiphrah and Puah, before Pharaoh, which occurs in the Synagogue at Dura Europos (before A.D. 256)

and in the 7th-century Ashburnham Pentateuch, to support the hypothesis that the four leaves reflect an early Christian cycle. However, the early examples quoted are not very similar and Shiphrah and Puah do in fact appear quite often in 11th–12th-century manuscripts (e.g. Stavelot Bible, B.L. Add. 28106, f. 23ᵛ; Lobbes Bible, Tournai, f. 29). A much rarer scene with a possible link with early cycles is that of the boy Moses stamping upon Pharaoh's crown which, like the scene of Herod's suicide (M. R. James, 1936, 6 f.; cf. also Lambach, c. 1089, O. Demus, *Romanesque Mural Painting*, 1970, 625, fig. 280) is derived from Josephus (*Antiquities*, II, 9. 7; see Gutman, 1952). However, on the present state of the evidence such considerations are quite inconclusive. Any proposed link with Early Christian cycles remains tantalizingly unproven, because so very few Early Christian manuscripts survive. All we know is that the four leaves are related to the St. Albans Psalter and Pembroke 120, and that the common source was related in some way to Ottonian and, particularly, to Echternach cycles.

To judge from their style, the leaves appear to be the work of at least two hands. The first, covering the first three leaves and the upper half of the recto of the fourth, is characterized by profile figures of the St. Albans Psalter type with the addition of damp fold drapery. A different hand has been detected in the lower half of the recto and in the whole of the verso of the V & A leaf. This is a more sophisticated style, linked with the Lambeth Bible in the treatment of the faces, hair, and beards and in the drapery folds. Pächt (*St. Albans Psalter*, 75) has also pointed to similarities with the St. Albans Calendar in Bodley MS Auct. D. 2. 6. (no. 71). The relationship with these manuscripts suggests a date c. 1140 for the four leaves.

PROVENANCE: All four leaves in W. Y. Ottley sale, Sotheby's, 12 May 1838, lots 130–3. Lot 130 bought by Tindall for £1; Holford collection, sold Sotheby's, 12 July 1927, lot 48, bought by the Morgan Library (MS 724). Lot 131 bought by Tindall for £1; David MacIntosh, sold Christie's, 20 May 1857, lot 771, bought by the British Museum (Add. 37472. 1). Lot 132 bought by Lloyd for £2. 2s.; N. P. Simes, sold Christie's, 9 July 1886, lot 1095; acquired by the Victoria and Albert Museum in 1894 (MS 661; no. 816-1894). Lot 133 bought by Payne for £2. 8s.; Bateman sale, Sotheby's, 25th May etc. 1893, lot 1152; J. Pierpont Morgan (MS 521).

LITERATURE: V & A Museum, *Catalogue of Miniatures, Leaves and Cuttings from Illuminated MSS*, 1st ed. 1908, MS 661, 2nd ed. 1923, 50, no. 816-1894; British Museum, *Reproductions from Illuminated MSS*, ser. III, 1908, pl. 11; Millar I, 46; R. H. Benson, *The Holford Collection, Dorchester House*, I, 1927, 15 f., pls. 1–2; *The Pierpont Morgan Library 1924–29*, 1930, 50; M. R. James, 'Four leaves of an English Psalter', *Walpole Society*, 25, 1936–7, 1–23; H. Swarzenski, 'Unknown Bible Pictures by W. de Brailes', *Journal of the Walters Art Gallery*, I, 1938, 65–9; J. Gutman, 'The Test of Moses', *The Student Zionist*, IX, no. 3, Spring 1952, 22 f., fig. 1; Dodwell, *Canterbury School*, 99 ff., 121, pl. 66; Boase, *English Art*, 109 f., 159, 289, pl. 95*a, b*; Rickert, *Painting in Britain*, 67–8, pl. 67; *St. Albans Psalter*, 75, 158 n. 3, 169; Schiller, *Iconography*, II, 1972, 80, 83, figs. 285; 300; III (German ed.), 96, 101, fig. 288; A. N. L. Munby, *Connoisseurs and Medieval Miniatures*, 1972, 149 f.

EXHIBITED: Morgan Library, *Exhibition of Illuminated MSS held at the New York Public Library*, 1933–4, no. 31; Brussels, 1973, no. 16, pl. 6 (V & A leaf).

67. London, British Library MS Harley 603
12th-century addition to the Harley Psalter
380 × 314 mm., ff. 29–38
c. 1140. Canterbury, (?)Christ Church
Ills. 170, 182

Twelve tinted drawings illustrating Psalms 52–62 and 65.

The text of each Psalm is illustrated in a literal, line-by-line fashion by oblong drawings extending across the page. For the history of this type of Psalter illustration see under Eadwine Psalter (no. 68). Harley 603 is the earliest of the English copies of the 9th-century Utrecht Psalter. The bulk of its illustrations date from the early 11th century and are close to the impressionistic style of the original, but the manuscript was left unfinished. Attempts were made to complete the illustrations, first at various times in the mid 11th century (ff. 28, 28ᵛ, 58–73ᵛ), and finally in the second quarter of the 12th century (ff. 29–38), but the cycle remains incomplete.
These 12th-century drawings are unframed, and stylistically they retain more of the impressionism of the Utrecht Psalter, both in the figures and the background, than do the illustrations of the near-contemporary Eadwine Psalter. However, as to the iconography, the Eadwine Psalter is a faithful copy of the original cycle, while these drawings in the Harley Psalter vary in many points of detail from the Utrecht Psalter compositions. Quite apart from the attempt to bring the *accoutrements* up to date—for example, the priest in f. 29ᵛ has acquired a clearly recognizable 12th-century habit—there are considerable divergences in the disposition of the figures. Most of these differences are fortuitous or due to misunderstandings, but A. Heimann (1966) has shown that the figure of God holding the sun on f. 33 (Psalm 60), (instead of a wreath as in Utrecht and Eadwine), represents a conscious emendation. For the change from wreath to sun has been made to illustrate the scene of the Lord showing the emblem of the sun to King Hezekiah.

PROVENANCE: Harleian manuscripts collected by Robert (1661–1724) and Edward Harley (1689–1741)

1st and 2nd Earls of Oxford. Bought by the British Museum in 1753.

LITERATURE: Wormald, *English Drawings*, 69 f., no. 34; Dodwell, *Canterbury School*, 27 f., 42, 123, pl. 1*c*; A. Heimann, 'Three illustrations from the Bury St. Edmunds Psalter . . .', *J.W.C.I.*, 29, 1966, 55, pl. 12*c*.

68. Cambridge, Trinity College MS R. 17. 1
Tripartite Psalter (Eadwine Psalter)
460 × 327 mm., ff. 286
c. 1147. Canterbury, Christ Church
Ills. 181, 183–7

One hundred and sixty-six framed, tinted drawings: one for each of the one hundred and fifty Psalms (ff. 5ᵛ–261), eleven for Canticles (ff. 262ᵛ–78), four for prayers (ff. 278ᵛ–9ᵛ) and one for Apocryphal Psalm 151 (f. 281).
Full-page miniature of the scribe (N.B. *not* illuminator) Eadwine (f. 283ᵛ); plan of Christ Church buildings showing the waterworks installed by Prior Wibert, *c.* 1160 (f. 284ᵛ–5), part of a second plan (f. 286).
Four hundred and seventy-four decorated initials: three for each of the one hundred and fifty Psalms; twenty-four for the Canticles and prayers.

Each page of the text is divided into three columns corresponding to three versions of the Psalter: the *Hebraicum*, St. Jerome's Latin version from the Hebrew, the *Romanum*, St. Jerome's Roman version, and the *Gallicanum*, St. Jerome's revision of his own *Romanum* text, which was first adopted by the Gallican church and later became the Psalter generally used in Western churches. In addition, there are interlinear versions in Anglo-Saxon and French, and there is a collect after each Psalm.
The text of each Psalm is illustrated in a literal, line-by-line fashion by oblong drawings extending across the page. This is one of four extant Psalters illustrated in this way, the earliest of which is the 9th-century Psalter from Rheims now at Utrecht (E. T. De Wald, *The Illustrations of the Utrecht Psalter*, Princeton, 1932). The Utrecht Psalter was at Canterbury in the Middle Ages, where it was much copied, and there are three extant manuscripts in which its picture cycle reappears: (1) B.L. MS Harley 603, *c.* 1000, unfinished, with later additions (see no. 67), (2) The Eadwine Psalter, (3) Paris, Bibl. Nat., lat. 8846, *c.* 1200. It is clear that all three are ultimately derived from the Utrecht Psalter, but there has been some controversy concerning the precise nature of the relationship. Recently, Adelheid Heimann has argued from a detailed analysis of the illustrations that Eadwine was not a direct copy of Utrecht, but rather that both it and the Paris manuscript were copied from a copy of Utrecht now lost. A similar conclusion was reached a century ago by Francisque Michel (*Le Livre des Psaumes, anciennes traductions françaises*,

1876, 10) from a study of the text: the French interlinear text which appears in Eadwine and Paris was derived from a lost intermediary manuscript and was not copied by Paris from Eadwine.

The relationship of the four extant manuscripts may therefore be tentatively reconstructed as follows:

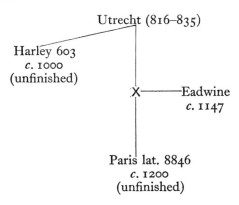

The Eadwine Psalter has the distinction, alone among all the derivatives of the Utrecht Psalter, of containing the complete set of illustrations to the Psalms. The Utrecht compositions have been followed very faithfully, except in the first seven Psalms, where new themes have been added to the illustrations. Occasionally an English feature is introduced, such as the frequently recurring dragon hell-mouth. In general terms, the pictures represent a hardened, Romanesque version of the Utrecht Psalter illustrations which are in a sketchy, impressionistic style derived from classical art. They are all framed, with outlines and tinting in red, blue, green and brown and with uncoloured backgrounds. The figures, with their slightly elongated bodies and profile heads craned forward, betray the influence of the St. Albans Psalter (no. 29). These characteristics are common to the whole manuscript, but Dodwell was able to distinguish three different hands (apart from the obviously cruder work on ff. 5ᵛ and 6ᵛ):

1. ff. 8–27, 70–84, 166–234: characterized by a considerable survival of the calligraphic technique of the Utrecht Psalter. Some of the figures (e.g. f. 9) are similar to those of the Dover Bible (no. 69).
2. ff. 32–6ᵛ, 49–68, 86–142ᵛ, 235ᵛ–81: characterized by brighter colours, more spirited figures, and more animated expressions.
3. ff. 144ᵛ–64ᵛ: a much cruder hand.

The portrait of the scribe Eadwine is one of the most monumental paintings to emerge from the Canterbury scriptorium. It is the only 12th-century picture in which the scribe is depicted, in the posture, size and setting of an evangelist portrait. The monumentality is a feature of the international Romanesque style, but the fine arabesque designs on the drapery are a distinctly English feature. There are stylistic links with the St. Matthew portrait in the Dover Bible (no. 69).

The date c. 1147 is suggested by a description of a comet (f. 10) which, according to contemporary sources, appeared in 1146 or 47. Such a date accords well with the style of the drawings, the Eadwine portrait, and the initials. This date does not, however, apply to the plans on ff. 284–6. These represent one of the very few examples of contemporary plans of monastic buildings; their importance in this respect is comparable to that of the 9th-century plan of the Abbey of St. Gall. Their purpose was to record the system of water distribution and drainage whereby the convent was supplied with pure water from nearby springs and the drainage system flushed by rainwater drawn from the roof of the Abbey Church. This intricate system was installed by Prior Wibert in c. 1160–5 and this is probably the date of the drawings (see below, Willis, 1868; Woodruff and Danks, 1912).

PROVENANCE: Christ Church, Canterbury (Eastry's Catalogue, 14th century); remained at Canterbury until presented to Trinity College by Thomas Nevile, Dean of Canterbury and Master of Trinity (1593–1615).

LITERATURE: James, *Catalogue*, II, no. 987; R. Willis in *Archaeologia Cantiana*, 7, 1868, 158–68, 174–81; C. E. Woodruff and W. Dank, *Memorials of Canterbury Cathedral*, 1912, 51–5; M. R. James, *The Canterbury Psalter*, 1935 (facsimile ed.); Millar, I, 32 f., pl. 43; G. Haseloff, *Die Psalter-illustration im 13. Jahrhundert*, 1938, 7; Boase, *English Art*, 158 ff. pl. 94*a*; Swarzenski, *Monuments*, fig. 4; Dodwell, *Canterbury School*, 36 f., chapt. 4, pls. 23, 27–9, 47; *Rickert, Painting in Britain*, 71, pl. 72B; D. Tselos, 'English Manuscript illustration and the Utrecht Psalter', *Art Bulletin*, 41, 1959, 141 ff.; *id.*, *Art Bulletin*, 49, 1967, 334 ff. esp. 340, figs. 5, 9, 10, 12, 19; S. Dufresne, 'Les copies anglaises du Psautier d'Utrecht', *Scriptorium*, 18, 1964, 185–97.

EXHIBITED: Manchester, 1959, no. 17, pl. 2; Barcelona, 1961, no. 173, pl. 11; Brussels, 1973, no. 17, pl. 7.

69. Cambridge, Corpus Christi College MS 3–4
Bible (The Dover Bible)
Vol. I, 550×370 mm., ff. 273
Vol. II, 533×355 mm., ff. 283
c. 1150. Canterbury, Christ Church
Ills. 188–91; Fig. 29

Vol. I:
Twenty-one historiated initials (initial to Genesis, f. 4, cut out): Exodus, H, busts of Jacob and the twelve patriarchs in scrolls (f. 26), Numbers, L, busts in medallions (f. 56ᵛ), Deuteronomy, H, Moses teaching, Judges, P, Joshua and Caleb, armed (f. 91ᵛ), Ruth, I, Ruth in medallion (f. 114), 1 Samuel, F, David and Goliath; below, David cutting off Goliath's head (f. 117ᵛ), 2 Samuel, F, David told of Saul's death; below, the Amalekite is killed (f. 133), 2 Kings, P, Ascension of Elijah; Elisha below (f. 161ᵛ), Isaiah, V, the Prophet (f. 174ᵛ), Jeremiah, V,

Christ and the Prophet (f. 196), Daniel, A, Prophet with scroll (f. 245ᵛ), Hosea, V, Prophet with scroll (f. 255), Joel, V, Prophet with scroll (f. 258), Amos, V, Prophet with scroll (f. 259ᵛ), Obadiah, V, Prophet with scroll (f. 261ᵛ), Jonah, E, Prophet, with fish below (f. 262), Micah, V, Prophet with scroll (f. 263), Habakkuk, U, Prophet with scroll (f. 265ᵛ), Zephaniah, V, Prophet with scroll (f. 266ᵛ), Haggai, I, bust of Prophet (f. 267ᵛ), Zechariah, I, bust of Prophet (f. 268ᵛ), Malachi, O, Prophet with scroll (f. 272).

Four decorated initials: Leviticus, V (f. 43ᵛ), Joshua, E (f. 91ᵛ), 1 Kings, E (f. 146ᵛ), Ezekiel, E (f. 222ᵛ).

Vol. II:

Seventeen historiated initials: Psalms, Beatus initial, David plays psaltery and bells; below, David as shepherd plays harp (f. 13), Proverbs, P, Solomon teaching (f. 43), Song of Songs, O, Solomon holds scroll emerging from a scroll case (f. 56), Wisdom of Solomon, D, Christ above; below, a nude criminal, tied, with judges, scroll inscribed: *Diligite iustitiam qui iudicatis terram* (f. 58), Ecclesiasticus, O, seated writer (f. 64ᵛ), Chronicles, A, descendants of Adam in three tiers of busts (f. 84ᵛ), 1 Maccabees, E, Alexander the Great dividing his kingdom (f. 139ᵛ), Matthew, L, three-quarter page, seated Evangelist (f. 168ᵛ), Luke, Q, a priest sacrificing a calf (f. 192ᵛ), John, I, bust of Evangelist (f. 208), Acts, P (?)St. Luke (f. 220ᵛ), 1 Peter, P, Peter enthroned (f. 237), 3 John, N, occupation of a painter, grinding colour and painting (f. 241ᵛ), Romans, P, Paul (f. 244), 2 Corinthians, P, Paul seated (f. 255ᵛ), Ephesians, P, Paul holding up book (f. 261), Apocalypse, A, John on Patmos (f. 276).

Decorated canon tables (ff. 164ᵛ–5) and fifteen decorated initials: Psalm 51, Q (f. 22ᵛ), Psalm 101, O (f. 32ᵛ), Ecclesiastes, V (52ᵛ), Ezra, I (f. 112ᵛ), Esther, I (f. 122ᵛ), Tobit, T (128ᵛ), Judith, A (f. 133ᵛ), 2 Maccabees, F (f. 154), Mark, I (f. 184), James, I (f. 235ᵛ), 2 Peter, S, fable of fox and cock; below, wolf and stork (f. 239), 1 John, Q (f. 240), Galatians, P (f. 259), 2 Thessalonians, P (f. 267), Hebrews, M (f. 271ᵛ).

The close palaeographical similarities with the Eadwine Psalter (no. 68) were stressed by Dodwell, who suggested that this Bible should be identified with the 'Eadwine Bible', listed in Eastry's catalogue of Christ Church manuscripts. Dover Priory was a dependent cell of Christ Church, and it is quite possible that the manuscript was transferred there from the mother house in the 14th century (see under Provenance, below).

The style of the figures is different in the two volumes. In the first, the figures are under strong Byzantine influence. The bodies are weighty, the draperies solidly modelled by damp folds made up of nested Vs and circles. Heavy ochre shading gives the faces a naturalistic appearance. In the second volume the figures have similar basic characteristics, but are differentiated by a more linear treatment and by highly unusual facial features. These are characterized by large, staring eyes, heavily accentuated eye-brows and long, curling moustaches. Dodwell (p. 58) suggested that these figures might be compared with Flemish manuscripts of the 11th and early 12th centuries, but, as he indicated, the closest parallel is provided by the Eadwine portrait in the Eadwine Psalter.

The iconography, though sometimes idiosyncratic, is in most initials paralleled in Mosan and French Bibles of the late 11th and 12th centuries. Dodwell was justified in pointing out that many of the narrative scenes, as well as the single figures of prophets, have their ultimate origin in Byzantine art. Yet it should be stressed that, iconographically, Byzantine influence was not direct, for these images had been adapted for use in Western Bibles well before the Dover Bible was illustrated. For example, the composition of Jacob and the twelve tribes depicted in foliage scrolls is paralleled in the Exodus initial in a French Bible of *c.* 1100 in Rheims (Bibl. de la Ville MS 22–3). The 1 Samuel initial with David told of Saul's death and the Amalekite killed is very similar to the one in the Bible of St. Bénigne at Dijon (MS 2, f. 114; see Introduction, p. 34). The Ascension of Elijah is, as Dodwell says, of Byzantine origin, but it had become the standard illustration to 2 Kings, where it appears in many Western Bibles in the 11th and 12th centuries, and the same can be said of the numerous standing prophets. Volume II contains, as one might expect from such an idiosyncratic artist, a number of unparalleled illustrations, such as the judgement scene for the Wisdom of Solomon. The descendants of Adam are occasionally shown elsewhere in the initial to Chronicles (e.g. St. Bénigne Bible, Dijon MS 2), but the way they are shown here, by three rows of busts is highly unusual. However, several of the other initials in this volume are paralleled in earlier Continental Bibles. Solomon teaching, for example, in the Proverbs initial, reappears in an identical composition in an early 12th century French Bible (Paris, Chambres des Deputés, f. 189ᵛ; *Bull. de la Soc. Fr. de Repr. de MSS à Peintures*, VI, 1922, 36 ff.). The initial of Alexander crowning his successors for Maccabees and the unusual representation of a priest sacrificing a calf are fully discussed by Dodwell (p. 86 ff., pls. 57–8).

PROVENANCE: Christ Church, Canterbury (probably identical with *Biblia Edwini* in Eastry's Catalogue of 1284–1331); Dover Priory (press mark A. 1. on f. 4, Vol. I; Dover catalogue of 1389). Bequeathed to his college by Matthew Parker, Archbishop of Canterbury.

LITERATURE: James, *Catalogue*, I, nos. 3–4; H. H. Glunz, *History of the Vulgate in England*, 1933, 180; N. Gray, *Jacob's Ladder*, 1949, pl. 20; Boase, *English Art*, 167 ff., pls. 56c, 57, 60a; Rickert, *Painting in Britain*, 72–4, 89, pls. 63a, 70; Swarzenski, *Monuments*, fig. 302; Dodwell, *Canterbury School*, 48 ff., 53, 57, pls. 33–4; V. W. Egbert, *The Medieval Artist at Work*, Princeton 1967, 34, pl. 7; H. Roosen-Runge, *Farbgebung & Technik Frühmittelalterlicher Buchmalerei*, 1967, I, 105–11, pls. 7–8.

EXHIBITED: Manchester, 1959, no. 18 (Vol. II).

70. London, Lambeth Palace Library MS 3 & Maidstone Museum

Bible (The Lambeth Bible)
Vol. I: Lambeth Palace, Genesis–Job,
518×353 mm., ff. 328
Vol. II: Maidstone Museum, 500×357 mm.,
ff. 310
c. 1140–50. (?)Canterbury, St. Augustine's
Ills. 192–5; Figs. 30, 32, 36

Vol. I:
Six framed miniatures: Genesis, full-page (double sheet of vellum), top, Abraham receives the three angels, below, right, Sacrifice of Isaac, left, Jacob's dream and Jacob anointing the stone of Bethel (f. 6), Numbers, two-thirds page, top, right, Moses communicating with God, centre and left Moses speaking to Israelites; centre, Levites carrying the Ark followed by (?)Eleazer, son of Aaron, and a group of Gershonites and Merarites carrying Columns, Key and Curtain; below, Princes with offerings of sheep, goats etc. at the Tabernacle (f. 66ᵛ), Ruth, one-third page, left, Ruth gleaning, Boaz speaks to four gleaners; centre, Ruth bringing grain to Naomi; right, Ruth at the feet of Boaz (f. 130), Prophets, full-page, Tree of Jesse, in medallions, lower register, four Prophets; centre, Mercy and Truth, Justice embracing Peace (Psalm 84); top, Ecclesia between two Apostles, Synagogue between (?)Abraham and Moses; above the Virgin, the seven gifts of the Holy Spirit (f. 198), Ezekiel, two-thirds page, top, God's hand on Ezekiel's head; Ezekiel lifted by his hair to the door of the inner gate (Ezek. 8: 1–3); below, the man with the writer's ink horn marking the forehead of the righteous while his companions slay the unrighteous (Ezek. 9) (f. 258), Daniel, full-page, top, Nebuchadnezzar's dream of the large image (Dan. 2: 1), Wise men consulted; centre, Daniel before Nebuchadnezzar; three Hebrew youths praying; Daniel's vision (Dan. 5: 19); below, Nebuchadnezzar venerates Daniel, adoration of the golden statue; the three youths in the furnace (f. 285ᵛ).

Twenty-four historiated initials: Jerome's letter, F, Jerome writing (f. 1), Genesis, I, Creation cycle in medallions (f. 6ᵛ), Leviticus, U, Moses communicating with God; aspersion of lamb's blood (Exod. 12: 7) (f. 52), Ruth, I, medallions with Ruth given barley by Boaz; Boaz' compact with kinsmen; Boaz seated (f. 130ᵛ), 2 Samuel, F, battle on Mount Gilboa, death of Saul (f. 151), 1 Kings, M, David enthroned (f. 164ᵛ), Isaiah, V, Isaiah sawn in half (f. 198ᵛ), Baruch, H, Prophet seated (f. 254), Jeremiah's letter P, King of Babylon seated (f. 256ᵛ), Ezekiel, E, Ezekiel eating the roll, and shaving (f. 258ᵛ), Prologue to Daniel, D, Prophet standing (f. 284ᵛ), second prologue to Daniel, D, bust of Prophet (f. 285), Daniel, A, the lions' den, with Habakkuk lowered by the angel (f. 286), Daniel 3: 24, I, Nebuchadnezzar (f. 289), Prologue to

Hosea, V, Prophet standing (f. 296ᵛ), Hosea, V, Prophet standing (f. 296ᵛ), Joel, V, Prophet seated on mountain preaching locust and worm (f. 300), Amos, V, Prophet as shepherd and prophesying destruction (f. 301ᵛ), Micah, V, Prophet standing (f. 304), Nahum, O, Prophet seated, two red streams emerge from city gate (f. 306), Prologue to Habakkuk, A, Prophet (f. 307), Habakkuk, O, Crucifixion with Synagogue and Ecclesia, bust of Habakkuk below (f. 307), Zechariah, I, medallions, top, vision of man on red horse (1: 8); centre, vision of gold candelabra between two olive trees (4: 2–3); below, coming of Christ (9: 9) (f. 310) Malachi, O, outline initial, Prophet seated (f. 314). (N.B. folios missing after ff. 117 and 133, openings to Judges and 1 Samuel, initials missing (? peeled off) on ff. 31ᵛ, Exodus; 105, Joshua; 197, Prologue to Isaiah; 22ᵛ, Jeremiah.)

Nineteen decorated initials, D (f. 4ᵛ), Numbers, L with grotesques (f. 67), Deuteronomy, H (f. 88), Prologue to Ruth, R (f. 130), Prologue to 1 Samuel (f. 312), 1 Kings, E (f. 165), 2 Kings, C (f. 182), Lamentations, E (f. 251), Daniel 13, E (f. 294ᵛ), Prologue to minor Prophets, N (f. 296ᵛ), Prologue to Nahum, N with climbing figures (f. 306), Habakkuk 3, D (f. 307ᵛ), Prologue to Sophonias, S with peacocks (f. 308), Sophonias, V (f. 308), Prologue and text of Haggai, A and I combined (f. 309), Prologue to Zechariah, Z (f. 310), Prologue to Malachi, M, outline only (f. 314), Prologue to Job, C (f. 315ᵛ).

Vol. II:
Five historiated initials at the liturgical divisions of the Psalms: Psalm 26, D David and lion (f. 14), Psalm 38, D, Christ (f. 17), Psalm 51, Q, Doeg killing Ahimelech, Solomon enthroned (f. 19ᵛ), Psalm 52, D, man pointing to his mouth (f. 19ᵛ), Psalm 109, D, God and Christ with feet on enemies (f. 32ᵛ).

Over seventeen decorated initials, Psalm 68, S, man butting goat and ram (f. 22ᵛ), Psalm 80, E, (f. 26), Psalm 119, A (f. 35ᵛ), and ff. 61ᵛ, 63, 139ᵛ, 205ᵛ (coloured initials), 61ᵛ, 63, 139ᵛ, 173ᵛ, 205ᵛ, 237ᵛ, 297, 298, 298ᵛ, 304 (outline only). Most of the illuminated pages and initials have been removed.

The illuminations of this great manuscript are not in a clearly recognizable Canterbury style, but Dodwell argued convincingly that the circumstantial evidence is sufficiently strong to warrant an attribution to Canterbury. He has analysed the family register at the end of the Maidstone volume and demonstrated the close links between Canterbury and the Hales and Colyar families. The fact that the Bible was apparently in the hands of the Colyars in 1538 suggests St. Augustine's—which was dissolved in that year—as the likely home, rather than Christ Church, which was not dissolved until 1541.

The figure style of the Lambeth Bible is derived from that of the Bury Bible. The clinging curvilinear folds by which the body beneath the drapery is delineated are essentially the same, but it is a mannered version of the style. The gently modulated curves of the Bury Bible have taken on a sharply independent life of their own, almost to the point of dominating the composition. However, the link with the Bury Bible does not necessarily imply a direct dependence, for this drapery style appears also, for example, in the Winchester Psalter and Bible and in the wall painting of St. Paul in Canterbury Cathedral. Like the drapery, the heads are strikingly linear in treatment. The faces tend to be round, and the curls on foreheads and beards are characteristically individualized.

The same artist was responsible for the illumination of a book of the Gospels written for Abbot Wedric of Liessies in Hainault in 1146. This book was in the Municipal Library at Metz (MS 1151) until its destruction in the last war. However, two detached leaves from it survive in the Société Archéologique, Avesnes (Dodwell, *Great Lambeth Bible*, pls. 7–8). These contain full-page miniatures of St. Mark and St. John—the latter together with Abbot Wedric—and there can be no mistaking the hand of the Lambeth Bible Master. The Liessies Gospels were written in France, and Dodwell has argued convincingly that the Lambeth Bible master, whose style was derived from an English tradition, was an English artist who worked in France. This conclusion is supported by the existence of other English manuscripts which show a similar treatment of the figures, though they are not necessarily by the same hand (see especially the two leaves in Corpus Christi College, Oxford, no. 72, and also nos. 71 and 66).

The Lambeth Bible shares with the Bury Bible the practice of having full-page miniatures as well as historiated initials but, as far as one can tell from the surviving parts of these books, there is little similarity between the two. Dodwell has stressed the Byzantine influence on the iconography of the Lambeth Bible; in most instances however the immediate influence was western. He has compared the scene of Ruth and Boaz with a similar composition in the Bible produced at Acre in the Crusader Kingdom in *c.* 1250–60 (Paris, Arsenal, MS 5211), but this illustration, as Hugo Buchthal has pointed out, is of Western rather than Byzantine origin. Other scenes, such as the initials with Isaiah sawn in half (see R. Bernheimer, *Art Bulletin*, 34, 1952, 19 ff.) and Daniel in the lions' den, may well have originally come to the medieval West from Byzantine art, but they had become standard in Western Bibles well before the period of the Lambeth Bible. Another initial, the illustration of the battle on Mount Gilboa and Saul falling on his sword, is closer to the Carolingian Bible in San Paolo fuori le Mura, Rome, than to the Byzantine Book of Kings in the Vatican (Vat. Gr. 333, f. 38). Most strikingly, the Lambeth Bible has detailed and extensive Prophet illustrations which do not occur in Byzantine art and which, indeed, are paralleled only in the 11th-century Bible from Roda in Catalonia (Paris, Bibl. Nat., lat. 6). The scene of Ezekiel lifted by his hair to the door of the inner gate, is extremely rare and the Roda Bible provides a very close comparison to the Ezekiel frontispiece, both

for the sequence of scenes and for their composition (see Introduction, p. 39, figs. 32, 33). The illustration of Ezekiel eating the scroll and Ezekiel shaving (f. 258ᵛ) is also closely paralleled in the Roda Bible. Daniel's story (f. 285ᵛ) was more frequently illustrated, but again the Roda Bible provides the most similar sequence of scenes. The upper register of the Lambeth miniature, in particular, is very close indeed to the upper register in the Roda Bible (figs. 36, 37). This is not to claim that the Lambeth Bible artist knew this particular Catalan Bible, but one can conclude that a similar cycle of Prophet illustrations was known in 12th-century England. An analysis of the Prophet initials in the Winchester Bible, furthermore, leads to the same conclusion.

Of the other full page miniatures, the Tree of Jesse is discussed at length by A. Watson and by Dodwell, who also draws attention to the typological significance of the Crucifixion in the initial to Habakkuk (see above, Introduction p. 42). The frontispiece to Numbers remains, as far as can be seen, unparalleled, though there are points of similarity with the Leviticus frontispiece in the San Paolo fuori le Mura Bible (f. 31ᵛ). Vol. II provides another early example of historiated initials at the liturgical divisions of the Psalms (see under Shaftesbury Psalter, no. 48 and cf. the tables in G. Haseloff, *Psalterillustration im 13. Jahrhundert*, 1938).

PROVENANCE: John Colyer of Lenham, near Maidstone, 1538; other references to the Colyar, Hales (of Canterbury) and Pery families to 1652 (inscriptions on last page of Maidstone vol.). Vol. I: Archbishop Bancroft, in foundation bequest to Lambeth Palace Library, 1610. Vol. II: Maidstone Parochial Library, then Maidstone Museum.

LITERATURE: M. Kershaw, 'On MSS and rare books in the Maidstone Museum', *Archaeologica Cantiana*, 11, 1877, 191 f.; E. G. Millar in *Bulletin de la Soc. Franç. de Repr. de MSS à Peintures*, 8, 1924, 15–31, pls. 2–10 (full description); Millar, I, 30 ff., pl. 41; A. Watson, *The Early Iconography of the Tree of Jesse*, 1934, 99–102, pl. 15; O. E. Saunders, *English Illumination*, pls. 39–40; Wormald, 'Development', 43, pl. 19a; Boase, *English Art*, 165–9, frontispiece, pls. 58, 62; Rickert, *Painting in Britain*, 68, 75, 77–9, pls. 69b, 73; A. Grabar and C. Nordenfalk, *Romanesque Painting*, 1958, 167 f. repr.; Swarzenski, *Monuments*, figs. 300 f.; Dodwell, *Canterbury School*, 48 ff., 81 ff., 92, 123, pls. 24c, 31a, 41b, 48a, 49b, 50–3, 59–61; id., *The Great Lambeth Bible*, 1959; E. Kitzinger, 'Norman Sicily as a source of Byzantine Influence . . .', in *Byzantine Art an European Art, Lectures*, 1966, 136 f.; H. Roosen-Runge, *Farbgebung und Technik Frühmittelalterlicher Buchmalerei*, 1967, I, 111–20, pl. 9; R. Mellinkoff, *The horned Moses in medieval art and thought*, 1970, 63, figs. 51–2; Schiller, *Iconography*, I, 1971, 19, fig. 35; E. Klemm, *Ein Romanischer Miniaturzyklus aus dem Maasgebiet*, 1973, 45, fig. 64.

EXHIBITED: Manchester, 1959, nos. 19–20.

**71. Oxford, Bodleian Library MS Auct. D. 2. 6
(S.C. 3636) Part I**
Calendar
241×155 mm., ff. 1–8
c. 1140. St. Albans Abbey   *Ills. 203, 204*

Historiated KL (Kalendae) initials with occupations of the months and roundels with signs of the Zodiac (February and March missing): January, Janus, feasting (f. 2ᵛ); April, pruning (f. 3); May, falconry (f. 3ᵛ); June, sheep shearing (f. 4); July, man with scythe, mowing (f. 4ᵛ); August, reaping (f. 5); September, vintage (f. 5ᵛ); October, feeding hogs with acorns (f. 6); November, killing hogs (f. 6ᵛ); December, feasting (f. 7).

The Calendar points to St. Albans and the Paschal Table (f. 7ᵛ) indicates that it was written in the lunar cycle 1140–58, possibly in 1149 (E. W. B. Nicholson). Otto Pächt (*St. Albans Psalter*, 158 n. 3) compared the style of the figures with that of the last of the four great Psalter leaves (Victoria and Albert Museum, MS 661, see no. 66) and the unfinished miniatures of the Crucifixion and the Three Marys at the Sepulchre from a St. Albans manuscript in Corpus Christi College, Oxford (no. 72). The latter has points of similarity with the Lambeth Bible, which, like the four Psalter leaves, is probably a Canterbury product, and Pächt suggested that these manuscripts form a link group between St. Albans and Canterbury. Certainly there are similarities, particularly in the treatment of the hair and beards. However, in the Pächt–Alexander Catalogue the Calendar is described as 'early work of the Master of the Lambeth Bible'. This is hardly tenable, considering that the Calendar is probably post-1140 and the Lambeth Bible style was already fully developed by 1146, when its artist illuminated the Liessies Gospels (see under no. 70). And if these manuscripts are nearly contemporary, the stylistic differences are too considerable to warrant this attribution. In particular the Calendar lacks the characteristic drapery treatment of the Lambeth Bible and it also differs in colour.
The occupations of the months, unlike those in the St. Albans Psalter, are not set in roundels, but six of the ten surviving scenes are similar to those in the Psalter. The occupations are fairly typical of the tradition as it had become established in England in the 12th century (see no. 39). Only sheep shearing (June) is unusual. This appears in an Italian example, on a capital in the Museum at Brescia (J. C. Webster, *The Labors of the Months*, 1938, p. 137, no. 37, pl. 23), but is otherwise seldom recorded.

PROVENANCE: Calendar suggests St. Albans (e.g. Invention of St. Alban, Aug. 2, in blue). Probably bound with the Psalter from Winchester (ff. 9–155) *c.* 1200 at which period St. Frideswide was added to both the Calendar and the Litany. Adam Basset of Littlemore (13th century inscription, f. 155); Littlemore Nunnery (15th century inscription f. 1ᵛ). Given to the Bodleian Library by

Richard Beswick, fellow of Exeter College, Oxford, in *c.* 1672.

LITERATURE: E. W. B. Nicholson, *Introduction to some of the oldest MSS in the Bodleian Library*, 1913, lxxx, pl. 48; Boase, *English Art*, 109; *St. Albans Psalter*, 158 n. 3, pl. 157c, *d*; Bodleian Picture Book, *English Rural Life*, 1965, pls. 7a, 10a, 18a.

72. Oxford, Corpus Christi College MS 2*
Two leaves (one bifolium) from a (?)Psalter
347×241 mm.; formerly bound with MS 2, a 13th-century Bible
c. 1140–50. (?)St. Albans Abbey
                                             Ills. 196, 197

Two miniatures, unfinished: the Deposition (f. 1ᵛ), the Marys at the Sepulchre (f. 2).
On the reverse (f. 2ᵛ and part of f. 1) a 13th-century map of Palestine.

Boase has rightly described these miniatures as 'shadowy masterpieces'. They appear to have been left unfinished, with only faint washes of colour applied, and subsequently damaged by rubbing. The 13th-century map of Palestine on the reverse (f. 2ᵛ) extends on to the opposite leaf, showing that the bifolium was used as a single sheet at that date. This indicates that the two miniatures on the other side had already been abandoned when the sheet was re-used for the map. The fact that the map is by Matthew Paris (Vaughan) suggests that the miniatures also originated at St. Albans.
Their style, in so far as this can still be gauged, is related to the Lambeth Bible (no. 70). The elongated figures, the facial types, the treatment of the curls on hair and beards and, to some extent, the drapery folds, are all paralleled in the Bible. The heads in medallions on the frames, a type which originated in Ottonian illumination, also occur in the Lambeth Bible and the Avesnes Leaves. Pächt (*St. Albans Psalter*) compared the figure style with the St. Albans Calendar (Bodleian Library, MS Auct. D. 2. 6; no. 71) and argued that these manuscripts form a link between the St. Albans and Canterbury scriptoria in the mid century.
The iconography of the scenes is similar to that of the St. Albans Psalter, but by no means identical. In the Deposition, Joseph of Arimathea holds Christ's body from the right instead of from behind, as in the Psalter. The St. Albans Psalter follows the Byzantine formula, which became current in the West in the 12th century, of having the Virgin and St. John holding Christ's hands in a gesture of sorrow, but this miniature is most unusual in showing only St. John in this attitude (for a discussion of the iconography of this scene, with bibliography, see *St. Albans Psalter*, 70 f.). The iconography of the Marys at the Sepulchre, on the other hand, is standard and differs from the St. Albans Psalter chiefly in omitting the baldachin.

LITERATURE: Coxe, *Catalogus*, II, 1852, 1; Boase, *English Art*, 178; Dodwell, *Canterbury School*, 56; *St. Albans Psalter*, 158 n., pl. 157e; R. Vaughan, *Matthew Paris*, 1958, 245 f., pl. 17.

EXHIBITED: Manchester 1959, no. 25.

73. Oxford, Bodleian Library MS Auct. F. 2. 13 (S.C. 27603)
Terence, Comedies
282 × 220 mm., ff. iv + 174
Mid 12th century. St. Albans Abbey

Ills. 198–202

One hundred and thirty-nine brown tinted drawings: author portrait (f. 2ᵛ), the others illustrating nearly every scene in the plays (each character is identified by an inscription in red or green ink); Andria (f. 3) 23 drawings (one folio cut out); Eunuchus (f. 35ᵛ) 26 (one folio cut out); Heautontimorumenos (f. 67ᵛ) 22; Adelphi (f. 97) 27; Hecyra (f. 128ᵛ) 19; Phormio (f. 153) 21 (three fols. cut out).

Written in the 2nd century B.C., the Comedies of Terence were enormously popular throughout the Roman period and their continued fame in the Middle Ages is attested by the survival of a considerable number of manuscripts, of which thirteen, dating from the 9th to the 12th centuries, are illustrated. The illustrations of these manuscripts derive from a classical archetype—the precise date of which is not known (Weitzmann, 159)—and they reflect the appearance of actors on the Roman stage, with their masks and characteristically exaggerated gestures and expressions. The Bodleian Terence appears to be a direct copy of one of the Carolingian manuscripts, Paris, Bibl. Nat., lat. 7899, which in turn was probably copied direct from a late classical manuscript, perhaps of the 5th century. Dating from the mid 12th century, it is one of the last products of this tradition. As in the case of the Prudentius manuscripts (see no. 30), the continuous sequence of such classicizing illustrations did not survive the coming of the Gothic style. Classical literature, both in the Latin and in vernacular versions, continued to be popular, but in the illustrations the Roman and Greek characters took on the guise of Gothic knights and ladies. The Bodleian Terence is still recognizably in the classical tradition, but, compared to the sketchy treatment of the figures in the Carolingian manuscript from which it was copied, it is characterized by much more solid, Romanesque forms with firm outlines and stylised drapery folds. Equally, the summary doorways of the Paris manuscript have been changed into elaborate portals typical of 12th-century conventional architectural background. These general characteristics are common to the whole manuscript, but Jones and Morey, analysing the style in detail, distinguished the hands of four different artists:

A. ff. 2ᵛ–17ᵛ: Characterized by figures with thick outlines, fine contours, parallel folds on the chest. Heads are set low on shoulders; the grotesque effect is achieved by the very large mouths and bulging eyes absent in the work of the other artists. This is the only artist to use a ground line.

B. ff. 19–99; 102–42; 161–164ᵛ: Simpler than A. There is more use of the damp fold, less attention to details of ornament.

C. ff. 10, 143ᵛ: More highly stylized folds, but derived from A.

D. ff. 144ᵛ–159: Rougher in execution, with two individual mannerisms: the toes are turned up and the fingernails carefully indicated.

Hand A is by far the most forceful and individual of these artists. As, furthermore, he reserved to himself the illustration of the first two quires of the manuscript, he may reasonably be identified as the head of the group. Morey and Jones connected hands A and B with the early artists of the Winchester Bible and Oakeshott subsequently identified hand A with the Bible's 'Master of the Apocrypha Drawings' (no. 83). In general terms, the fine, linear treatment of the draperies, with parallel folds across the chest, and the emphatic gestures recur in both the Terence and the Bible, and Oakeshott (1950, p. 51) has also compared details, such as the serrated edge at the foot of the garments and the architectural feature, like two ears, at the top of turrets with a trident above (ills. 198–202). The influence of St. Albans on the emergent Winchester School in the mid 12th century is noted elsewhere (nos. 79, 80) and the evidence provided by the products of the St. Albans scriptorium in the first half of the century suggests that the Master of the Apocrypha Drawings came to Winchester from St. Albans rather than the other way round.

PROVENANCE: St. Albans Abbey (13th-century inscription, f. 1); Roger Walle, Canon of Lichfield, d. 1488 (f. iiᵛ).

LITERATURE: Waagen, *Treasures of Art in Great Britain*, III, 1854, 68; L. W. Jones and C. R. Morey, *The Miniatures of the Manuscripts of Terence*, 1931, 68–93, pls. *passim* (all drawings); *New Pal. Soc.*, I, pl. 63; W. Oakeshott, *The Artists of the Winchester Bible*, 1945, 18; *id.*, *The Sequence of English medieval art*, 1950, 19, 24, 51, pl. 53b, c; K. Weitzmann, *Illustrations in roll and codex*, 1947, 159, fig. 153; Bodleian Picture Book, *English Romanesque illumination*, 1951, pl. 8 f.; Boase, *English Art*, 156 f., 165, 177, pl. 63b; Rickert, *Painting in Britain*, 64, 79, 84, pl. 82; W. Oakeshott, *Classical inspiration in medieval art*, 1959, 97 f., pls. 102, 104; Swarzenski, *Monuments*, fig. 297; Pächt and Alexander, III, no. 132, pl. 14.

EXHIBITED: William College, Mass., *Terence Illustrated*, 1955; Manchester, 1959, no. 26; Barcelona, 1961, no. 186; Brussels, 1973, 32, pl. 17.

74. Oxford, Bodleian Library MS Digby 83 (S.C. 1684)

Astronomical treatise (*Opusculum de Ratione Sphaerae*)
203 × 150 mm., ff. 76
Mid 12th century   *Ills. 205–7, 211*

Geometrical diagrams of the world, seasons, elements etc. (ff. 2ᵛ–39)
Forty tinted pen drawings, unframed, of constellations and signs of the Zodiac (ff. 44–67; detailed description in Saxl and Meier, III).

The text of Books I–III, which deals with astronomers (Bk. I) and geography (Bk. II), as well as astronomy, is a compilation containing extracts from Pliny, Isidore of Seville, Bede and Abbo of Fleury. This part of the manuscript differs from MS Bodley 614 (no. 38), but the text of Book IV and all but a few of the astronomical illustrations are identical in the two manuscripts. The illustrations of both manuscripts go back to a model similar to the Anglo-Saxon MS Cotton, Tiberius B. V., which in turn was derived from the Carolingian MS Harley 647 (see under nos. 37 and 38).
To judge from the style of the figures, with their draperies shown in fully developed clinging curvilinear folds, Digby 83 should be dated in the mid 12th century, perhaps a decade or two after Bodley 614. It is the last of the English astronomical cycles to descend from Harley 647 and the last manuscript to contain the texts most in vogue before the large scale penetration into Western Europe of Arabic and Greek science in the 12th century. Indeed, in Books I–III, it already contains the Arabic names of the stations of the moon and the Hebrew and Arabic names of the planets, and Saxl has also pointed out that it is the first medieval Western manuscript to include a reference to astrological theory.

PROVENANCE: Robert Colshill, 15th century (inscription f. iii); Sir Kenelm Digby (1603–65; arms on front cover), presented his library to the Bodleian in 1634.

LITERATURE: L. Thorndike, *A History of Magic and Experimental Science*, I, 1923, 705–7; J. Millàs Vallicrosa, *Assaig d'Historia de les idees fisiques i matemàtiques a la Catalunya medieval*, I, Barcelona, 1931, 259 ff., pl. 20; A. van de Vyver, 'Les plus anciennes traductions latines médiévales de traités d'astronomie et d'astrologie', *Osiris*, I, 1936, 689–91; Saxl and Meier, III, 345 f.; F. Saxl, *Lectures*, 1957, 108 ff., pl. 61; Bodleian Picture Book, *English Romanesque Illumination*, 1951, fig. 11; M. Destombes, *Mappemondes*, Amsterdam 1964, no. 25. 7; M. W. Evans *Medieval Drawings*, 1969, pl. 65; Pächt and Alexander, III, no. 196, pl. 19.

EXHIBITED: Manchester, 1959, no. 24; Brussels, 1973, no. 30, pl. 15.

75. Oxford, Bodleian Library MS Auct. D. 2. 6 (S.C. 3636)

St. Anselm, Prayers and Meditations
241 × 155 mm., ff. 156–200, bound with no. 71
c. 1150   *Ills. 208–10*

Eighteen historiated initials and small miniatures joined to initials:
Opening initial O with St. Anselm; supplicant female figure before Christ (f. 156), Oratio 51 (Prayers to the Virgin), Virgin and Child, female supplicant at her feet (f. 158ᵛ), Oratio 50, S, Virgin standing (f. 160), Oratio 49, S, female supplicant before the Virgin (f. 161), Oratio 52, M with the Virgin (f. 162ᵛ), Prayer to St. John: Herod's feast, beheading of the Baptist, his head on a charger (f. 166ᵛ), Prayer to St. Peter: Christ handing keys to St. Peter, Peter receiving souls in heaven (f. 169), Prayer to St. Paul: the conversion of St. Paul (f. 170ᵛ), Prayer to St. John the Evangelist: Legend of Drusiana, she is carried to her burial and raised from the dead by St. John (f. 176), Prayer to St. Nicholas: St. Nicholas raising the three youths (f. 180ᵛ), Prayer to the monastery's patron saint: a white canon before St. Peter (f. 184), Prayer to St. Augustine: St. Anselm hands his book to Countess Mathilda (above) and to his monks (below) (f. 185ᵛ), Prayer to Mary Magdalen: she annoints Christ's head; Noli me tangere (f. 186ᵛ), Oratio 23, D with Christ and angel (f. 188ᵛ), Meditatio 2, Christ enthroned with a couple before him (f. 189ᵛ), Meditatio 3, Christ blessing a couple (f. 191ᵛ), Oratio 9, O, with a female supplicant before Christ (f. 193ᵛ), Oratio 27, D with a priest celebrating Mass (f. 194).
One decorated initial (f. 196ᵛ).

Using the evidence provided by two other 12th-century Anselm manuscripts (Verdun, Bibl. Mun. MS 70, St. Albans *c.* 1130, with one remaining miniature, no. 31, and Admont, Stiftsbibliothek, MS 289, Salzburg *c.* 1160, with eleven framed drawings), Otto Pächt arrived at the following conclusions:

1. The female supplicant who appears five times in the Bodley manuscript may be identified as Mathilda, Countess of Tuscany. She had asked Anselm for a collection of his Prayers and Meditations which he had sent her from his exile at Lyons in 1104. The Admont manuscript is a copy of Mathilda's exemplar and it contains three dedication miniatures (Pächt, pls. 16*a*, *d*, 17*a*) which parallel those in the Bodley manuscript.
2. On the same analogy, the supplicant couple on ff. 189ᵛ and 191ᵛ may be tentatively identified as Anselm and Mathilda (cf. Admont f. 2ᵛ, Pächt, pl. 17*a*)
3. Although these dedication miniatures are similar in Admont and Bodley, the illustrations to the prayers to the Apostles and Saints do not correspond. For these illustrations, the Bodleian manuscript appears to belong to the tradition of the

Verdun manuscript, whose sole surviving minia-ture—Christ handing the keys to St. Peter (see ill. 77)—is related to the Bodleian illustration. Both Verdun and Bodley belong to the Bec–Canterbury recension of the Prayers and Medita-tions, which contains the same selection but in a slightly different order from the Mathilda re-cension. The Bodleian manuscript thus belongs to the English tradition with the addition of the Mathilda illustrations derived from a Continental source.

Pächt is on more controversial ground when he goes on to argue that the original manuscript sent in 1104 by Anselm to Mathilda in Italy was already illustrated. But if this were the case, it would provide perhaps the earliest English example of a medieval text being illustrated during the author's lifetime.

Stylistically, the facial types, in particular the prevalent profile, descend from the St. Albans Psalter tradition. This provides another link with the Verdun manuscript, which was illustrated by the Master of the St. Albans Psalter. However, the drapery, with its complex damp folds, and the foliage decoration, with the occasional large, luxuriant blossom (especially f. 191ᵛ, Pächt, pl. 17c), belong to the post-Bury Bible period.

PROVENANCE: written for use in a house of White Canons dedicated to St. Peter (illustration f. 184); 13th century, Adam Basset of Littlemore, Oxon (inscription f. 155). Given by Richard Beswick, Fellow of Exeter College, Oxford, 1672.

LITERATURE: A. Wilmart, 'La Tradition des prières de Saint Anselme', *Revue bénédictine*, 26, 1924, 53; O. Pächt, 'The illustrations of St. Anselm's prayers and meditations', *J.W.C.I.*, 19, 1956, 68–83, pls. 15–24; Boase, *English Art*, 107, pl. 50b; Bodleian Library, *English Romanesque illumination*, 1951, pl. 15; id., *Scenes from the Life of Christ*, pl. 12; Pächt and Alexander, III, no. 154, pl. 16.

76. Durham University, Bishop Cosin's Library MS V. III. 1.

Laurence of Durham, Works
241 × 152 mm., ff. ii+107
c. 1150. Durham Cathedral Priory

Ill. 215

Full page, framed author portrait, f. 22ᵛ; four decorated initials: P (f. 23), H (f. 27), E (f. 32), C (f. 42ᵛ).

Laurence was Prior of Durham 1149–54 and this edition of his works was probably produced at about this time. The miniature, like all such author portraits, is derived from the traditional Evangelist portrait, though the manner in which the desk is joined to the chair is highly idiosyncratic. Prior Laurence seems to be writing in a bound book, but,

as G. S. Ivy has pointed out, this is an artistic convention, for there is evidence to show that the scribe usually wrote on separate sheets which were bound after the work was completed.

The initials, which have floral decorations with very large flowers and some gold, are not typical of Durham manuscripts of this period.

PROVENANCE: Durham Cathedral Priory (listed in the catalogues of 1391 and 1416); 1670 given by Nic. Frevyle to George Davenport, Chaplain to Bishop John Cosin (inscription f. ii); given by Davenport to Bishop Cosin's (1660–72) library (now incorporated in the University Library).

LITERATURE: *Catalogues of the Library of Durham Cathedral*, Surtees Society Publications, 7, 1838, 26, 102, 160; Mynors, *Durham*, no. 110; Boase, *English Art*, 287, pl. 53A; G. S. Ivy, in *The English Library before 1700*, ed. F. Wormald and C. E. Wright, 1958, 48, pl. 6B.

77. Madrid, Biblioteca Nacional MS Vit. 23–8

Psalter; Prayers and Meditations of St. Anselm
210 × 144 mm., ff. 1–161
Mid 12th century. (?)Winchester, Cathedral Priory of St. Swithun
Zodiac roundels in Calendar (ff. 2ᵛ–8)

Ills. 216–19

Two miniatures after the Psalter text: two registers of armed, mounted knights in battle inscribed *Arma ferunt plagas nec non simul arma ferentes nec tutela virum se valet ipsa tueri* and *Iam iam rarescunt qua vulnera multa crebrescunt* (f. 81ᵛ); a bishop before St. Peter illustrating the *Oratio episcopi vel abbatis* of St. Anselm (f. 144ᵛ).

Eleven decorated initials: Beatus, Psalm 1 (f. 15), D, Psalm 21 (f. 24ᵛ), D, Psalm 26 (f. 27ᵛ), D, Psalm 38 (f. 35), Q, Psalm 51 (f. 44), D, Psalm 52 (f. 44ᵛ), S, Psalm 68 (f. 52), E, Psalm 80 (f. 61), C, Psalm 97 (f. 69), D, Psalm 101 (f. 72), C, Canticle of Isaiah (f. 101).

The Calendar, which has been published in part by H. Buchthal, and the Litany, indicate a Winchester origin. St. Swithun's appearance in gold capitals throughout suggests the Cathedral Priory, of which he was the titular saint, as the likely home of the manuscript. However, prominence is also given to the translation of St. Judoc (1 Jan. in capitals) whose relics were housed in the New Minster (Hyde Abbey) and the Calendar is similar to that of the late 13th century Hyde Abbey Breviary (J. B. Tol-hurst, *The Monastic Breviary of Hyde Abbey, Winchester*, Bradshaw Society, 71–5, 1932–42, especially vol. 5, 1934). Confirmation of the Win-chester provenance is provided by the decorated initials. The Beatus in particular, with its naked figures enmeshed in foliage spirals, is very similar to Winchester initials of the mid-century: Bodleian Library, MS Auct. D. 2. 4 (no. 81) and MS Auct. D. 2. 6., f. 94ᵛ.

Each Psalm is followed by a collect, a relatively rare practice in England though it occurs in the Eadwine Psalter (no. 68). However, the series of collects in this manuscript is not the one derived from the Mozarabic Breviary which appears in the Eadwine Psalter (James, *Canterbury Psalter*, 3), but it does follow a recognized pattern derived from earlier manuscripts (see Cardinal G. M. Tomasi, *Psalterium cum canticis*, 1735, also contained in his *Liturgia antiqua Hispanica, Gothica*, etc., Rome, 1746, II, 137 ff., where these collects are given in full, as the first of several such series: opening *Effice nos, Domini, tamquam fructuosissimum lignum* . . . after Psalm 1).

The miniature containing battle scenes (f. 81ᵛ) follows the collect to Psalm 108 (109). Neither the inscription (trans.: 'The arms strike wounds as at the same time do those bearing arms; nor does man's defence avail to protect himself', and 'Now they become fewer as their wounds increase in number'), nor the miniature itself have any obvious connection with the Psalm or the collect. The following Psalm is missing and the Psalter text continues after the miniature with Psalm 110 (111). It is conceivable that the miniature is a later interpolation, but this is unlikely, as the figure style is the same as that of the Beatus initial.

St. Anselm's Prayers and Meditations begin on f. 112ᵛ and the dedication miniature on f. 144ᵛ illustrates one of the Prayers. The same composition, again with St. Peter as the Saint addressed, appears in a mid-century Anselm manuscript contained in Bodleian MS Auct. D. 2. 6 (no. 75; Pächt, pl. 15*b*).

PROVENANCE: Cardinal F. X. Zelada (*c.* 1717–1801) in Rome; bequeathed to Toledo Cathedral Library; passed to the Biblioteca Nacional.

LITERATURE: J. Dominguez Bordona, *Manuscritos con Pinturas*, I, 1933, 403 no. 960, fig. 344; O. Pächt, 'The Illustrations of St. Anselm's Prayers and Meditations', *J.W.C.I.*, 19, 1956, 83; H. Buchthal, *Miniature Painting in the Latin Kingdom of Jerusalem*, 1957, 123.

EXHIBITED: Barcelona, 1961, no. 189.

78. London, British Library, MS Cotton, Nero C. IV

Psalter in Latin and French (Winchester Psalter)
320 × 230 mm., ff. 142
c. 1150. Winchester, (?)Cathedral Priory of
St. Swithun   *Ills. 220–4*

Thirty-eight full-page miniatures, damaged and mounted with paper edges, with two or three registers on each page surrounded by inscriptions in Anglo-Norman French: the Expulsion from Paradise; Adam and Eve working; Cain and Abel sacrificing, Cain slaying Abel (f. 2), Noah commanded to build the ark; the ark at sea; Sacrifice of Isaac (f. 3), Moses and burning bush, and reviewing the tablets of the law; God with two kings (? the division of Ecclesiastical and Secular authority, see W. Cahn, 1969) Annunciation to Joachim (f. 4), Jacob wrestling with the angel and Jacob's dream; Joseph and Potiphar's wife, Joseph accused by Potiphar's wife; Joseph sold to the Ishmaelites, and honoured by Potiphar (f. 5), Saul and David; David kills Goliath (f. 6), David takes lamb from lion's jaw; Samuel annoints David (f. 7), Annunciation to Anna; Anna and Joachim at the Golden Gate; Birth of the Virgin; the infant Mary presented in the Temple (f. 8), Tree of Jesse (f. 9), God sending out Gabriel; Annunciation; Visitation; Nativity (f. 10), Annunciation to Shepherds; the Magi before Herod (f. 11), Magi follow the star; Adoration of the Magi (f. 12), the Magi warned; an angel warns Joseph (f. 13), Flight into Egypt; Massacre of the Innocents (f. 14), Presentation in the Temple; Christ among the doctors (f. 15), Christ between his parents; the Baptism (f. 16), Wedding at Cana; water turned into wine (f. 17), the three Temptations (f. 18), Raising of Lazarus; Entry into Jerusalem (f. 19), Last Supper; Christ washing the Disciples' feet (f. 20), Betrayal; Flagellation (f. 21), Crucifixion; Deposition (f. 22), Entombment; Marys at the Sepulchre (f. 23), Harrowing of Hell; Noli me tangere (f. 24), Christ handing the key to St. Peter; Journey to Emmaus (f. 25), Supper at Emmaus; Incredulity of Thomas (f. 26), The Ascension (f. 27).) Pentecost; Christ in Majesty (f. 28), Death of the Virgin (f. 29), Virgin enthroned between two angels (f. 30), the Last Judgment (in nine sections, ff. 31–39).

Calendar with signs of the Zodiac and occupations of the months (ff. 40–5): January, Janus with a key; February, warming; March, sowing; April, flower-bearer; May, hawking; June, mowing; July, reaping; August (damaged); September, pruning trees; October, gathering acorns; November, killing hogs; December, feasting.

Historiated Beatus initial: David writing; David playing viol (f. 46). Two-decorated initials: Psalm 26, D (f. 57ᵛ), Psalm 101, D (f. 98).

This famous manuscript has traditionally been known as the St. Swithun's Psalter, from the evidence of the Calendar and of the prayer addressed to St. Swithun (Warner, 1903). Recently, however, Francis Wormald re-examined the Calendar and concluded that it was not possible to be sure whether the manuscript had been made for Hyde Abbey or St. Swithun's, though St. Swithun's remains the likelier alternative. The inclusion of two Abbots of Cluny in the Calendar (Hugh 20 April, Maiolus 11 May) suggests that the Psalter was commissioned by Henry of Blois, Bishop of Winchester 1129–71, brother of King Stephen and collector and patron of the arts, who had been a monk at Cluny. Yet the Litany is more typical of Abingdon than Winchester (Wormald, 123).

The miniatures are now on the rectos only, but Wormald demonstrated that they were originally on the rectos and versos, so that the pictures faced one another. At some stage, presumably after the manuscript was damaged in the Cotton Library fire in 1731, the leaves were split and the pictures mounted as rectos. From the evidence of the two sets of numeration, Wormald concluded that two folios, probably with Creation illustrations, have been lost. Apart from the damage sustained by them in the fire, the miniatures suffered when the blue background was scraped. Whatever their original appearance, the figures now look like lightly tinted drawings, the faces and parts of the drapery left uncoloured, against a pale blue background. All except two of the miniatures are in the clinging curvilinear drapery convention of the Bury Bible, which is in a less mannered form here than in the Winchester Bible. Characteristic of this manuscript are the recurrent caricatures, particularly in the Passion scenes, which are among the most expressive in the whole of English art. The two miniatures of the Virgin (ff. 29, 30) are in a different style, closely copied from a Byzantine model, perhaps from an icon. These two miniatures would originally haved faced each other to form a diptych. The decoration of the initials and also of the Tree of Jesse is dominated by large, luxuriant flowers of the octopus type, with fine striations and hanging berries. Both the figure style and the decoration indicate a date *c.* 1150.

The iconography shows some links with Winchester manuscripts of the Anglo-Saxon period. Most of the scenes in the David cycle, for example, are paralleled in the 11th-century Winchester Psalter (B.L. Cotton, Tiberius, C. VI). The Presentation of the Virgin, the Entry into Jerusalem, the Holy Women at the Sepulchre and Pentecost—illustrated without the Virgin—are all close to the late 10th-century Benedictional of St. Ethelwold (B.L. Add. 49598; facsimile ed. by G. F. Warner and H. A. Wilson, Roxburghe Club, 1910). The mouth of hell in the Last Judgment is similar to that in the New Minster register (B.L. Stowe 944; Millar, I, pl. 25*b*). However, in the majority of New Testament scenes the Winchester Psalter follows the tradition evolved in England in the first half of the 12th century. The Shaftesbury Psalter (see no. 48) contains the unusual scene of God sending out Gabriel, as well as a similar composition of the Tree of Jesse. The Annunciation with the Virgin holding a book, the Annunciation to the Shepherds, the Baptism and the third Temptation, with a beak-headed devil, are all close to the St. Albans Psalter. Of the Passion and Resurrection cycle, there are seventeen scenes in common with the so-called Bury Gospels (Pembroke College, MS 120), of which the Last Supper, the Crucifixion with three crosses, the Deposition, the Harrowing of Hell, Doubting Thomas and the Ascension are very similar indeed.

PROVENANCE: 13th century Shaftesbury Abbey (additions to Calendar). Sir Robert Cotton Bt. (1571–1631); his library presented to the nation by Sir John Cotton Bt. in 1700; incorporated in the British Museum in 1753.

LITERATURE: Pal. Soc., *Facsimiles*, ser. i, 1873–83, III, pl. 124; E. M. Thompson, *English Illuminated MSS*, 1895, 29–33, pl. 9; G. F. Warner, *Illuminated MSS in the British Museum*, 1903, pl. 12; *id.*, *Reproductions*, . . . III, 1908, pl. 7–9; Millar, I, 84, pl. 44; A. Watson, *The Early Iconography of the Tree of Jesse*, 1934, 103 f., pl. 17; Wormald, 'Development', 41 f., pls. 27–9; Boase, *English Art*, 172, 178 f., pl. 64; Rickert, *Painting in Britain*, 79 f., pls. 80–1; F. Saxl and R. Wittkower, *British Art and the Mediterranean*, 1949, pl. 24; F. Saxl, *English Sculptures of the 12th century*, 1954, 66, figs. 47 f.; A. Grabar and C. Nordenfalk, *Romanesque Painting*, 1956, 114, 192, pl. p. 157; E. B. Garrison, *Studies in Medieval Italian Painting*, III, 1957–8, 201, 204; E. H. Kantorowicz, 'The Baptism of the Apostles', *Dumbarton Oaks Papers*, 9–10, 1956, 235, fig. 37; Swarzenski, *Monuments*, figs. 323–4; G. Zarnecki, 'A Romanesque bronze candlestick and the problem of Belts of Strength', *Oslo, Kunstindustrimuseet Årbok* 1963–4, 54, figs. 15–16; W. Cahn, 'The Tympanum of the Portal of St. Anne at Notre-Dame de Paris,' *J.W.C.I.*, 32, 1969, 64, pl. 10*a*; R. Mellinkoff, *The horned Moses in medieval art and thought*, 1970, 63, fig. 53; F. Wormald, *The Winchester Psalter*, 1973 (all miniatures reproduced).

79. Oxford, Bodleian Library MS Auct. D. 1. 13 (S.C. 2098)
St. Paul, Epistles, with gloss 'Pro altercatione'
298 × 190 mm., ff. vi+154
Mid 12th century. (?)Winchester

Ill. 212

Large historiated opening initial P: St. Paul teaching; St. Paul lowered down the wall, and (below) beheaded (f. 1).

The style of the figures, with their expressive, mask-like faces, is reminiscent of the St. Albans Terence (no. 73) and the Apocrypha drawings of the Winchester Bible (no. 83). The likelihood of a Winchester, rather than a St. Albans, provenance is supported by the scrollwork initials (e.g. ff. 28, 28ᵛ, 83ᵛ) which are generically similar to those in the Winchester Bible but which are not paralleled in the St. Albans Terence. The way in which the structure of the historiated initial is fully exploited for the illustrative purpose also forms a link with the earlier initials of the Winchester Bible. Although body colour is used, the technique is essentially that of a tinted drawing.

The centre of the initial shows his disciples lowering St. Paul down the walls of Damascus in a basket to escape the plot of the Jews against him (Acts 9: 25; 2 Corinthians 11: 33). This is a relatively rare scene, but Erika Dinkler-von Schubert lists a dozen examples of the period up to 1300, half of which are like Auct. D. 1. 13 in showing the Saint lowered frontally and symmetrically. The earliest example occurs in the Carolingian Bible at San Paolo fuori le Mura, Rome, where it is one of the scenes in the frontispiece to the Epistles of St. Paul. A similar composition was used in Byzantine art to illustrate David's flight from Saul (1 Kings, 19: 12) and in the later Middle Ages to show Virgil suspended in a basket by his mistress.

PROVENANCE: Exeter Cathedral (Catalogue of 1506); given by the Dean and Chapter to the Bodleian Library in 1602.

LITERATURE: Bodleian Picture Book, *English Romanesque Illumination*, 1951, pl. 16; Boase, *English Art*, 178 f.; Rickert, *Painting in Britain*, 231 n. 82; E. Dinkler-von Schubert, 'Per murum dimiserunt eum', *Studien zur Buchmalerei und Goldschmiedekunst des Mittelalters. Festschrift K. H. Usener*, 1967, 80; Pächt and Alexander, III, no. 130, pl. 12.

EXHIBITED: Brussels, 1973, no. 33, pl. 18.

80. Oxford, Bodleian Library MS
Auct. D. 2. 15 (S.C. 4096)
Gospels
287 × 187 mm., ff. 86
Mid 12th century. (?)Winchester   *Ill. 214*

Historiated initial Q to Luke: the angel appearing to Zacharias at the altar, Luke 1: 11 (f. 42); decorated initials to the other Gospels: Matthew, L (f. 2), Mark, I (f. 26), John, I (f. 67).

Oakeshott was the first to link this initial with the Master of the Apocrypha drawings in the Winchester Bible (no. 83), attributing it to the assistant responsible for three initials in the Bible (ff. 198, 200ᵛ, 342). These initials he subsequently ascribed to the Master of the Apocrypha drawings himself (*The Sequence of English Medieval Art*, 1950, 51, pl. 56) and this is supported by Pächt and Alexander. It is a reasonably convincing attribution. The fine linear patterning of the drapery is paralleled in the Apocrypha drawings in the Winchester Bible and details of the facial treatment, such as the heavy, pointed hooked eyebrows, recur in the Bodleian Terence (no. 73) which is considered to be by the same hand. With the three initials in the Bible, it shares a predilection for profiles reminiscent of the St. Albans school, a similar technique of highlighting the drapery and the same gestures, but it is much more sophisticated in execution. The foliage on the decorated initials (e.g. f. 2, Pächt and Alexander, pl. 13), with its fleshy stems and thick curling ends, is also paralleled in the Bible (f. 342) and this forms another link with Winchester.

PROVENANCE: William Laud, Archbishop of Canterbury, (?)1635 (inscription, f. 2) who gave it to the Bodleian Library.

LITERATURE: Wormald, 'Development', 47, pl. 22a; W. Oakeshott, *Artists of the Winchester Bible*, 1945, 18; Bodleian Picture Book, *English Romanesque illumination*, 1951, pl. 14; Pächt and Alexander, III, no. 131, pl. 13.

81. Oxford, Bodleian Library MS
Auct. D. 2. 4 (S.C. 2105)
Psalter with gloss
283 × 173 mm., ff. xii+116
Mid 12th century. Winchester   *Ill. 213*

Historiated initial D, Psalm 101, with a bust of Christ (f. 69); three decorated initials: B, Psalm 1 (f. 1), Q, Psalm 51 (f. 34ᵛ), D, Psalm 109 (f. 79ᵛ).

The year 1168 is marked with a dot on one of the calendarial tables (f. xiᵛ). However, this is not necessarily relevant to the date of origin of the manuscript and, indeed, to judge from the decoration, it could be somewhat earlier. The initials appear to be by the principal artist of Vol. I of the 'Auct.' Bible (no. 82) and similar, also, to those in the Winchester Psalter bound with Bodley, MS Auct. D. 2. 6 (ff. 9–155) and to one of the hands of the Winchester Bible (no. 83; e.g. f. 342).

PROVENANCE: Winchester, New Minster (13th-century marginal additions to Calendar ff. ixᵛ, x, e.g. *Gaufridus Coridon dedit . . . hoc Psalterium ecclesie Wintoniensi*, and other obits of Winchester monks). Given to the Bodleian Library by William Harwood, prebendary of Winchester, 1611.

LITERATURE: H. M. Bannister, 'Signs in Kalendarial Tables', *Mélanges offerts à M.E. Chatelain*, 1910, 145; Boase, *English Art*, 179; Pächt and Alexander, III, no. 129, pl. 13.

82. Oxford, Bodleian Library MS
Auct E. inf. 1–2 (S.C. 2426–7)
Bible (2 vols.)
E. inf. 1 Genesis to Job 525 × 360 mm. ff. 315
E. inf. 2 Psalms to end 527 × 362 mm. ff. 318
Mid 12th century and *c*. 1180. Winchester
          Ills. 225–8

One historiated initial for Psalms (Beatus) with David writing and playing the harp (Auct. E inf. 2 f. 2).
Auct. E inf. 1; thirty-seven decorated initials: F (f. 1) D (f. 5) I (f. 6ᵛ) H (f. 31), V (f. 51ᵛ), L (f. 66), V (f. 84), H (f. 85ᵛ), P (f. 104), E (f. 104ᵛ), I (f. 127ᵛ), F (f. 132ᵛ), F (f. 149), S (f. 161ᵛ), E (f. 162ᵛ), C (f. 178ᵛ), V (f. 192ᵛ), I (f. 214), V (f. 214ᵛ), E (f. 241), E (f. 241ᵛ), D (f. 264), A (f. 264ᵛ), V (f. 274ᵛ), V (f. 277ᵛ), V (f. 278ᵛ), V (f. 281), E (f. 281ᵛ), V (f. 282ᵛ), O (f. 284ᵛ), O (f. 285), I (f. 287), I (f. 288), O (f. 291ᵛ), S, H (f. 292ᵛ), V (f. 304.)
Auct. E inf. 2; twenty-two decorated initials: B,

second Beatus initial (f. 2), E (f. 67), P (f. 67ᵛ),
V (f. 77), O (f. 83), M (f. 90), O (f. 90ᵛ), C (f. 122ᵛ),
V (f. 139), C, T (f. 155ᵛ), A (f. 160), E (f. 173), P,
Acts, (f. 198), P (f. 215ᵛ), Q (f. 218), A (f. 220ᵛ),
Gospels, C (f. 261), M (f. 276ᵛ), Q (f. 288ᵛ), I
(f. 306).

The most inventive decoration in this splendidly
decorated manuscript is by the principal artist of
Vol. I whose initials are characterized by thick
foliage coils inhabited by elongated figures and
dragons, and terminating in luxuriant blossoms. A
distinctive feature are the profile heads emerging
from the petals of flowers which end in long curling
spurs. These characteristics recur in a manuscript of
undoubted Winchester provenance, Bodleian Library MS Auct. D. 2. 4 (no. 81) and the scrollwork
initials may be compared with those in a Cassiodorus
still at Winchester Cathedral (MS 4). The naked
figure, shown in profile, clambering in foliage coils is
paralleled in a Winchester Psalter contained in MS
Auct. D. 2. 6 (cf. no. 75) and in certain initials of the
Winchester Bible (e.g. f. 342). As Pächt has pointed
out (*St. Albans Psalter*), the facial characteristics
of this figure are strongly influenced by the profile figures of the St. Albans Psalter and provide
one of several indications of a link between St.
Albans and Winchester in the mid 12th century.
On the other hand, the parallel folds and pleated
skirt of the figure on f. 264ᵛ is not readily paralleled
in English illumination, but may be influenced by
French models (e.g. St. Omer MS 698; J. Porcher,
French Miniatures from illuminated MSS, 1960,
p. 30 f., pl. XXII).
Initials in a different style, but of about the same
period, occur in Vol. I, ff. 214, 214ᵛ; a later type
of initial, with large flowers outlined in fine white
lines and white dots, appears in Vol. I, ff. 161ᵛ,
162ᵛ, and predominates in Vol. II (Auct. E. inf. 2).
This probably belongs to about the same period as
the historiated Beatus initial (E. inf. 2, f. 2), which
shows a strong and apparently direct Byzantine
influence and belongs to the phase of Byzantinizing
naturalism of the last quarter of the century.
Although not by the same hand, the style of the
figures is comparable to that of the Master of the
Morgan Leaf of the Winchester Bible (no. 83).
The Winchester provenance, indicated by stylistic
links with manuscripts of undoubted Winchester
origin, is supported by textual considerations as
well as by the fact that the manuscript belonged,
in the late 16th century, to a canon of Winchester.
Ker (p. 52) has demonstrated that the Winchester
Bible was corrected from the 'Auct.' Bible, and,
furthermore, that the alterations in the text of the
'Auct.' Bible are probably written by the same hand
as three supply leaves in the Winchester Bible (ff. 13,
134, 214).

PROVENANCE: Given to the Bodleian Library by
George Rives, Warden of New College (1599–1613)
and Canon of Winchester in 1601.

LITERATURE: Millar, I, 115; Bodleian Picture

Book, *English Romanesque Illumination*, 1951, pls.
12, 17, 18; Rickert, *Painting in Britain*, 84; Boase,
English Art, 43, 85, 89, 179, pls. 28c, 29, 66a, 76b;
A. Grabar, C. Nordenfalk, *Romanesque Painting*, 1959,
174, 177, fig. p. 175; Ker, *English MSS*, 35, 43, 45,
48, 50–2, pls. 22a, 23b; *St. Albans Psalter*, 168, 170,
pl. 156b, e; Swarzenski, *Monuments*, fig. 271; O.
Pächt, 'The Pre-Carolingian Roots of early Romanesque Art', *Acts of the 20th International Congress
of the History of Art*, I, 1963, pl. xviii–xix; Pächt
and Alexander, III, no. 128, pls. 13–14.

EXHIBITED: Brussels, 1973, no. 34, pl. 19.

83. Winchester, Cathedral Library
Bible (The Winchester Bible)
The original two volumes bound in three volumes
in early 19th century and rebound in four volumes
in 1948:
Vol. I (1) 578×400 mm., ff. 1–128
I (2) 583×396 mm., ff. 129–214
Vol. II (1) 578×396 mm., ff. 215–330
II (2) 583×396 mm., ff. 331–468
c. 1150–*c*. 1180. Winchester, Cathedral Priory of
St. Swithun

Ills. 229–39; Figs. 26, 34, 38

Two full-page drawings in Vol. II:
Frontispiece to Judith, upper register: Achior
before Holofernes; Achior tied to a tree; middle
register: Feast of Holofernes; Judith decapitates
Holofernes; lower register: Judith returns to
Bethulia with Holofernes' head; the Israelites defeat
the Assyrians (f. 331ᵛ);
Frontispiece to 1 Maccabees, upper register:
Antiochus commanding sacrifices; Mattathias slay-
ing the Jew sacrificing at the pagan altar (1: 44–52,
2: 24–5), middle register: battle of Adasa; Nicanor's
head hung up beside Jerusalem (7: 43–7), lower
register: battle of Eleasa; King Demetrius defeats
Judas Maccabeus; burial of Judas Maccabeus (9:
17–19) (f. 350ᵛ).
Fifty-one historiated initials:
Vol. I (1):
Prologue, F, Frater Ambrosius brings letter to St.
Jerome (f. 1), Jerome's letter, D, St. Jerome (f. 3),
Genesis, I, Creation cycle, with the Nativity and
Christ of the Last Judgment (f. 5), Exodus, H,
Egyptian smiting the Hebrew; Moses slaying the
Egyptian (f. 21ᵛ), Leviticus, V, two sons of Aaron
offer unholy fire; fire from the Lord devours them
(Lev. 10. 1) (f. 34ᵛ), Numbers, L, Moses and the
brazen serpent (f. 44), Joshua, E, God's charge
to Joshua: he speaks to his officers (f. 69), 1 Samuel,
F, Elkanah, Hannah and Penninah at table; Hannah
praying below (f. 88), 2 Samuel, F, battle of Mount
Gilboa; Amalekite takes Saul's crown, below the
Amalekite offers Saul's bracelet to David; the
young man slays the Amalekite (f. 99ᵛ), 1 Kings,
E, David's charge to Solomon; David and Abishag
(f. 109), 2 Kings, P, Elijah and the messenger of
Ahaziah; Ascension of Elijah (f. 120ᵛ); Initials of

Deuteronomy (f. 57) and Judges (f. 77ᵛ) have been cut out.

Vol. I (2):

Isaiah, V, calling of Isaiah (f. 131), Jeremiah, V, calling of Jeremiah (f. 148), Lamentations, R, Jeremiah and Christ (f. 169), Baruch, H, reading to King Jechonias; preaching (f. 169), Prologue to Ezekiel, E, Ezekiel taken prisoner (f. 170ᵛ), Ezekiel, E, vision of the tetramorph (f. 172), Daniel, A, Belshazzar's Feast (?) (f. 190), Hosea, V, preaching (f. 198), Joel, V, preaching (f. 200ᵛ), Amos, V, fighting a lion (f. 201ᵛ), Obadiah, V, Obadiah giving bread to the prophets in the cave (1 Kings 18: 4) (f. 203ᵛ; restored to the Bible in 1947), Micah, V, fighting the lion (? decorative) (f. 205), Habakkuk, D, standing (f. 208), Zephaniah, V, disputing (f. 209), Haggai, I, God, Haggai, Zerubbabel in medallions (f. 210), Zechariah, I, medallions with the calling of Zechariah; vision of the man with the measuring line; vision of carpenters and four horns; Joshua reclothed (f. 210ᵛ), Malachi, O, calling of Malachi (f. 213ᵛ).

(Initials on ff. 167, 200, 204ᵛ, 206ᵛ, 207ᵛ cut out.)

Vol. II (1):

Psalms, two Beatus initials: 1. David slays bear and lion, 2. Christ casting out a devil; Harrowing of Hell (f. 218), Psalm 51, Q, 1. Doeg before Saul, 2. Doeg slaying the priests (f. 232), Psalm 101, D, 1. Angel of death slaying the firstborn, 2. Abraham receiving the covenant (f. 246), Psalm 109, O, outline only, 1. Trinity, 2. Christ and David (?) (f. 250), Proverbs, P, Solomon with scribes (f. 260), Ecclesiastes, V, outline, Ecclesiastes the preacher (f. 268), Song of Songs, O, *Sponsus Sponsa*: Christ and Ecclesia (f. 270ᵛ), Wisdom of Solomon, D, Solomon discussing (f. 272ᵛ), Ecclesiasticus, O, outline, Wisdom enthroned (f. 278ᵛ), 2 Chronicles, C, outline, Solomon at altar (f. 303).

Vol. II (2):

Ezra, I, King Cyrus; Zerubbabel and Joshua, Ezra preaching (f. 342), the remaining initials are in outline or outline and gold only: 2 Maccabees, F, fire kindled at altar (f. 363), Jerome's prologue to the Gospels, P, Jerome writing (f. 375), Mark, I, beast-headed Evangelist; Baptism; Temptation (f. 387ᵛ), Luke, Q, Zacharias with angel at the altar (f. 395), John, I, Christ; eagle-headed Evangelist; Virgin and Child (f. 407), James, I, St. James Minor shouting from the roof that Jesus is the son of God (f. 429), Peter, P, Peter enthroned (f. 430ᵛ), Romans, P, Paul disputing (f. 436ᵛ), Titus, P, Paul (f. 458ᵛ).

Sixteen decorated initials: ff. 85ᵛ, 193, 197ᵛ, 204, 209ᵛ, 210, 210ᵛ, 376ᵛ, 434 (2), 435ᵛ, 452, 453ᵛ, 456, 456ᵛ, 459.

The illumination of this great Bible was carried out over a number of years and in the end was never completed, as is testified by the numerous uncoloured initials and blank spaces in Vol. II. Walter Oakeshott (1945) differentiated six main artists, and both his analysis and his nomenclature have been widely accepted:

1. *Master of the Leaping Figures*: an artist working in the clinging curvilinear drapery convention of the Bury Bible and the Winchester Psalter, whose figures are constantly poised for movement. The decoration of the initials with large acanthus leaves and bunches of fruit, as well as details such as the rock-formation in the Elijah scene, are very similar to the Bury Bible. Working in a mid-century style, this is the principal of the earlier artists collaborating on the illumination of the Bible. He was responsible for the design of some forty initials though he only completed seven. Surprisingly, perhaps, considering that he is one of the early artists, his work appears more consistently in Vol. II than in Vol. I. The following initials may be attributed to him: ff. 21ᵛ, 120ᵛ, 148, 232 (2), 268, 270ᵛ, 272ᵛ, 278ᵛ, 303, 363–459 (ten historiated and seven decorated initials, outline only).

2. *Master of the Apocrypha drawings*, who was responsible for the full-page uncoloured drawings to Judith and Maccabees. He has been identified with one of the principal artists of the St. Albans Terence manuscript in the Bodleian Library (see no. 73) and it may be presumed that he came to Winchester from St. Albans. This is also a mid-century style characterized by a more finely linear, less patterned treatment of the drapery.

3. *A more 'primitive' St. Albans artist*, not separately categorized by Oakeshott, whose style was derived ultimately from the St. Albans Psalter: ff. 198, 200ᵛ, 342. The decoration of the initial on f. 342 may be linked with that of other mid-century Winchester manuscripts such as Bodleian Library, Auct. D. 2. 6. Some of the drapery conventions, such as the double hook at the knee and thigh, are derived from the Master of the Apocrypha drawings.

4. *Master of the Morgan Leaf*, who was so named because of his work on the single leaf illustrating the Book of Samuel in the Morgan Library, New York (no. 84). Carefully modelled, bearded faces and a more naturalistic, less patterned, treatment of the drapery show the renewed Byzantine influence of the last third of the 12th century. The backgrounds tend to be gold rather than blue as in the earlier illustrations. Some of the initials are on a framed outer panel, a feature unknown before the 1170s. This is the artist most closely linked with the frescoes from Sigena now in the museum at Barcelona. His initials appear on ff. 169, 170ᵛ, 172, 190, 208, 260.

5. *Amalekite Master*, so called as the author of the initial to 2 Samuel showing the Amalekite taking Saul's crown (f. 99ᵛ, and also ff. 69, 109). This is less satisfactory than Oakeshott's other categories, but it does cover the work of an artist who was probably an assistant of the Master of the Morgan Leaf.

6. *Master of the Genesis initial*, an artist of the same generation as the Master of the Morgan Leaf, whose work is characterized by more violently expressive faces, with bulging eyes and furrowed brows, and fluttering drapery: ff. 1, 3, 5, 34ᵛ, 44, 203ᵛ, 205, 209, 210, 211, 213ᵛ (the last five perhaps by an assistant).

7. *Master of the Gothic Majesty*, (referring to the Trinity initial on f. 250 see also ff. 131, 250). This artist also is akin to the Master of the Morgan Leaf,

but the calm classicism of his figures looks forward to the transition style of the late 12th century.

When the work of the Master of the Leaping Figures on the Winchester Bible came to an end, he left many initials uncoloured. Over twenty of these remained unfinished, but others were painted by the second generation of artists over designs by the Master of the Leaping Figures. Of these, Oakeshott identified the following:
Master of the Morgan Leaf over Master of the Leaping Figures: ff. 88, 201ᵛ, 246 (2), Amalekite Master over Master of the Leaping Figures: ff. 99ᵛ, Master of the Gothic Majesty over Master of the Leaping Figures: f. 218 (2).
There are no secure dates for the Winchester Bible and, although there is general agreement on the stylistic variations, dating has fluctuated considerably. Oakeshott, who originally proposed *c.* 1150 for the Master of the Leaping Figures and up to 1225 for the Master of the Gothic Majesty, now suggests that there may not have been more than a decade between the two. Certainly, the styles of the three earlier hands suggest that the illumination was begun in the 1150s. Equally, the later hands could hardly be earlier than *c.* 1170. These dates are supported by Neil Ker's conclusions concerning the palaeography. The main script is of a mid-century type, while the corrections, which were apparently made from the text of the 'Auct.' Bible in the Bodleian Library (no. 82), and the two supply leaves, one of which contains the Isaiah initial, date from the 1170s (Ker, 35, 51 f.; and quoted by Oakeshott, *Sigena*, 142). A date in the 1170s for the second generation of Winchester Bible artists is inherently likely, for this was the period of renewed Byzantine influence in other centres, such as St. Albans under Abbot Simon (1155–83) (see nos. 90, 91) and London (or wherever the Psalter now in Paris was produced apparently before 1173, see no. 89). The Byzantine figures of the Master of the Morgan Leaf are, as Oakeshott has pointed out (*Sigena*, 98) close to those in the mosaics of the Cappella Palatina, Palermo (1150s). On the other hand, the more dramatic style of the Master of the Genesis initial has been linked by Ernst Kitzinger with what he has called the 'late Comnenian baroque' of the mosaics at Monreale (1183–9). Yet if this were the case, the work on the Winchester Bible would have to be placed *c.* 1190, which hardly fits with the other evidence discussed. However, Kitzinger himself has placed the beginnings of this Byzantine dynamic style in the 1160s (Nerezi, 1164) and if its influence can be traced in the West in the 1170s, there seems little reason to insist that the Master of the Genesis initial is dependent on the mosaics of Monreale. (See also Kitzinger, *Gesta*, IX, 2, 1970, 49 ff.).
A final fragment of evidence concerning the Winchester Bible is provided by a well known passage in the *Magna Vita* of St. Hugh of Lincoln. Hugh became Prior of Henry II's new foundation at Witham in Somerset probably in 1179, and after he had seen to the structure of the building, he asked the king for help with the formation of a library. Henry II had 'heard that the monks of St. Swithun had made a fine and beautifully written Bible, which they intended for reading at meals in the refectory . . .' and he insisted that this Bible should be given to Witham. When they received it, the monks of Witham were delighted: 'The correctness of the text pleased them especially, even more than the delicacy of the penmanship and the general beauty of the manuscript' (*The Life of Hugh of Lincoln*, ed. D. L. Douie and H. Farmer, 1961, I, 85–7). This description fits well with the Winchester Bible, which must have been widely known and which was corrected and accented for reading aloud, though the possibility that it refers to the Auct. Bible in the Bodleian Library (no. 82) cannot be entirely excluded. St. Hugh subsequently discovered from a Winchester monk how the Bible had been obtained and he in turn insisted that it should be returned to its rightful home. Both transactions took place between 1180 and 1186, when Hugh left Witham to become Bishop of Lincoln. If, therefore, this story does refer to the Winchester Bible, it further indicates that the work on the manuscript as we know it to-day was more or less complete by 1180–6.

Although the style of the Winchester Bible is permeated with Byzantine influence, the iconography is largely derived from Western sources. The scenes in the Genesis initial and the Harrowing of Hell in the Beatus initial are modelled on the Winchester Psalter (no. 78). The composition of Moses and the brazen serpent is reminiscent of the four Psalter leaves (Morgan MS 724; no. 66). English Bibles have comparable scenes to those of Elkanah and his wives, the Ascension of Elijah (Rochester Bible), David rending his clothes (Dover and Lambeth Bibles) and to the illustrations to the Song of Songs and Ecclesiasticus (Laud Misc. 752). Other initials are paralleled in Continental and, in particular, French and Mosan Bibles. For example, the Joshua initial, the calling of Jeremiah and the unusual scene of St. James shouting from the roof top (f. 429) are all similar in the great Bible of 1097 from Stavelot (B.L. Add. 28106–7). The Stavelot Bible also contains a Genesis initial with typological scenes, though the choice of scenes differs. The figure of Ecclesiastes the Preacher is very closely paralleled in the Stephen Harding Bible (Dijon 12–15, III, f. 56). For the Vision of Ezekiel, the tetramorph occurs in the Lobbes Bible of 1084 (Tournai Seminary, f. 226) while the position of Ezekiel is very similar in the Bourges Bible (Bourges MS 3, f. 216ᵛ). Other scenes, such as David and Abishag (1 Kings) are very common in Continental Bibles (closest in the 11th-century Arras Bible, Boutémy, *Scriptorium*, 4, 1950, pl. I). Among the Prophet initials, however, there are several that illustrate obscure scenes which do not occur in the initials of Romanesque Bibles. The compositions for Baruch, Obadiah, and Zechariah find a parallel only in the 11th-century Roda Bible (Paris, Bibl. Nat., lat. 6; see Introduction, figs. 34, 39). This link is also to be found in the Prophet scenes of the Lambeth Bible and it is discussed in the introduction (see p. 39). Finally, the Winchester Bible is distinguished by its two full-page drawings of the Apocryphal books of Judith and Maccabees. It is interesting that these form the subject of the last two Old Testament illustrations in the Carolingian Bible at San Paolo fuori le Mura and it is likely that the Master of the Apocrypha Drawings had recourse to full page illustrations of this kind.

PROVENANCE: Probably at St. Swithun's, Winchester, throughout the Middle Ages (perhaps obtained by Henry II for his new foundation at Witham and subsequently returned).

LITERATURE: W. Neuss, *Das Buch Ezechiel...*, 1912, 234, fig. 44; Roger Fry, 'English Illuminated MSS at the B.F.A.C.', *Burlington Magazine*, 13, 1908, 267, pl. I; L. W. Jones and C. R. Morey, *The Miniatures of the Manuscripts of Terence*, 1931, 92 f., fig. 35; Millar, I, 34 f. pls. 45–7; Wormald, 'Development', 45 ff.; W. Oakeshott, *The Artists of the Winchester Bible*, 1945; *id.*, *Sequence of English Medieval Art*, 1950, 18, pl. 27–8; E. Kantorowicz, 'The Quinity of Winchester', *Art Bulletin*, 29, 1947, 73 ff., fig. 10; O. Demus, *Mosaics of Norman Sicily*, 1950, 450 f.; Boase, *English Art*, 175 ff., pls. 61, 63*a*; Rickert, *Painting in Britain*, 80–4, pls. 83–5; Swarzenski, *Monuments*, figs. 304, 308–11; H. J. Dow, 'The Rose Window', *J.W.C.I.*, 20, 1957, 276; E. B. Garrison, *Studies in the History of Mediaeval Italian Painting*, III, 1957–8, 201, 204, 207 f., 210; A. Grabar and C. Nordenfalk, *Romanesque Painting*, 1958, 163, 167 f., 176; W. Oakeshott, *Classical Inspiration in Medieval Art*, 1959, 101 ff.; O. Pächt, 'A cycle of English frescoes in Spain', *Burlington Magazine*, 1961; Ker, *English MSS*, 35, 48, 51 f., pls. 22–3; A. Heimann, 'Jeremiah and his girdle', *J.W.C.I.* 25, 1962, 7 f., pl. 3*c*; E. Kitzinger, 'Norman Sicily as a source of Byzantine influence . . .', *Byzantine Art, an European Art: Lectures*, Athens 1966, 137 f., figs. 108 ff.; O. Demus, *Byzantine Art and the West*, 1970, 154 f., fig. 169; D. H. Turner in *The Year 1200*, II, Metropolitan Museum, New York, 1970, 134 f., W. Oakeshott, *Sigena*, 1972, esp. 80 ff., figs. 138 ff.; *id.*, in *Kunsthistorische Forschungen, Otto Pächt zu seinem 70. Geburtstag*, ed. A. Rosenauer, G. Weber, 1972, 90–8; L. M. Ayres in *Art Bulletin*, 56, 1974, 201.

EXHIBITED: B.F.A.C., *Illuminated MSS*, 1908, no. 106; R.A., *British Primitive Paintings*, 1923 no. 100; R.A., *British Art*, 1934, no. 1079–81; Manchester, 1959, no. 31 (Vol. II. 2).

84. New York, Pierpont Morgan Library MS 619
Single leaf related to the Winchester Bible
575 × 388 mm.
c. 1160–1180. Winchester, Cathedral Priory of St. Swithun

Ills. 240, 241; Colour Plate, p. 9

Recto: Chapter heading to 1 Samuel; painted on right side and lower half: left, Hannah praying in the Temple; Hannah before Eli; right top: Hannah presenting Samuel in the Temple; Samuel before Eli and called by God; Saul meeting Samuel; Saul anointed by Samuel.
Verso, full page: top: Saul with army; David meets and kills Goliath; centre: Saul hurling javelin at David; Samuel anointing David; bottom: Joab kills Absalom caught in the tree; David sorrowing.

Eric Millar was the first to recognize that this leaf is closely linked with the Winchester Bible, and Oakeshott devised the name Master of the Morgan Leaf to describe one of the Bible's principal artists. The chapter headings on the recto begin at precisely the same place in the text as in the Winchester Bible, and in all likelihood this leaf was originally intended as a frontispiece to 1 Samuel, on the lines of the full-page illustrations to Judith and Maccabees. For some reason, this plan must have been subsequently changed and this leaf omitted. Recently, Oakeshott (*Sigena*) has returned to the problem and has concluded that the drawing on both sides of the leaf is by the Master of the Apocrypha Drawings and that the colouring was carried out later by the Master of the Morgan Leaf—in the same way as he coloured earlier initials in the Bible itself. The drawback to this conclusion lies in the fact that the two sides look rather different. In particular, the drapery on the verso is much more naturalistic in treatment, indicating a date c. 1180 or later. Oakeshott recognized this difference and suggested that it is due to the Master of the Morgan Leaf faithfully following the underdrawing on the recto, whereas on the verso the original contours have been completely obliterated.
Like the two Apocrypha drawings, this leaf is, to some extent, iconographically related to the Carolingian Bible at San Paolo fuori le Mura (1 Samuel frontispiece, f. 81ᵛ). The choice of scenes is similar and a few of the individual compositions, such as that of David and Goliath, are quite close. More strikingly, however, the verso of the leaf is related to the David cycle in the early 12th-century Bible of Stephen Harding, Abbot of Cîteaux (Dijon, MS 14, f. 13; C. Oursel, *La Miniature du 12e Siècle à l'Abbaye de Cîteaux*, 1926, pl. 4). All the scenes are paralleled in the Harding Bible and those of Saul hurling the javelin and Absalom's death, with David weeping, have almost identical compositions. This concordance supports Hanns Swarzenski's thesis that a cycle of illustrations to the Book of Kings was available in the West and was drawn upon for the frontispieces of Romanesque Bibles.

PROVENANCE: Bought by J. Pierpont Morgan from L. Olschki in 1912.

LITERATURE: Millar, I, p. 85, pl. 48; W. Oakeshott, *Artists of the Winchester Bible*, 1945, 18 f.; Boase, *English Art*, 177 f.; Rickert, *Painting in Britain*, 82–3, pl. 86; H. Swarzenski, 'A Chalice and the Book of Kings'; *De Artis Opuscula XL. Essays in Honor of Erwin Panofsky*, ed. M. Meiss, 1961, 441; W. Oakeshott, *Sigena*, 1972, 82–90, figs. 144–6, 149; L. M. Ayres in *Art Bulletin*, 56, 1974, 201.

EXHIBITED: Morgan Library, *The Bible*, 1947, no. 28; Metropolitan Museum, New York, *The Year 1200*, 1970, no. 256.

85. Winchester, Cathedral Library MS XIII
Lives of Saints
304×215 mm., ff. 91, of which ff. 50–82 Life of Edward the Confessor
c. 1170. Winchester   *Ills. 250, 251*

Historiated initial C in outline, with King Edward holding scroll and sceptre (f. 51ᵛ); decorated initial M to prologue in outline on pale brown ground (f. 50).

The figure of the king is in the style of the Master of the Morgan Leaf (cf. Oakeshott, *Winchester Bible*, pl. xxviii), but the decoration with its large, hairy acanthus leaves is closer to the Winchester Psalter and the other manuscripts of the mid 12th century.

PROVENANCE: Winchester Cathedral Library, at least since 17th century, probably since the Middle Ages.

86. Cambridge, St. John's College MS H. 6
Bede, Commentary on the Apocalypse
270×178 mm., ff. iii+213
c. 1160–1170. (?)Ramsey Abbey
Ills. 244, 245; Fig. 2

Four full-page, framed, uncoloured pen drawings, preceding the text: author portrait, a bearded Apostle (?St. John) (f. ii); John vested as a bishop with a monk, the scribe, kneeling at his feet (f. iiᵛ), a vaulted building with seven towers, representing the seven churches, and a seven-branch candlestick (*Septem ecclesie*; *septem candelabra*) (f. iii), Christ enthroned, the sword emerging from his mouth (Revelation 1: 16) (f. iiiᵛ).
Decorated opening initial A (f. 2ᵛ).

There is no evidence to show whether this manuscript was actually produced at Ramsey. G. Swarzenski compared the linear treatment of the folds, and the way in which the drapery is drawn across the body, with the enamels on the candlestick in Brunswick Cathedral. The Brunswick candlestick is now generally dated *c.* 1170 (H. Swarzenski, *Monuments*, fig. 46) and the manuscript may also be placed in this period or slightly earlier.
The picture of Christ with the sword proceeding from his mouth is common in Apocalypse illustrations, both in the cycles and in opening initials. The other Apocalypse drawing (f. iii), however, is most unusual. The seven churches are usually shown as separate entities and the *septem candelabra*

of Rev. 1: 20 are, strictly speaking, seven candlesticks which symbolize the seven churches. They are invariably depicted as seven separate candlesticks in illustrated manuscripts of the Apocalypse. In telescoping them into a single seven-branch candlestick, the artist appears to be depicting a type of object actually in contemporary use. Comparable seven-branch candlesticks still exist in Essen and Milan cathedrals (O. Homburger, *Der Trivulzio Kandelaber*, 1949, 16, pl. 1) and in the 11th and 12th centuries they were recorded in Winchester, St. Augustine's Canterbury, Bury St. Edmunds, Westminster, Lincoln, Hereford, York and Durham. They appear to have been introduced under the influence of Jewish ritual (J. Wickham Legg and W. H. St. John Hope, *Inventories of Christ Church, Canterbury*, 1902, 45 ff.; 'The Rites of Durham', *Surtees Society*, 107, 1902, 11, 202).

PROVENANCE: Ramsey Abbey in later Middle Ages (15th or 16th-century inscription, erased, f. 1), William Crashaw (1572–1626) Puritan Divine; *c.* 1615, Henry Wriothesley, Earl of Southampton, presented by his son Thomas in 1635.

LITERATURE: James, *Catalogue*, no. 209; Saunders, *English Illumination*, pl. 46; G. Swarzenski, 'Aus dem Kunstkreis Heinrichs des Löwen', *Staedel Jahrbuch*, 7–8, 1932, 355 f., fig. 299; Charles Oman, 'The Trivulzio Candlestick', *Apollo*, 56, 1952, 54, figs. 4 and 6; Rickert, *Painting in Britain*, 78, pl. 78, M. W. Evans, *Medieval Drawings*, 1969, pl. 50.

EXHIBITED: B.F.A.C., *Illuminated MSS*, 1908, no. 20; Victoria and Albert Museum, *Medieval Art*, 1930; Manchester, 1959, no. 23.

87. Camarillo, California, Doheny Library MS 7
Zacharias Chrysopolitanus, In Unum ex Quatuor
330×225 mm., ff. 179
c. 1170–80. (?) Abbotsbury Abbey, Dorset
Ills. 246–9

Four historiated initials: first preface, D with seated scribe (f. 5), third preface, U (*Unum ex quatuor evangelistarum dictus*) with tetramorph (f. 12ᵛ), Book III, V, Christ with twelve apostles; Peter receives key; Christ stands on lion and dragon (f. 81), Book IV, E, above, Last Supper, below, Christ washing disciples' feet, with part of the Betrayal on the right (f. 130ᵛ). Five pages of decorated Canon tables (ff. 2–5).

Zacharias Chrysopolitanus has been identified with the Zacharias who taught at the school of the Church of S. Jean at Besançon (Chrysopolis) in 1144. This treatise, which attempts to provide a concordance of the four Gospels, is a commentary on Victor of Capua's Latin version of the *Diatessaron* of Tatian (Migne, P.L., 186, col. 11). The Abbotsbury provenance is secure, but as this is the only extant 12th-century book from this abbey, there is no means of knowing whether it was actually produced there.

These drawings are executed in a delicate grisaille technique in brown with shading of the same colour. The figures have naturalistic, flowing robes and expressive, individualized faces. Boase associated the style with the later hands of the Winchester Bible and a comparison can also be made with the drawing in the Winchester *Life of Edward the Confessor* (no. 85, ill. 251), though this is more static. For complexity of draughtsmanship, the scene of Christ with the apostles (ill. 249) is almost comparable with the seated physicians in the Mosan medical manuscript of *c.* 1170 in the British Library (Harley 1585; D. H. Turner, *Romanesque Illuminated Manuscripts in the British Museum*, 1966, pl. 6). The large, hairy octopus flowers are reminiscent of mid-century manuscripts (e.g. Pembroke College MS 16, from Bury St. Edmunds, no. 57), but as the last initial has an outer framing panel, a date after 1170 is likely.

The manner in which the Betrayal is cut off at the edge of this initial suggests that the composition was adapted, not with complete success, from a Passion cycle. The tetramorph on fol. 12, illustrating the unity of the four Gospels, is similar to the one in the Ezekiel initial of the Winchester Bible.

PROVENANCE: 15th century, Benedictine Abbey of Abbotsbury, Dorset (inscription f. 179); 16th century, Geoffrey Bevenew (name scribbled ff. 5, 35ᵛ, 36, 60, etc.); Michel family, Dewlish, Dorset, sold by family of Field Marshal Sir John Michel, Sotheby's, 27 July 1925, lot 201, bt. A. Chester Beatty; Sotheby's, 9 May 1933, lot 43.

LITERATURE: E. G. Millar, *Library of A. Chester Beatty*, I, 1927, 99 ff., no. 28, pls. 75–7; Boase, *English Art*, 178 n. 1.; N. Ker, *Medieval Libraries*, 1964, 1.

88. Oxford, Bodleian Library MS Bodley 494 (S.C. 2108)

Richard of St. Victor, Commentary on the Visions of Ezekiel

245 × 155 mm., ff. 128–67

c. 1160–75   *Ills. 242, 243*

Coloured diagrams ff. 131ᵛ, 132, 133, 135, 136ᵛ, 137ᵛ, 139, 165ᵛ, and four full page coloured architectural drawings representing the Temple of Ezekiel's vision (Ezek. 40–47): elevation of a building, *Representatio porticus quasi a fronte videretur* (f. 155ᵛ), section of a building, *Representatio porticus quasi a latere videratur* (f. 156), ground plan (f. 158ᵛ), section of a building, *Edificium vergens ad aquilorem* . . . (f. 162ᵛ).

The Temple of Ezekiel's vision, which is described at considerable length in the Bible, shares essential features both with Solomon's Temple (1 Kings, 6, 5–9; 2 Chronicles 3: 1–7, 11) and with the second and third Jewish Temples in Jerusalem. It consisted of oblong buildings divided into three rooms flanked by storage chambers and surrounded by courtyards. The Temple of Jerusalem was depicted frequently in medieval art, but in a wide variety of guises, none of which was related to the written description of the actual building. Indeed, as one might expect, artists used conventional representations of buildings current in their time and passed on from generation to generation (C. H. Krinsky, 'Representations of the Temple of Jerusalem before 1500', *J.W.C.I.*, 33, 1970, 1–19; for the later period see W. Herrmann in *Essays in the History of Architecture presented to Rudolph Wittkower*, 1967, 143–58). The same generalization applies to the Temple of Ezekiel's vision, though it was only rarely depicted. There is a splendid example in the Farfa Bible (MS Vat. lat. 5729) a Spanish manuscript of the 11th century; an elaborate structure consisting of a series of conventionalized arcades, gables and turrets arranged in a symmetrical order (W. Neuss, *Das Buch Ezechiel in Theologie und Kunst*, 1912, 224 f., fig. 40).

The illustrations in Bodley 494 contrast sharply with this convention in having the appearance of real architectural drawings; an elevation, two sections and a ground plan. They are much closer to the tradition of diagrammatic plans of monastic buildings, such as that of Christ Church Canterbury, contained in the Eadwine Psalter (no. 68, ill. 181) than to the current stereotypes of the Temple. The reason for this lies in the character and aims of the author of this Commentary. Richard of St. Victor was a Scot who came to the Abbey of St. Victor of Paris during the abbacy of Gilduin (1113–55), studied under Hugh of St. Victor, became prior in 1162, and died there in 1173. His commentaries are characterized by a strong interest in architecture which is expressed in greatest detail in his minute descriptions of Solomon's Temple and the Temple of Ezekiel's vision (B. Smalley, *Study of the Bible in the Middle Ages*, 1964, 106 ff.). These architectural drawings embody an attempt to follow Ezekiel's description—as can be seen from the explanatory inscriptions—and at the same time to interpret the building in terms of contemporary architecture. The drawings have close affinities with sections of actual 12th-century castles (S. Toy, *Castles*, 1939, e.g. Etampes, p. 15), and they may be seen as the nearest approach we have to genuine architectural drawings of the period. An English origin for Bodley 494, suggested by its provenance, is attested by its script (information kindly supplied by R. W. Hunt). It was presumably copied from a near-contemporary French manuscript, possibly the one now in the Bibliothèque Nationale, Paris (lat. 14516, cf. illustrations in Migne, P.L., 196, cols. 527–600).

PROVENANCE: bound up with other manuscripts given to Exeter Cathedral by Hugo, Archdeacon of Taunton, 1219–44 (inscription f. iii); Exeter Cathedral catalogues of 1327 and 1506. Given to the

Bodleian Library by the Dean and Chapter of Exeter in 1602.

LITERATURE: Pächt and Alexander, III, no. 185, pl. 18.

89. Paris, Bibliothèque Nationale, MS lat. 10433
Psalter and Book of Hours
275×175 mm., ff. 249
c. 1170.   *Ills. 252–5*

Full page miniature of the Crucifixion (f. 1ᵛ) not part of the original manuscript, stuck on in the 13th century.
Two full page miniatures: frontispiece to Psalm 1, The Last Judgment, with the Temptation at the bottom (f. 9), Psalm 26, Samuel anointing David, within initial D; below, Daniel and Jesus, son of Sirach, holding scrolls (f. 38).
Two historiated initials: Canticles, C, washing of the feet (f. 193ᵛ), Hours of the Virgin, D, bust of Christ with kneeling supplicant (f. 226).
The opening pages to Psalms 1, 38, 51, 68, 80, and 109 were left blank; in some instances they have been filled in by 17th-century engravings (ff. 56ᵛ, 113).

This is an early example of a Psalter combined with a book of hours (Hours of the Virgin, ff. 226–46). From the prominence given to English saints in the Calendar and Litany, the Abbé Leroquais decided that this was an English manuscript and he was the first to publish it as such (*Livres d'Heures*, 1927). Subsequently (*Psautiers*, 1940) he concluded that the Calendar and Litany were essentially the same as those of a Westminster manuscript (J. W. Legg, *Missale ad usum ecclesie Westmonasteriensis*, Bradshaw Society, 1, 1891, v–xvi) and attributed this Psalter to Westminster also. However, a close examination of the Calendar does not fully support this conclusion. It is true that the Psalter's Calendar contains SS. Mellitus and Erconwald who are particularly relevant to London, but if the Calendar as a whole is compared with those of two undoubted Westminster manuscripts, the Westminster Psalter (B.L. Royal 2. A. XXII) and the Nicholas of Lytlington Missal (Westminster Abbey) the relationship is not sufficiently close to warrant a firm attribution to Westminster. Above all, the Paris manuscript does not contain any references to St. Edward the Confessor who refounded Westminster and who figures so prominently in Calendars of the Abbey (Jan. 5 and Oct. 13; canonized in 1161).
With the exception of the single leaf of the Crucifixion stuck onto f. 1ᵛ in the 13th century, the illumination is all in the same style and of the same period. The style is Byzantinizing, the figures characterized by heavy, greenish facial shading and fierce expressions emphasized by furrowed brows. This dramatic Byzantinism provides a link with the later hands of the Winchester Bible (no. 83), in particular with the 'Master of the Genesis initial'.

However, the draperies in the Paris manuscript are organized into a pattern of ovoid folds, less naturalistic than the Winchester Bible and perhaps, therefore, slightly earlier. The absence of Becket in the original Calendar suggests a date before 1173, but the style of the figures and of the initials, with their panel backgrounds, can hardly be dated before 1170.
The surviving illustrations for Psalms 1 and 26 and the empty spaces at the beginning of Psalms 38, 51, 68, 80, and 109 indicate that this manuscript was intended to be illuminated at all the liturgical divisions of the Psalter. This is, therefore, an early example of what was to become a standard practice. The possibility that the empty pages originally contained opening initials that were stripped off cannot be entirely excluded. Of the extant illuminations, the Anointing of David was already the standard illustration to Psalm 26 (compare, for example, the Glasgow Psalter, no. 95, and see G. Haseloff, *Die Psalterillustration im 13 Jahrhundert*, 1938, tables p. 100 ff.), but the Last Judgment as a frontispiece to Psalm 1 is exceedingly rare. It appears, for example, in the Huntingfield Psalter of *c.* 1200 (Pierpont Morgan Library, M. 16).

PROVENANCE: 14th century, Abbey of S. Pierre-le-Vif, diocese of Sens (Saints added to Calendar); acquired by the Bibliothèque Nationale in 1860.

LITERATURE: L. Delisle, *Le Cabinet des Manuscrits*, II, 1874, 306; V. Leroquais, *Les Livres d'Heures MSS*, I, 1927, 311–14, pl. I; *id.*, *Les Psautiers MSS Latins*, II, 1940–1, 93; Boase, *English Art*, 286, pl. 85a.

90. Cambridge, Trinity Hall MS 2
Ralph of Flavigny (Radulphus Flaviacensis), Commentary on Leviticus
453×283 mm., ff. 182
c. 1167–83. St. Albans Abbey   *Ill. 277*

One historiated initial: V, Bk. I, God and Moses (the inscription on the scroll is a later addition) (f. 3); five decorated initials: C (f. 2), Q, Bk. II (f. 13), S, Bk. III (f. 21ᵛ), P, L, Bk. IV and prologue (f. 30ᵛ).

The figures are characterized by heavy, grey facial shading in the Byzantine manner, soft, naturalistic treatment of the drapery and great solemnity. The initials contain thin foliage spirals on gold ground and are framed by blue or red panels. Those on f. 30ᵛ are made up of large, attenuated dog-like creatures, but the others have foliage decoration only. Similar initials appear in another St. Albans manuscript with the inscription of Abbot Simon, a volume of St. Gregory's homilies at Stonyhurst College. The style of both the figures and the decoration is related to that of two northern French manuscripts: a large Bible of disputed provenance plausibly connected with both St. Bertin and Troyes (Paris, Bibl. Nat., lat. 16743–6, Vols. II and IV), and a Psalter from St. Bertin (St. John's College, Cambridge, C. 18; see Introduction, figs. 16, 17). The close link with northern French art may be explained by the patronage of Abbot Simon who was renowned as a bibliophile and during whose abbacy St. Albans became a centre of artistic production (L. F. R. Williams, *History of the Abbey of St. Alban*, 1917, 79–82; C. C. Oman, 'The Goldsmiths of St. Albans Abbey during the 12th and 13th centuries', *Transactions of the St. Albans and Hertfordshire Architectural & Archaeological Society*, 1932, 221 ff.). The St. Bertin Psalter may be dated before 1173 as it contains no reference to the canonization of Thomas Becket and it is reasonable to propose a date *c.* 1170 for this manuscript also. Certainly it appears to be earlier than a New Testament at St. John's College (MS G. 15), another Abbot Simon book, in which the tiny initials are in a more proto-Gothic style.

PROVENANCE: St. Albans Abbey, made for Abbot Simon, 1167–83 (inscribed with his name f. 1ᵛ); given to Trinity Hall by the Cambridge antiquary Robert Hare in 1603 (inscription f. 1).

LITERATURE: James, *Catalogue*, no. 2; Boase, *English Art*, 182; L. M. Ayres, 'A Tanner MS in the Bodleian Library . . .', *J.W.C.I.*, 32, 1969, 47, pl. 7a.

91. Cambridge, Corpus Christi College MS 48
Bible
315 × 205 mm., ff. 276
c. 1180. St. Albans Abbey   *Ills. 258, 278*

Thirteen historiated initials: Jerome's prologue, St. Jerome as a black monk (f. 7), Genesis, I, full length of page, with eight medallions of the Creation: God the Father; creation of angels, heaven and earth, plants, sun and moon, birds, Eve, (the Creator only appears in the last scene); God giving tablet to Moses (f. 7ᵛ), Job, V, Job with his wife (f. 149), Song of Songs, O, Ecclesia (f. 160ᵛ), Ecclesiasticus, O, Solomon (f. 173), Four Gospels, parallel in 4 columns, 4 initials with Evangelist symbols (f. 205ᵛ), James I with James in profile (f. 243), Peter, P with Peter half length (f. 244), Revelation, A, Christ with sword emerging from his mouth (f. 246ᵛ), Romans, P, with bust of Paul (f. 250ᵛ).
Some seventy decorated initials, mostly small, with foliage scrolls and small flowers characterized by rows of white dots at the outlines. Canon tables under arcades (ff. 200ᵛ–201ᵛ).

For its small script and unusual layout of three columns per page, this book has long been recognized as a sister manuscript of another Bible, Eton College MS 26 (and cf. also a third, Trinity College,

Dublin, MS A. 2. 2) which was commissioned, as we know from an inscription, under Abbot Warin of St. Albans (1083–95). However, the style of the figures and of the decoration is closely related to that of a group of manuscripts apparently written at St. Bertin Abbey, S. Omer, and at St. Albans: the St. Bertin (Troyes) Bible (Paris, Bibl. Nat., lat. 16743–6, Vols. II and IV), the St. Bertin Psalter (St. John's College, Cambridge, C. 18) and the Radulphus Flaviacensis at Trinity Hall (see no. 90 for a discussion of these manuscripts). The type of initial with large, attenuated beasts (ff. 57, 154ᵛ, 263ᵛ) is also paralleled in the Trinity Hall manuscript. The St. Bertin Psalter may be dated before 1173 and the Trinity Hall manuscript was made for Abbot Simon of St. Albans (1167–83). The stylistic connections with these manuscripts would appear to indicate a date *c.* 1180 for the Corpus Christi Bible, in spite of the paleographical links with the manuscripts of Abbot Warin's period (1183–95).
This is a beautifully illuminated book, but it contains little illustrative material. The Creation roundels are, with the exception of the Creation of Eve, copied from an earlier St. Albans Book (B.L. Royal 13. D. 6; no. 32, cf. also the Lambeth Bible, no. 70) and the other historiated initials are mainly of single figures only.

PROVENANCE: St. Albans Abbey; bequeathed to his college by Matthew Parker, Archbishop of Canterbury (1504–75).

LITERATURE: James, *Catalogue*, I, no. 4–8; H. H. Glunz, *History of the Vulgate in England*, 1933, 177 f.; Boase, *English Art*, 182; L. M. Ayres, 'A Tanner MS in the Bodleian Library . . .', *J.W.C.I.*, 32, 1969, 46 f., pl. 6a.

EXHIBITED: New York, Metropolitan Museum, *The Year 1200*, 1970, no. 247.

92. London, British Library MS Royal 10. A. XIII
Commentary on the Rule of St. Benedict ascribed to Smaragdus, Abbot of St. Mihiel (809)
245 × 176 mm., ff. 156
c. 1170. Canterbury, Christ Church

Ill. 256

Full-page miniature of St. Dunstan writing the Rule in a book inscribed above *Scs Dunstanus* (f. 2; now bound separately).

After the flowering of book production at Canterbury in the first half of the 12th century there was a sharp decline, and this is one of the very few illuminated manuscripts produced there in the second half of the century. The gold background, multiple fold drapery decorated with small red circles and heavy, Byzantinising facial shading suggests a date not earlier than c. 1170. On the other hand, the figure still has an essentially Romanesque, hieratic quality and both the posture and the throne—decorated with registers of arcades—are reminiscent of the great portrait of Eadwine (no. 68). The same figure in a more Gothic form appears in a late 12th-century Christ Church manuscript at Corpus Christi College (Dodwell, *Canterbury School*, pl. 68b).

PROVENANCE: Christ Church, Canterbury (14th-century inscription, f. 1; listed in early 14th-century catalogue, see M. R. James, *The Ancient Libraries of Canterbury and Dover*, 1903, p. 31, no. 139). Archbishop Thomas Cranmer, (name on f. 3); John Lord Lumley (d. 1609) whose library was bought by James I; royal library given to the British Museum by George II in 1757.

LITERATURE: J. Strutt, *Dress and habit of the People of England*, new ed., 1842, I, pl. 50; Warner and Gilson, I, 309, pl. 65; Millar, I, 89, pl. 59a; Dodwell, *Canterbury School*, 112, 122, pl. 68a.

93. London, British Library MS Cotton, Claudius B. II

John of Salisbury, Life of St. Thomas Becket; Letters of St. Thomas Becket
328 × 215 mm., ff. 356
c. 1180. Canterbury, Christ Church

Ills. 257, 259

Miniature, half-page, framed: upper register: servant announces the arrival of the four knights to Becket who is seated at table; the knights stand outside the door; lower register: the martyrdom; on the right, the four knights in penitence at Becket's tomb.
One historiated initial: Letters, Bk. III, I, containing three medallions: Becket argues with the knights; the martyrdom; the burial (f. 214ᵛ).
Seven decorated initials: Prologue, S (f. 2), beginning of the Life, P (f. 2ᵛ), introduction to Letters, O (f. 9), Letters Bk. II, Q (f. 142), Letters Bk. IV, A (f. 268), Letters Bk. V, D (f. 300), S (f. 319).
17th-century drawing of Becket on f. 2.

John of Salisbury (c. 1110/20–80), perhaps the most distinguished scholar and political thinker of 12th-century England, was a friend of Becket from the time they worked together in Archbishop Theobald's household in 1154. His Life of Becket is short and his account of the murder, which he witnessed, is a repetition of a letter he wrote in 1171, shortly after the event. Becket's letters, which form the bulk of this manuscript, were collected by Prior Alan, later Abbot of Tewkesbury.
The identification of this manuscript with the *Epistola Sancti Thome Alani Prioris* listed in Eastry's

catalogue was first suggested by M. R. James and it has been accepted as a Christ Church book by Mynors (see Dodwell), Dodwell, and Ker (*Medieval Libraries of Great Britain*, 2nd ed. 1964, p. 356). Dodwell suggested that the small marginal doodles of animals and human heads (esp. frequent from f. 140) were copied from the Eadwine Psalter or Dover Bible (nos. 68–9), thereby providing further support for a Canterbury provenance. The style of the figures in the miniature is similar to that of MS Royal 10. A. XIII of c. 1170–80 (no. 92) and differs from the tiny figures in the initial on f. 214ᵛ. The decoration of the initials consists of tight spirals with tiny white beasts on gold ground, on a blue or purple framing panel, and is typical of the style of the last quarter of the century.

The miniature of Becket's martyrdom is placed before John of Salisbury's letter describing that event (Robertson, VII, 462; Migne, P.L., 199, col. 335). Becket was killed on 29 December 1170. After the archbishop had refused to make any concessions, the four knights took up their swords, followed him to the cathedral and slew him there. He was canonized in 1173; his cult at once became popular in the whole of Europe and his martyrdom illustrated in a variety of media. Among the earliest examples are a Psalter in the British Library (Harley 5102) of c. 1190–1200, a reliquary casket with niello plaques in the Metropolitan Museum, New York (c. 1180), a window of c. 1190 in Sens Cathedral and a seal of Archbishop Hubert Walter, 1193–1205 (see T. Borenius, *St. Thomas Becket in Art*, 1932, pls. 27, 29, 37).
As early as about 1190, the iconography of the martyrdom had become fairly standardized: the knights approach from the left, one of them strikes the archbishop, who is kneeling near the altar, while his crucifer, later identified as Edward Grim, stands on the right. To judge from the style, which places the manuscript in c. 1180, Claudius B. II is one of the earlier representations of this scene and it is certainly the earliest extant occurrence of it in a manuscript. Reginald Fitzurse, the leader of the knights who strikes the fatal blow, is distinguished by his armorial bearings, a bear rampant, as in Harley 5102. The scene of St. Thomas at table, told by a messenger of the knights' arrival, is not uncommon in later cycles (Borenius, pl. X), but the last scene, apparently showing the penance of the four knights, seems to have inspired few followers (cf. Borenius, 106 f.).

PROVENANCE: Christ Church, Canterbury (probably No. 358 in Eastry's catalogue of c. 1300); Sir Robert Cotton, Bt. (1571–1631) his library presented to the nation by his grandson Sir John Cotton, Bt. in 1700, incorporated in the British Museum in 1753.

LITERATURE: J. C. Robertson, *Materials for the History of Thomas Becket*, Rolls Series, II, 1876, 299; V, 1881, xxii; M. R. James, *The Ancient Libraries of Canterbury and Dover*, 1903, 52 no. 358, 525; Dodwell, *Canterbury School*, 112 n.

94. Oxford, Bodleian Library MS Douce 293 (S.C. 21867)

Psalter
260×171 mm., ff. 139
Mid or third quarter 12th century. Northern
England   *Ills. 268, 269*

Sixteen full-page, framed miniatures preceding Psalter text: Annunciation (f. 8), Nativity (f. 8ᵛ), Annunciation to Shepherds (f. 9), Adoration of the Magi (f. 9ᵛ), Flight into Egypt (f. 10), Presentation in the Temple (f. 10ᵛ), Last Supper and Christ washing the Disciples' feet (f. 11), the Betrayal (f. 11ᵛ), Christ crowned with thorns (f. 12), the Flagellation (f. 12ᵛ), the Crucifixion (f. 13), the Entombment (f. 13ᵛ), Harrowing of Hell (f. 14), the Marys at the Sepulchre (f. 14ᵛ), Virgin and Child enthroned (f. 15), Christ enthroned, with Evangelist symbols (f. 15ᵛ).
Three historiated initials: Psalm 26, D, with David (f. 33), Psalm 97, C, with Annunciation to the Shepherds (f. 87ᵛ), Psalm 109, D, with God and Christ seated, their feat on their enemy below (f. 100ᵛ).
Eight decorated initials: Beatus, full-page (f. 16), Psalm 22, D (f. 29), Psalm 38, D (f. 44), Psalm 51, Q (f. 54), Psalm 52, D (f. 54ᵛ), Psalm 68, S (f. 65), Psalm 80, E (f. 78), Psalm 114, D (f. 103).

An origin in northern England is indicated by the preponderance of northern saints in the Calendar (ff. 1ᵛ–7): Wilfrid, Oswald, Paulinus and Kentigern are included, while Cuthbert is commemorated twice. There are several Northern French and Flemish saints in the Calendar, which may indicate a link with a Continental model. The absence of Thomas Becket suggests a date before his canonization in 1173.
The style is strikingly primitive: lively, but utterly lacking in the usual sophistication of Romanesque art. Enormous goggle eyes dominate the faces, while the figures are flat, with simple pleats or chevron folds on the drapery. The appearance of liveliness is accentuated by unusually bright colours, with a preponderance of orange and red. The use of horizontal painted bands for the backgrounds (e.g. f. 9) suggests that the artist may have used a Continental model of the 11th century. If this was the case, it might, to some extent, explain the stylized faces and two-dimensional patterned drapery. It is not possible to find close parallels for the figure style in 12th-century England, but the decoration fits with mid-century usage.
The miniature cycle is related to two other northern Psalters, those in Copenhagen (no. 96) and in the Bodleian Library (MS Gough Liturg. 2; no. 97), but it differs considerably in detail. An analysis of the iconography will be included in the forthcoming study of this manuscript by Elizabeth Temple. There are historiated initials at three out of the eight liturgical divisions. The illustration to Psalm 109–God and Christ triumphant—follows the pattern of the Shaftesbury Psalter (no. 48). For Psalm 97 this is the earliest example of the Annunciation to the Shepherds, which was to become the usual type in the 13th century. It refers to the opening words of the Psalm: *Cantate domino novum quia mirabilia fecit*: the greatest wonder referred to being the Nativity of Christ which is announced in this scene.

PROVENANCE: Francis Douce (1757–1834), antiquarian, Keeper of manuscripts at the British Museum.

LITERATURE: C. Nordenfalk, 'Insulare und Kontinentale Psalterillustrationen aus dem 12. Jahrhundert', *Acta Archaeologica*, 10, 1939, 116; Boase, *English Art*, 245, pl. 79b; Bodleian Picture Books, *English Romanesque Illumination*, 1951, pl. 24, *Scenes from the Life of Christ*, 1951, pls. 7, 14; Pächt and Alexander, III, no. 168, pl. 17.

EXHIBITED: Bodleian Library, *Latin Liturgical MSS*, 1952, no. 44.

95. Glasgow University Library MS Hunter U. 3. 2

Psalter
290×184 mm., ff. 210
c. 1170. Northern England (? diocese of York)
                                           Ills. 260–7

Calendar with occupations of the months and signs of the Zodiac (ff. 1–6ᵛ): January, fasting; February, warming; March, digging; April, man and women; May, hawking; June, pruning; July, mowing; August, reaping; September, vintage—picking grapes; October, vintage—treading grapes; November, gathering acorns for hogs; December, killing hogs.
Thirteen full-page framed miniatures, of which eight have two registers. These are on facing pages, each pair followed by two blank pages: Creation of Adam; The Temptation (f. 7ᵛ), Expulsion from Paradise; Adam digging, Eve spinning (f. 8), Angel instructing Abraham to sacrifice his son; sacrifice of Isaac (f. 9ᵛ) (faces a blank page), Temptation of Christ, raising of Lazarus (f. 11ᵛ), Supper at Emmaus; Christ showing wounds to Apostles (f. 12); doubting Thomas; Christ walking on the waters (f. 13ᵛ), Ascension (f. 14), Pentecost (f. 15ᵛ), Christ in majesty (f. 16), Virgin receives palm from angel; Virgin hands palm to Apostles (f. 17ᵛ), death of the Virgin; Apostles carry her sarcophagus (f. 18), Burial of the Virgin; angels carry her to heaven (f. 19ᵛ) (faces a blank page), David and his musicians (f. 21ᵛ).
Full-page, splendidly decorated Beatus initial with angels in medallions at corners of the frame.
Ten historiated initials: Psalm 26, D, Samuel anointing and crowning David (f. 46), Psalm 35, I, a mailed crusader, holding a shield (f. 54), Psalm 51, Q, Doeg whispering to Saul and pointing to David (f. 75), Psalm 65, I, the Church triumphant (f. 86ᵛ), Psalm 66, D, Christ nimbed (f. 87ᵛ),

Psalm 71, D, woman suckling two tonsured men (? Mother Church) (f. 94), Psalm 81, D, bust of Christ (f. 109), Psalm 82, D, bust of Christ holding orb and book (f. 109ᵛ), Psalm 90, Q, Christ trampling on lion and dragon (f. 119ᵛ), Psalm 99, I, David pointing up to Christ (f. 127).

Six large decorated initials at the remaining liturgical divisions: Psalm 38, D (f. 61ᵛ), Psalm 52, D (f. 75ᵛ), (Psalm 68 cut out), Psalm 80, E, (f. 108), Psalm 97, C (f. 125ᵛ), Psalm 101, D (f. 128), Psalm 109, D (f. 145).

About one hundred and fifty decorated initials to the remaining Psalms and to the prayers at the end.

An origin in northern England is indicated by the inclusion of several northern saints (Cuthbert and his translation, Wilfrid, John of Beverley, Oswald) in the Calendar and Litany, which are similar to those of the Copenhagen Psalter (no. 96). Most of these are national saints, but John of Beverley (Archbishop of York, d. 721) occurs rarely outside northern manuscripts and the appearance of Paulinus (Bishop of York, d. 644) in the Litany (though not in the Calendar) further supports the arguments for a northern origin. York is certainly a reasonable attribution, but the evidence does not permit a firm conclusion (cf. the Calendar in the York Breviary, *Publications of the Surtees Society*, 71 and 75, 1880–3). The fact that there is no entry in the Calendar for Thomas Becket suggests a date before his canonization in 1173.

The style of the figures represents a more rigid and stylized version of the mid-century damp fold convention. Elongated and stiff with long faces and staring eyes, these figures are silhouetted against a tooled gold background. Compared to the figures in, for example, the Bury Bible and the Winchester Bible, they are somewhat lacking in sophistication, and yet they are immensely expressive. Most of the miniatures and historiated initials are probably by the same artist (though the David miniature may be by another hand) who was also responsible for some of the initials in the Copenhagen Psalter. Like the style of the figures, the floral decoration belongs to the mid-century type, with thick stems, large blossoms and inhabited scrolls. There is as yet no sign of the later initials, with fine spirals and tiny white beasts, which came into prominence in the 1170s and which appear in the Copenhagen Psalter. From a study of the script, Boase suggested a date in the 1160s and this is confirmed by the style of the initials.

The cycle of full-page miniatures differs from that of the Copenhagen Psalter with which this manuscript is related in so many ways. In particular, the lack of any scenes between the Raising of Lazarus and the Supper at Emmaus is strange. But as fols. 11–12, which contain these scenes, form a quire of only two leaves, whereas all the others consist of four, it is possible that two leaves illustrating the Passion are missing. Iconographically, the Old Testament illustrations are fairly standard, though the scene of the angel instructing Abraham to sacrifice his son is unusual. Isaac naked on the

altar is an Early Christian motif which was revived in the 11th and 12th centuries (St. Sever Apocalypse, Paris, Bibl. Nat., lat. 8878; Fulda Sacramentary, Göttingen, Univ. Libr. MS 231; capital, Autun Cathedral). But the principal novelty of the cycle lies in the six scenes at the end dealing with the death and assumption of the Virgin. This has been examined by Boase who connected it with the writings of Honorius Augustodunensis and, in particular, of Elisabeth of Schönau (1129–64) who specifically relates her vision of how Mary was carried to heaven in body and spirit by a multitude of angels (cf. f. 19ᵛ with the standard representation of the death of the Virgin, derived from Byzantine art, e.g. in the Winchester Psalter).

Historiated initials occur at two of the major divisions: Psalm 26, Samuel anointing David, and Psalm 51, Doeg and Saul. These illustrations appear also in the Copenhagen Psalter and ultimately became standard for these Psalms. Yet this system of Psalter illustration (see Introduction, p. 16) was still in its infancy and most of the historiated initials have no connection with the liturgical divisions. Some of them are related to the text. For example, the armed knight at Psalm 34 is relevant to 'Disarm the enemies who rise in arms against me; grip thy weapons and thy shield', and Psalm 90, depicting Christ treading on a dragon and a serpent, illustrate the verse: 'Thou shalt tread safely on asp and adder', but some of the other scenes are less clearly appropriate to the Psalter text.

PROVENANCE: Dr. William Hunter (1718–83) left his museum to Glasgow University; it was moved from London to Glasgow in 1807.

LITERATURE: J. Young and P. H. Aitken, *Catalogue of Manuscripts in the Hunterian Museum, University of Glasgow*, 1908, no. 229; *New Pal. Soc.*, I, pls. 189–91; Millar, I, 41 f., pl. 60 f.; G. Haseloff, *Die Psalterillustration im 13 Jahrhundert*, 1938, 8 ff.; Boeckler, *Abendländische Miniaturen*, 92, pl. 89; Wormald, 'Development', 44; Boase, *English Art*, 241–3, pls. 31c, 55b, 80; Rickert, *Painting in Britain*, 86, pl. 89; T. S. R. Boase, *The York Psalter*, 1962; Schiller, *Iconography*, III (German ed.), 111, figs. 353, 375.

EXHIBITED: B.F.A.C., *Illuminated MSS*, 1908, no. 31; R.A., *British Primitive Painting*, 1923, no. 101; V & A, *English Medieval Art*, 1930, no. 34; R.A., *British Art*, 1934, no. 1083; B.F.A.C., *British Medieval Art*, 1939, no. 153; Manchester, 1959, no. 36. Brussels, Bibliothèque royale, *Trésors des Bibliothèques d'Écosse*, 1963, no. 6, pls. I, 2–3; Brussels, 1973, no. 35, pl. 20.

96. Copenhagen, Royal Library MS Thott 143 2°

Psalter
286 × 198 mm., ff. 199
c. 1170. Northern England

Ills. 272–6; Colour Frontispiece

Sixteen full-page, framed miniatures preceding Psalter text: Annunciation (f. 8), Visitation (f. 8ᵛ), Annunciation to Shepherds (f. 9), Nativity (f. 9ᵛ), Magi before Herod (f. 10), Magi follow the star (f. 10ᵛ), Adoration of the Magi (f. 11), Massacre of Innocents (f. 11ᵛ), Flight into Egypt (f. 12), Presentation in the Temple (f. 12ᵛ), Baptism (f. 13), Entry into Jerusalem (f. 13ᵛ), Betrayal (f. 14), Crucifixion (f. 14ᵛ), Marys at the Sepulchre (f. 15), Christ in Majesty with Evangelist symbols (f. 15ᵛ).

Some fifteen historiated initials, including: Psalm 5, U, man in *orans* gesture (f. 19), Psalm 26, D, Samuel anointing David (f. 40), Psalm 50, M, David and Bathsheba admonished by Nathan; defenders of the town stone Uriah (f. 68), Psalm 51, Q, Doeg whispers to Saul that David is sheltering with Ahimelech; Doeg kills Ahimelech's family (f. 69ᵛ), Psalm 56, M, King in *orans* gesture (f. 74), Psalm 70, I, man with scroll (f. 88), Psalm 81, D, Christ preaching (f. 104), Psalm 85, I, man appealing to Christ (f. 107ᵛ), Psalm 87, D, Christ admonishing man (f. 109), Psalm 90, Q, Christ standing on dragon and monster (f. 114ᵛ), Psalm 91, Christ; two musicians below (f. 115ᵛ), Psalm 137, C, King holding scroll (f. 163); Canticles: C, with Isaiah (f. 174), D, with Habakkuk (f. 178).

The manuscript contains altogether one hundred and sixty-six initials. Apart from those listed above, and the large Beatus initial (f. 17), Mackeprang interprets several others as having illustrative content (see below): Psalm 16, E (f. 28), Psalm 42, I (f. 60ᵛ), Psalm 47, M (f. 64ᵛ), Psalm 55, M (f. 73), Psalm 59, D (f. 77), Psalm 67, E (f. 83), Psalm 69, D (f. 87ᵛ), Psalm 72, Q (f. 91), Psalm 77, A (f. 96ᵛ), Psalm 78, D (f. 100ᵛ), Psalm 80, E (f. 103ᵛ), Psalm 88, M (f. 110), Psalm 93, D (f. 116ᵛ), Psalm 101, D (f. 123), Psalm 103, B (f. 126), Psalm 107, D (f. 135), Psalm 111, B (f. 138ᵛ), Psalm 123, N (f. 155), Psalm 138, D (f. 163ᵛ), Psalm 148, L (f. 172).

The Calendar and Litany indicate an origin in an Augustine house in the North of England. St. Augustine is commemorated three times in the Calendar (feast, 28 Aug.; octave, 4 Sept.; translation, 11 Oct.) and northern saints predominate in both Calendar and Litany. Of these, Cuthbert and Oswald are national saints who appear in most calendars throughout the country; Wilfrid occurs less frequently and John of Beverley relatively rarely. The same saints appear in the Litany, with the addition of Paulinus, first Archbishop of York. The absence of Northumbrian saints, such as Benedict Biscop, Bede, Carilef, Boisilus, and Aidan, would appear to rule out Durham. The Calendar and Litany are very similar to those of the Glasgow Psalter (no. 95) and this, together with the stylistic links between the two manuscripts, raises the possibility that they were written in the same scriptorium. The absence of Thomas Becket from the Calendar suggests a date before 1173; but, as Boase pointed out, in a northern Augustine house this cannot be considered conclusive proof.

Two hands have been differentiated in the minia-tures (Mackeprang). Those on ff. 8, 8ᵛ, 9ᵛ, 10, 10ᵛ, 11, 12ᵛ, 13, 13ᵛ, 15ᵛ are by the main artist; the remainder are wholly or in part by an assistant, whose work may be readily recognized by his thick, crude outlines. The main artist is one of the great masters of the English 12th century. In the figures, the emphasis is on curves formed by the contours and by the softly indicated pear-shaped damp folds, and accentuated by arabesques in white or light tones. This form of surface decoration on draperies, which had been a recurrent feature in English illumination since the 1130s, when it appeared in the Bury Bible (no. 56), reached its apogee in the Copenhagen Psalter. The backgrounds are gold with panels of blue, red, or pink. The figures retain a Romanesque solidity and the draperies are still defined by damp fold abstractions, but there is a neatness and grace in some of the figures which presages the Gothic style.

The miniatures form a cohesive group of essentially one style in spite of the collaboration of two artists, but the initials present a wider variety of styles. Mackeprang, following Bruun, distinguished four different hands: I, initials to Psalms 1–54 (ff. 17–71ᵛ), II, Psalms 55–96 (ff. 73–119ᵛ), III, Psalms 97–117 (ff. 120ᵛ–42ᵛ) IV, Psalms 118–50 and Canticles (ff. 144–90). These fall into two main groups. Hands I and II are characterized by fleshy foliage decoration and acanthus leaves on a blue background, with a predominance of large luxuriant flowers, typical of the decoration current in the middle and third quarter of the century. In contrast, hands III and IV have fine spiral stems with small leaves stippled with white dots on gold ground, the whole initial placed on a framing panel of blue or red. The animal world is represented by small white lions, larger animals reminiscent of late 12th-century Bestiaries, and elongated creatures extending the length of initial shafts. These are typical of post-1170 initials and they belong to a distinctly later stylistic phase than hands I and II. As the earlier hands worked on the first half of the manuscript it may well be that the illumination was begun by c. 1170 and was then completed by two younger artists in the course of the 1170s. Most of the large historiated initials are the work of hand I and it is this artist who is closest to the style of the Glasgow Psalter (no. 95). A comparison can be made between the Beatus initials of the two manuscripts and the figure style of the Saul and Doeg initial (f. 69ᵛ), which reflects the long faces, staring eyes, and deep greenish facial shading of the Glasgow Psalter. The figures in some of the later historiated initials (ff. 163, 174, 178; ills. 275–6), resemble those of the St. Albans manuscripts of Abbot Simon's period and the related St. Bertin manuscripts (see no. 90 and Introduction, figs. 16, 17).

The iconography of the full-page miniatures is almost identical with the somewhat later northern Psalter in the Bodleian Library (Gough Liturg. 2; no. 97). The latter has a longer cycle, twenty-two miniatures as against the sixteen in this manuscript, and this may indicate that the two were based on a larger cycle available in the North in the second half of the century. Very rarely does the Copenhagen Psalter diverge from the iconography of the Gough Psalter, the most striking instance being the angel with the jewelled cross in the Entry into Jerusalem. J. J. G. Alexander has shown that this is derived from a composition of the Return of the Holy Cross, such as the one in the 11th-century sacramentary from Mont-Saint-Michel (New York, Morgan Library, M. 641). The jewelled candelabra, looking like crowns, which occur in several miniatures (ff. 9ᵛ, 12ᵛ) are also unusual. These northern Psalters with their large cycles of full-page prefatory miniatures, belong ultimately to the tradition of the St. Albans Psalter, with which they share a similar selection of scenes, but the compositions differ in detail. Of the 12th-century English cycles, there are more links with the Winchester Psalter, in which, for example, the Annunciation (with the Virgin standing) and the Marys at the Sepulchre are very similar indeed.

The iconography of the principal initials (Psalms 26, 51, 81, 90) follows the same pattern as that of the Glasgow Psalter. Some of these illustrations, for example Samuel and David (Psalm 26) and Doeg and Ahimelech (Psalm 51), were to become standard at these liturgical divisions. However, this Psalter also contains historiated initials other than those at the liturgical divisions, for this method of illustration was not yet as standardized as it was to become in the following century. Mackeprang, indeed, interpreted some 35 initials as having illustrative content, usually referring to a particular line of the text, as in the St. Albans Psalter. For Psalm 57 (f. 75) the initial shows a lion devouring a man, which Mackeprang connected with v. 7: *molas leonem confunget Dominum*. This is a possible identification, but in other cases such interpretations are perhaps carried too far. Psalm 55 (f. 73), for example, shows a nude, clambering man surrounded by dragons and beasts, which Mackeprang interpreted as an illustration to the line *Miserere mei Deus*, but for which the intention was, more probably, purely decorative.

PROVENANCE: Augustine house in the north of England (Calendar and Litany, see above), early 13th century, Sweden, Convent associated with 'Birger Jarl'—probably Birger Jarl Brosa of the Folkungar stock, d. 1202—(dedication prayer, f. 16ᵛ); later 13th century, (?) Eric, duke of Sleswig (d. 1272), son of King Abel of Denmark and Queen Mechtilde (obit added in Calendar). 18th century, Count Otto Thott; 1786, Royal Library, Copenhagen.

LITERATURE: Ch. Bruun, *Aarsberetninger og Meddelelster fra det store kongelige Bibliothek*, III, 1876, 40; J. Strzygowski, *Ikonographie der Taufe Christi*, 1885, 52; M. Mackeprang, V. Madsen, C. S. Petersen, *Greek and Latin manuscripts in Danish collections*, 1921, 32 ff., pls. 48–60; G. Haseloff, *Die Psalterillustration im 13. Jahrhundert*, 1938, 8 ff., 100; H. Swarzenski, *The Berthold Missal*, 1943, 44 ff., fig. 46; Boase, *English Art*, 243 f., 279,

pls. 56b, 81, 86; Rickert, *Painting in Britain*, 86; Swarzenski, *Monuments*, figs. 316, 508; T. S. R. Boase, *The York Psalter*, 1962; J. J. G. Alexander, *Norman illumination at Mont St. Michel 966–1100*, 1970, 159, n. 1.

EXHIBITED: Brussels, 1973, no. 36, pl. 21.

97. Oxford, Bodleian Library MS Gough Liturg. 2 (S.C. 18343)
Psalter
260 × 184 mm., ff. 153
Late 12th century. Northern England

Ills. 270, 271

Twenty-two full-page, framed miniatures preceding Psalter text; each miniature faces a prayer on the opposite page: Annunciation (f. 11), Visitation (f. 12), Nativity (f. 13), Annunciation to the Shepherds (f. 14), Adoration of the Magi (f. 15), Presentation in the Temple (f. 16), Flight into Egypt (f. 17), The Magi before Herod (f. 18), Massacre of the Innocents (f. 19), Wedding at Cana (f. 20), The Baptism (f. 21), First Temptation (f. 22), Second Temptation (f. 23), Third Temptation (f. 24), Last Supper (f. 25), The Betrayal (f. 26), The Flagellation (f. 27), The Crucifixion (f. 28), The Marys at the Sepulchre (f. 29), The Ascension (f. 30), Pentecost (f. 31), David and choir (f. 32).

The miniatures on ff. 16, 19, 22–6, 31–2 are much rubbed.

Six historiated initials: Beatus, almost full-page, decorated with foliage spirals; prophets with scrolls at corners of frame (f. 33ᵛ); Psalm 26, D, with David (f. 50), Psalm 51, Q, David and the devil (f. 71ᵛ), Psalm 52, D, mounted knight (f. 72), Psalm 68, S, two men in a boat, ? Jonah (f. 82), Psalm 109 D, David enthroned (f. 120).

Each Psalm has a small decorated initial; larger decorated initials at the remaining liturgical divisions: Psalm 38, D (f. 61ᵛ), Psalm 80, E (f. 95), Psalm 97, C (f. 107).

The Calendar (formerly ff. 1–9) is missing, but the Litany has been taken as evidence of a northern provenance. It contains Oswald, Cuthbert, Wilfrid and Hilda, not in itself sufficient evidence were not the northern provenance supported by stylistic and iconographical considerations.

The execution is crude, in particular the thick contours and outlines make for a heavy and at times rustic appearance. Yet the style is clearly in the late 12th-century Byzantinising tradition, with heavy ochre facial shading, and drapery showing the transition from Romanesque panel folds to the more naturalistic multi-folds of the earlier Gothic period. The faces, and in particular the profiles, are reminiscent of the Puiset Bible at Durham (no. 98), but the drapery suggests a slightly later date, though not necessarily as late as the sculptures in the museum at York (c. 1200) with which these miniatures have been compared. The decoration of the initials, consisting of thin spirals on gold ground with a blue framing panel also indicates a late 12th-century date.

The Life of Christ cycle is very closely dependent on that of the Copenhagen Psalter (no. 96), another northern manuscript. These two manuscripts have thirteen scenes in common and these are all but identical in composition. However, the Gough manuscript cycle is considerably longer than that of the Copenhagen Psalter, which would indicate a common model rather than a case of direct copying. The simplified compositions of another northern Psalter, MS Douce 293 (no. 94), are also, to some extent, related to this group.

Most of the historiated initials are placed at the liturgical divisions of the Psalter, but they do not follow the standard types. David reappears several times: at Psalm 51, he is grasped by a devil, a scene which occurs elsewhere for Psalm 38 (see G. Hase-loff, *Die Psalterillustration*, 1938, 104). The two men in a boat at Psalm 68 might refer to Jonah or be intended as a more general illustration to the plea *salvum me fac*.

PROVENANCE: John Blyth, 15th century (inscription f. 33ᵛ; bequeathed to the Bodleian Library by Richard Gough (1735–1809) author of *British Topography*, etc.

LITERATURE: Boase, *English Art*, 244, pl. 79a: Bodleian Picture Book, *English Romanesque Illumination*, 1951, pl. 23; *Scenes from the Life of Christ*, 1951, pls. 6, 8, 9, 11, 12; *Rural Life*, 1965, pl. 8; Pächt and Alexander, III, no. 290, pl. 26.

98. Durham, Cathedral Library MS A. II. 1

Bible (Bishop Hugh du Puiset Bible)
Vol. I: Genesis–2 Kings, 465×312 mm., ff. 224
Vol. II: Prophets–Psalms, 453×310 mm., ff. 189
Vol. III: Proverbs–Maccabees, 480×332 mm., ff. 162
Vol. IV: New Testament, 477×330 mm., ff. 148
Rebound incorporating the original covers.
c. 1170–80. Durham Cathedral Priory

Ills. 279–82, 285

Vol. I:
Eleven initials cut out: Prologue (f. 4), Genesis (f. 8), Exodus (f. 34), Leviticus (f. 67), Numbers (f. 74), Deuteronomy (f. 100ᵛ), Joshua (f. 121ᵛ), Judges (f. 136), 1 Sam. (f. 154), 1 Kings (f. 188), 2 Kings (f. 206ᵛ).
Historiated initial to 2 Sam.: F, David, seated, mourning, Saul and Jonathan lie before him (f. 173); decorated initial to Ruth (f. 150ᵛ).
Vol. II:
Twelve initials cut out: Isaiah (f. 2), Ezekiel (f. 62), Daniel (f. 90ᵛ), Joel (f. 107), Micah (f. 113ᵛ), Nahum (f. 116), Habakkuk (f. 117), Haggai (f. 119ᵛ), Zechariah (f. 120ᵛ), Malachi (f. 125ᵛ), Job (f. 128), Psalms (f. 152).
Two historiated initials: V, Amos seated (f. 109),

V, Obadiah kneeling (f. 112); six decorated initials: E (f. 101), N (f. 103), C (f. 112ᵛ), D (f. 118), C (f. 126ᵛ), P (f. 142ᵛ).
Vol. III:
Eight initials cut out: Proverbs (f. 2ᵛ), Song of Songs (f. 20ᵛ), Wisdom of Solomon (f. 23), Ecclesiasticus (f. 32), Chronicles (f. 57), Ezra (f. 95), Tobit (f. 116ᵛ), Judith (f. 123ᵛ).
Five historiated initials: Proverbs, P, Solomon speaking to his son (f. 4), Ecclesiastes, V, shrouded corpse lying on a tomb before a king who is saying *Vanitas* (f. 16), prologue to Esdras, V, Ezra seated (f. 94ᵛ), Esther, I, Esther and Ahasuerus, Haman hanging (f. 109), 1 Maccabees, E, execution of the renegade Jew, battle scene (f. 131ᵛ).
Vol. IV:
Ten initials cut out: ff. 2ᵛ, 3, 11ᵛ (Matthew), 92ᵛ, 94, 96ᵛ, 131, 134ᵛ, 135, 139ᵛ.
Ten historiated initials: Jerome's letter, B, Jerome and Pope Damasus (f. 2), Prologue, P, Jerome seated (f. 10), Mark, I, with lion (f. 29), Prologue to Luke, L, with ox (f. 40), Luke, Q, with ox; F, Zacharias at the altar (f. 41), Prologue to Acts, L, seated figure (f. 72), 1 Corinthians, P, Sosthenes seated before the city (f. 114ᵛ), 2 Corinthians, P, messenger with scroll (f. 121ᵛ), Ephesians, P, angel with scroll (f. 128ᵛ).
Eight decorated initials, M (f. 28ᵛ), S (f. 95ᵛ), S (f. 96), E (f. 105), P (f. 126ᵛ), P (f. 133), P (f. 137ᵛ), P (f. 140ᵛ).
Decorated canon tables under arcades, ff. 4–9ᵛ.

Bishop Hugh du Puiset (c. 1125–95), kinsman of the powerful Blois family and a great patron and connoisseur, gave some seventy-five books to the Priory Library. The Bible is incomparably the finest, though it must be said that not many of them are illuminated (see nos. 99–100). Of the figured initials only one (I, f. 173) is of a quality comparable with the better work produced elsewhere at this period. The draperies are carefully modelled with white highlights and the faces with shades of ochre, while David's sorrow is competently conveyed. It is a great pity that this is the only figured initial to survive in Vol. I. The initials in the other volumes, while not quite uniform (the Maccabees initial in particular is better than the others) are all much cruder, characterized by rustic figures with bulbous noses, rougher facial modelling, and simple indications of drapery by white parallel lines. These figures are similar to those of the Gough Psalter in the Bodleian Library (no. 97) as well as of the other Puiset manuscripts, and there are points of contact also with St. Albans manuscripts of the Abbot Simon period (no. 90). The decorated initials are of greater variety. Some are in a mid-century style with large octopus flowers (e.g. II, ff. 101, 142ᵛ), but the majority have gold backgrounds and tight foliage spirals with small animals, and are placed on red framing panels typical of the period after 1170. Similar initials occur in other Durham manuscripts apart from those listed here (e.g. MS A. IV. 35, Mynors, pl. 46c; cf. Vol. IV, f. 96).

Our knowledge of the illustrations reaches beyond the relatively few remaining initials for in several instances there are marginal inscriptions, which were probably intended as instructions to the artists, for example *Joel et Senes* (II, f. 107), *Abbacuc et Deus* (II, f. 117), *Tobias et filius et angelus* (III, f. 116ᵛ), *Judith et rex* (III, f. 123ᵛ). On the whole, the subjects of the illustrations are the standard ones and compare closely, for example, with the Winchester and Laud Misc. 752 Bibles (nos. 83, 103; see Introduction, p. 40 f.). The inscription *rex et regina* to the last Song of Songs initial describes the *Sponsus Sponsa* theme which occurs in both the other Bibles. Apart from the curious allegory of Vanitas (III, f. 16), only the Esther initial, showing Haman hanging in the shaft, is an unusual composition, perhaps adapted from a fuller Esther cycle.

PROVENANCE: given to Durham Cathedral Priory by Hugh du Puiset, Bishop of Durham, 1153–95 (inscription *Hugonis episcopi* on fly-leaf of each volume).

LITERATURE: Mynors, *Durham*, no. 146, pls. 49–53; Millar, I, 86, pl. 50; Boase, *English Art*, 229 f., pl. 76*a*; Rickert, *Painting in Britain*, 86 f., pl. 88*b*; G. V. Scammell, *Hugh du Puiset, Bishop of Durham*, 1956, 105; J. Plummer, *The Glazier Collection of Illuminated Manuscripts*, Pierpont Morgan Library, 1968, no. 19. For the binding: Weale, *Bookbindings and Rubbings*, II, 84; G. D. Hobson, *English Bindings before 1500*, 1929, 5, 29, pl. 9; Swarzenski, *Monuments*, fig. 487.

EXHIBITED: B.F.A.C., *Bindings*, 1891, nos. 2–3; Manchester, 1959, no. 37.

99. Durham, Cathedral Library MS A. II. 19
Epistles of St. Paul with gloss of Peter Lombard
396×265 mm., ff. 317
c. 1180. Durham Cathedral Priory

Ills. 286, 287

Four historiated initials (all P): 1 Corinthians, St. Paul and Sosthenes (f. 87ᵛ), Galatians, St. Paul (f. 175), Philippians, SS. Paul and Timothy (f. 218), 2 Thessalonians, Martyrdom of St. Paul (f. 250).
Ten decorated initials (mostly Ps): fols. 3, 4ᵛ, 143, 200, 230, 240ᵛ, 255, 274ᵛ, 277ᵛ, 279 (M).

The *Magna Glosatura* of Peter Lombard on the Pauline Epistles was written in Paris between 1135 and 1142 and superseded all the previous glosses (see Beryl Smalley, *The Study of the Bible in the Middle Ages*, 1964 ed., esp. 51, 64, 73). Typically for such manuscripts of the period after *c.* 1170, each page contains a few lines of the biblical text surrounded by columns of commentary in a smaller hand. For a similar book see the Pauline Epistles from St. Peter Mancroft, Norwich (no. 101). The figures, with their greyish-green facial modelling in the Byzantine manner, are similar in style but superior to those in the Puiset Bible (no. 98). The splendid decorated initials, set against coloured framing panels, are also similar to those in the Bible (cf. esp. Vol. IV, ff. 126ᵛ, 133, 137ᵛ, 140ᵛ). However, the Bible lacks the highly individualized animals in medallions which are a feature of this manuscript and which suggest that it may be slightly later in date.

PROVENANCE: Given to Durham Cathedral Priory by Hugh du Puiset, Bishop of Durham, 1153–95 (inscription f. iᵛ).

LITERATURE: Mynors, *Durham*, no. 149, pls. 54 f.; Millar, I, 86, pl. 51; Boase, *English Art*, 230; Rickert, *Painting in Britain*, 87, pl. 88*a*.

100. Durham, Cathedral Library MS A. II. 9
Peter Lombard Gloss on the Psalter
374×260 mm., ff. 382
c. 1180. Durham Cathedral Priory

Ills. 283, 284

Four decorated initials: C (f. 2), D (f. 99), S (f. 163ᵛ), D (f. 248ᵛ).
Two historiated initials: Psalm 26, D, Samuel anointing David (f. 63), Psalm 51, Q, Doeg slaying the priests (f. 130ᵛ).
Several initials cut out: ff. 3ᵛ, 207, 243ᵛ, 280.

The decorated initials, characterized by thin, tight spirals with small rabbits and hounds, are different from those of the Puiset Bible and the Pauline Epistles, but the style of the figures in the historiated initials is very close to that of the Bible (see no. 98).

PROVENANCE: Given to Durham Cathedral Priory by Johannes de Insula *miles* (inscription f. 381).

LITERATURE: Mynors, *Durham*, no. 130.

101. Norwich, Church of St. Peter Mancroft
Epistles of St. Paul, with gloss of Peter Lombard
386×260 mm., ff. 202
c. 1180. (?)Northern England   *Ills. 288–90*

Two initials to each Epistle, one for the text, another for the gloss, several rubbed:
Nine historiated initials, nearly all P: Romans, beheading of St. Paul (f. 2), 2 Corinthians, St. Paul with scroll (f. 86), Galatians, (1) St. Paul, (2) conversion of St. Paul (f. 106ᵛ), Ephesians, SS. Peter and Paul holding up a tonsured figure which grips two devils (f. 123), Philippians, St. Paul (f. 135ᵛ), Colossians, SS. Paul and Timothy (f. 144), Thessalonians, St. Paul seated (f. 147), Timothy, martyrdom of St. Paul (f. 170ᵛ).
Twenty decorated initials, nearly all P, extending down the margins: ff. 1, 2, 53 (2), 86, 123, 135ᵛ

144, 147, 153 (2), 156 (2), 165^v (2), 170^v, 173 (2), 174, M (2).

The attribution to Norwich Cathedral Priory has been rejected by Neil Ker. Although there is no firm evidence, the possibility of a northern origin must be considered in view of the close stylistic similarities with the Puiset Pauline Epistles in Durham (no. 99). The figure style, with heavy facial modelling and fine white striations on the draperies is very close. St. Paul seated, on f. 147, for example, is almost identical in posture and treatment of drapery with the same figure on f. 87^v of the Durham manuscript. Equally, the initials placed on background panels and decorated with large flowers, fine foliage scrolls and small animals are paralleled in the Durham *Epistles*. These are features common to the whole of English and northern French illumination of the period, but the relationship between the two manuscripts extends beyond these generic similarities. The animals in medallions (ff. 144, 147), for example, which are reminiscent of English late 12th-century Bestiaries, reappear in the Durham manuscript (f. 87^v) and the palmette shaft fillings are also similar.

Iconographically, the links between the two manuscripts are less close. The Durham manuscript has only four historiated initials of which two—the beheading of St. Paul and SS. Paul and Timothy—are paralleled in the Norwich manuscript.

PROVENANCE: Robert de Novell (f. 1); Geoffrey Parishe (*c.* 1513–88), Vicar of Lilford, Northamptonshire, formerly a monk (f. 172), given to St. Peter Mancroft by William and Alice Gargrave.

LITERATURE: Ker, *Medieval Libraries*, 1964, 139.

EXHIBITED: Manchester, 1959, no. 38.

102. Cambridge, Corpus Christi College MS 66, Vol. I
Imago Mundi; History of England etc.
Vol. II: Cambridge University Library MS Ff. 1. 27
300×210 mm., ff. 58
c. 1180–90. Sawley Abbey, Yorkshire

Fig. 42

Five illustrations: world map at the beginning of the *Imago Mundi* (p. 2), Fortune turning her wheel showing ascending and descending figures, a crowned king at the top; Wisdom stands on the right, framed miniature at the opening of the history of England (p. 66), line of descent from Adam to Woden, figured diagram with bust of Adam at top (p. 67), figure of Woden with busts of his seven sons, drawing in coloured outline (p. 69), six-winged cherub inscribed with names of virtues, full-page drawing in coloured outline (p. 100).

The Chronicle is taken up to 1181 and a date in the 1180s fits well with the style of the Fortuna miniature. Both the figures on the wheel and the medallions on the frame recall the Puiset manuscripts produced at Durham *c.* 1180 (nos. 98 and 99).

This splendid Fortune miniature is an early example of a theme that was to become very popular in the later Middle Ages. Others of the same period are in the *Hortus Deliciarum* of Herrad of Landsberg and in the Sicilian Chronicle of Peter of Eboli (repr. in F. P. Pickering, *Literature and Art in the Middle Ages*, 1970, figs. 3, 6, and in A. Doren, 'Fortuna im Mittelalter und in der Renaissance', *Vorträge der Bibliothek Warburg*, 1922–3, I, p. 71 ff., pls. 2–3). The concept of Fortune's wheel had existed in classical antiquity, but it was Boethius who transmitted it to the Middle Ages as an instrument of Divine providence. Fortune's relevance as the arbiter of the rise and fall of dynasties was frequently stressed in medieval chronicles and the crowned king seated at the top of the wheel appears in the other contemporary examples. The presence of Wisdom, as the means by which kings rule, is explained in the inscription round the frame.

It was Alanus de Insulis (d. 1202) who first attached particular virtues to the plumage of a winged cherub (*De sex alis cherubim*, Migne, P. L., 210, col. 266). The drawing on p. 100, showing the names of virtues inscribed on the wings and feathers, is very similar to those illustrating this text in late 12th- and 13th-century manuscripts (see Katzenellenbogen, *loc. cit.*).

PROVENANCE: Cistercian Abbey of Sawley, Yorkshire (inscription p. 2). Bequeathed to his College by Matthew Parker, Archbishop of Canterbury (1504–75).

LITERATURE: James, *Catalogue*, I, no. 66; H. R. Patch, *The Goddess Fortuna in mediaeval literature*, Cambridge, Mass., 1927, pl. 5; Millar, I, pl. 54; Saxl, Meier, III, 421; A. Katzenellenbogen, *Allegories of the Virtues and Vices in Medieval Art*, Norton paperback ed. 1964, 62 n. 3; N. R. Ker, *Medieval Libraries of Great Britain*, 1964, 177; M. Destombes, *Mappemondes AD 1200–1500*, Amsterdam 1964, no. 25. 3.

103. Oxford, Bodleian Library MS Laud Misc. 752
Bible
520×358 mm., ff. 418
Last quarter 12th century; early 13th century
(?)West Country

Ills. 291–3

Three miniatures (head-pieces) with Evangelist portraits: St. Mark (f. 350), St. Luke (f. 357), St. John (f. 367^v). The original opening page to St. Matthew has been replaced by a 17th-century leaf containing a drawing of the Evangelist.

Forty-nine historiated initials: Jerome's preface, D, Jerome enthroned (f. 4), Genesis, I, six Creation medallions (f. 5ᵛ), Exodus, H, Moses, before the burning bush, takes off his shoes (f. 24), Leviticus, V, Moses at the Tabernacle, communicating with God (f. 39), Numbers, L, destruction of Korah (Numbers 16: 31–3), Moses holds up a scroll inscribed *Reredite a tabernaculis impiorum* (Numbers 16: 26) (f. 49ᵛ), Deuteronomy, H, Moses asleep; below, talking to the Israelites (f. 64ᵛ), Joshua, E, above: God's charge to Joshua, below: he pierces his enemies (? men of Ai) with a lance (f. 78ᵛ), Judges, P, Ehud kills Eglon (Judges 3: 21–2) (f. 87ᵛ), 1 Samuel, F, Hannah's prayer in the Temple (f. 99ᵛ), 2 Samuel, F, above: David offered Saul's crown by the Amalekite, below: the Amalekite killed (f. 112), 1 Kings, E, above: anointing of Solomon by Zadok the priest, below: burial of David (f. 122), 2 Kings, P, Ascension of Elijah, with Elisha just below (f. 134ᵛ), Isaiah, V, Isaiah sawn in half (f. 146ʳ), Jeremiah, V, lowered into the well (f. 165ᵛ), Ezekiel, E, the calling of Ezekiel (f. 186), Daniel, A, the lions' den with Habakkuk bringing bread above (f. 204ᵛ), Joel, V, preaching locust and worm (f. 214ᵛ), Obadiah, V; Jonah, E, prophet portraits (f. 217ᵛ), Job, V, scraping boils, three friends below (f. 227), Psalms, Beatus, David with choir (f. 236ᵛ), Proverbs, P, Solomon teaching (f. 249ᵛ), Ecclesiastes, V, Ecclesiastes the preacher enthroned (f. 256), Song of Songs, O, Christ and Ecclesia, *Sponsus Sponsa* (f. 258ᵛ), Wisdom of Solomon, D, Solomon writing (f. 260), Prologue to Ecclesiasticus, M, son of Sirach (f. 265), Ecclesiasticus, O, Wisdom enthroned with feet on two beasts (f. 265ᵛ), 1 Chronicles, A, David dancing before the ark (f. 279ᵛ), 2 Chronicles, C, Solomon communicating with God (f. 288), Ezra, I, Cyrus the Great, standing (f. 299ᵛ), Baruch, H, seated (f. 308), Esther, I, standing (f. 310), Tobit, C, comforting his fellow prisoners (f. 314), Judith, A, cutting off Holofernes' head (f. 317ᵛ), Maccabees I, E, above: Mattathias beheading the Jew worshipping, below: battle of horsemen (f. 372), Maccabees II, F, massacre (f. 332), St. Luke, Q, Annunciation to Zacharias and to the Virgin (f. 357), Acts, P, Pentecost (f. 376), author portraits to the Epistles: James, I (f. 386), Peter, P (f. 387ᵛ), John, Q (f. 388), Romans, P, Paul (f. 391ᵛ), Corinthians, P, Conversion of St. Paul (f. 399ᵛ), Galatians, P (f. 402), Ephesians, P (f. 403ᵛ), Colossians, P (f. 405ᵛ), Thessalonians, P (f. 407), Timothy, P, Paul and Timothy (f. 408), Titus, P, Paul and Titus (f. 410). Thirty-two decorated initials: full-page F (f. 1), and ff. 78, 97, 98, 146, 212, 215ᵛ, 216, 218ᵛ, 220, 220ᵛ, 221, 222, 222ᵛ, 225ᵛ, 235, 249 (2), 278ᵛ, 299, 310, 314, 321ᵛ, 349, 386, 387ᵛ, 389ᵛ, 404ᵛ, 406ᵛ, 407ᵛ, 409ᵛ, 410ᵛ.

Four main styles may be differentiated in this large and lavishly illuminated book; all except the fourth can be placed in the last quarter of the 12th century:

1. The principal hand, which is to be found in the greater part of the manuscript,
2. A much cruder hand, characterized by enormous eyes and sausage folds: ff. 249ᵛ–65ᵛ, 299ᵛ, 310,

3. Another fairly rustic but better artist working in an earlier style: f. 279ᵛ,
4. A Gothic hand, early 13th century: ff. 214–225ᵛ, 404ᵛ, 406ᵛ, 407ᵛ, 409ᵛ, 410ᵛ (three historiated and thirteen decorated initials).

A date *c.* 1180–90 for the main hand is suggested by the decoration, best represented by the first initial on folio 1. Small white animals are clambering in fine spiral foliage stems on gold ground, very much in the manner of the Bosham manuscripts. In the historiated initials, the faces, hair, and beards are carefully modelled in the Byzantine manner, but the Byzantine style has been interpreted in an unsophisticated way. The somewhat wooden effect of the figures is balanced by recurrent caricatures which enliven many of the initials. The same or a closely related hand was responsible for the initials of a Prophets manuscript from Buildwas in Shropshire (Trinity College, Cambridge, MS B. 4. 3; see Pächt and Alexander). A West Country origin seems likely, therefore, and this is confirmed by stylistic similarities with the late 12th-century Psalter in Munich (Clm. 835), the calendar of which has been connected with St. Peter's Abbey, Gloucester (Boase, p. 279; Saxl, fig. 38).

Iconographically, as much as stylistically, the manuscript is, in places, eccentric. A few of the scenes, such as Tobit comforting his fellow prisoners, are extremely rare and difficult to parallel before the 13th century. Others have prototypes in Byzantine art—such as the dance of David before the Ark (f. 279ᵛ), discussed by A. Heimann (1965)—but the compositions have been treated in a highly individual manner. Yet the majority of illustrations are closely based on earlier models. The scene of Ehud killing Eglon (f. 87ᵛ) is more similar to the Byzantine Octateuchs than to Western examples, such as the Bible at Bourges (MS 3, f. 68ᵛ). In most of the illustrations, however, the Laud 752 Bible follows the tradition evolved for the initials of Western Bibles in the 11th and 12th centuries. Thus, the Ascension of Elijah (2 Kings), Daniel in the lions' den, Solomon teaching (Proverbs), and Christ and Ecclesia (Song of Songs) are the standard illustrations for these books (see Introduction p. 40 f.). Moses before the burning bush, taking off his shoe, occurs in the Exodus initial of the Walsingham Bible (no. 59), and Isaiah sawn in half appears in the Lambeth Bible (no. 70; for the Byzantine origin of this scene see R. Bernheimer, *Art Bulletin*, 34, 1952, 19 ff.). Where a scene does not occur in earlier English Bibles, it is in Mosan and French manuscripts that the closest parallels are found. For example, the scene of Jeremiah lowered into the well reappears in a very similar form in a Clairvaux manuscript of *c.* 1200 (Troyes MS 436, Morel-Payen, *MSS Bibl. Troyes*, 1935, pl. xiv, fig. 55), Cyrus the Great standing (Ezra) can be compared with the initial in the Stavelot Bible (B.L. Add. 28106–7, Vol. II, f. 93ᵛ), and the destruction of Korah with a Mosan Josephus in Merton College, Oxford (W. Cahn, *Zeitschrift für Kunstgeschichte*, 29, 1966, 298, fig. 2). Finally both Judith and

Holofernes and the illustration to 1 Maccabees are closely paralleled in the S. Bénigne Bible at Dijon (MS 2, ff. 370, 380ᵛ).

PROVENANCE: George Giffard, 16th century (inscription f. 1 partially erased): Archbishop William Laud bequeathed it to the Bodleian Library.

LITERATURE: M. R. James and S. C. Cockerell, *A Book of Old Testament Illustrations*, Roxburghe Club 1927, 23; Wormald, 'Development', 48, pl. 22*b*; F. Saxl, *English Sculptures of the 12th century*, 1954, 57; E. B. Garrison, *Studies in the History of Medieval Italian Painting*, III, 1957–8, 202 n.; Boase, *English Art*, 193, 230, pls. 60*b*, 66*b*; Rickert, *Painting in Britain*, 84; Bodleian Picture Book, *English Romanesque illumination*, 19, 20, 22; A. Heimann, 'A 12th century Manuscript from Winchcombe', *J.W.C.I.*, 28, 1965, 100 f., pl. 15*c*; Pächt and Alexander, III, no. 254, pl. 25.

EXHIBITED: Oxford, *The Bodleian Library in the 17th Century*, 1951, no. 74.

104. Cambridge, Corpus Christi College MS 22

Isidore, Etymologies etc.
375 × 255 mm.,
ff. 20+181, of which Bestiary, ff. 162–9.
Third quarter 12th century

Ills. 294, 295; Fig. 3

Two columns per page.
Thirty-five unframed, tinted outline drawings, column width: unicorn speared; beaver hunt; hydrus (dragon) and crocodile (f. 162), crocodile devouring man; hyena stands on tomb (f. 162ᵛ), donkeys; monkeys; goat (f. 163), panther attracting other beasts with its breath (f. 163ᵛ), winged dragon; weasels; deer (f. 164), elephants, one with a castle on its back (f. 164ᵛ), wolves (f. 165), dog assaults a murderer; ibex (f. 165ᵛ), male and female stones, shown as man and woman, causing a fire; winged fish attacking boat, caladrius bird looking away from sick man; pelicans (f. 166), night crow; eagles; phoenix, burning nest (f. 166ᵛ), hoopoes pull out parents' feathers; ants (f. 167), sirens; ibis bringing food to its young; coot (f. 167ᵛ), whale, with a ship anchored to it; partridges; viper, with a man and, on right, a woman and a dog (f. 168), ostrich; doves; salamander, two men carrying tub, probably containing the apples poisoned by the salamander's breath (f. 168ᵛ), doves, a dragon lies in wait for them.

The contents and illustrations are very similar to those of the Bodleian Bestiary, Laud Misc. 247 (no. 36) and it clearly belongs to the same group even though the order of the chapters is different. Seven drawings found in Laud Misc. 247 do not appear here but some new beasts have been added, including the wolf, dog, ibex, and crocodile. These additions are also found in B.L. Stowe 1067.

PROVENANCE: Bequeathed to his College by Matthew Parker, Archbishop of Canterbury (1504–75).

LITERATURE: James, *Catalogue*, I, no. 22; James, *Bestiary*, 10; Boase, *English Art*, 292 n. 2; Florence McCulloch, *Mediaeval Latin and French Bestiaries*, N. Carolina, 1960, 30; Loren MacKinney, *Medieval Illustrations in Medieval MSS*, 1965, 22, 113, fig. 16.

EXHIBITED: Manchester, 1959, no. 39.

105. London, British Library MS Add. 11283

Bestiary
300 × 178 mm., ff. 41
c. 1170

Ills. 296–8

Ninety-nine unframed pen drawings, a few of them tinted, several pricked for copying: lion (f. 1), tiger, huntsman carrying off whelp; leopard; panther (f. 2), antelope speared; unicorn captured (f. 3), lynx; griffin carrying off pig (f. 3ᵛ), elephant, with a castle containing soldiers on its back (f. 4), beaver hunt (f. 4ᵛ), ibex; hyena devours corpse in tomb (f. 5), bonnacon, a lion with curling horns; monkeys (f. 5ᵛ), satyr; stag (f. 6), wild goat (f. 6ᵛ), goat; rhinocerous (f. 7), bear; leucrota, horse-like animal (f. 7ᵛ), crocodile, eating a man; manticora, beast with a human head (f. 8), parandrus, beast with stag's antlers; fox; eale, beast with curved horns (f. 8ᵛ), wolf (f. 9), dogs (f. 9ᵛ), a king freed by his dogs (f. 10), dogs attacking a murderer (f. 10ᵛ), Adam naming the animals (f. 11ᵛ), sheep; ram; lamb; goat (f. 12), boar; bull; ox (f. 12ᵛ), camel with two humps; dromedary without humps (f. 13), donkey; onager, a wild ass; horse (f. 13ᵛ), cat and mouse; weasel; mole (f. 15); hedgehogs; ants (f. 15ᵛ).
Birds: eagles (f. 16ᵛ), vulture; cranes (f. 17), parrot; caladrius bird looks away from sick man (f. 17ᵛ), stork; swan; ibis feeding young (f. 18), ostrich; coot (f. 18ᵛ), halcyon; phoenix (f. 19), cinomolgus, hunted by a man with a sling (f. 19ᵛ), ercinea aves, a bird like a cock; pelicans attacking their parents; night crow (f. 20), siren; partridges (f. 20ᵛ), magpie; hawk; nightingale (f. 21), bats; raven; crow (f. 21ᵛ), dove; turtle-dove (f. 22), turtle-doves; peacock; hoopoe; cock (f. 23), duck; bees (f. 23ᵛ), perindens tree, with doves in its branches, and a dragon (f. 24ᵛ).
Reptiles: dragon (f. 25), basilisk, cock with serpent's tail; viper (f. 25ᵛ), asp, with enchanter (f. 26), scitalis, a dragon; amphuiema, a winged dragon (f. 26ᵛ), hydrus; boas, a snake; iaculus, a winged serpent; syrena, a dragon; seps, a snake (f. 27), lacertus, a lizard; salamander poisoning fruit; saura, a lizard (f. 27ᵛ), serpent scraping off its old skin (f. 28), male and female stones, shown as man and woman, causing a fire (f. 41).

Although it follows the technique of the earlier manuscripts in having unframed outline drawings, this manuscript is in fact one of the earliest surviving members of the second family of Bestiaries, most of which are late 12th–14th centuries. The second family differs from the first (see nos. 36, 104) in containing new textual material, in following a system of classification into beasts, birds, and reptiles and in the addition of some sixty illustrations, bringing up the total to about a hundred.

The animals have a more naturalistic appearance than those in the earlier 12th-century Bestiary, Laud Misc. 247 (no. 36). The style of the figures is reminiscent of Mosan illumination of the period immediately preceding that of Nicholas of Verdun, c. 1160–70. The figure of Adam on f. 11ᵛ, for example, may be compared with the physician on f. 13 of the medical MS Harley 1585. However, the English origin of this manuscript is confirmed by the adherence to an English textual tradition.

PROVENANCE: 17th–18th century, P. H. Mainwaringe (inscription f. i); bought by the British Museum from Pickering in 1837.

LITERATURE: G. C. Druce, 'The Mediaeval Bestiaries and their influence on ecclesiastical decorative art', *Journal Brit. Archaeol. Asscn.*, 15, 1919, 52, pl. 5; James, *Bestiary*; D. J. A. Ross 'A lost painting in Henry II's palace at Westminster', *J.W.C.I.*, 16, 1953, 60; Boase, *English Art*, 295 n. 2; F. McCulloch, *Mediaeval Latin and French Bestiaries*, N. Carolina, 1960, 34.

106. New York, Pierpont Morgan Library M 81
Bestiary
216×165 mm., ff. 120
c. 1185. (?) Lincoln   *Ills. 299–303*

Historiated initial, Christ standing (f. 8);
One hundred and five framed miniatures: lions (f. 8), antelope speared (f. 9ᵛ), centaur holding snake; hedgehog (f. 10ᵛ), fox pecked by birds (f. 11ᵛ), unicorn speared (f. 12ᵛ), beaver hunt (f. 13ᵛ), hyena devours corpse in tomb (f. 14ᵛ), hydrus, a dragon, and crocodile (f. 15ᵛ), hydra, five-headed serpent (f. 16), sirens (f. 17), wild goats (f. 18), onager, a wild ass (f. 19), man shoots at monkeys (f. 19ᵛ), bearded satyr (f. 20ᵛ), panther attracting other beasts with its breath (f. 21), elephant with a castle on its back (f. 23), wolf and sheep (f. 25), king protected by dog; dogs swimming a river (f. 27), dog attacking a murderer (f. 28), stag and doe (f. 30), weasels (f. 30ᵛ), ants (f. 31ᵛ), ibex leaps headlong from rock (f. 33), male and female stones shown as man and woman, causing fire (f. 33ᵛ), eagles (f. 34), tiger looks into mirror, rider carries off whelp (f. 35), leopard (f. 35ᵛ), lynx (f. 36), griffin carrying off pig; two boars (f. 36ᵛ), bonacon, a lion with curling horns, attacked by men (f. 37), bear licking cubs (f. 37ᵛ), manticora, beast with

human head (f. 38ᵛ), parandrus, beast with deer's antlers; eale, beast with curved horns (f. 39), sheep, horned (f. 39ᵛ), ram; two lambs (f. 40), goat (f. 40ᵛ), ox (f. 41), bullock (f. 41ᵛ), camel with two humps (f. 42), dromedary without humps (f. 43), donkey (f. 43ᵛ), horse (f. 44), cats and mice (f. 46ᵛ), mouse; mole (f. 47), leucrotta, horse-like animal (f. 47ᵛ). Birds: eagles (f. 48), vultures (f. 48ᵛ), swan (f. 49ᵛ), cranes (f. 50), parrot (f. 50ᵛ), stork (f. 51), halcyon (f. 51ᵛ), cinomolgus, hunted by man with a sling (f. 52), avis ercinea, a bird like a cock (f. 52ᵛ), partridge (f. 53), hawk; two magpies (f. 53ᵛ), nightingale (f. 54), bats (f. 54ᵛ), raven; crow (f. 55), swallow (f. 56), quail (f. 56ᵛ), peacock (f. 57), cock; duck (f. 57ᵛ), bees (f. 58), caladrius bird looks at sick man (f. 60ᵛ), pelicans (61ᵛ), night crow (f. 62), phoenix (f. 62ᵛ), hoopoe (f. 63ᵛ), ibis (f. 64), coot (f. 65), partridge (f. 65ᵛ), two turtle doves billing (f. 66), Amos with goats (f. 68).
Fish: winged fish, serra, attacking a boat (f. 69), crocodile devouring man (f. 70), dragon and elephant (f. 78), basilisk, cock with serpent's tail; regulus, a lizard (f. 79), snakes (f. 79ᵛ), viper (f. 80), asp with enchanter (f. 81ᵛ), emorois, dragon; enchanter on right (f. 83), hydrus and crocodile (f. 83ᵛ), lacertus, lizard; salamander (f. 84ᵛ), scitalis, a dragon; amphisbaena, a dragon (f. 85ᵛ), boas, snake; jaculus, winged serpent; syrena, dragon (f. 86), seps, lizard; lacertus, lizard (f. 86ᵛ), saura, winged lizard; stellis, blue snake (f. 87), serpent scraping off old skin (f. 87ᵛ).

In appearance this manuscript, with over a hundred framed miniatures, most of them on gold ground, is typical of the late 12th-century second family of Bestiaries. Indeed, it looks more like a second family manuscript than does Add. 11283 (no. 105). However, Florence McCulloch has described the text as belonging to a transitional group, not containing quite all the material of the fully developed second family recension. Other manuscripts belonging to this group include Leningrad, State Library, Qu. V. I, B.L. Royal 12. C. XIX (late 12th century) and the 13th-century Alnwick Bestiary published by Millar.
The inscription on f. 1ᵛ dates this manuscript before 1187 and places its likely origin in the vicinity of Lincoln. Stylistically it is closest to the Leningrad MS; Royal 12. C. XIX is more elegantly Gothic in appearance and probably dates from c. 1200.

PROVENANCE: Given, with other books, in 1187 to the Augustinian Priory of Radford (now Worksop) by Philip, Canon of Lincoln (inscription, f. 1ᵛ). 19th century: 10th Duke of Hamilton; Prussian Government 1882–9; 1889 bought by William Morris; Richard Bennett; 1902, J. Pierpont Morgan.

LITERATURE: M. R. James, *Catalogue . . . of the Library of J. Pierpont Morgan, Manuscripts*, 1906. 165 ff., no. 107; James, *Bestiary*, no. 11; Millar I, 38, 88, pl. 55; *id., A 13th Century Bestiary in the Library at Alnwick Castle*, Roxburghe Club, 1958, 1 f.; Boase, *English Art*, 294; Rickert, *Painting in*

Britain, 88, pl. 91*b*; L. M. Ayres, 'A miniature from Jumièges and trends in manuscript illumination around 1200', *Festschrift Hanns Swarzenski*, Berlin, 1973, 133 f., fig. 25.

EXHIBITED: B.F.A.C., *Illuminated MSS*, 1908, no. 80, pl. 69; Pierpont Morgan Library, (1), *Exh. of Illuminated MSS held at the New York Public Library*, 1933–4, no. 33, pl. 33; (2) *Exh. held on the occasion of the New York World Fair*, 1939, no. 55, pl. IIIA; (3) *The Animal Kingdom*, 1940–41, 14 f., no. 1, pl. 1; (4) *Treasures from the Pierpont Morgan Library: 50th Anniversary Exhibition*, 1957, no. 15, pl. 13.

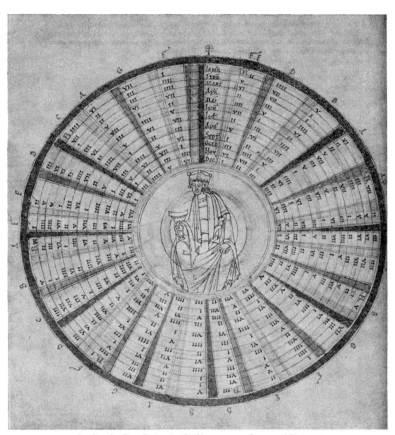

Oxford, St. John's College 17, f. 27ᵛ (Cat. 9)

1. Beatus Initial. London, B.L., Arundel 60, f. 13 (Cat. 1)

[*slightly enlarged*]

2. Crucifixion with Evangelist symbols. London, B.L., Arundel 60, f. 52ᵛ (Cat. 1)

[slightly enlarged]

3. St. Matthew.
Paris, Bibl. Nat., lat. 14782, f. 16ᵛ (Cat. 2)

4. St. Mark.
Paris, Bibl. Nat., lat. 14782, f. 52ᵛ (Cat. 2)

5. St. Luke.
Paris, Bibl. Nat., lat. 14782, f. 74 (Cat. 2)

6. St. John.
Paris, Bibl. Nat., lat. 14782, f. 108 (Cat. 2)

7. Initial Q.
Cambridge, Clare College 30, f. 2 (Cat. 4)

8. David playing the harp.
Cambridge, Corpus Christi College 391, p. 24 (Cat. 3)

9. Initial V.
Cambridge, Clare College 30, Bk. I (Cat. 4)

10. Initial P.
Cambridge, Clare College 30, Bk. IV (Cat. 4)

11. Beatus Initial.
Cambridge, Trinity College, B.5.26, f. 1 (Cat. 6)

12. Initial R.
London, B.L., Arundel 16, f. 2 (Cat. 7)

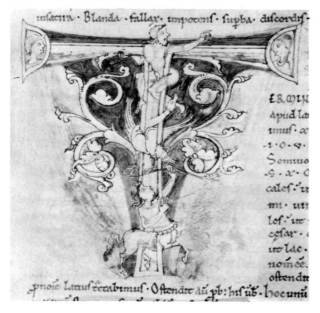

13. Initial T.
Cambridge, Trinity College, O.2.51, f. 46 (Cat. 8)

14. Initial V.
Cambridge, Trinity College, O.2.51, f. 58 (Cat. 8)

15. Initial Q.
Cambridge, Trinity College, O.2.51, f. 91 (Cat. 8)

16. Initial C.
Cambridge, Trinity College, O.2.51, f. 100 (Cat. 8)

17. St. Matthew.
Oxford, Wadham College, A.10.22, f. 12ᵛ (Cat. 5)

18. Three Marys at the Sepulchre.
Oxford, Wadham College, A.10.22, f. 104ᵛ (Cat. 5)

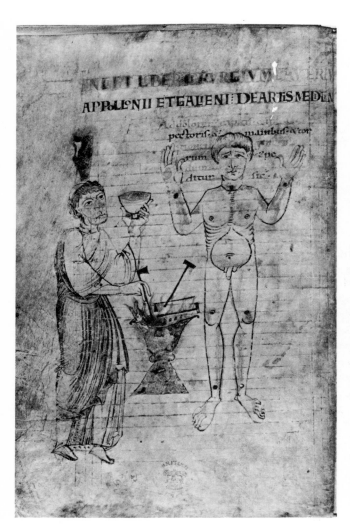

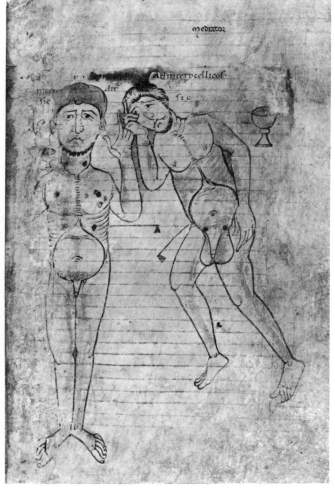

19–20. Cautery scenes. London, B.L., Sloane 2839, f. 1ᵛ, f. 2 (Cat. 12)

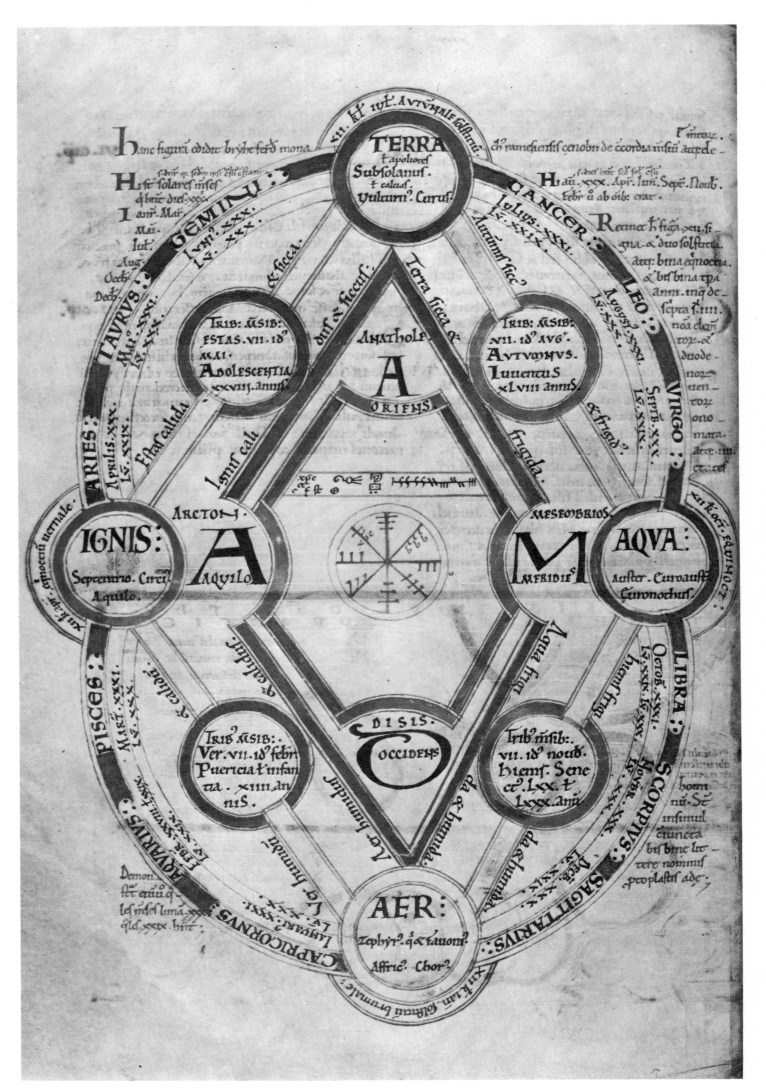

21. Byrhtferth's diagram. Oxford, St. John's College 17, f. 7ᵛ (Cat. 9)

22–23. Mandrake. Oxford, Bodl. Lib., Ashmole 1431, f. 31, f. 34 (Cat. 10)

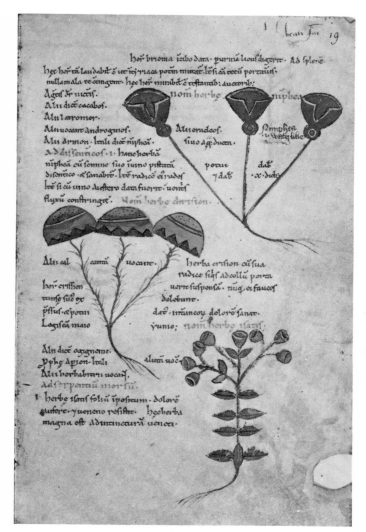

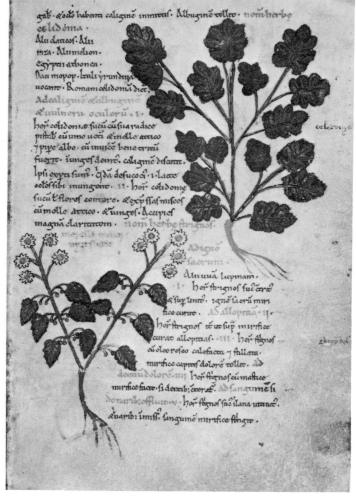

24–25. Plants. Oxford, Bodl. Lib., Ashmole 1431, f. 19, f. 20 (Cat. 10)

26. Horse.
Oxford, Bodl. Lib., Bodley 130, f. 76 (Cat. 11)

27. Wild boar.
Oxford, Bodl. Lib., Bodley 130, f. 93 (Cat. 11)

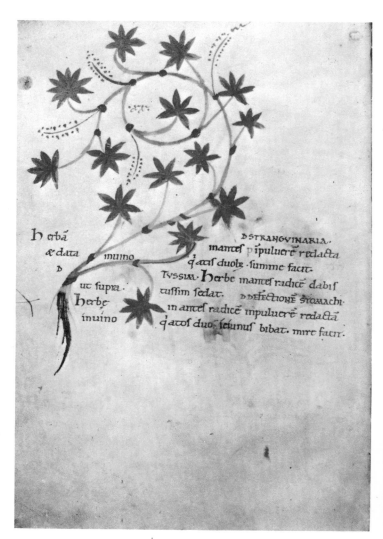

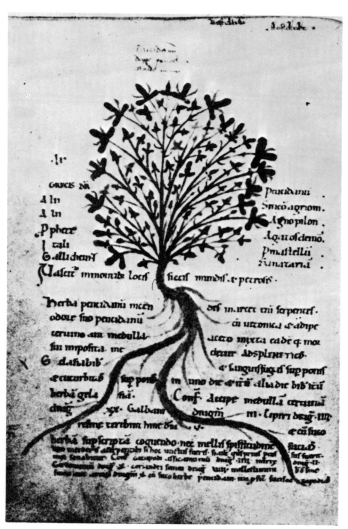

28–29. Plants. Oxford, Bodl. Lib., Bodley 130, f. 10ᵛ, f. 36ᵛ (Cat. 11)

30. Initial T.
Lincoln, Cath. Lib., A.1.2, f. 70ᵛ (Cat. 13)

31. Initial I.
Lincoln, Cath. Lib., A.1.2, f. 85ᵛ (Cat. 13)

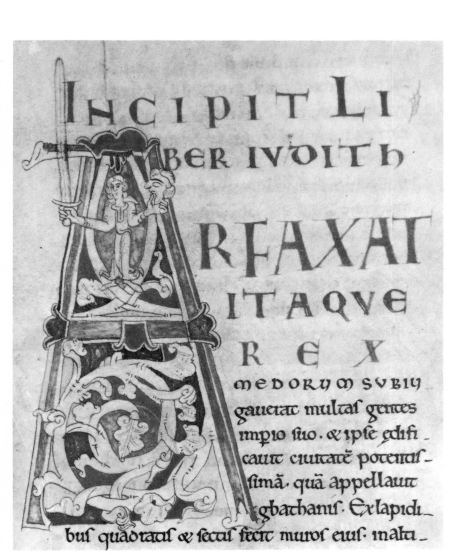

32. Initial A.
Cambridge, Trinity College, B.5.2, f. 70 (Cat. 13)

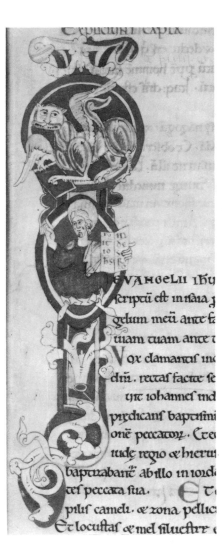

33. Initial I.
Cambridge, Trinity College, B.5.2, f. 110 (Cat. 13)

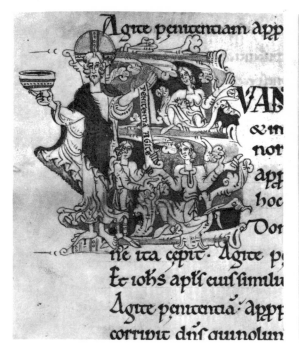

34. Initial E.
Lincoln, Cath. Lib., A.3.17, f. 8ᵛ (Cat. 14)

35. Initial D.
Lincoln, Cath. Lib., A.3.17, f. 142 (Cat. 14)

36. Initial Q.
Lincoln, Cath. Lib., A.3.17, f. 233 (Cat. 14)

37. Initial P. London, B.L., Royal 6.C.VI, f. 79ᵛ (Cat. 15)

38. Initial P. London, B.L., Royal 5.D.I, f. 1 (Cat. 16)

39. Initial M. London, B.L.,
Royal 5.D.II, f. 70ᵛ (Cat. 16)

40. Initial B. London, B.L.,
Arundel 91, f. 179 (Cat. 17)

41. Initial I. London, B.L.,
Arundel 91, f. 190 (Cat. 17)

42. March, Pisces, pruning trees.
London, B.L., Cotton,
Vitellius C. XII, f. 121 (Cat. 18)

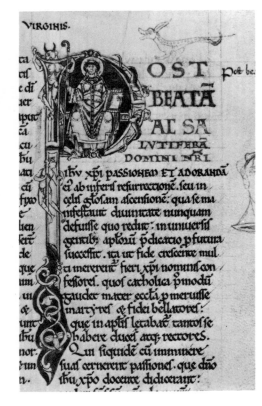

43. Initial P. London, B.L.,
Arundel 91, f. 86 (Cat. 17)

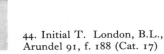

44. Initial T. London, B.L.,
Arundel 91, f. 188 (Cat. 17)

45. Initial B.
Cambridge, Trinity College, R.3.30, f. 1 (Cat. 24)

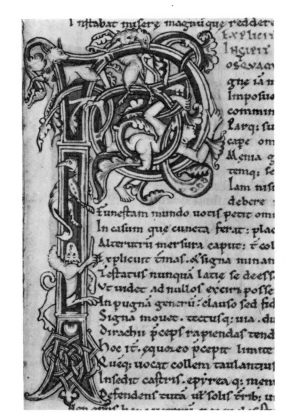

46. Initial P.
Cambridge, Trinity College, R.3.30, f. 54 (Cat. 24)

47. Initial A. Cambridge, Trinity College, O.4.7, f. 48ᵛ (Cat. 23)

48. Initial A.
Cambridge, Trinity College, O.4.7, f. 75 (Cat. 23)

49. Weighing of souls; bad regiment; good regiment.
Florence, Biblioteca Mediceo–Laurenziana, Plut. XII. 17, f. 1ᵛ (Cat. 19)

50. The City of God.
Florence, Biblioteca Mediceo–Laurenziana, Plut. XII. 17, f. 2ᵛ (Cat. 19)

51. Initial A. London, B.L.,
Cotton, Claudius E.V, f. 28 (Cat. 21)

52. Initial U. London, B.L.,
Cotton, Claudius E.V, f. 49 (Cat. 21)

53. Initial N. London, B.L.,
Harley 624, f. 108ᵛ (Cat. 22)

54. Initial T. London, B.L., Harley 624, f. 106ᵛ (Cat. 22)

55. Initial R. London, B.L., Cotton, Cleopatra E.1, f. 40 (Cat. 20)

56. Initial Q. Florence, Biblioteca Mediceo–Laurenziana,
Plut. XII. 17, f. 174ᵛ (Cat. 19)

57. Initial Q.
New York, Pierpont Morgan Lib. 777, f. 38 (Cat. 25)

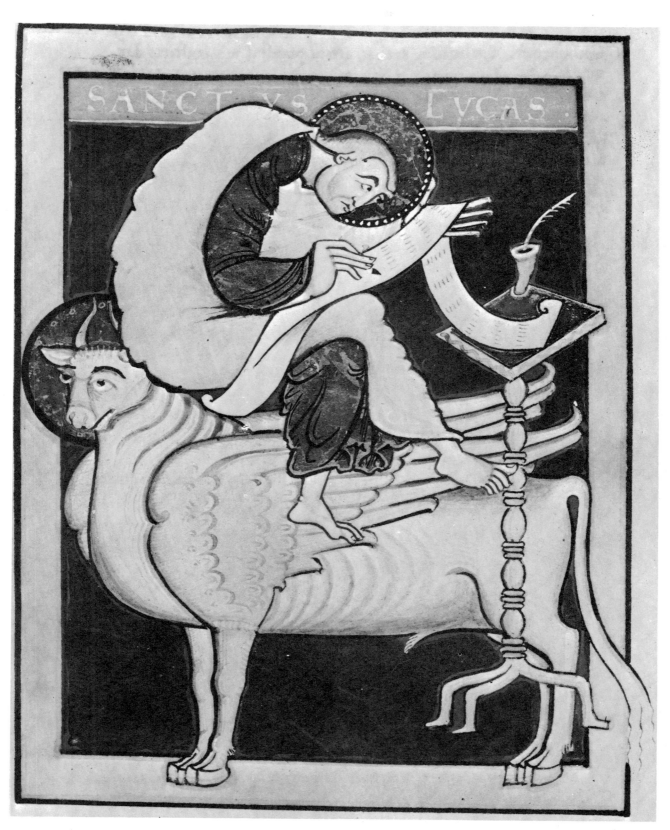

58. St. Luke. New York, Pierpont Morgan Lib. 777, f. 37ᵛ (Cat. 25)

59. Cuthbert as a boy.
Oxford, University College 165, p. 8 (Cat. 26)

60. Cuthbert extinguishes a fire through prayer.
Oxford, University College 165, p. 45 (Cat. 26)

61. Cuthbert entertains an angel. Oxford, University College 165, p. 26 (Cat. 26)

62. Cuthbert sees the soul of Bishop Aidan carried to heaven.
Oxford, University College 165, p. 18 (Cat. 26)

63. The boat carrying Cuthbert's body.
Oxford, University College 165, p. 143 (Cat. 26)

64. Constellations.
Durham, Cath. Lib., Hunter 100, f. 62 (Cat. 27)

65. Initial A. Durham, Cath. Lib.,
B.II.26, f. 90 (Cat. 28)

66. Gemini. Durham, Cath. Lib., Hunter 100, f. 4 (Cat. 27)

67–68. Cautery scenes. Durham, Cath. Lib., Hunter 100, f. 119, f. 119ᵛ (Cat. 27)

69. Superbia attacks Humilitas.
London, B.L., Cotton, Titus D.XVI, f. 14 (Cat. 30)

70. Prudentius offers prayers.
London, B.L., Cotton, Titus D.XVI, f. 34 (Cat. 30)

71. Superbia falls into a pit.
London, B.L., Cotton, Titus D.XVI, f. 14ᵛ (Cat. 30)

72. Initial E.
Hildesheim, St. Albans Psalter, p. 184 (Cat. 29)

73. Initial I.
Hildesheim, St. Albans Psalter, p. 304 (Cat. 29)

74. The Entombment. Hildesheim, St. Albans Psalter, p. 48 (Cat. 29)

[slightly enlarged]

75. St. Mark.
Hereford, Cath. Lib., O.1.VIII, f. 46 (Cat. 33)

76. Pentecost.
Hildesheim, St. Albans Psalter, p. 55 (Cat. 29)

77. Christ handing the keys to St. Peter.
Verdun, Bibl. Mun. 70, f. 68ᵛ (Cat. 31)

78. The Annunciation.
Hildesheim, St. Albans Psalter, p. 19 (Cat. 29)

79. Angles, Saxons and Jutes divide Britain between them.
New York, Pierpont Morgan Lib. 736, p. 13 (Cat. 34)

80. Edmund bestows alms on the poor.
New York, Pierpont Morgan Lib. 736, p. 15 (Cat. 34)

81. Edmund scourged and mocked.
New York, Pierpont Morgan Lib. 736, p. 24 (Cat. 34)

82. Edmund's head cut off and hidden in a thicket.
New York, Pierpont Morgan Lib. 736, p. 26 (Cat. 34)

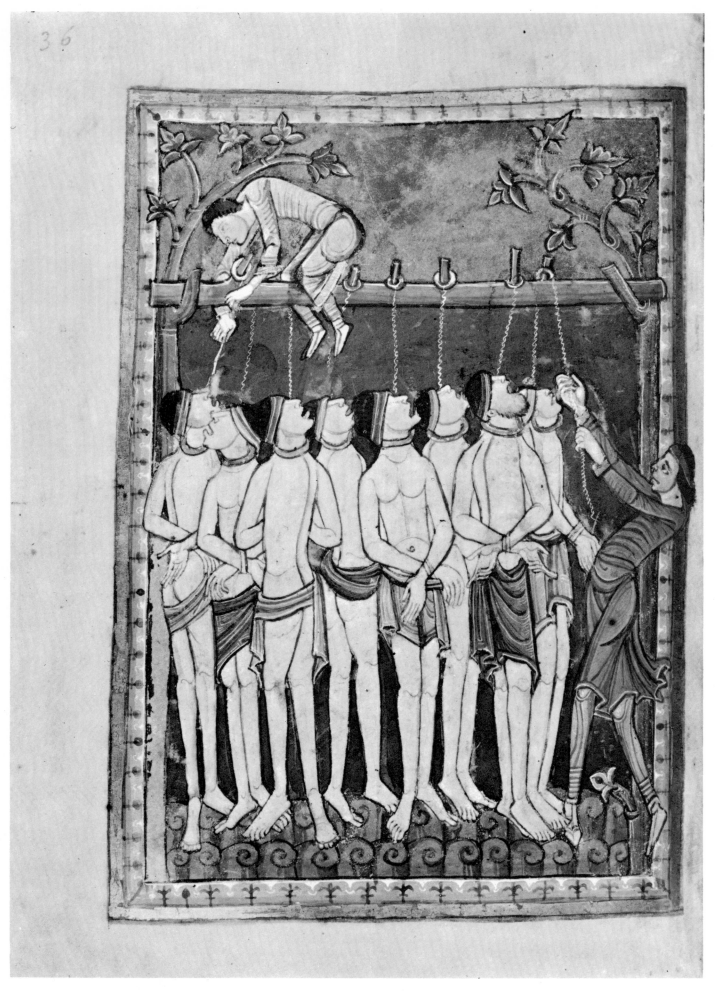

83. The hanging of the eight thieves. New York, Pierpont Morgan Lib. 736, p. 36 (Cat. 34)

84–85. Initial D. Initial S. Verdun, Bibl. Mun. 70, f. 39ᵛ, f. 42ᵛ (Cat. 31)

86–87. Initial M. Initial V. Verdun, Bibl. Mun. 70, f. 33, f. 54 (Cat. 31)

88. Initial M. London, B.L., Royal 13.D.VI, f. 61ᵛ (Cat. 32)

89. Initial T. London, B.L., Royal 13.D.VI, f. 77ᵛ (Cat. 32)

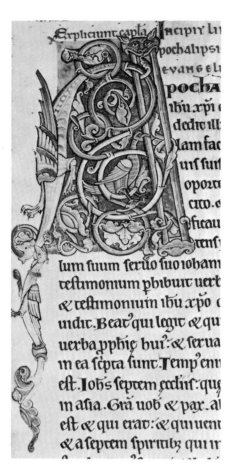

precario munere in preciosum auxilium tres q
populi. hoc: saxones. iuti. & angli. primu bri
diu fuere presidii. Qui cu sepius bello lacessir
defensarent fortiter illi u ignauie opam dat
pletarii ad solam uoluptate domi residerent
uicta fortitudine stipendiarios militu qs sib
ipsos miseros indigenas domo patriaq; pelle
Factuq; est. Et exclusis britonib; staciuint uie
uictores aliengene insulam bonis omnib; fecu
in dignu iudicantes eam ignauios domino det

sum suum seruo suo ioham
testimonium phibuit uerb
& testimonium ibu xpo c
undit. Beat qui legit & qui
uerba pphie hui: & serua
in ea scpta sunt. Temp cui
est. Iohs septem ecclif: qu
in asia. Gra uob & pax. a
est & qui erat: & qui uent
& a septem spiritib; qui ir

90. Initial A.
New York, Pierpont Morgan Lib. 736, p. 153 (Cat. 34)

91. Initial A.
Cambridge, Pembroke College 120, f. 174 (Cat. 35)

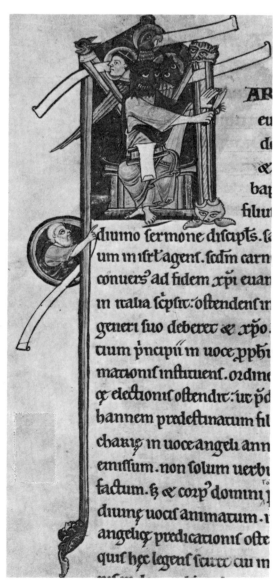

diuino sermone disciptos. sa
um in isrl agens. scdm carn
conuers ad fidem xpi euar
in italia scpsit: ostendens ir
generi suo deberet & xpo.
tium principiu in uoce pphi
mationis instituens. ordine
& electionis ostendit: ut pd
hannem predestinatum fil
charis in uoce angeli ann
emissum. non solum uerbi
factum. sz & corp domini j
diuine uocis animatum. i
angelice predicationis oste
qui hec legens scient cui in

92. Initial L.
Cambridge, Pembroke College 120, f. 11 (Cat. 35)

93. Initial M.
Cambridge, Pembroke College 120, f. 31ᵛ (Cat. 35)

94. Scenes from Christ's Ministry. Cambridge, Pembroke College 120, f. 2ᵛ (Cat. 35)

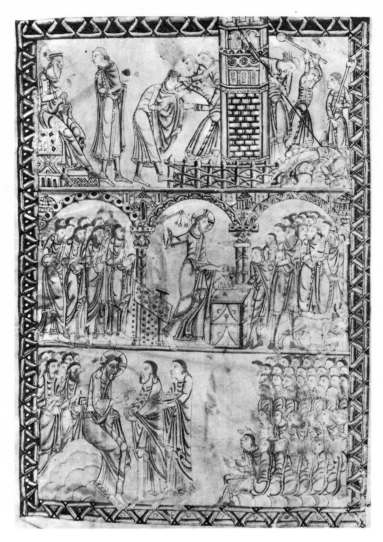

95–96. Scenes from Christ's Ministry. Cambridge, Pembroke College 120, f. 1, f. 1ᵛ (Cat. 35)

97–98. Scenes from the Passion. Cambridge, Pembroke College 120, f. 3, f. 3ᵛ (Cat. 35)

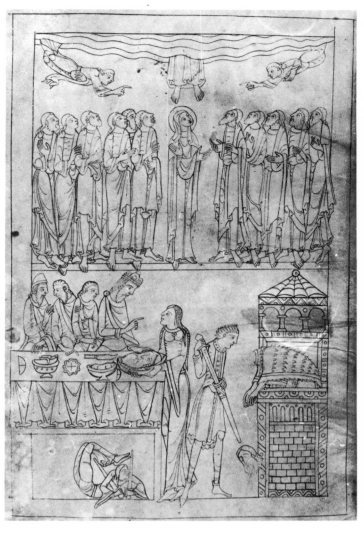

99. Scenes after the Resurrection.
Cambridge, Pembroke College 120, f. 4ᵛ (Cat. 35)

100. The Ascension; the beheading of John the Baptist.
Cambridge, Pembroke College 120, f. 5ᵛ (Cat. 35)

101. God and Christ between Cherubim; Pentecost.
Cambridge, Pembroke College 120, f. 6 (Cat. 35)

102. The Last Judgment.
Cambridge, Pembroke College 120, f. 6ᵛ (Cat. 35)

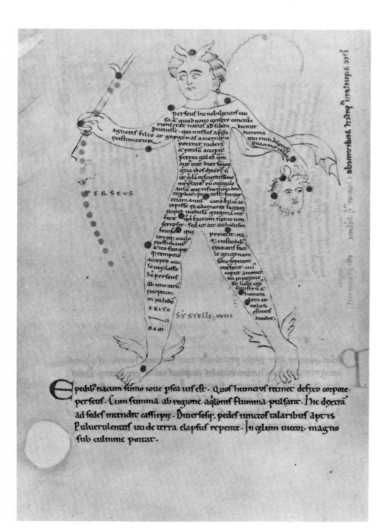

103. Capture of a Unicorn.
Oxford, Bodl. Lib., Laud. Misc. 247, f. 149ᵛ (Cat. 36)

104. Elephants.
Oxford, Bodl. Lib., Laud. Misc. 247, f. 163ᵛ (Cat. 36)

105. Perseus.
London, B.L., Cotton, Tiberius C.I, f. 22ᵛ (Cat. 37)

106. Sagittarius.
London, B.L., Cotton, Tiberius C.I, f. 25ᵛ (Cat. 37)

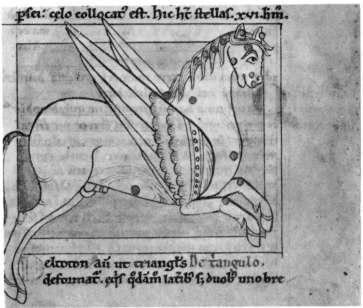

psei celo collocar̄ est. hic hr̄ stellas. xvi. hm̄

elcoton aū ut eriangl̄s De tangulo.
deformac̄. eis q̄dam latib̄ s; duob̄ uno bre

107–108. Constellations. Oxford, Bodl. Lib.,
Bodley 614, f. 19ᵛ, f. 30 (Cat. 38)

109. Sun and moon in chariots.
Oxford, Bodl. Lib., Bodley 614, f. 17ᵛ (Cat. 38)

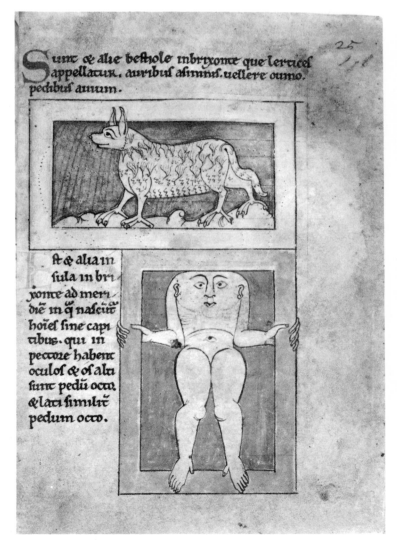

Sunt & alie bestiole inbrixonte que lerticel
appellatur. auribus asininis. uellere ouino.
peclibus auium.

St & alia in
sula in bri
xonte ad meri
die in q̄ nascū
hōes sine capi
tibus. qui in
pectore habent
oculos & os. alti
sunt pedū octo.
& lati similit̄
pedum octo.

ciopodū gens. ē. in ethiopia singulis cruribz;
& celericate mirabili. q̄s īde sciopodas greci
uocant. eo q̄ p estū in terra resupini iacentes.
pedū suoꝛ magnitudine ad ūbrentur.

Arcapodes
sō in libia
plancas ū̄sas
post crura
habentes. &
octonos digi
tos in plantis
Yppopodes
in scithia
sunt huma
nā formam
habentes. &
eqinos pedes.

110–111. Marvels of the East. Oxford, Bodl. Lib., Bodley 614, f. 41, f. 50 (Cat. 38)

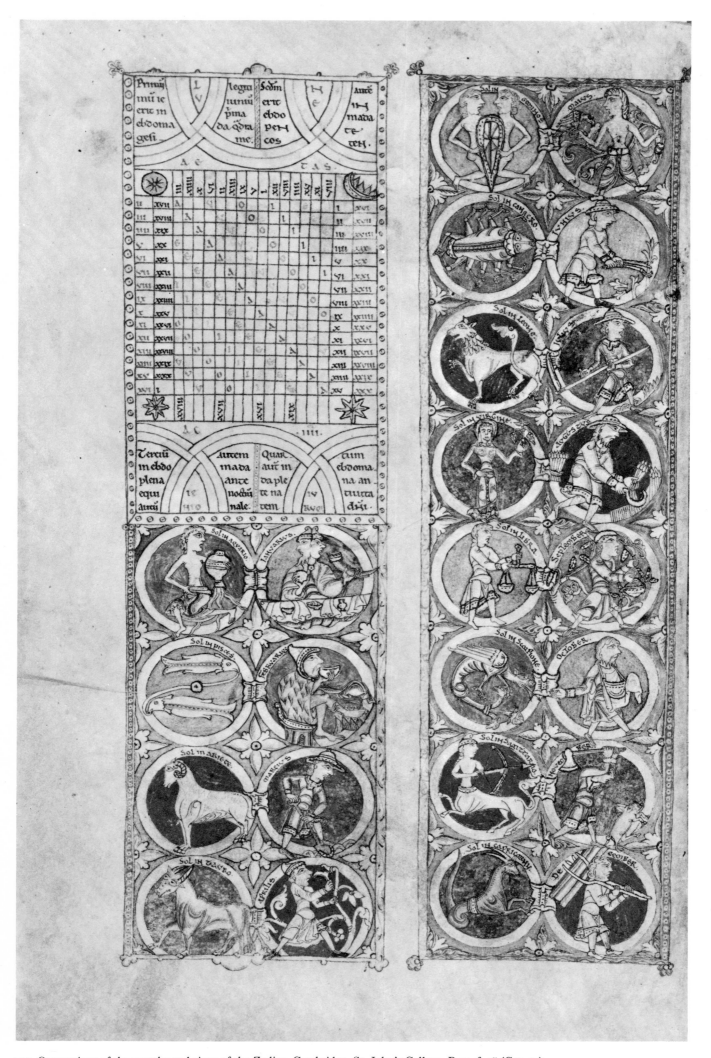

112. Occupations of the months and signs of the Zodiac. Cambridge, St. John's College, B.20, f. 2ᵛ (Cat. 39)

113. Boethius, Pythagoras, Plato and Nichomachus. Cambridge, University Lib., Ii.3.12, f. 61ᵛ (Cat. 41)

114. Initial O.
Cambridge, Corpus Christi College 393, f. 59 (Cat. 40)

115. Initial O. Cambridge, University Lib.,
Ii.3.12, f. 62ᵛ (Cat. 41)

116. Initial M. Cambridge, University Lib.,
Dd.1.4, f. 64ᵛ (Cat. 43)

119. Initial T.
Oxford, Bodl. Lib., Bodley 271, f. 36 (Cat. 42)

120. Initial Q.
Oxford, Bodl. Lib., Bodley 271, f. 43ᵛ (Cat. 42)

121. Initial A.
Cambridge, St. John's College, A.8, f. 39ᵛ (Cat. 44)

122. Initial A.
Cambridge, University Lib., Dd.1.4, f. 220 (Cat. 43)

117. (*far left*) Initial M. Cambridge, St. John's College, A.8, f. 91 (Cat. 44)

118. (*left*) Initial C. Cambridge, St. John's College, A.8, f. 103ᵛ (Cat. 44)

FVIT VIR VNVS

DE RAMATHAIM
sophim de monte e
phraim: & nomen el
helchana. filius iero
boam filu helui. filu
thau. filu suph ephra
teus. & habuit duas
uxores. Nomen uni an
na. & nomen secunde
fenenna. fueruntq;
fenenne filu. anne n
erant liberi. Et ascen
debat uir ille de cui
tate sua statutis die
b;. ut adoraret & sa
crificaret dno exer
cituum in sylo.

Erait autem ibi
duo filu hely:

123. Initial F.
London, B.L., Royal 1.C.VII, f. 58 (Cat. 45)

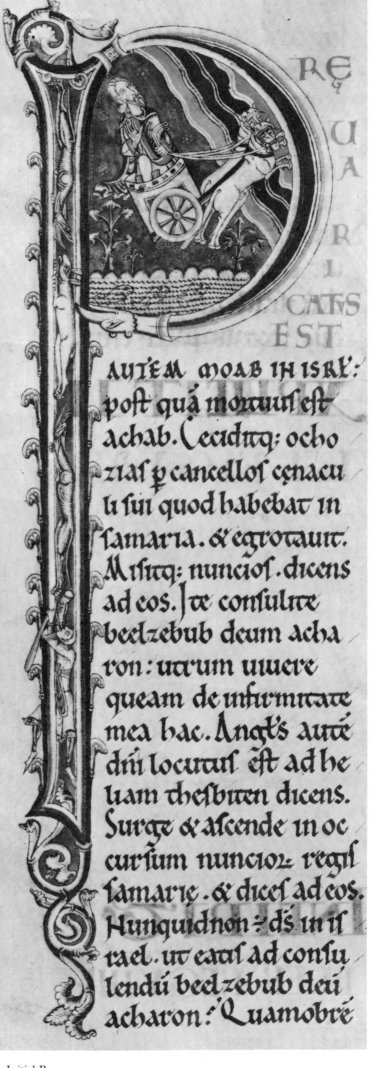

REQVARL CATVS EST

AVTEM MOAB IN ISRL:
post quá mortuus est
achab. Ceciditq; ocho
zias p cancellos cenacu
li sui quod habebat in
samaria. & egrotauit.
Misitq; nuncios. dicens
ad eos. Ite consulite
beelzebub deum acha
ron: utrum uiuere
queam de infirmitate
mea hac. Angl's auté
dni locutus est ad he
liam thesbiten dicens.
Surge & ascende in oc
cursum nuncior regis
samarie. & dices ad eos.
Hunquidnon ÷ ds in is
rael. ut eatis ad consu
lendu beelzebub deu
acharon: Quamobré

124. Initial P.
London, B.L., Royal 1.C.VII, f. 154ᵛ (Cat. 45)

125. Initial E.
London, B.L., Royal 1.C.VII, f. 120ᵛ (Cat. 45)

126. Initial Q.
London, B.L., Royal 1.C.VII, f. 126 (Cat. 45)

127–128. Initial V. Initial I.
Durham, Cath. Lib., B.II.8,
f. 1ᵛ, f. 34ᵛ (Cat. 46)

129–130. Initial A. Initial S.
Durham, Cath. Lib., A.I.10,
f. 170, f. 227 (Cat. 47)

131. God sending forth the angel Gabriel.
London, B.L., Lansdowne 383, f. 12ᵛ (Cat. 48)

132. Pentecost.
London, B.L., Lansdowne 383, f. 14 (Cat. 48)

133. Tree of Jesse.
London, B.L., Lansdowne 383, f. 15 (Cat. 48)

134. Beatus Initial.
London, B.L., Lansdowne 383, f. 15ᵛ (Cat. 48)

135. Virgin and Child. Oxford, Bodl. Lib., Bodley 269, f. iii (Cat. 52)

Quid me felicem totiens iactastis amici?
Qui cecidit stabili non erat ille gradu.

136. Boethius in prison.
Cambridge, University Lib., Dd.6.6, f. 2ᵛ (Cat. 50)

137. Boethius in prison.
Oxford, Bodl. Lib., Auct. F.6.5, f. 1ᵛ (Cat. 49)

138. Initial C.
Oxford, Bodl. Lib., Auct. F.6.5, f. viiᵛ (Cat. 49)

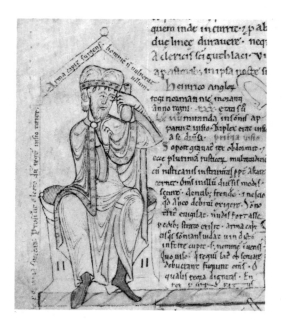

139. The Physician Grimbald. Detail of
Oxford, Corpus Christi College 157, p. 382 (Cat. 55)

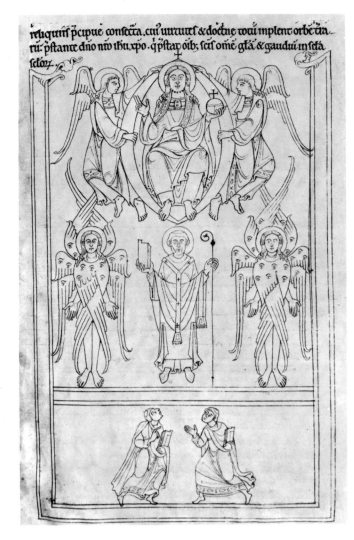

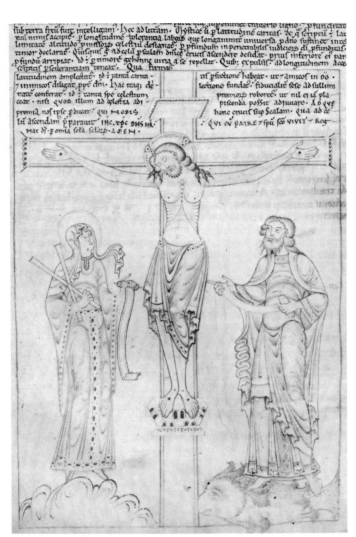

140. St. John Chrysostom in heaven.
Hereford, Cath. Lib., O.5.XI, f. 147 (Cat. 51)

141. Crucifixion.
Oxford, Corpus Christi College 157, p. 77b (Cat. 55)

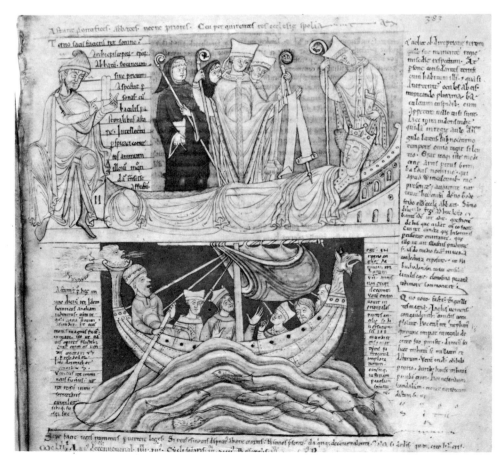

142. Visions of Henry I of Normandy.
Oxford, Corpus Christi College 157, p. 383 (Cat. 55)

143. Initial E. Oxford, Bodl. Lib.,
Bodley 269, f. iii^v (Cat. 52)

144. Initial Q.
Dublin, Trinity College 53, f. 36 (Cat. 53)

145. St. Matthew; Initial L.
Dublin, Trinity College 53, f. 7^v (Cat. 53)

146. Beatus Initial.
Dublin, Trinity College 53, f. 151 (Cat. 53)

147. The City of God; struggle for a dead man's soul. Oxford, Bodl. Lib., Laud. Misc. 469, f. 7ᵛ (Cat. 54)

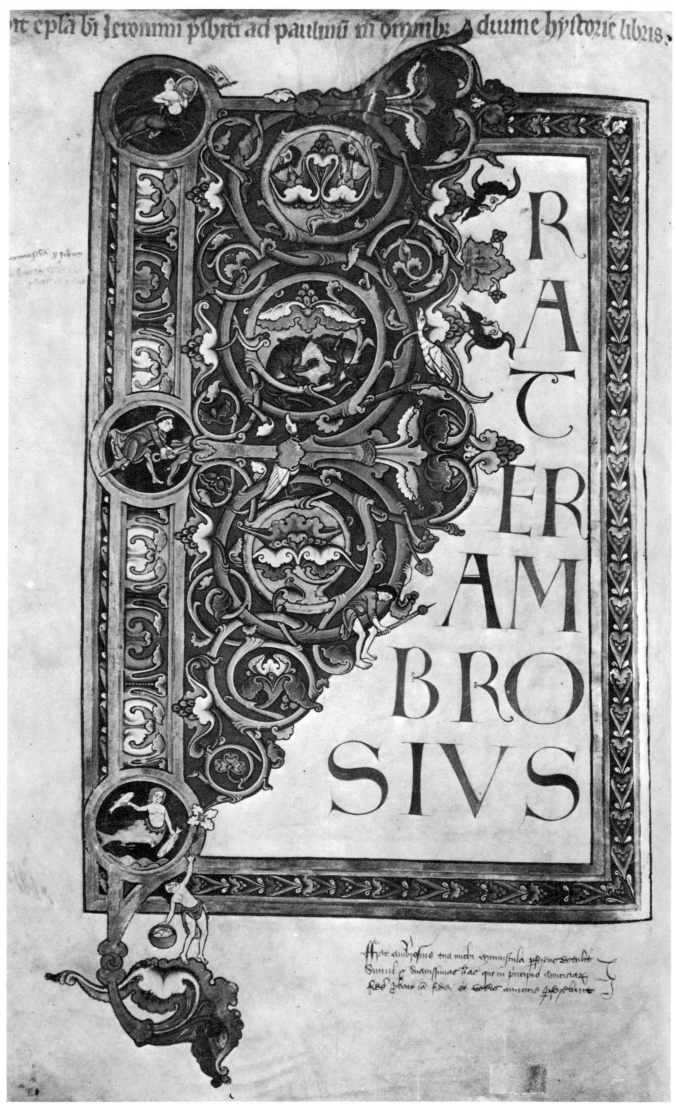

148. Decorated page with initial F. Cambridge, Corpus Christi College 2, f. 1ᵛ (Cat. 56)

149. Moses and Aaron. Cambridge, Corpus Christi College 2, f. 94 (Cat. 56)

150–151. Initial D. Initial C. Cambridge, Corpus Christi College 2, f. 5ᵛ, f. 201ᵛ (Cat. 56)

152. Elkanah, Hannah and Penninah. Cambridge, Corpus Christi College 2, f. 147ᵛ (Cat. 56)

153. Ezekiel's vision of God. Cambridge, Corpus Christi College 2, f. 281ᵛ (Cat. 56)

154. Initial Q.
Cambridge, Pembroke College 16, f. 71ᵛ (Cat. 57)

155. St. John. London, B.L.,
Add. 46487, f. 52ᵛ (Cat. 60)

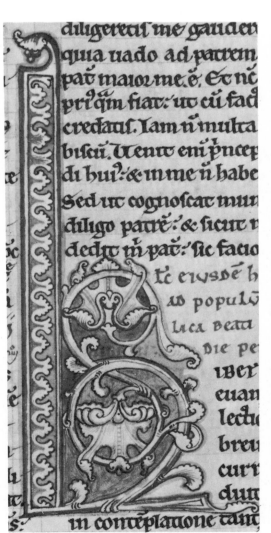

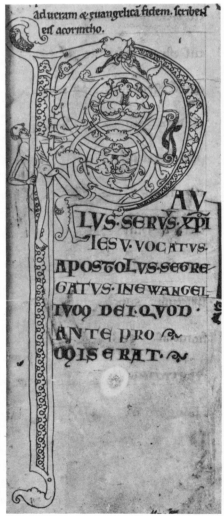

156–157. Initials L.
Cambridge, Pembroke College 16, f. 75, f. 70 (Cat. 57)

158. Initial P. Cambridge,
Pembroke College 78, f. 1 (Cat. 58)

159. Initial E.
Dublin, Chester Beatty Lib. 22, f. 108 (Cat. 59)

160. Initial H.
Dublin, Chester Beatty Lib. 22, f. 89ᵛ (Cat. 59)

161. Initial H.
Dublin, Chester Beatty Lib. 22, f. 32ᵛ (Cat. 59)

162. Initial L.
Dublin, Chester Beatty Lib. 22, f. 67ᵛ (Cat. 59)

163. Initial I. Lincoln, Cath. Lib.,
A.1.18, f. 45ᵛ (Cat. 61)

164. Initial P. Lincoln, Cath. Lib.,
A.1.18, f. 80 (Cat. 61)

165. Initial O. Lincoln, Cath. Lib.,
A.1.18, f. 135ᵛ (Cat. 61)

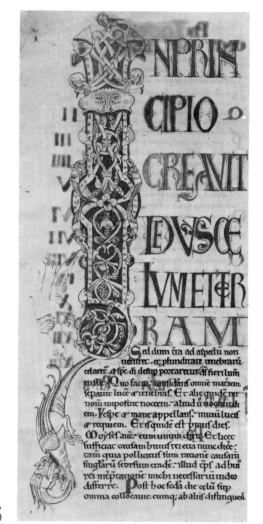

166. Initial I. Cambridge,
Trinity Hall 4, f. 2ᵛ (Cat. 63)

167–168. Initial V. Initial O.
Hereford, Cath. Lib., P.4.III, f. 3, f. 93 (Cat. 64)

169. Initial Q.
Hereford, Cath. Lib., O.6.XII, f. 63ᵛ (Cat. 62)

est usque ad unum ;
onne cognoscent omnes:

non erat timor
uio df diffipat offa hominu

xultabit iacob: & letabi
tur iffrabel

SINFINEM INCARMINIBUS
INTELLECTUS DAVID
SINNOMINE
uio saluum mefac:
& inuirtute tua libera

CUM UENISSENT ZIPHELET
DIXISSENT ADSAUL · ECCE DD
nime : & fostter quefierut
animam meam · & nonp
posuerunt dm ante con

LATITAT APUD NOS · LIII ·

& inueritate tua disspde
illos
uoluntarie sacrificabo ubi

170. Psalm 53. London, B.L., Harley 603, f. 29ᵛ (Cat. 67)

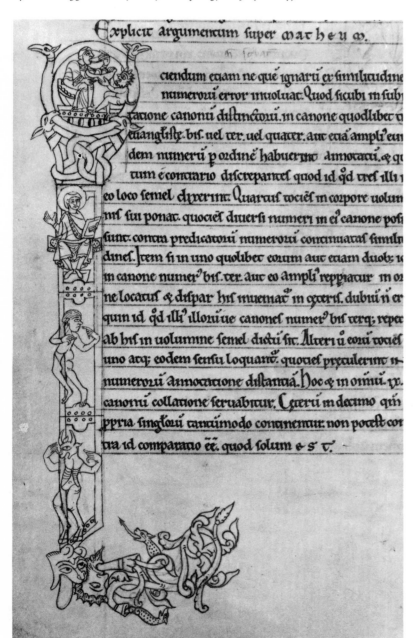

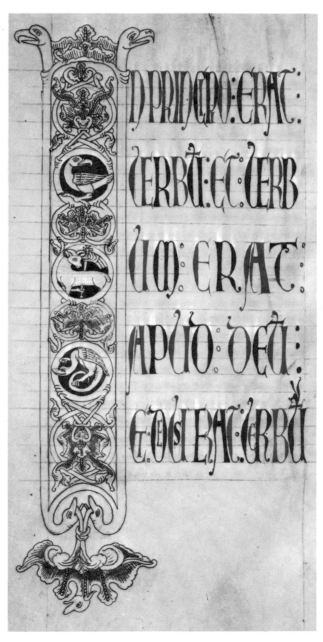

171–172. Marginal decoration. Initial I. London, B.L., Royal 1.B.XI, f. 6ᵛ, f. 114 (Cat. 65)

173. Moses and David. New York, Pierpont Morgan Lib. 724, recto (Cat. 66)

174. Tree of Jesse; opening scenes of New Testament. New York, Pierpont Morgan Lib. 724, verso (Cat. 66)

175. Infancy of Christ. London, B.L., Add. 37472, recto (Cat. 66)

176. Ministry of Christ. London, B.L., Add. 37472, verso (Cat. 66)

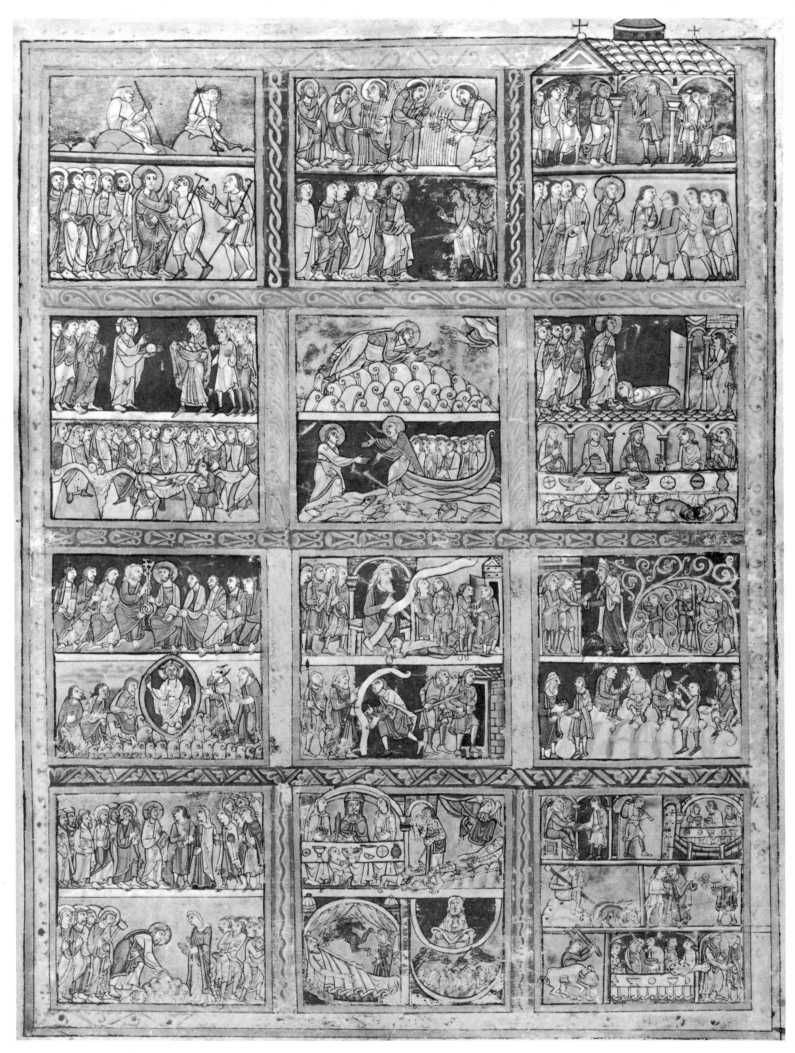

177. Ministry of Christ. New York, Pierpont Morgan Lib. 521, recto (Cat. 66)

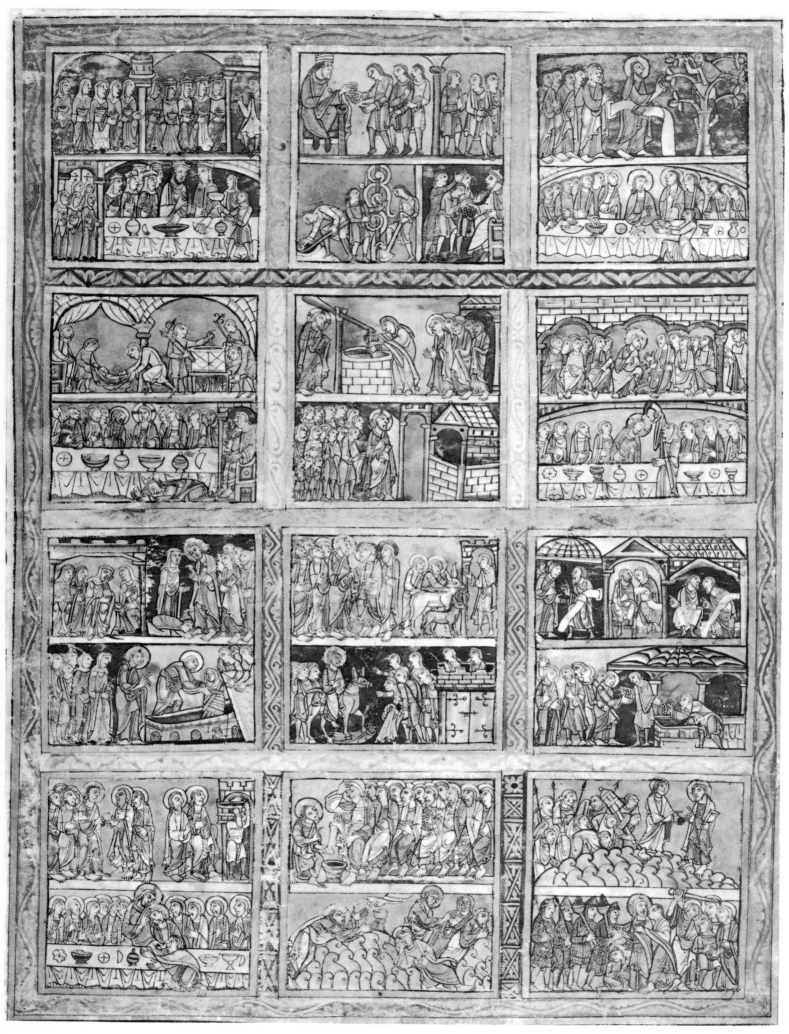

178. Ministry of Christ; the Passion. New York, Pierpont Morgan Lib. 521, verso (Cat. 66)

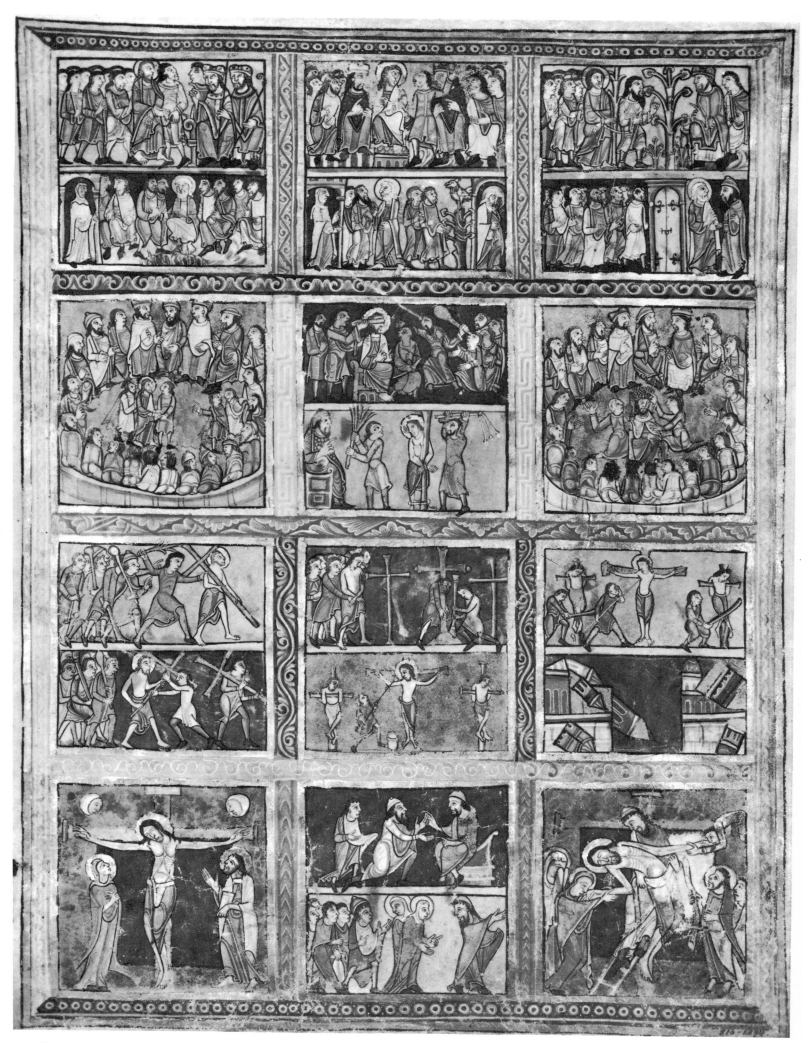

179. The Passion. London, Victoria and Albert Museum 661, recto (Cat. 66)

180. Life of Christ: Entombment to Pentecost. London, Victoria and Albert Museum 661, verso (Cat. 66)

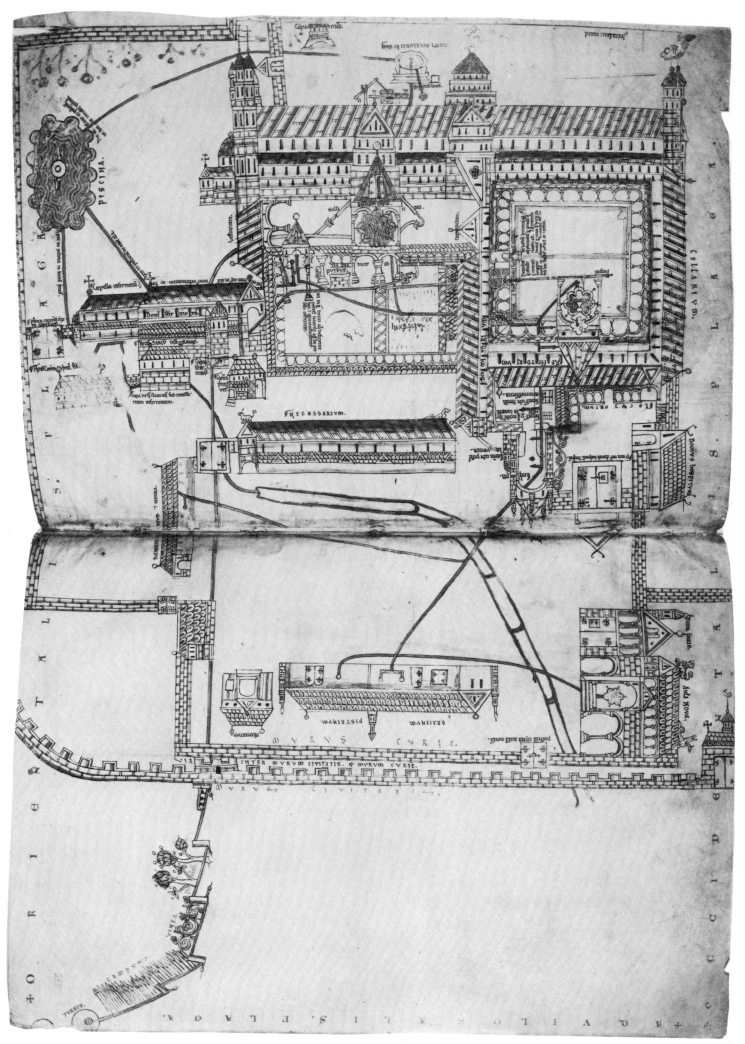

181. Plan of Christ Church water works. Cambridge, Trinity College, R.17.1, f. 285 (Cat. 68)

ota die iuiufticiam cogi   tuo · &iudicem tuam de   onfitebor tibi dñe infcm
tauit lingua tua ficut   temx miuentium   quia fecifti · &exfpectabo
nouacula acuta fecifti   idebunt iufti & timebunt·   nomen tuu qm bonum eft·
dolum   x fup eum ridebunt &dicet   ante confpectum fcoru tuoy·

INFINEM PRO   AMALEH INTELLE   GENTIAE DAUID · LII
IXIT INSIPIENS   mnabiles facti funt in   non eft ufq: adunum

182. Psalm 52. London, B.L., Harley 603, f. 29 (Cat. 67)

183. Psalm 52 (53). Cambridge, Trinity College, R.17.1, f. 92 (Cat. 68)

184–186. Psalms 4, 11 (12), 65 (66). Cambridge, Trinity College, R.17.1, f. 9, f. 20, f. 111 (Cat. 68)

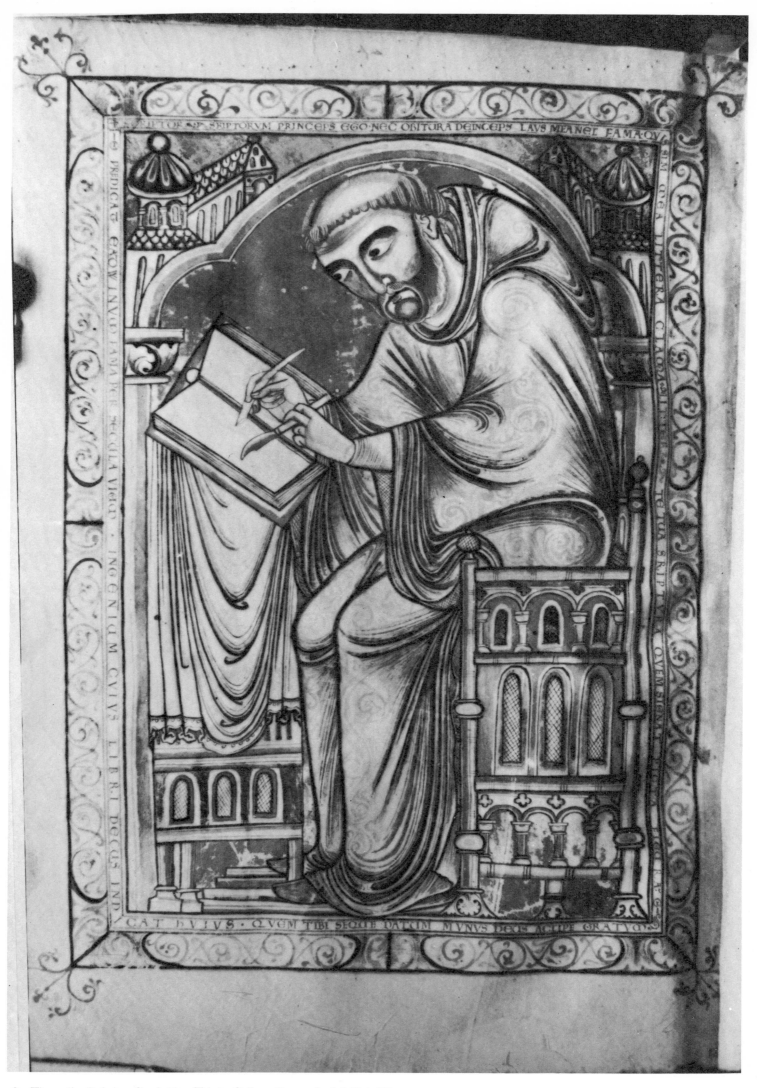

187. The scribe Eadwine. Cambridge, Trinity College, R.17.1, f. 283ᵛ (Cat. 68)

188. Initial L with St. Matthew.
Cambridge, Corpus Christi College 3, f. 168ᵛ (Cat. 69)

189. Initial H.
Cambridge, Corpus Christi College 3, f. 26 (Cat. 69)

190. Initial A.
Cambridge, Corpus Christi College 4, f. 84ᵛ (Cat. 69)

191. Initial E.
Cambridge, Corpus Christi College 4, f. 139ᵛ (Cat. 69)

192–193. Initial V. Initial O. London, Lambeth Palace 3, f. 198ᵛ, f. 307 (Cat. 70)

194. Ruth and Boaz. London, Lambeth Palace 3, f. 130 (Cat. 70)

195. Tree of Jesse. London, Lambeth Palace 3, f. 198 (Cat. 70)

196. The Deposition. Oxford, Corpus Christi College 2, f. 1ᵛ (Cat. 72)

197. The Marys at the Sepulchre. Oxford, Corpus Christi College 2, f. 2 (Cat. 72)

SYMO   SOSIA

of istec & cetera. Quia Simo nuptias simulabat se uelle celebrare. serui illius eulogias ei detulerunt.

& ministri qd unusquisq: poterat. quidam pisces. quidā aues. quidā uinū. quidā lac. & cetera

SYMO   DAVOS   PAMPHILOS

Reuiso quid agant Dauus & filius meus Pamphilus. Dauo recedente a conspectu Simonis. cepit

secum Simo cogitare ac dicere. Scio qa Dauus omīa ista renuntiat filio meo. simulq: hortatur ne

ducat Philumenā quā ego uolo ei dare. Vadam q̄ & iudebo quid tractent;

Reuiso quid agant aut quid captent consilii.

198–199. Scenes from the *Comedies* of Terence. Oxford, Bodl. Lib., Auct. F.2.13, f. 4ᵛ, f. 16 (Cat. 73)

GNATHO · Ridiculum · non enim cogitaras · ceterum · idem hoc tu te
meliuf quanto inuenisses thraso ;

GNATO · THRASO · MILES · THAIS · PARMENO SERUUS · THAIS ·

THAIS · MERETRIX · CHREMES · ADULESCENS · PYTHIAS · ANCILLA ·

CREDO equidem illu̅ · i · Trasone̅ iam affuturu̅ esse · ut illā puellā quam michi dedit · a me accipiat ·

Meretryx ista ueniens a domo Trasonis · ubi se mutuo uerbis concitauerant · tam in domo sua

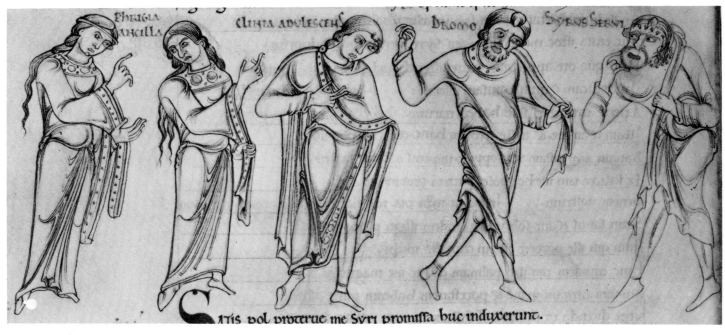

PHRIGIA ANCILLA · CLINIA ADULESCENS · DROMO · SYROS SERVI ·

SATIS uol protrue me Suri promissa huc induxerunt ·

200–202. Scenes from the *Comedies* of Terence. Oxford, Bodl. Lib., Auct. F.2.13, f. 47, f. 54ᵛ, f. 85ᵛ (Cat. 73)

203–204. Occupations of the months. Oxford, Bodl. Lib., Auct. D.2.6, f. 4, f. 6ᵛ (Cat. 71)

205. Perseus. Oxford, Bodl. Lib., Digby 83, f. 48ᵛ (Cat. 74)

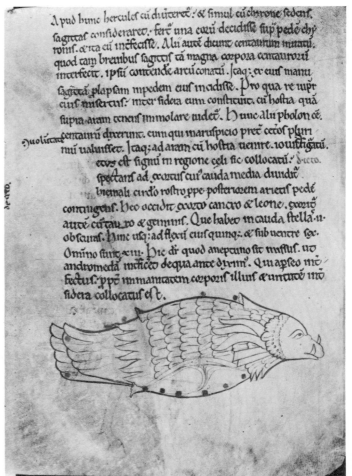

206–207. Sagittarius; Pisces. Oxford, Bodl. Lib., Digby 83, f. 65, f. 65ᵛ (Cat. 74)

208. Herod's feast; beheading of St. John.
Oxford, Bodl. Lib., Auct. D.2.6, f. 166ᵛ (Cat. 75)

209. Christ and St. Peter.
Oxford, Bodl. Lib., Auct. D.2.6, f. 169 (Cat. 75)

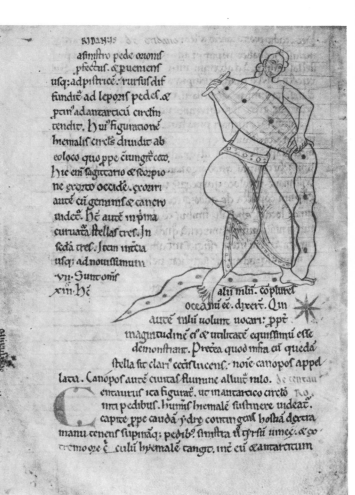

210. Supplicant before the Virgin.
Oxford, Bodl. Lib., Auct. D.2.6, f. 158ᵛ (Cat. 75)

211. Eridanus.
Oxford, Bodl. Lib., Digby 83, f. 64ᵛ (Cat. 74)

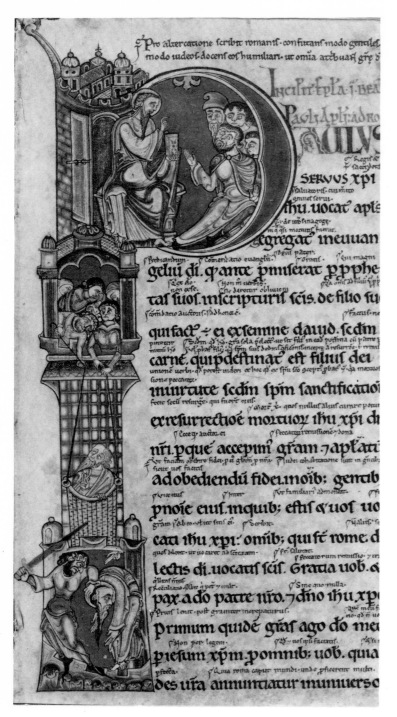

212. Initial P.
Oxford, Bodl. Lib., Auct. D.1.13, f. 1 (Cat. 79)

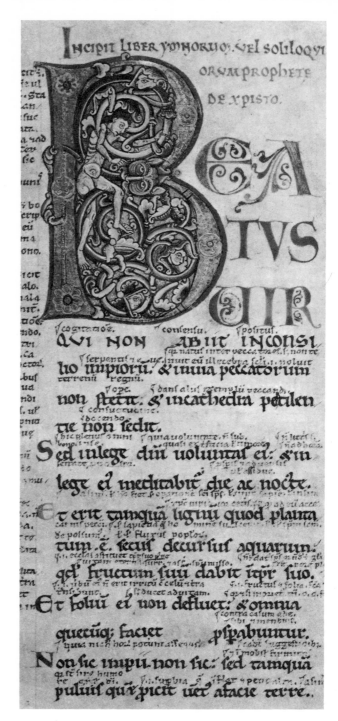

213. Beatus Initial.
Oxford, Bodl. Lib., Auct. D.2.4, f. 1 (Cat. 81)

214. Initial Q.
Oxford, Bodl. Lib., Auct. D.2.15, f. 42 (Cat. 80)

215. Laurence of Durham.
Durham, University Lib.,
Bishop Cosin's V.III.1, f.22ᵛ (Cat. 76)

216. Beatus Initial.
Madrid, Biblioteca Nacional, Vit. 23–8, f. 15 (Cat. 77)

217. Initial D.
Madrid, Biblioteca Nacional, Vit. 23–8, f. 72 (Cat. 77)

218. A Bishop before St. Peter.
Madrid, Biblioteca Nacional, Vit. 23–8, f. 144ᵛ (Cat. 77)

219. Knights in battle.
Madrid, Biblioteca Nacional, Vit. 23–8, f. 81ᵛ (Cat. 77)

220. Tree of Jesse. London, B.L., Cotton, Nero C.IV, f. 9 (Cat. 78)

221. The Death of the Virgin.
London, B.L., Cotton, Nero C.IV, f. 29 (Cat. 78)

222. Virgin enthroned.
London, B.L., Cotton, Nero C.IV, f. 30 (Cat. 78)

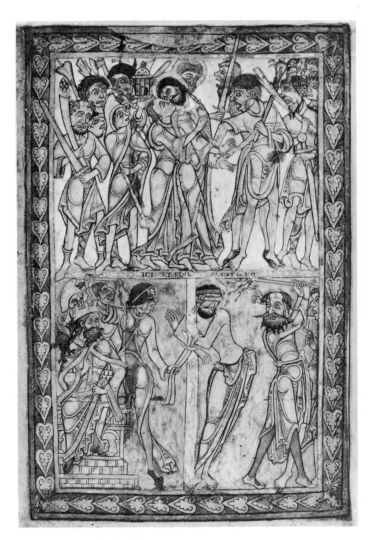

223. Betrayal and Flagellation.
London, B.L., Cotton, Nero C.IV, f. 21 (Cat. 78)

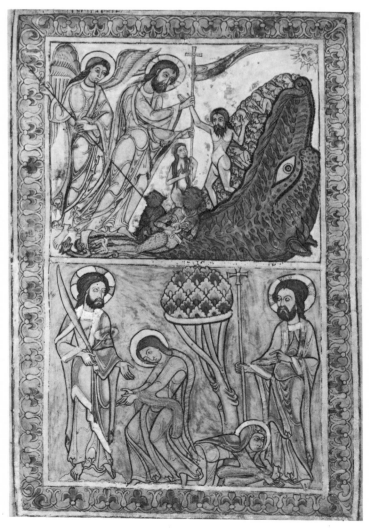

224. Harrowing of Hell.
London, B.L., Cotton, Nero C.IV, f. 24 (Cat. 78)

225. Initial V.
Oxford, Bodl. Lib., Auct. E. inf. 1, f. 281 (Cat. 82)

226. Initial V.
Oxford, Bodl. Lib., Auct. E. inf. 1, f. 304 (Cat. 82)

227. Beatus Initial.
Oxford, Bodl. Lib., Auct. E. inf. 1, f. 2 (Cat. 82)

228. Initial A.
Oxford, Bodl. Lib., Auct. E. inf. 1, f. 264ᵛ (Cat. 82)

229. Initial P. Winchester, Cath. Lib.,
Winchester Bible, f. 120ᵛ (Cat. 83)

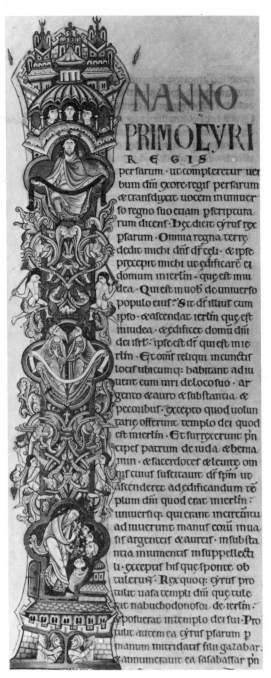

230. Initial I. Winchester, Cath. Lib.,
Winchester Bible, f. 342 (Cat. 83)

231. Initial H. Winchester, Cath. Lib.,
Winchester Bible, f. 21ᵛ (Cat. 83)

232. Initial V. Winchester, Cath. Lib.,
Winchester Bible, f. 200ᵛ (Cat. 83)

233. Illustration to Judith. Winchester, Cath. Lib., Winchester Bible, f. 331ᵛ (Cat. 83)

234. Illustration to Maccabees. Winchester, Cath. Lib., Winchester Bible, f. 350ᵛ (Cat. 83)

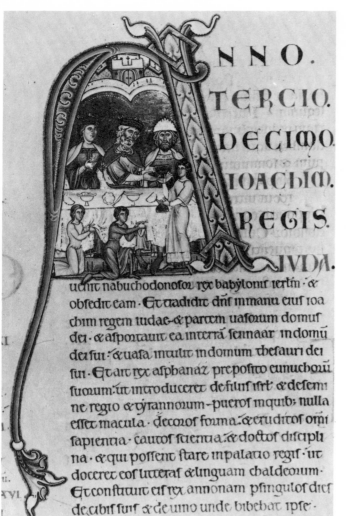

235. Initial A. Winchester, Cath. Lib.,
Winchester Bible, f. 190 (Cat. 83)

236. Initial R. Winchester, Cath. Lib.,
Winchester Bible, f. 169 (Cat. 83)

237. Initial E. Winchester, Cath. Lib.,
Winchester Bible, f. 69 (Cat. 83)

238. Initial V. Winchester, Cath. Lib.,
Winchester Bible, f. 131 (Cat. 83)

INCIPIT
LIBER GE
NESIS:
IN PRIN
CIPIO CRE
AVIT DEUS
CELV̄ ET T̄RRĀ.

Terra autem erat inanis &
uacua · & tenebrę erant
sup faciem abyssi · & spc̄
dei ferebatur sup aquas.
Dixitq: ds̄ · Fiat lux · Et
facta est lux · Et uidit ds̄
lucem quod ē̄t bona · &
diuisit ds̄ lucē atenebris ·
Appellauitq: lucē diē̄ · &
tenebras noctem · Factūq:
est uespe & mane · dies un̄ ·
Dixit quoq: ds̄ · Fiat firma   II
mentum in medio aquarū ·
& diuidat aquas ab aqui ·
Et fecit ds̄ firmamentum ·
diuisitq: aquas quę erāt
sub firmamento · ab iis
quę erant sup firmamtū ·
Et factum est ita · Voca
uitq: ds̄ firmamentū cę
lum · & factū est uespe &
mane · dies secundus ·
Dixit uero ds̄ · Congre   III
gentur aquę quę sub
celo sunt in locū unum ·
& appareat arida · Fac
tumq: est ita · Et uocauit
ds̄ aridam terrā · congre
gationesq: aquarū appel
lauit maria · Et uidit ds̄
quod ē̄t bonum · & ait · Germinet terra herbā
uirentē & facientē semen · & lignū pomiferū
faciens fructum iuxta genus suū · cuius semen
in semetipso sit sup terram · Et factū est ita ·

239. Initial I. Winchester, Cath. Lib.,
Winchester Bible, f. 5 (Cat. 83)

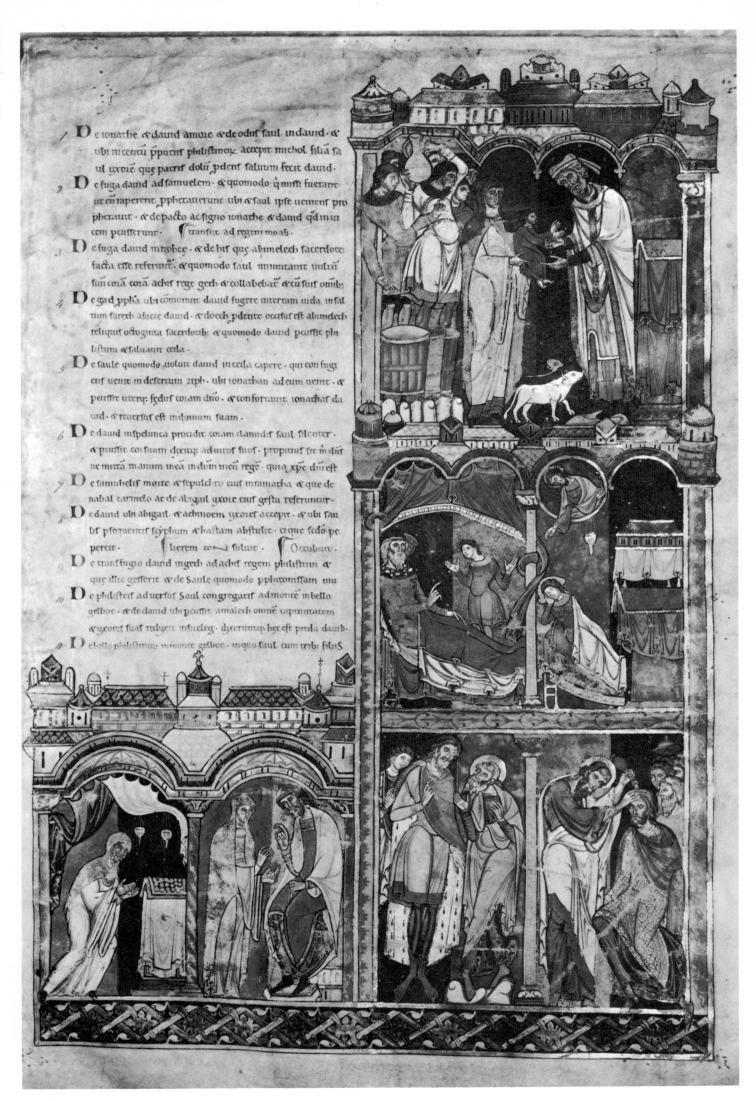

1 De ionathe & dauid amore & de odiis saul in dauid. &
ubi incentu pputiis philistinox accepit michol filia sa
ul uxore que patris dolu pdens saluum fecit dauid.

2 De fuga dauid ad samuelem. & quomodo qmissi fuerant
ut eu raperent pphetauerunt ubi & saul ipse ueniens pro
phetauit. & de pacto ac signo ionathe & dauid qd inui
cem puisserunt. Transiit ad regem moab.

3 De fuga dauid in nobee. & de his que abimelech sacerdoti
facta esse referunt. & quomodo saul immutauit uultu
suu cora coia achis rege geth & collabebat & cu suis omib;

4 De gad ppha ubi comonuit dauid fugere interram iuda. in sal
tum sareth a facie dauid. & doech pdente occisus est abimelech
reliquis octoginta sacerdotib; & quomodo dauid puissit phi
listium & saluauit ceila

5 De saule quomodo uoluit dauid in ceila capere. qui confugi
ens uenit in desertum ziph. ubi ionathan ad eum uenit. &
puissit uterq; fedus cora dno. & confortauit ionathas da
uid. & reuersus est in domum suam.

6 De dauid in spelunca procidit cora clamidis saul silenter.
& puissit con suum dixitq; ad uiros suos. propicius sit m dns
ne mitta manum mea in dnm meu rege. quia xpe dni est

7 De samuelis morte & sepulchro eius inramatha & que de
nabal carmelo ac de abigail uxore eius gesta referuntur

8 De dauid ubi abigail & achinoem uxores accepit. & ubi sau
lis psequentis scyphum & hastam abstulit. eique scdo pe
percit. Ierem cor i soluit. Occubuit.

9 De transfugio dauid ingreth ad achis regem philistim &
que illic gessit & de saule quomodo pphitonissam mu

10 De philisteis aduersus saul congregatis ad monte in bello
gelboe. & de dauid ubi puissit amalech omne captiuitatem
& uxores suas reduxit insceleg. dixeruntq; hec est preda dauid.

11 De bello philistinox in monte gelboe. in quo saul cum trib; filiis

240. Opening to I Samuel. New York, Pierpont Morgan Lib. 619, recto (Cat. 84)

241. Story of David. New York, Pierpont Morgan Lib. 619, verso (Cat. 84)

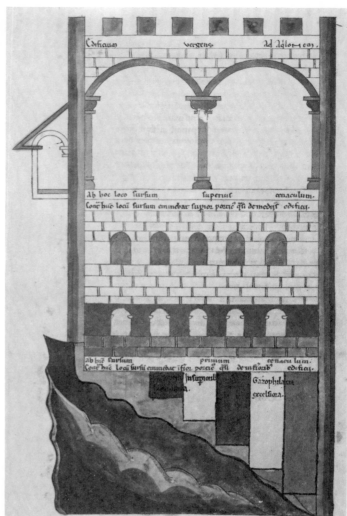

242–243. Sections of a building. Oxford, Bodl. Lib., Bodley 494, f. 156, f. 162ᵛ (Cat. 88)

244. The seven towers and seven-branched candlestick.
Cambridge, St. John's College H.6, f. iii (Cat. 86)

245. St. John with the scribe.
Cambridge, St. John's College H.6, f. iiᵛ (Cat. 86)

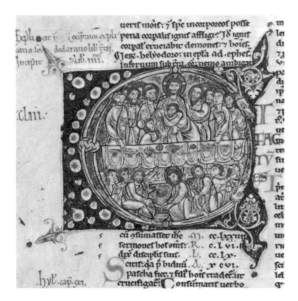

246. Initial D. Camarillo (Calif.),
Doheny Lib. 7, f. 5 (Cat. 87)

247. Initial U. Camarillo (Calif.),
Doheny Lib. 7, f. 12ᵛ (Cat. 87)

248. Initial E. Camarillo (Calif.),
Doheny Lib. 7, f. 139ᵛ (Cat. 87)

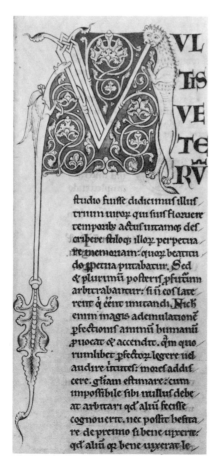

249. Initial V. Camarillo (Calif.),
Doheny Lib. 7, f. 81 (Cat. 87)

251. Initial C. Winchester, Cath. Lib. XIII, f. 51ᵛ (Cat. 85)

250. Initial M. Winchester, Cath. Lib. XIII, f. 50 (Cat. 85)

252. Initial C.
Paris, Bibl. Nat., lat. 10433, f. 193ᵛ (Cat. 89)

253. Initial D.
Paris, Bibl. Nat., lat. 10433, f. 226 (Cat. 89)

254. The Last Judgment.
Paris, Bibl. Nat., lat. 10433, f. 9 (Cat. 89)

255. Initial D: Samuel anointing David.
Paris, Bibl. Nat., lat. 10433, f. 38 (Cat. 89)

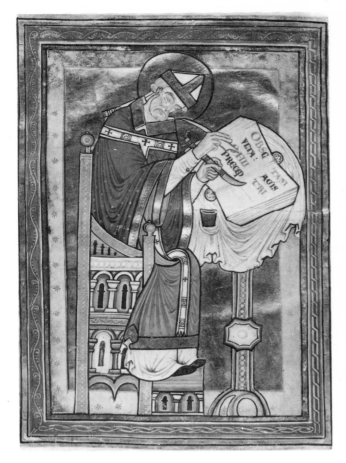

256. St. Dunstan.
London, B.L., Royal 10.A.XIII, f. 2 (Cat. 92)

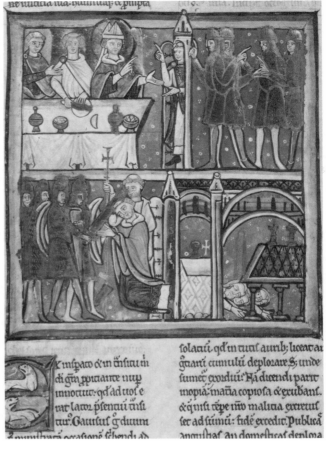

257. The murder of Becket.
London, B.L., Cotton, Claudius B.II, f. 341 (Cat. 93)

258. Initial I.
Cambridge, Corpus Christi College 48, f. 7ᵛ (Cat. 91)

259. Initial P. London, B.L., Cotton, Claudius B.II, f. 2ᵛ (Cat. 93)

260. Creation of Adam; the Temptation.
Glasgow, University Lib., Hunter U.3.2, f. 7ᵛ (Cat. 95)

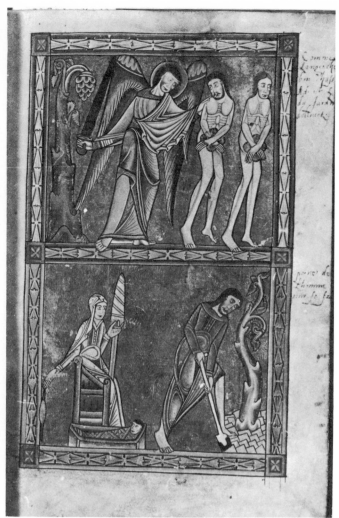

261. The Expulsion; Adam digging, Eve spinning.
Glasgow, University Lib., Hunter U.3.2, f. 8 (Cat. 95)

262. Abraham and Isaac.
Glasgow, University Lib., Hunter U.3.2, f. 9ᵛ (Cat. 95)

263. Temptation of Christ; raising of Lazarus.
Glasgow, University Lib., Hunter U.3.2, f. 11ᵛ (Cat. 95)

264. Supper at Emmaus; Christ and the Apostles.
Glasgow, University Lib., Hunter U.3.2, f. 12 (Cat. 95)

265. The Ascension.
Glasgow, University Lib., Hunter U.3.2, f. 14 (Cat. 95)

266. Pentecost.
Glasgow, University Lib., Hunter U.3.2, f. 15ᵛ (Cat. 95)

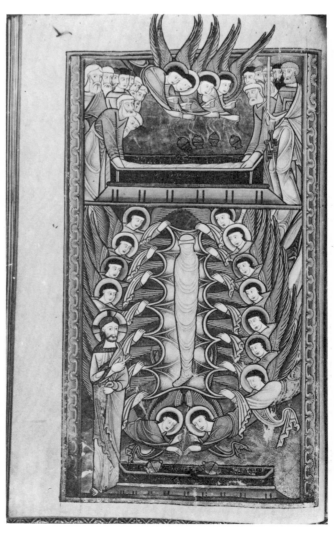

267. Burial of the Virgin.
Glasgow, University Lib., Hunter U.3.2, f. 19ᵛ (Cat. 95)

268. Flight into Egypt.
Oxford, Bodl. Lib., Douce 293, f. 10 (Cat. 94)

269. Harrowing of Hell.
Oxford, Bodl. Lib., Douce 293, f. 14 (Cat. 94)

270. Flight into Egypt.
Oxford, Bodl. Lib., Gough Liturg. 2, f. 17 (Cat. 97)

271. Flagellation.
Oxford, Bodl. Lib., Gough Liturg. 2, f. 27 (Cat. 97)

272. The Magi follow the star. Copenhagen, Royal Lib., Thott 143 2, f. 10ᵛ (Cat. 96)

273. Adoration of the Magi. Copenhagen, Royal Lib., Thott 143 2, f. 11 (Cat. 96)

274–276. Initial Q. Initials C. Copenhagen, Royal Lib., Thott 143 2, f. 69ᵛ, f. 163, f. 174 (Cat. 96)

277. Initial V.
Cambridge, Trinity Hall 2, f. 3 (Cat. 90)

278. Initial D.
Cambridge, Corpus Christi College 48, f. 7 (Cat. 91)

279. Initial V.
Durham, Cath. Lib. A.II.1, Vol. II, f. 109 (Cat. 98)

280. Initial V.
Durham, Cath. Lib. A.II.1, Vol. III, f. 16 (Cat. 98)

281. Initial I. Durham, Cath. Lib.
A.II.1, Vol. III, f. 109 (Cat. 98)

282. Initial E.
Durham, Cath. Lib. A.II.1, Vol. III, f. 131ᵛ (Cat. 98)

284. Initial Q. Durham, Cath. Lib.
A.II.9, f. 130ᵛ (Cat. 100)

283. Initial D. Durham, Cath. Lib. A.II.9, f. 63 (Cat. 100)

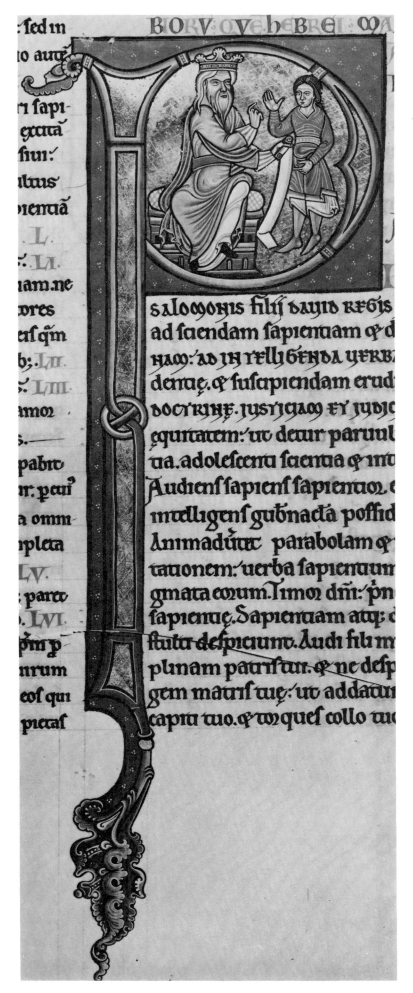

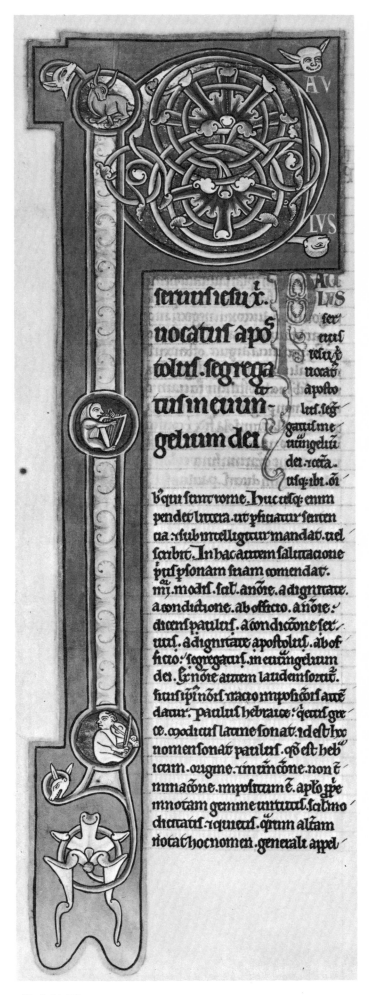

285. Initial P.
Durham, Cath. Lib. A.II.1, Vol. III, f. 4 (Cat. 98)

286. Initial P.
Durham, Cath. Lib. A.II.19, f. 4ᵛ (Cat. 99)

287. Initial P.
Durham, Cath. Lib. A.II.19, f. 87ᵛ (Cat. 99)

288. Initial P.
Norwich, Church of St. Peter Mancroft, f. 106ᵛ (Cat. 101)

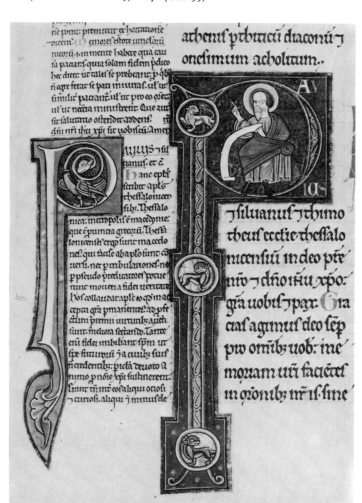

289–290. Initials P. Norwich, Church of St. Peter Mancroft, f. 147, f. 123 (Cat. 101)

291. St. Mark. Oxford, Bodl. Lib., Laud Misc. 752, f. 350 (Cat. 103)

292. Detail of initial F.
Oxford, Bodl. Lib., Laud. Misc. 752, f. 99ᵛ (Cat. 103)

293. Initial V.
Oxford, Bodl. Lib., Laud Misc. 752, f. 146 (Cat. 103)

294–295. Bestiary scenes. Cambridge, Corpus Christi College 22, f. 162, f. 166 (Cat. 104)

297. Adam naming the animals.
London, B.L., Add. 11283, f. 11ᵛ (Cat. 105)

296. Sheep; ram; lamb; goat.
London, B.L., Add. 11283, f. 12 (Cat. 105)

298. Dogs attacking a murderer.
London, B.L., Add. 11283, f. 10ᵛ (Cat. 105)

Est aïal qd grece monoceros. latine ñ unicor
nus dr. Phisiologus dicit unicornē hanc
habere naturā. Pusillum aïal est. simile hedo
acerrimū nimis. unū cornu habens in medio
capite. ce nullus omnino uenator eū cape p̄.
S; hoc argumento eū capiunt. puellā uirgi
nem ducunt in illo loco ubi morat̄. ce dimit
tunt illam in siluā solam. At ille uisa uigine
ce complectit̄ eam. ce dormiens in gḿo eī
sic cōp̄hendit̄ ab explorator̄ib; eī. ce exhibet̄
in palatio regis. Sic rōns ñr ihc ̄x sp̄ualis
unicornis descendens in uterū uirginis p
carnē ex ea sumptā capt̄ a iudeis morte crucis

Est aïal qd dr castor mansuetū nimis.
cui testiculi in medicina pficiunt adu̅
uersas inualitudines. Phisioloḡ exponit
naturā eī dicens q̄a cum uenator inuesti
gaut̄ eū. sequit̄ post eum. Castor ū cū res

301–302. Unicorn speared. Beaver hunt. New York, Pierpont Morgan Lib. 81, f. 12ᵛ, f. 13ᵛ (Cat. 106)

fructus sp̄uales. i. caritatē gaudium. pacem.
patientiam. castitatē inbonis opib; idē ele
mosinā ī uisitationib; infirmoᷓ. in curis
paupium. in laudib; dei in orationib; ī g̅raᷓū
actione. ce cetis que dei sunt. Castores a castra
do dicti sunt. Nam testiculi eoᷓ apti sunt me
dicaminib;. P̄p̄ qd cum p̄secuti eos uenato
res fuint: ipsi se castrant. ce morsib; utilia
sua amputant. De quib; ciceᷓo in scauriana.
redimunt sua parte corp̄; p̄p̄ qd maxime ex
petunt̄. Et iuuenat̄. Qui se eunuchū facit cū
piens euadere dampna testiculoᷓ. Ipsi s̄e ce
tibri qui etiam pontici canes uocantur.

Est aïal qd dr hiena in sepulc̄s mortuoᷓ ha
bitans. eoᷓq; corpa uescens. Cui natā ē ut

delectan̄. consecutam sue nequitie corda
coᷓ timoris aculeus semp pungit. ce eodē
usu ad pp̄trata retrahunt̄. Supiora oᷓis
moᷓ q̄a hiscoᷓ patrū opa aliis in ūbo oste
dunt. cū minime eoᷓ que dicunt in sese ha
beant. De sterore ē unguentū fit qᷓ plerūq;
mali de pp̄cto malo. ab impiis laudantur.
ac uelut unguento huᷓ mundi fauoᷓib; ex
tollun̄. S; cum districtus iudex de pp̄tra
tis malis ualam sue ultionis ad feriendum
p̄mouet. tunc omnis ille decoᷓ laudis ue
lud fumus euanescit.

301–302. Hyena devours corpse in tomb. Sirens. New York, Pierpont Morgan Lib. 81, f. 14ᵛ, f. 17 (Cat. 106)

ANALYSIS OF MANUSCRIPTS IN THE CATALOGUE

I. TYPES OF BOOKS

Apocalypse commentaries: nos. 47, 86
Astronomical MSS: nos. 27, 37, 38, 74
Bestiaries: nos. 36, 104–6
Bibles: nos. 13, 45, 56, 59, 69, 70, 82–4, 91, 98, 103
Book of Hours: no. 89
Calendars (*see also* Psalters): nos. 39, 71
Cartularies; Canon Law: nos. 20, 21, 60
Chronicles: nos. 40, 55, 102
Church Fathers
    St. Augustine: nos. 6, 14, 16, 19, 28, 52, 54, 61
    St. Gregory: nos. 4, 15, 57
    St. Jerome: nos. 23, 46
    St. John Chrysostom: no. 51
Classical authors
    Boethius: nos. 41, 49, 50
    Josephus: nos. 32, 43, 44, 63
    Lucan: no. 24
    Priscian: no. 8
    Prudentius: no. 30
    Terence: no. 73
Gospels: nos. 2, 5, 25, 33, 35, 53, 65, 80

Herbals: nos. 10, 11
Lives of Saints; martyrologies: nos. 7, 17, 18, 22, 26, 34, 85, 93
Marvels of the East: no. 38
Medical MSS: nos. 12, 27
Medieval Theologians
    St. Anselm: nos. 31, 42, 75, 77
    Bede: no. 26
    Berengaudus: no. 47
    John of Salisbury: no. 93
    Laurence of Durham: no. 76
    Peter Lombard: nos. 99–101
    Ralph of Flavigny: no. 90
    Richard of St. Victor: no. 88
    Smaragdus: no. 92
    Zacharias Chrysopolitanus: no. 87
Natural science MS: no. 9
Prophets: no. 64
Psalters: nos. 1, 3, 29, 48, 53, 62, 66–8, 72, 77, 78, 81, 89, 94–7
St. Paul Epistles: nos. 58, 79, 99

II. PLACES OF ORIGIN

Abbotsbury Abbey, Dorset: no. 87
Bury St. Edmunds Abbey: nos. 11, 34, 35, 56–8
Canterbury
    Christ Church: nos. 6, 7, 20–2, 41–4, 66–9, 92, 93
    St. Augustine's Abbey: nos. 8, 10, 17–19, 65, 70
Durham Cathedral Priory: nos. 26–8, 46, 47, 76, 98–100
Ely Cathedral Priory: no. 40
Exeter Cathedral: no. 2
Eynsham Abbey: no. 52
Hereford: nos. 62–4
Lincoln: nos. 13, 14, 61, 106
Northern England: nos. 94–7, 101
Peterborough Abbey: no. 37

Ramsey Abbey: nos. 9, 86
Rochester Cathedral Priory: nos. 15, 16, 23, 24, 45
St. Albans Abbey: nos. 29–33, 71–3, 90, 91
Sawley Abbey, Yorks.: no. 102
Sherborne Abbey, Dorset: no. 60
Walsingham Priory, Norfolk: no. 59
West country: nos. 48, 49, 51, 103
Winchcombe Abbey, Glos.: no. 53
Winchester: nos. 8, 79–82, 85
    St. Swithun's: nos. 77, 78, 83, 84
    New Minster (Hyde Abbey): no. 1
Worcester Cathedral Priory: nos. 3, 4, 39, 55

GENERAL INDEX

This index should be used in conjunction with the Analysis of Manuscripts in the Catalogue, p. 233

British Museum
Education Office